Terrorism and Human Rights

Terrorism and Human Rights aims to reinforce our knowledge and understanding of the problems involved in balancing human rights protection and security concerns. It considers how these human rights issues have been raised by the various international debates and policy issues which have been created by the continuing global war on terrorism.

In the shadow of 9/11 the threat of terrorism is an ever increasing global preoccupation. This book discusses the effects of the legal and social aspects of terrorism. It does this by examining the relation between security issues and human rights from the angle of international organisations, political bodies and different countries. Some of the examples covered and which are examined in light of their approach and reaction to terrorism include the European Union, the UN, Russia and the United States.

This book will be useful for all students of security, politics and terrorism studies, but also for policy-makers, legislators, and the law-enforcers.

This was previously published as a special issue of *Terrorism and Political Violence*.

Dr Magnus Ranstorp is Research Director of the Centre for Asymmetric Threat Studies at the Swedish National Defence College.

Paul Wilkinson is Professor of International Relations and Chairman of the Centre for Study of Terrorism and Political Violence at the University of St Andrews.

Terrorism and Human Rights

Edited by Magnus Ranstorp and Paul Wilkinson

LONDON AND NEW YORK

First published 2008
by Routledge
2 Park Square, Milton Park, Abingdon, Oxon, OX14 4RN

Simultaneously published in the USA and Canada
by Routledge
270 Madison Avenue, New York, NY 10016

Routledge is an imprint of the Taylor and Francis Group, an informa business

Transferred to Digital Printing 2009

© 2008 Magnus Ranstorp and Paul Wilkinson

Typeset in Times New Roman by
RefineCatch Limited, Bungay, Suffolk

British Library Cataloguing in Publication Data
A catalogue record for this book is available from the British Library

Library of Congress Cataloging in Publication Data
A catalog record for this has been requested

ISBN10: 0-415-41479-2 (hbk)
ISBN10: 0-415-49524-5 (pbk)

ISBN13: 978-0-415-41479-1 (hbk)
ISBN13: 978-0-415-49524-0 (pbk)

Contents

Balancing Security and Civil Liberties Since 9/11

Human Rights Protection and Issues from Regional Perspectives

Foreword

From a law enforcement perspective there are three key conclusions from the development of the threat of international terrorism since the 1990s. The first is a new dimension of potential harm to the public. The agenda is mass murder. The second is that this dimension is enduring. Endeavours to contain the worst dangers will require many years of effort. The third is that a new balanced normality is achievable but it will require a major commitment of leadership and sustained hard work.

Cumulatively, this is a strategic shift. The current threat of international terrorism requires defences beyond the traditional criminal justice response. Aspects of terrorism are crimes. However, if the potential impact is on the catastrophic scale, effective defence can only be provided by multinational, multiagency and multidisciplinary measures. The threat is not only a crime but also a national security issue. That is why this conference and the long-standing work of the Centre for the Study of Terrorism and Political Violence at St Andrews University are so important.

It is immediately apparent that the importance of the academic contribution will only grow in the months and years ahead. This is entirely welcome and produces benefits on many fronts. These include: a systematic and rigorous analysis of the subject; independent research of key areas of development; creation of individual skills and talents; contact with a broad range of essential actors across a spectrum of disciplines providing a unique and vital network; and stimulating balanced debate between private and public sectors.

The contribution of the academic community is demonstrated by the work being conducted through Economic and Research Council grants into the domestic management of terrorist attacks in the UK. We look forward to the conclusion of these projects, which include work by the Centre for the Study of Terrorism and Political Violence at St Andrews University; the Mountbatten Centre for International Studies at Southampton University; Kings College, London; and Lancaster University.

One of the key strategic challenges to be addressed by both public and private contributions is to integrate defences which have evolved from different disciplines. These include: intelligence; proactive pursuit; prevention; community support; crisis management; consequence management; disaster recovery; restoration of normality; and long-term impact.

The activities of international terrorists now present a global threat and the opportunity exists to strengthen a global response based upon a cohesive strategy. The strategy must be based in national competence and capability. The operational components of a counterterrorist strategy will include: political will; military action; diplomatic endeavour; international/national intelligence; international/national law enforcement; target hardening (defence and protection); efforts to address root causes; and degrading the terrorists' financial infrastructure on both the macro- and micro-levels.

Within the UK we see a greater involvement through key sectors of the national economy and infrastructure ranging from the public health and transport sectors; commerce; financial institutions; telecommunications; and utilities. The breadth and diversity of these "unlikely counterterrorists" underlines the importance of crosscutting efforts such as this conference which has demonstrated that academia can provide a valuable forum for the discussion of issues involved in terrorism and human rights as we adjust to the new security environment.

David Veness
New Scotland Yard

Introduction

This special issue of *Terrorism and Political Violence* is based on a selection of papers presented at an International Conference on Terrorism and Human Rights held in St Andrews between 13–15 July 2003, organised by the Centre for the Study of Terrorism and Political Violence (CSTPV) at St Andrews University and generously supported by the Economic and Social Research Council (ESRC). The conference was of major importance as it came at a time when British and international debates and policy initiatives concerning terrorism were raising human rights issues in the aftermath of 9/11 and as a consequence of the continuing global war on terrorism. There had been no comparable effort in the United Kingdom, bringing together over 120 specialists and experts in the fields of terrorism studies, human rights studies and practitioners in government, international organisations and NGOs.

The primary aim of the conference and ultimately this collection of contributions is to enrich our knowledge and understanding of the difficult problems involved in balancing human rights protection and security concerns. In particular it seeks to highlight a multiplicity of dilemmas on many fronts: the conceptual and definitional problems constantly encountered in the processes of drafting national and international laws and agreements; the difficulties involved in ensuring that the rights of terrorist suspects and defendants facing terrorist charges at trial are upheld; the dilemmas involved in the vital work of intelligence agencies and the police in the prevention of terrorism while avoiding overreaction and the creation of a repressive climate with damaging effects to the rights and liberties of the public at large; the impact of emergency laws, antiterrorism laws and measures on the rights and liberties of the public at large; and the problems faced by democracies in preserving the rights of minorities (ethnic, religious, asylum seekers and refugees) during periods of terrorist emergencies.

Addressing the New Terrorism – The Vital Role of Human Rights Protection

It may be helpful to begin by comparing the two key concepts that are the subject of this volume – terrorism and human rights. Terrorism is the systematic use of coercive intimidation usually, though not exclusively, to service political ends. It is used to create and exploit a climate of fear among a wider group than the immediate victims of the violence, often to publicise a cause, as well as to coerce a target into acceding to terrorist aims. Terrorism may be used on its own or as part of a wider conventional war. It can be employed by desperate and weak minorities, by states as a tool of domestic or foreign policy, or by belligerents as an accompaniment or additional weapon in all types and stages of warfare. A common feature is that innocent civilians, sometimes foreigners who know nothing of the terrorist political quarrel, are killed or injured. The weapon of terror can be used for an almost infinite variety of causes and purposes. Hence, although it is quite wrong to regard terrorism as synonymous with violence in general, it is a rather broad political-strategic concept and it is therefore useful to distinguish between basic forms and contexts of terrorism based on their underlying causes or political motivation. One basic distinction is between the use of terror by states, and its use as a weapon by substate groups. The former has been vastly more lethal and has often been an antecedent to, and contributory cause of, terrorism by substate groups.

The concept of human rights has a number of modern variants, such as 'collective rights' and 'minority rights'. However, in the liberal democratic context the predominant concept, and the one adopted in this discussion, is human rights defined as universal fundamental rights inherent in *individuals* by virtue of their status as human beings, such as the right to liberty, the right to justice, the rights to freedom of opinion, speech and religion and so on.

It is interesting to observe that the concepts of terrorism and human rights have some features in common: Both entered into political discourse roughly at the time of the French Revolution. Edmund Burke's passionate denunciation of the Jacobin Reign of Terror in his *Reflections of the French Revolution* and his opponent Thomas Paine's equally impassioned polemic *The Rights of Man*, helped to bring these ideas into the English political vocabulary. (There is tragic irony in the fact that Thomas Paine narrowly escaped the guillotine at the hands of the extremists of the French revolutionary regime he had so admired from afar!) Terrorism and human rights have been bitterly contested concepts from the outset, but this does not render them any less indispensable as part of our modern moral and political vocabulary. Both are value laden: In the vocabulary of liberal democracy, particularly since the terrible atrocities of 9/11, 'terrorism' has become what the philosopher T. D. Weldon[1] called a 'boo' word, while 'human rights' is now a virtually universal 'hurrah' word. To be 'against' human rights would be as bad as being opposed to motherhood and apple pie. Yet if we are honest we will recognise that virtually all the key political concepts – justice, liberty, tyranny, democracy, imperialism and dictatorship are heavily impregnated with values. The search for a value-free language is in any case, as the philosopher Bertrand Russell long ago discovered,[2] a complete dead end. The fact that political and moral/philosophical concepts are constantly subject to arguments about their precise definition and the contexts and circumstances in which they apply does not make them any less essential to any meaningful political or moral discourse.

However, the similarities between the concepts of terrorism and human rights end there. For unless you wish to argue that there is an inherent human right to blow up or shoot your fellow human beings or to hold them hostage or to terrorise them by other means, then terrorism is a fundamental threat to human rights. After all, what could be a more fundamental human right than the right to life itself?

Regime Terror and Human Rights

It is a matter of record that tyrannical rulers, regimes and modern dictatorships have been responsible for the vast majority of acts of terror throughout history. Despotic and oppressive regimes have been able to exploit the means of violence by which they acquired and sustained their power to inflict mass terror as a weapon for suppressing any actual or putative opposition within their borders or as a tool of ideological or foreign policy objectives. Hence regime terror has been, and remains to this day, a far more dangerous threat to human rights than the use of terrorism by substate groups. The rise of the totalitarian states of Hitler's Germany and Stalin's Soviet Union, of Pol Pot, Milosevic and Saddam Hussein, justify describing the twentieth century as truly an 'Age of Terror'.[3] We can all give thanks that these regimes have been defeated or have collapsed.

But alas, the problem of regimes using terror and violating human rights on a major scale is still very much with us. North Korea, Liberia, Burma, Vietnam and Zimbabwe are just a few examples. As the valuable reports of Amnesty International remind us, there are dozens of countries which suffer political oppression and a climate of fear at the hands of a cruel regime.

What can the international community do to at least reduce if not eradicate regime terror? The honest answer is that in a world of sovereign states where there is no global system of justice and human rights enforcement there is very little that can be done in the short term. The few exceptions, such as the Bosnia, Kosovo and East Timor conflicts, have occurred when the UN has been, if somewhat belatedly, persuaded to authorise a humanitarian intervention with an international force under a UN mandate, and where the intervention has led to a massive reduction in the level of violence and an increase in human security. However, member states have proved increasingly reluctant to get involved in humanitarian peacekeeping missions of this kind, and the UN budget for this type of task is ludicrously inadequate. A major factor in discouraging member states from contributing to these blue-helmet missions is their fear of becoming involved in protracted deployments without any clear exit strategy.

In launching their invasion of Iraq in 2003, the US and UK governments showed that they were prepared to take the unusual step of intervening unilaterally without specific UN Security Council authorisation. In the wake of the Iraq invasion and the toppling of the Saddam Hussein regime it has become clear that the gloomy predictions of the opponents of the war to the effect that it would be extremely difficult and costly to win peace and that it would be an even more daunting task to achieve a democratic and stable Iraq and economic recovery were all too accurate. Other contributors to this symposium discuss the Iraq War and its implications. Much of the debate in the immediate aftermath of the war has been about the decision to go to war and whether or not the US and UK governments and intelligence agencies exaggerated the threat of Saddam's weapons of mass destruction.

Far less attention has been given to what we would regard as a much more serious aspect of the US/UK invasion of Iraq. The US government employed its new strategic doctrine of preemptive attack as a justification for the invasion of Iraq, but what are the wider long-term implications of this controversial doctrine for the peace and security of the international community? What is sauce for the goose is sauce for the gander. What if *other* governments decide to take a leaf out of the US book? The North Korean regime could decide to strike out at South Korea on the grounds that the latter threatens its security. China could use the doctrine to justify a preemptive attack on Taiwan. The Indian government might use it to provide a rationale for a preemptive attack on Pakistan, or vice versa. Let us bear in mind that China, India and Pakistan already have nuclear weapons and that the nuclear weapons programmes of North Korea and Iran are much further advanced than Saddam's covert programme was. Hence, the doctrine of preemptive attack carries with it the real risk of triggering wider conflicts, including possibly the use of nuclear weapons, with all the concomitant loss of life, destruction and curtailment of human rights.

We would argue that in an age of weapons of mass destruction war should not be regarded as a stock-in-trade tool of foreign policy. It is not appeasement but sheer common sense that should cause us to revive the strategic doctrines of containment and deterrence, combined with constructive dialogue, the very means which enabled the US and its allies to *manage* Cold War conflict without resort to a war (which at its height could have led to mutual annihilation). We should remind ourselves that this is the policy which the US and the European NATO allies also adopted in relation to China, with considerable success.

In the light of the real dangers of conflict escalation in a world of weapons of mass destruction proliferation the use of nonmilitary tools in conflict management has a compelling logic. Political and diplomatic pressures and incentives, economic sanctions and aid and trade incentives, and moral support for dissident movements and NGO campaigns provide useful options for dealing with 'rogue regimes' using terror. Other more specific and often-useful tools which can work when combined with other pressures are: bans on arms-related exports and sales to designated terrorist regimes; strict controls on exports of dual-use items (of potential use in manufacturing weapons of mass destruction), banning defence contracts with companies controlled by terrorist states; and banning citizens from entering into business transactions with any government on the terrorist list.

Substate Terrorism and Human Rights

Some wish to argue that substate terrorism has entirely different implications for human rights. They prefer to see all terrorists as freedom fighters, compelled to use terror because they are the underdogs in an asymmetric conflict with an oppressive regime and have no other methods of resistance or rebellion open to them. But, as the courageous efforts of dissidents in the former Soviet Union and Communist Eastern Europe remind us, there are *always* other ways of struggling against oppressive regimes. With the exception of the brief period of anticolonial struggles in Palestine, Cyprus, Algeria and Aden from the 1940s to the early 1960s, terrorism has *never* been successful in overthrowing authoritarian governments and dictatorships.

As Timothy Garton Ash argues in his excellent analysis of the 'velvet revolution',[4] what was remarkable about the collapse of the Communist regimes in Eastern Europe was the *absence* of violence. Terrorist violence did not enter the picture. Indeed, if groups like Solidarity in Poland or Charter 88 in Czechoslovakia had used terrorist tactics against the Communist regimes it is likely that they would have provoked a draconian backlash by the authorities and the shift to democracy would have been delayed for decades.

A key paradox of terrorism is its power to corrupt its perpetrators. This was evident in the French revolutionaries' use of terror. They began by using it against the *ancien regime*, but it was eventually turned against the people, devouring the Revolution's own children. A dramatic example, which symbolises the self-corrupting effect of the terror, was the case of Madame Roland.

Madame Roland was the wife of Jean Roland, a French statesman who was a strong critic of royal corruption. However, eventually Madame Roland was sent to the guillotine. Jean Roland committed suicide when he heard the news of her death. Madame Roland's bravery and coolness at the time of her execution became famous. As she looked at the statue of liberty in the Place de Revolution she called out: 'O Liberte, O Liberte, que de crimes on commet en ton nom'.

Of course it is often true that we sympathise with the *aspirations* of rebels in cases where we recognise that they have been victims of major injustice. But support for the strategic *goals* of a group does not imply that we should be ready to support the use of utterly immoral *means* to achieve such ends. The method of terror should always be rejected, in our view, because it inherently involves deliberate attacks on civilians.

Long established and 'traditional' terrorist groups such as ETA, FARC and Shining Path have murdered on a smaller scale than terror regimes but this does not make their crimes against human rights 'acceptable'. Between them, 'traditional' groups have killed and injured many thousands of civilians.

What of the New Terrorism, of which the archetype is Al-Qaeda and its network of cells and affiliates? This form of terrorism is infinitely more lethal than the violence of the traditional groups. Its hallmarks are coordinated, simultaneous, no-warning suicide attacks. As so tragically demonstrated by their attacks on 11 September 2001, Al-Qaeda has no compunction about killing thousands of innocent civilians. Unlike traditional groups, all of which observed *some* limits on the scale of their violence, Al-Qaeda and its affiliates are hell-bent on the mass murder of their designated 'enemies', 'infidels' and 'apostles'. Moreover they have expended considerable efforts in indoctrinating and training a whole generation of terrorists, deployed in a global network unprecedented in its global reach and its ability to utilise its links with local and regional cells and affiliates.[5] Al-Qaeda has suffered considerable damage from the war in Afghanistan, the capture of many of its upper echelon, and the blocking of at least a part of its finances. It would be foolish to exaggerate the danger posed by Al-Qaeda, but equally dangerous to underestimate it. The recent lethal attacks in Bali, Riyadh, Casablanca and Madrid show that the New Terrorist network is still capable of deadly and destructive terrorism. Al-Qaeda set in motion a phenomenon that will take years, if not decades, to confront, disrupt and degrade. In many ways, the West is challenged by the daunting prospect of battling an enemy that is more ideological than tangible, more a vapour than an army, and more a lethal virus than an overt frontal assault.

The protection of human rights is a vital part of any effective strategy against the New Terrorism. It is first and foremost a moral imperative: Commitment to upholding individual human rights is inextricably linked to the principles of democracy and the rule of law. These values are the very foundation of our liberties and to suspend or abandon them in the name of security would be to give the terrorists a victory they could never achieve by themselves.

The protection of human rights is moreover, a potent asset of great *practical* significance in the battle of ideas, the struggle for the hearts and minds of the young Muslims Al-Qaeda and its affiliates are trying to recruit. The winning strategy against the New Terrorism must be intelligence led, as multinational as possible and genuinely multipronged. But it will be totally undermined if the authorities are perceived as condoning the violation of human rights or actively curtailing human rights of Muslim communities. Draconian measures such as detention without trial and denial of the right to a fair trail will only give Al-Qaeda more recruits, more financial contributions and a big gratuitous propaganda boost. As Joe Nye, Yukio Satoh and Paul Wilkinson concluded in a recent report:

> Dialogues about the protection of civil liberties in the face of security threats should be a regular feature of the meetings of home security officials and should be reinforced by meetings of judicial officials and parliamentarians. Assistance programmes must include attention to human rights issues. Not only are such issues central to the definition of the civilisation that we seek to protect, but over-reactions to insecurity that infringe civil liberties undercut the soft or attractive power that is essential to maintain the support of moderate opinion and to deprive terrorists from recruiting new converts.[6]

At the beginning of the twenty-first century it is a tragic reality that terrorism has become a ubiquitous component of warfare. In these 'terror wars' we witness time and again gross violations of human rights against the civilian population and against members of the armed forces, often on both sides. In this age of terror and weapons of mass destruction the international community needs to be reminded of the requirement to ensure that everything possible is done to uphold and enforce the Geneva Conventions. As Hugo Grotius, the great founder of international humanitarian law, rightly perceived,[7] it is precisely at times of especially bitter conflict that we need to strive to ensure that the international community does not abandon the effort to uphold, at the very least, basic humanitarian principles. This volume on terrorism and human rights provides overwhelming evidence to support this conclusion.

Magnus Ranstorp and Paul Wilkinson
CSTPV, St. Andrews University

Notes

1. T. D. Weldon, *The Vocabulary of Politics* (Harmondsworth, Middlesex, Pelican 1953, p.5).

2. See Bertrand Russell, *Principia Mathematica* (1920, 1912 and 1913) and also *The Analysis of Mind* (1921).

3. The phrase was first used as a book title by the English philosopher Leslie Paul, who published *The Age of Terror* (London: Faber 1950).

4. See the conclusions of Timothy Garton Ash, *The Polish Revolution* (Harmondsworth, Middlesex, Pelican, 2000).

5. See Jane Corbin, *The Base: Al Qaeda and the Changing Face of Global Terrorism*, updated edition (London: Pocket Books 2003) and Rohan Gunaratna, *Inside Al Qaeda: Global Network of Terror* (London: C. Hurst & Co. 2003).

6. Joseph S. Nye, Jr., Yukio Satoh, and Paul Wilkinson, *Addressing the New International Terrorism: A Report to the Trilateral Commission*, Washington, DC: The Trilateral Commission, 2003) p.30.

7. This is the major theme of the classic work by Hugo Grotius, *De Jure Belli et Pacis*.

Global Threat and International Response

1

The Challenges of Strategic Terrorism

GIANDOMENICO PICCO

GDP Associates, New York, New York, USA

The Al Qaeda type of terrorist is quite different from that of those of the IRA or Hezbollah. The former is seeking a clash of civilizations or at least a clash between the Islamic world and the West or at least between Islam and the US. The latter used and use terrorism to pursue a specific objective and a limited one at that in scope and geography. Terrorism is not a one dimensional phenomenon.

Truth is the first victim of war. Intelligence is not yet a science. One could argue that foreign policy is at least partially out of sync with democracy. Foreign policy does involve a level of secrecy, or at least discretion, which is at odds with transparency. How many foreign policy practitioners, dealing with specific issues of human rights, have found themselves confronted with the dilemma of taking the matter to the streets or keeping it quiet to obtain better results?

How does one use knowledge in this case? To a large extent, that is what we are talking about in different dimensions. When is knowledge shared? Why should it even be shared if its unveiling can be counterproductive? This of course is an old debate. It is not the theory that bothers me—it is the practice.

During the Cold War many individuals found themselves caught up, literally in jail, in the direct violation of human rights. Quiet diplomacy was invoked by some in order to help them; street demonstrations and even trade retaliation was called for by others. I met the dogmatists of both approaches.

Well after the Soviet Union had become part of history, those dealing with cases in other regimes faced the same dilemma. Having dealt with some similar situations during the Cold War and after, I came to the conclusion that either approach can work or fail. Each case requires a judgment call on the part of those who are asked to help. But there are no assurances of success by choosing one approach or the other. There are no templates no matter what the dogmatists may say.

How to use knowledge? Even in the defense of human rights it is not always so clear.

A few years ago one of the victims of a kidnapping in Lebanon, an American, took advantage of US legislation and sued the Iranian government for his suffering in Beirut during the 1980s. I knew him well as he was one of the hostages I had the good fortune to help regain his freedom. I was perhaps more than others familiar with the reality and the fantasy of an Iranian role in the case. Could I or should I be asked to take the stand as a witness in the trial? I would not argue with a man who had been deprived of many years of his freedom and made to suffer for absolutely no reason. The question was simply unanswerable at a human level. Had he asked me I would have obliged. But before putting the question to me, he was good enough to ask me something else. 'Are you still involved in helping other human beings in or in relation to Iran', he queried? Yes, it was indeed so. Then, the former hostage replied, I will not ask you to testify for me.

On the other side of the coin, acquisition of new knowledge may well help others from suffering unjustly. At what price should that knowledge be acquired? What if, to acquire that knowledge, others will suffer?

One of the most difficult ethical and practical questions I had to answer in my life was in 1991. I was asked by the Israeli authorities to halt my negotiations and arrangements for the release of the American hostages in Lebanon until I could put together a package which also included Israeli MIAs. Indeed I had tried to do so all along but with scarce success. So the time came when the choice had to be made between giving back freedom (a rather major human right) to some individuals or to leave them in captivity with the possibility that other human cases could be resolved. There was clearly no assurance that this could happen even given more time. I wish no one to be put in that position for, at an ethical level, one cannot ever overcome that dilemma.

I am aware that I am referring here to human rights in a different context than some have spoken about during this conference, but human rights nevertheless. Basic human rights, I would say. The issue of human rights needs, of course, to be looked at from many other angles, but to me the angle of operational interest is that of knowledge and human rights. Knowledge, of course, can also be acquired through contacts and *negotiations*. Repeat. Negotiations are a way to acquire knowledge.

While a number of western hostages were killed during their captivity in Lebanon, the majority were released in different stages and fashions. The purpose of the taking of hostages in Lebanon was directly connected with the imprisonment of the seventeen Lebanese in Kuwait in 1983. The hostage idea was an instrument to achieve an end, or as I would prefer to call it, was a tactic to achieve an end (ironically the end was achieved with the help of Saddam Hussein, whose army invading Kuwait opened the prison cells of that country).

The instrument having become superseded by events, it was a matter of time to free those unfortunate people. If that was (and it was) terrorism I would submit it was *tactical terrorism*. Indeed throughout the years the kidnappers sought contact with those governments that would negotiate with them. Not only was there a consistent and clear explanation of the hostage phenomenon in Lebanon during those years, but negotiations about it became possible and at different times brought about results. More than that, when the objective of releasing the seventeen Lebanese in Kuwait was unfeasible (in the early years, that is), other *quid pro quo* actions were found (Iran-Contra for the US and money for the French).

It would appear that contrary to public declarations by government leaders, institutions have dealt with terrorist groups almost consistently as long as the groups were prepared to deal with them. In other words, the crucial decision to enter into negotiations was not made by the governments but by the groups themselves. If they were ready, then the governments would find a way to communicate and engage. But if they were not, then no negotiations were to be had. Accepting to enter into negotiations seems to be a necessary aspect of tactical terrorism. By indicating availability to talk about an issue of confrontation it is the first, though not necessarily the only, indication that we are confronting terrorism as a tactic. From Colombia to Lebanon, from Northern Ireland to Palestine, negotiations have been pursued with different results but with a common meaning: Those groups were prepared to reach some kind of adjustment, some kind of deal and most of all were prepared to take some risks by the very fact of placing themselves in a line of two-way communication. Tactical terrorism implicitly rests on the perception (declared or not) that a deal can be struck with the other side, whoever that is. Not everything is negotiable, of course, even for those who operate on the basis of tactical terrorism. But the question here is: Can what is not negotiable always be defined as still a political objective or is it simply a philosophical one? Is it a flag, a call to arms, a slogan or is it an operational target?

Groups that have built a social structure around them, a welfare organization which involves and benefits large numbers of civilians, will over time become more and more interested in negotiations and less and less in a clash to the end. To operate as if groups, even terrorist groups, do not change is to operate as if time did not exist.

A tension between the two wings of a movement – those who see the changes and embrace the responsibilities of their constituency, and those who remain loyal to the militancy of their origins – is almost unavoidable over time for any group which has embraced tactical terrorism. To judge when the time is to live in between the two so as to accelerate the victory of the former is key in the fight against terrorism, I believe. The US negotiations with the IRA were based on this approach: engaging the political wing to 'bring home' the military wing of the movement.

At a different level the question is can groups which have been defined as terrorist survive without an enemy? I suppose the answer is to be found in what they have to offer to their constituency. If it is social welfare and the like, chances are their future does not depend on their enemy. They need not pursue a military struggle in order to exist both politically and existentially. Groups involved in tactical terrorism would tend to fit in this category.

Can Al-Qaeda exist without an enemy? I doubt it. Indeed, Al-Qaeda may well be in the business of *strategic terrorism;* the perpetual war, the struggle to the end (a never-ending end), for it appears to be a struggle against the 'other', yesterday the Hazaras Shiite or the Tajiks in Afghanistan, then the Russians, then the Chinese, then the Indians, then the West and so forth – and since the 'other' will always be there, the perpetual war is guaranteed. Is this strategic terrorism?

The very structure of Al-Qaeda allows for no welfare state to be created anywhere unless, of course, it succeeds in taking over a failed state of some sort. Its disconnection from a nation or a state or a tribe represents advantages but also risks. Strategic terrorism *per se* has nothing to loose in a perpetual struggle. In fact it feeds on it. It represents part of the appeal for those who join as the ultimate real battle – a confrontation that includes no compromise or other options. Indeed no occasion has arisen so far where we have seen any negotiation attempted, sought or even imagined with Al-Qaeda. Why? Because there is nothing to negotiate about.

The very inability or impossibility to enter into negotiations tells a bit about the inherent difference between a group like Hizballah (whose leader stated to an Italian journalist in the summer of 2002: 'There are members of the US Administration with whom we are in a quasi-constant contact') and Al-Qaeda.

Negotiations and strategic terrorism are a contradiction in terms. Indeed the political objectives themselves are only instruments and thus keep shifting.

If tomorrow the Palestinian-Israeli situation was to be solved, and if the last US military personnel were to leave Saudi Arabian soil, Al-Qaeda would very likely use other issues to rally its troops. The political issues are chosen insofar as issues of confrontation with the 'other'.

The objective being a perpetual war, the items on the table seem to serve that purpose for they are chosen in order to play on the so-called 'civilization' or religious divide. Strategic terrorism is not interested in the veniality of the single political issue. They are tools to be used to make sure that the confrontation goes on and the appeal of the confrontation never ends. We all remember that during the hostage saga in Lebanon, the victims were very much the focus of the systems of communications and the governments and public opinions of their respective countries. As Jessica Stern writes in an issue of *Foreign Affairs*, in the case of Al-Qaeda's type of terrorism:

> The real target audience of violent attacks is therefore not necessarily the victims and their sympathizers, but the perpetrators and their sympathizers . . .

Hizballah has no apparent interest in a war between the West and the Arab world nor has it sought one. Al-Qaeda by contrast has consistently moved in that direction: The early targets of Al-Qaeda have been India, Russia and China and other non-Sunni groups inside Afghanistan before moving to America. To use a different terminology, Al-Qaeda could not be happier than in a real clash among civilizations.

Perhaps few groups today have constructed an entire *raison d'etre* on a profound and deep sense of exclusion both at the practical and philosophical level like Al-Qaeda. Exclusion contains by itself the very opposite of human rights. Unlike groups which have chosen over time to use terrorism as a tactic, those that have chosen terrorism as a strategy have to be sure to be rooted on *an insurmountable sense of exclusion*, on an *unbridgeable gap with the 'other'* and on a *dogmatic perception* of being in the sole possession of the truth, and that those who do not agree need to be restrained or worse.

To strategic terrorism the foundation of the so-called ideology is more important than the tactical political objectives. Indeed those political objectives shift over time, which proves by itself that they do not constitute the essence but only the facade of Al-Qaeda.

The Soviet invasion of Afghanistan, the US presence in Saudi Arabia, the Palestinian cause, the Chechen situation, the Iraqi case and so forth are only some of the instruments which we have been presented with as the reasons for the actions of strategic terrorism.

It is of interest to me that over time Al-Qaeda has listed the UN as an enemy.

The UN as a global human endeavor is based on the exact opposite philosophy.

Inclusion, diversity, and bridge building are at the core of the charter; the tools are also diametrically different: negotiation, conventions, existing laws, political and economic pressure and only as a last resort military action. It would not be a surprise if the UN were to become a more direct target of Al-Qaeda in the future. In an ideological sense the UN is the nemesis of Al-Qaeda. More than any state and any religion, the UN must be blasphemy for Osama bin Laden. If he thought so he would be right.

Devoted to the perpetual war, strategic terrorism represents the antithesis of the United Nations project. It would be a mistake to underestimate the UN's so-called philosophical component and impact on the strategic terrorism sector of the world population. Its actions have a larger effect than the disastrous loss of human life or economic damage.

Its impact on the mindset of many in different parts of the world may very well have immeasurable effects. An example: How much has Pakistan's society been Talibanized or Al-Qaedaized? What other failed states are going to be hijacked next by groups seeking the perpetual war and inspiring the hatred of the 'other' as a fundamental component of their ideological baggage? Will it be in Africa or simply a portion of a Southeast Asian state? Portion of African and Southeast Asian states can possibly be estranged from central government control to offer new sanctuaries or bases for operations if necessary.

A proper analysis of how many believe that the differences with the 'other' are simply irreconcilable to the point that an armed confrontation, or rather the suppression of the other, is the only way to pursue justice cannot perhaps be done.

For sure, the spreading of such a philosophy by itself is making the terrain for human rights around the world less fertile. It is equally sad to observe that in the political discourse over this matter the religious scholars and leaders seem to be absent, or at least rather low key. With very few exceptions religious leadership does not appear to have substantially succeeded in opposing the theology of exclusion. Indeed their visibility on the entire issue of terrorism seems to have been very low.

From the Balkans to the Middle East and South Asia, from the South of the US to Russia, the voices of people of faith in favor of inclusion have not been very loud. The question that I ask is why such reluctance, why such an invisible role there, where religion and civilization and ethnicity are being used as justification, openly or not, for exclusion and disregard of the 'other'?

Tactical terrorism may well have been a subject that religious leaders shied away from as exclusively a political issue. But strategic terrorism is another matter, for it fuels the theology of 'we and them', of perceiving diversity as a threat and the 'other' as enemy.

It seems to me that to mistake strategic terrorism as any other terrorism would mean to miss its deeper effect at a level of the hearts and minds: The action matters more than its result, the clash more than its effect. The generalization we often make in speaking of terrorism as one phenomenon is not only analytically incorrect but also operationally unwise. We do not combat tactical terrorism as we combat strategic terrorism. The real challenge that strategic terrorism has launched to all is the creation of an operative ideology of exclusion. This ideology seems to have captivated the hearts and minds of some.

It would seem to me that all the 'others', irrespective of political and religious differences around the world, could find it appropriate to face up to that challenge and on that basis even find an ideological common ground. Indeed in a world ever smaller the *ideology of inclusion* should surely find more supporters. We may need also an anti-strategic terrorist manifesto that unifies all those 'others' that Al-Qaeda and company seem to find so unacceptable. Al-Qaeda has really called for a clash of civilizations and more. I can only express regret here that the call for a 'dialogue among civilizations' by the United Nations was not seized after 11 September by member states as a platform to a world antiterrorist manifesto. For different reasons, from Africa to Europe to America, it was not seen as a useful soft tool in the struggle against terrorism. It was, in fact, the right tool in the battle for the hearts and minds of the young people across the world who cannot possibly embrace the sectarian, and at times, racist overtone of strategic terrorism. It would be a further mistake, in my view, if in our fight against terrorism we would let those who seek a perpetual war, coalesce with tactical terrorism that has no interest in a confrontation at the global level.

2

The United Nations' Response to 9/11

JAYANTHA DHANAPALA

Sri Lanka

The United Nations has been at the forefront of the global campaign against terrorism after the events of September 11, 2001, giving the campaign legitimacy and universality. The Security Council acted with remarkable speed with its Resolution 1373 and set up the Counter Terrorism Committee with extensive powers. Its UK Chairman provided able leadership but reservations over human rights issues, lack of funding for assistance, and the danger of duplicating the work of other UN bodies with specific mandates have been revealed as deficiencies. The General assembly condemned the events of 9/11 and held debates on the subject later. The Secretariat's views were expressed by several eloquent statements of the Secretary-General and in a policy working group report that advocated a tripartite strategy of "discussion–denial–cooperation" and made 31 recommendations. Counter terrorism is only one tool in tackling terrorism. Human rights concerns must be addressed. A separate, functional commission under the Economic and Social Council is recommended to provide the international community with a universal forum for a focused discussion on terrorism.

Introduction

The terrorist attacks in the United States on 11 September 2001, by their unexpected boldness, their diabolically elaborate intercontinental planning and the tragic scale of the death and destruction they wrought, are now widely regarded as a watershed in the global history of terrorism and political violence. This does not minimize the impact of terrorism in other countries prior to 9/11. Nor does it trivialize the importance of the twelve international treaties and conventions on terrorism adopted well before the events of 11 September. It is, however, a realistic assessment of the repercussions of a terrorist attack on the nerve centres of the sole superpower in the world and the global reaction to it. Nothing after 9/11 will be as it was before. A wounded superpower has not only been driven to act globally on the issue of terrorism but the entire world has responded to what is being seen as a global campaign against terrorism. The United Nations, as the only universal global body empowered by its 191 member states to maintain international peace and security, has been at the forefront of this renewed effort to combat the scourge of terrorism. This has helped to provide legitimacy and universality to the campaign as well to establish forums to discuss some of its drawbacks and omissions.

Beyond the formal condemnations of the events of 11 September 2001 adopted both by the Security Council one day afterwards (S/RES/1368(2001)) and by the UN General Assembly on 18 September (A/RES/56/10) the United Nations moved swiftly to adopt practical and effective measures through international cooperation to prevent future acts of terrorism. In this connection UN Secretary-General Kofi Annan underlined three important principles when he addressed the opening of the fifty-sixth session of the UN General Assembly one day after the tragic events and again on 1 October. These principles are as follows:

(1) 'Terrorist acts are never justified no matter what considerations may be invoked'. At the same time the counterterrorist campaign should not distract from action on other UN principles and purposes, the achievement of which could by itself reduce and eliminate terrorism.
(2) The adoption of preventive measures to be undertaken on a cooperative basis should be 'in accordance with the Charter and other relevant provisions of international law'.
(3) The search for legal precision must be subordinated to 'moral clarity' on the subject of terrorism.

This approach ensured that the UN reaction was not one of revenge or retribution but based, as to be expected in a norm-based organization, on legal concepts and values. It also placed the action to be taken in the context of the antiterrorism conventions already adopted within the UN framework. Moreover the secretary-general focused on the protection of civilians – a vital theme in the UN – pointing significantly to the indiscriminate nature of terrorist attacks.

The Security Council

The Security Council, vested with 'primary responsibility for the maintenance of international peace and security' under Article 24 of the UN Charter, moved within three weeks of 9/11 to adopt Resolution 1373 unanimously. In a body that has been accused of fractious and dilatory behaviour the speed and sweep of this resolution was truly remarkable, surprising many member states who had hoped that the General Assembly could have acted more decisively on the subject before the Security Council did. There is no doubt that politically, the Security Council with the five permanent members (P5) dominating its decision-making, had wrested the initiative and was going to be in the driving seat in the prevention and countering of terrorism. It was in an aggressive mode since all the P5 members, to a greater or lesser degree, had their own domestic and foreign policy reasons for providing the Security Council with the powers to pursue terrorists wherever they may be.

The range of actions required of member states by Security Council Resolution 1373 was extensive and detailed. From the very specific prohibitions regarding the financing of terrorism through the recruitment of terrorists and supplies of weapons to them, to the actual exchange of information in tracking the activities of terrorist groups, the resolution had the cumulative impact of setting rigorous barriers against global terrorism under Chapter VII of the charter which are mandatory for all member states to observe. Operative paragraph 6 of the resolution was perhaps the most important in practical terms because it set up a committee–later to be called the Counter Terrorism Committee (CTC)–which was to ensure and monitor the implementation of Resolution 1373. A specific timetable was recommended for member states to report to the committee and for the committee to submit a work programme to the Security Council.

The CTC has now been in existence for over two years and for a greater part of this period it has been ably led by Sir Jeremy Greenstock, the permanent representative of the United Kingdom to the UN in New York, as its chairman. The decision on the chairmanship of the CTC was a departure from the well-established convention that representatives of the P5 countries do not chair Security Council committees. It is still to be seen whether Sir Jeremy Greenstock's successor, the permanent representative of Spain–a non-permanent member of the Security Council–will be as effective and dynamic. The influence and energy generated by the CTC is not only because of the personal leadership of the chairman but also to the fact that his country is one of the P5 members. An elaborate programme of activities, an infrastructure of support staff and a weighty documentation output that has strained the UN's resources are among the CTC's achievements. On the latter issue the secretary-general has been constrained to note on 18 January 2002 that 'We are currently using more than 25 per cent of our resources allocated to documentation to processing the national reports submitted to the committee by member states, in order to facilitate the committee's review of them. This is an unprecedented effort, which I fear cannot be sustained for long when those very same resources are being reduced by the General Assembly'. Not being a Sanctions Committee, the CTC has had to work on the basis of a broad mandate to strengthen the capacity of member states against terrorism. The reporting required from governments on their national legislation and implementation machinery and process enables the committee to assess what assistance is needed in individual countries with regard to their counter-terrorism efforts. A ministerial level meeting of the Security Council on 20 January 2003 gave further impetus to the CTC by calling for all countries to take urgent action to prevent and suppress all active and passive support for terrorism, as well as by stressing the importance of complying fully with the council's resolutions in this regard.

Concerns voiced over the maintenance of human rights in the counterterrorism campaign have resulted in the High Commissioner for Human Rights (HCHR) addressing the Security Council on this issue. Links, on a continuous basis, for cooperation and information exchange have also been established between the Office of the HCHR and the CTC. In addition, a website has been designed to function as a 'one stop shop' for states looking for support in their efforts to fight terrorism, especially through the Directory of Counter Terrorism Information and Sources of Assistance. The CTC is not without its deficiencies. Two of them could be seen as a result of the experience of the period of the committee's existence. They are:

(a) The CTC itself cannot provide assistance. It can only put member states in contact with potential donors or providers of assistance.

(b) The CTC runs the grave risk of becoming an operational arm of the UN duplicating or overlapping the work of the UN Office on Drugs and Crime located in Vienna or other components of the UN system that are already mandated to work on different aspects of terrorism.

Nonetheless the CTC claims credit for member states upgrading their domestic laws, encouraging states to ratify the twelve international conventions and protocols relating to terrorism as well as offering guidelines and models for adoption and implementation of the existing legal instruments. A significant development was the CTC meeting held in March 2003 with representatives of several international, regional and subregional organizations. Opened by the UN secretary-general, the meeting was designed, he said, to consolidate global cooperation against terrorism with a rational division of labour based on comparative advantages of the participating organizations. The meeting discussed global standards on counter-terrorism as well as the role of regional and subregional organizations in strengthening global counterterrorism capacity and the assistance they could provide the states. A subsequent meeting limited to a discussion of the terrorism threat with regard to weapons of mass destruction (WMD) was held with relevant organizations and technical agencies in May 2003. Among those participating were the International Atomic Energy Agency (IAEA), the Organization for the Prohibition of Chemical Weapons (OPCW), the World Customs Organization (WCO) and Interpol. This meeting was seen as duplicating the efforts of others in the field and was only valuable as an attempt to identify who does what in terms of information-sharing.

An important feature of the CTC's intense activity has been the personality of the chairman. Whether the committee can sustain this level of activity without actually providing any resources to assist member states is doubtful. There is also the fact that member states outside the Security Council may not feel the same sense of ownership and participation in the CTC's activities in the long term. Their role in submitting information to the CTC may not be sufficient for them since decision-making is confined to members of the Security Council only. Individual components of the UN system such as the UN Office on Drugs and Crime, the IAEA and other operational bodies are perceived to be more likely to be responsive to the needs of member states than the CTC. The CTC may, on the other hand, move from a post-office or intermediary function to a more assertive one.

The General Assembly

The General Assembly's response to the events of 11 September 2001 was firstly the adoption of a resolution one week after the tragedy condemning the acts of terrorism. Thereafter in a general debate a large number of member states participated in making it abundantly clear that there was broad unanimity on condemning the acts of terrorism against the US but differences persisted over the definition of terrorism and ways and means to combat the phenomenon. Moreover, the General Assembly held a separate debate from 1–5 October on measures to eliminate international terrorism. As a consequence of the speedy action on the part of the Security Council a separate resolution was considered redundant on the part of the General Assembly.

The Secretariat

The response of the UN Secretariat to the events of 9/11 was of course embodied mainly in the many eloquent statements of the secretary-general. Among the themes he emphasized was the need to build on the wave of solidarity that 9/11 had caused so that the momentum would not be lost in developing a long-term counterterrorism strategy. The need to implement the twelve international legal conventions already in existence to combat terrorism was another theme. The need to agree on a comprehensive convention on international terrorism was also stressed. On this the secretary-general was unambiguous. He said, 'I understand that there are outstanding issues, which until now have prevented agreement on this convention. Some of the most difficult issues relate to the definition of terrorism. I understand and accept the need for legal precision ... But let me say frankly, that there is also a need for moral clarity. There can be no acceptance of those who would seek to justify the deliberate taking of innocent civilian life, regardless of cause or grievance'.

The secretary-general has also frequently warned against the potential use of weapons of mass destruction in future acts of terrorism by urging the adoption of measures to prevent this.

A more coordinated Secretariat response to the challenges posed by 9/11 came through a policy working group established in October 2001 by the secretary-general 'to identify the long-term implications and broad policy dimensions of the issue of terrorism for the United Nations'. The group convened by the undersecretary-general for political affairs included senior officials of the Secretariat and a few outside experts. In fulfilling its mandate the policy working group had as its objectives the task of placing the role of the UN within the context of the struggle against terrorism, prioritizing the UN's activities in this regard and formulating a set of recommendations on how the UN system could function more coherently and effectively. Eight subgroups were formed for a more detailed examination of the issues involved and extensive links were established within the UN system and with outside groups including research bodies. The group submitted its report to the secretary-general on 28 June 2002 and the report was made public on 10 September with the secretary-general's endorsement one day before the first anniversary of 9/11. It was later introduced in the Security Council on 4 October 2002 when the CTC held its one-year anniversary meeting.

The group's report, while wisely recommending that the UN should focus on areas where it had a clear comparative advantage, emphasized how terrorism stood to undermine the purposes and principles of the UN Charter and had therefore to be effectively countered. The tripartite strategy proposed was as follows:

(a) Dissuade affected groups from embracing terrorism.
(b) Deny groups or individuals the means to carry out acts of terrorism.
(c) Cooperate internationally in the struggle against terrorism and its multifaceted nature.

While recognizing the enormous complexity of terrorism and its multifaceted nature the group did not attempt to define terrorism. It acknowledged that terrorism was both a political and a criminal act and that both dimensions had to be addressed. Thus a multilayered and coherent strategy was necessary. Under the rubric of 'dissuasion' the report examined international legal instruments, human rights and behavioral norm setting. In the 'denial' aspect of the strategy the work of the Counter Terrorism Committee, UN efforts at disarmament and arms limitation and the prevention and resolution of armed conflicts were addressed. The third section on 'cooperation' considered non-UN multilateral initiatives and coordination within the UN system. The problem of coordination has been the bane of the UN system under normal circumstances in many areas of its laudable work and the need for this in the urgent task of combating terrorism cannot be overemphasized. The report admits frankly that in the rush to incorporate counterterrorism in all areas of work UN bodies have caused overlaps, duplication and gaps. The under-resourcing of the Terrorism Prevention Branch of the Centre for International Crime Prevention in the Office on Drugs and Crime was highlighted. This has since been remedied to some extent.

In the thirty-one recommendations made by the group within the tripartite strategy of 'dissuasion–denial–cooperation', some could be implemented without delay while others would need additional resource allocations through complex budgetary procedures. Such constraints do not apply to the Security Council's CTC to the same extent. Despite the months that have elapsed since the publication of the group's report, implementation of the recommendations has been slow. It is clear that action by the Secretariat is being overshadowed by the CTC.

Conclusion

Following the foregoing survey of the UN's response to the gauntlet thrown down by the terrorists on 11 September 2001 it is necessary to evaluate this record as a basis for future action. Terrorism must be seen in context. It is undoubtedly a pernicious evil that affects all nations big and small, rich and poor. Counterterrorism is but one of the tools we must use in ushering in a better and safer world. It cannot diminish efforts in other priority areas of work such as the war on poverty, the struggle to eliminate HIV/AIDS, the promotion of human rights and disarmament. The very complexity of terrorism as a phenomenon requires a broader approach than is offered today by the CTC. As Secretary-General Kofi Annan has stated "the reality is that, like war, terrorism is an immensely complicated phenomenon with multiple objectives and causes, a multitude of weapons and agents, and virtually limitless manifestations'.

Another important aspect is that the vital relationship between countering terrorism and maintaining human rights has not been fully explored in the CTC. Mary Robinson, her successor as HCHR, Sergio Vieira de Mello, and numerous human rights NGOs have all spoken out against the circumvention of due process of the law, the secrecy surrounding counterterrorist measures (especially when directed against foreigners in countries) and the racial and religious profiling directed especially against Arabs and Muslims. Democracies as well as dictatorships have been guilty of this curtailment of civil liberties, justifying their actions on the basis of countering terrorism. Let me quote UN Secretary-General Kofi Annan again– 'there is no trade-off between effective action against terrorism and the protection of human rights'.

The problem is evidently a serious preoccupation among human rights experts today. From a meeting held by special rapporteurs, human rights experts, chairpersons of working groups of the special procedures of the UN Commission on Human Rights and chairpersons of human rights treaty bodies from 23–27 June in Geneva a joint statement was issued which contained the following – 'Although they share in the unequivocal condemnation of terrorism, they voiced profound concern at the multiplication of policies, legislations and practices increasingly being adopted by many countries in the name of the fight against terrorism, which affect negatively the enjoyment of virtually all human rights – civil, cultural, economic, political and social'.

> They draw attention to the dangers inherent in the indiscriminate use of the term 'terrorism', and the resulting new categories of discrimination. They recall that, in accordance with the International Covenant on Civil and Political Rights, and pursuant to the Convention against Torture and Other Cruel, Inhuman or Degrading Treatment or Punishment, certain rights are non-derogable and that any measures of derogation from the other rights guaranteed by the Covenant must be made in strict conformity with the provisions of its article 4.
> The Special Rapporteurs/Representatives, Experts and Chairpersons of the Working Groups of the special procedures of the Commission and the

Chairpersons of human rights treaty bodies deplore the fact that, under the pretext of combating terrorism, human rights defenders are threatened and vulnerable groups are targeted and discriminated against on the basis of origin and socio-economic status, in particular migrants, refugees and asylum-seekers, indigenous peoples and people fighting for their land rights or against the negative effects of economic globalization policies.

They strongly affirm that any measures taken by States to combat terrorism must be in accordance with their obligations under the international human rights instruments.

They are determined, in the framework of their respective mandates, to monitor and investigate developments in this area and call upon all those committed to respect for human rights, including the United Nations, to be vigilant to prevent any abuse of counter-terrorism measures.

Precisely for these reasons it is the view of this writer that in parallel with the useful work done by the CTC and complementary to it, a functional commission of the UN's Economic and Social Council (ECOSOC) should be established on terrorism. This would be analogous to other ECOSOC functional commissions such as the Commission on Human Rights and would help harmonize the work of the two bodies. Article 68 of the UN Charter empowers ECOSOC to 'set up commissions in economic and social fields for the promotion of human rights and such other commissions as may be required for the performance of its functions'. The international situation requires that a separate commission be established on international terrorism. It would provide the international community with an annual opportunity of a session devoted to a detailed examination of individual terrorist issues and situations in a coordinated effort to reduce and eliminate the scourge of terrorism. The Commission on Terrorism should ideally meet in Vienna serviced by the Office on Drugs and Crime located there. It should have all relevant UN departments, funds and programmes and specialized agencies address it from their individual perspectives together with intergovernmental, regional and subregional organizations, such as the International Committee of the Red Cross (ICRC) and NGOs. This rich kaleidoscope of views and presentations could benefit member states greatly in their struggle against terrorism beyond the purely law-and-order approach. Without in any way justifying terrorism, a multifaceted approach which sees the root causes as well as the manifestations and ramifications of the problem will better equip the international community in the critical task of preventing terrorism. This approach will also give member states not in the Security Council a greater sense of participation and ownership in the UN's efforts to combat terrorism. It will be consonant with the spirit of Article 1 of the UN Charter by being an effective collective measure and a peaceful means to prevent and remove a threat to international peace and security.

3

Terrorism and Human Rights:
A Perspective from the United Nations

ALEX P. SCHMID[1]

Senior Crime Prevention Officer, United Nations,
Office on Drugs and Crime, Vienna, Austria

The chapter begins with a discussion of the draft definition of terrorism in the UN Ad Hoc Committee on Terrorism, a definition which covers both terrorist blackmail and intimidation of target audiences but does not address the terrorist goal of impressing potential and actual constituencies with their "propaganda by the deed". It distinguishes then between a military response to terrorism, based on maximum force within the framework of the laws of war, and a law enforcement response, based on minimal use of force, within the framework of the rule of law. Subsequently twelve principles of the rule of law are outlined and their relationship to human rights is clarified. Next a discussion of specific human rights and how they relate to terrorism and countering terrorism follows. The activities of the Terrorism Prevention Branch of the UN Office on Drugs and Crime are discussed in the framework of the three-pronged UN Strategy against international terrorism. The chapter ends by stressed that upholding human rights and effective anti-terrorist measures are not exclusive. On the contrary: human rights and the rule of law are essential tools in the effort to combat terrorism.

By its very nature, terrorism is an assault on the fundamental principles of law, order, human rights, and peaceful settlement of disputes upon which the United Nations is established.

K. Annan, 4 October 2002

Introduction

Before turning to human rights issues and their relationship with terrorism, it is useful to make some broader observations on terrorism. When one talks about terrorism one talks about a sensitive issue, one on which the member states of the United Nations could not agree on a definition in more than thirty years. Currently the Ad Hoc Committee on International Terrorism in New York is negotiating a Comprehensive Convention against International Terrorism. At the moment, the following draft definition is on the table:

Any person commits an offense within the meaning of this Convention if that person, by any means, unlawfully and intentionally, causes:
(a) Death or serious bodily injury to any person; or
(b) Serious damage to public or private property, including a place of

        public use, a State or government facility, a public transportation sys-
        tem, an infrastructure facility or the environment; or
  (c) Damage to property, places, facilities, or systems referred to in para-
        graph 1 (b) of this article, resulting or likely to result in major
        economic loss, when the purpose of the conduct, by its nature or con-
        text, is to intimidate a population, or to compel a Government or an
        international organization to do or abstain from doing any act.[2]

While this draft text correctly identifies intimidation of the public and bringing pressure to bear on state authorities to accede to political demands as key purposes of terrorism, it does not address another major objective of terrorist groups, namely, to bring, (or keep) a particular issue in the forefront of public consciousness by means of perpetrating acts of violence which the news media cannot ignore. The idea of 'propaganda by the deed' is central to terrorism. In the French Revolution the guillotine was the instrument of terror; later the dynamite bomb allowed terrorists to achieve disproportionate resonance with their deeds. Later still came hijackings, truck bombs and suicide bombers.

    Terrorists create terror – but not only terror. Terrorism polarizes as it addresses different audiences simultaneously: while trying to immobilize one, it tries to mobilize the others by making them stiff with fear. Terrorism targets:

- Those who already identify positively with the terrorist group (goal: to increase their support);
- those who are their declared opponents (goal: to demoralize, intimidate or blackmail them);
- the noncommitted bystanders (goal: to impress them);
- the terrorists' own organization (goal: to keep it united through planning 'the big one');
- rival groups (goal: to show them who is 'No. 1').

    Audiences tend to give different interpretations to terrorist acts. Depending on whether people identify with the perpetrators or the victims of such acts they are viewed as heroic by some and as cowardly by others.

    The attacks of 11 September were serving the purpose of mobilization of discontent at least as much as the purpose of intimidation. According to a treatise titled *The Reality of the New Crusade*, it was meant 'to inflame the hearts of Muslims against America', in the hope of 'inspiring thousands of others to this type of operation'.[3] Terrorism, then, must also – and some think primarily – be seen as a form of violent and coercive communication.[4]

    When we try to evaluate the terrorist menace, we therefore not only have to look at terrorism's potential for intimidation and blackmail, we also have to look at the mobilization bold acts of terrorism can potentially produce in groups vulnerable to the terrorist temptation. In this regard, those responsible for 9/11 were manifestly wrong in their expectations: they did not manage to ignite a war between civilizations. We have seen relatively few copycat crimes and, more importantly, we have not seen a mass movement in the Islamic world marching under the banner of Al-Qaeda.[5] Its aim of being catalytic – able to provoke a wider conflict and mobilize a larger constituency – has not (or not yet) been reached.[6]

However, terrorists attempt to mobilize their constituencies not only by their own brazen deeds. As much, if not more, they rely on an overreaction of the opponent, which in turn might mobilize resistance against those opposing the terrorists.[7] That is the terrorist trap – a trap in which we will not be caught if we adhere to the principles of the rule of law, respect for human rights and minimal and proportionate use of force.

There is a difference between a military response to terrorism and a criminal justice response to terrorism. The military attempts to use maximum force to overwhelm an opponent within a framework of the *laws of war*, while the police try to use minimal force within a framework of the *rule of law*.[8]

Principles of the Rule of Law

The UN Office on Drugs and Crime very much uses the rule of law paradigm. In fact, the recent reorganization of the office has led to the creation of a new rule of law section. The human rights discourse focuses primarily on the rights of individual citizens and noncitizens, and to a lesser extent on group rights. The rule of law paradigm, on the other hand, is broader than the human rights paradigm. The ideas behind the concept are quite old but have been codified only at the end of the nineteenth century. Here are the main principles:

There are various interpretations of the concept 'rule of law'. A major influence in the original conceptualization was A. P. Dicey (*Introduction to the Study of the Law of the Constitution* [1885]). Drawing from Dicey and others, a dozen characteristics of the Rule of Law can be identified:

1. **Common ethics**: An underlying moral value orientation (e.g., towards equality and fairness) of all laws.
2. **The supremacy of the law**: All persons are subject to the law (i.e., those holding state power are also bound by a common law or constitution).
3. **Restraint of arbitrary power**: No power can be exercised except according to procedures, principles and constraints contained in the law.
4. **Separation of powers**: Parliament exercises legislative power; there are restrictions on the exercise of legislative power by the executive.
5. **The principle of 'habeas corpus'**: Arbitrary or preventive detention is prohibited.
6. **The principle nulla poena sine lege (no punishment without a law)**: Legislation should be prospective and not retroactive.
7. **Judicial independence**: An independent and impartial judiciary, with no special courts.
8. **Equality before the law**: Redress for breaches of the law must in principle be open to any citizen against any other citizen or officer of the state.
9. **State protection for all**: Just as nobody should be above the law, nobody should be outside the protection of the laws of the land.
10. **Supremacy of civilian authority**: Military and police forces must be subject to civilian control or oversight.
11. **Prohibition of summary justice**: Crimes are viewed as individual acts; there must be no collective punishment of a group for acts of individuals.
12. **The principle of proportionality**: Only minimum force should be used to stop lawbreakers; punishment must be relative to the seriousness of the offense.

The rule of law establishes a framework for the conduct and behaviour of both members of society and officials of the government. At the core of the concept there are three basic notions:

(a) that people should be ruled by the objective determination of general laws;
(b) that nobody should stand above the law, and that ordinary citizens can find redress against the more powerful for any act which involves a breach of the law;
(c) that nobody should fall outside the protection of the law.

Where the rule of law is firmly in place, it ensures the responsiveness of government to the people as it enables enhanced critical civil participation. The more citizens are stakeholders in the political process, the less likely it is that some of them form a terrorist organization. In this sense, it can be argued that the rule of law has a preventive effect on the rise of terrorism – at least on the domestic front.

As there is a growing awareness that there is a relationship between the rule of law and a nation's internal stability and its ability to manage conflict, the concept of the rule of law has also become a focus of international technical assistance. In order to help countries in transition to reach a higher level of law enforcement, judges, prosecutors, lawyers and police need to be instructed or trained to bring national practices in line with recognized international standards. In their technical cooperation programmes, UN agencies like the Office on Drugs and Crime focus, *inter alia*, on advancing the development of an independent judiciary and promoting more just legal systems.

As emphasized earlier, rule of law principles include human rights principles. Human rights are often conceived of as rights of individuals (and sometimes also groups) against the state. Rule of law principles, on the other hand, can be seen as more state-centered rather than individual-centered. In a way both conceptual frameworks look at the obligations that exist between the state and members of society.

Terrorism and Human Rights

Let us now turn to the relationship between terrorism and human rights. Human rights are codified in several international and regional instruments on human rights. Human rights instruments are:

1. International Covenant on Civil and Political Rights (ICCPR)
2. International Covenant on Economic, Social and Cultural Rights (ICESCR)
3. International Convention on the Elimination of All Forms of Racial Discrimination
4. Convention on the Elimination of All Forms of Discrimination against Women
5. Convention against Torture and Other Cruel, Inhuman or Degrading Treatment or Punishment
6. Convention on the Rights of the Child

The most famous one is the Universal Declaration of Human Rights from 1948 which is, however, only a declaration, not a treaty. Nevertheless, over the years many of its provisions have gained some customary law status, at least in some countries. These rights can be listed as, in a dozen major rights, namely:

The Right to Life
The Right Not to Be Tortured
The Right Not to Be Arbitrarily Arrested

The Right to a Fair Trial
The Right Not to Be Discriminated Against
The Right to Freedom of Association
The Right to Political Participation
The Right to Freedom of Expression
The Right to Food
The Right to Health Care
The Right to Education
The Right to Fair Working Conditions

Terrorists violate human rights, including the right to life, and in the case of hostage-taking and kidnapping, the right not to be arbitrarily arrested. However, terrorist crimes are usually punished under national penal laws.

Suspected terrorists often claim respect for human rights – some of the very same rights they have violated themselves in their acts of focused or indiscriminate victimization. This raises the question of whether terrorists too should be allowed to enjoy human rights. The answer is 'yes'. People accused of terrorist acts have human rights. That is exactly the difference between a situation of the rule of law and a situation where law is arbitrary. Do they have the same rights as victims? Again, the answer is 'yes', although this might go against our own feelings of justice. Everybody is equal before the law.

While states can derogate during an emergency certain human rights, like the right to freedom of association, there are rights which cannot be derogated – for instance, the right not to be tortured or the right to a fair trial. Extraordinary measures should be limited in scope and time. Stern and broad repressive measures alienate large sectors of society from the government and tend to produce new recruits for terrorist organizations.

Terrorists know very well that an overreaction by the government to their provocative attacks can play into their hands – though at times overreaction has also led to the elimination of the terrorist organization. The price some governments paid for overreactions involving gross violations of human rights were truth commissions and sometimes criminal court procedures against those who went beyond what the law allowed.

The UN advocates a human rights – based approach to fighting terrorism. In the words of the secretary-general:

> We should all be clear that there is no trade-off between effective action against terrorism and the protection of human rights. On the contrary, I believe that in the long run we shall find that human rights, along with democracy and social justice, are one of the best prophylactics against terrorism.[9]

Such statements were made amidst concerns about the erosion of fundamental rights in countries engaged in the fight against terrorism since the attacks of 11 September 2001. There has been a tendency to resort to a war model of fighting terrorism. Yet when we look at successful measures against terrorism since September 2001, we find that criminal justice measures have been prominent.

There are four pillars on which successful antiterrorist measures should build:

I.   Good Governance
II.   Democracy

III.   Rule of Law
IV.   Social Justice

Why these four? The reason for this is simple:

(i)   When governance is bad, resistance against corrupt rule gains followers and support.
(ii)   When unpopular rulers cannot be voted away in democratic procedures, advocates of political violence find a wide audience.
(iii) When rulers stand above the law and use the law as a political instrument against their opponents, the law loses its credibility.
(iv)   When long-standing injustices in society are not resolved but allowed to continue for years without any light in sight at the end of the tunnel, we should not be amazed that desperate people – and others championing their cause – are willing to die and to kill for what they perceive to be a just cause.

These then, are the foundations on which one should build policies aimed at the prevention and suppression of terrorism. These views were expressed by the late UN high commissioner for Human Rights (HCHR) who himself fell victim to a terrorist attack. The late UN HCHR Sergio Vieira de Mello said in October 2002:

> I am convinced that the best – the only – strategy to isolate and defeat terrorism is by respecting human rights, fostering social justice, enhancing democracy and upholding the primacy of the rule of law. We need to invest more vigorously in promoting the sanctity and worth of every human life; we need to show that we care about the security of all and not just a few; we need to ensure that those who govern and those who are governed understand and appreciate that they must act within the law.[10]

On 6 March 2003, the Counter Terrorism Committee convened a special meeting with some fifty international and regional organizations and at the end of the day the participants agreed that 'they would remain aware of the interaction between their activities and human rights concerns, and of the need for respect for the rule of law and human rights obligations'.

Activities of the Terrorism Prevention Branch of the UN Office on Drugs and Crime in the Framework of the Strategy of the United Nations

Let me now turn to the activities of the UN Office on Drugs and Crime and its Terrorism Prevention Branch. The Centre for International Crime Prevention in Vienna has, for many years, engaged in standard-setting. As a reminder, here are some of the standards developed by the UN, Crime Prevention and Criminal Justice Programme over the years, mainly in the quinquennial UN Congresses which are also relevant when it comes to dealing with terrorists and their victims:

1.   The Standard Minimum Rules for the Treatment of Prisoners (1957)
2.   The Declaration on the Protection of All Persons from Being Subjected to Torture and Other Cruel, Inhuman or Degrading Treatment or Punishment (1975)
3.   The Code of Conduct for Law Enforcement Officials (1979)

4. The Capital Punishment Safeguards (1984)
5. The Basic Principles on the Independence of the Judiciary (1985)
6. The Declaration of Basic Principles of Justice for Victims of Crime and Abuse of Power (1986)
7. The Principles on the Effective Prevention and Investigation of Extra-Legal, Arbitrary, and Summary Executions (1989)
8. The Basic Rules for the Treatment of Prisoners (1991)
9. The Basic Principles on the Use of Force and Firearms by Law Enforcement Officials (1990)[11]

In recent years, the UN Office on Drugs and Crime and its Centre for International Crime Prevention have engaged more and more in technical cooperation activities to make these and other standards work. In 1999 a small unit, the Terrorism Prevention Branch, was added to the centre. It engaged mainly in research and analysis before September 2001, when its mandate was strengthened and when the UN defined its role in the prevention and suppression of terrorism. Before turning to the Terrorism Prevention Branch's current activities, let us have a brief look at the wider UN strategy.

The Strategy of the United Nations

The overall strategy of the United Nations has been outlined in a report of a high-level policy working group on the United Nations and terrorism, which was made public on 10 September this year.[12] It is a three-pronged strategy which suggests that the United Nations should set for itself three goals: dissuasion, denial and cooperation.

UN Strategy 1 is to dissuade disaffected groups from embracing terrorism. That means:

- the UN ought to continue to make its contribution through norm setting, human rights and communications;
- the UN has a primary role in preparing for the adoption and effective implementation of legal instruments;
- the UN must ensure that the protection of human rights is conceived of as an essential concern;
- the UN should project a clear and principled message, underscoring the unacceptability of terrorism;
- these messages must be targeted to key audiences – particularly to achieve a greater impact in dissuading would-be supporters of terrorist acts.

UN Strategy 2 is to deny groups or individuals the means to carry out acts of terrorism. That means:

- The Counter Terrorism Committee is at the center of UN activities to deny opportunities for the commission of acts of terrorism;
- the UN system as a whole must ensure its readiness to support the committee's efforts to achieve the implementation of measures to counter terrorism;
- the UN agencies can provide assistance in this process through the development of model legislation for member states' compliance with international instruments and pertinent resolutions;

- the Department of Disarmament Affairs should draw public attention to the threat posed by the potential use of weapons of mass destruction in terrorist acts;
- preventive measures, especially measures to strengthen the capacity of states, can help to create inhospitable environments for terrorism.

UN Strategy 3 is to sustain broad-based international cooperation in the struggle against terrorism. That means:

- cooperation between the United Nations and other international actors must be made more systematic;
- an appropriate division of labour based on comparative advantage should be ensured;
- the next high-level meeting between the United Nations and regional organizations in early 2005 should establish terrorism as an agenda item, with the goal of developing an international action plan;
- the United Nations family must ensure a higher degree of internal coordination and coherence;
- consideration should be given to strengthening some UN offices, notably the Office for Drug Control and Crime Prevention of the UN Secretariat.

In line with the last recommendation, the Terrorism Prevention Branch of the UN Office on Drugs and Crime in Vienna has been elaborating a Global Programme against Terrorism, which envisages three types of activities.

UN Office on Drugs and Crime activities that relate to the promotion of the ratification and implementation of the international instruments to suppress and prevent terrorism include:

- analysis of existing relevant universal instruments and prioritisation of international cooperation provisions;
- assistance in drafting enabling laws and preparation of model legislation;
- strengthening the legal regime against terrorism with new tools contained in the conventions against illicit drugs and transnational organized crime;
- study of the compatibility between the relevant universal legal instruments and bilateral cooperation agreements;
- preparation of legislative guidelines on the basis of relevant instruments;
- preparation of implementation kits;
- analysis of the effectiveness of antiterrorist legislation;
- organization of regional workshops to review national legislation.

First, the global programme assists countries in taking concrete steps towards becoming parties to, and implementing, the international instruments relating to the prevention and suppression of international terrorism. The global programme will, to this effect, develop legislative guidelines and implementation kits.

Many countries have put in place measures to prevent and suppress terrorism. Not all of these mechanisms work in a satisfactory manner. The Global Programme against Terrorism provides advice on possible weaknesses of existing institutional structures and assists in the upgrading of old structures or the establishment of new institutions, providing training to staff in specific areas.

UN Office on Drugs and Crime activities of the centre for International Crime Prevention that relate to national administration measures include:

- facilitating mentorship programmes for capacity building;
- technical assistance for capacity building for international cooperation;
- collection of 'best practices' on international cooperation;
- promoting enabling operational structures for international cooperation;
- promoting counter-money-laundering structures;
- strengthening international cooperation for common border control;
- establishment of coordination agencies;
- provision of early warning checklist.

Finally, the new Global Programme against Terrorism also uses its information and databases in order to inform policy-makers on measures that can be taken to control terrorism. The information it collects also serves to establish national profiles in the fields of drugs, crime and terrorism and will contribute to the development of recommendations for national strategies.

UN Office on Drugs and Crime activities related to advocacy and prevention include:

- public awareness and civil society mobilization;
- public service announcements on prevention;
- contribute to the Office on Drugs and Crime's National Profiles (on drugs, crime and terrorism);
- contribute to National Country Strategies (as above);
- create 'best practices' kits.

Conclusion

The Secretary-General, when speaking to the Counter Terrorism Committee of the Security Council on 6 March 2003, said:

> We need to develop an international programme of action, founded on an unshakeable commitment to upholding the rule of law. As terrorism involves the calculated use of violence in violation of the law, our response to terrorism should aim to ensure the rule of law ... Terrorist acts, particularly those involving the loss of life, constitute grave violations of human rights. Our responses to terrorism, as well as our efforts to thwart it and prevent it, should uphold the human rights that terrorists aim to destroy. Human rights, fundamental freedoms and the rule of law are essential tools in the effort to combat terrorism – not privileges to be sacrificed at a time of tension.

When combating terrorism, we can therefore not do away with human rights, the rule of law, and principles of the peaceful settlement of disputes and the laws of war. It took so long to establish these norms and we have to defend them, even when this means, at times, defending the rights of terrorists. It is significant to find this line of thought also in a recent resolution of the Security Council:

> States must ensure that any measure taken to combat terrorism comply with all their obligations under international law, and should adopt such

measures in accordance with international law, in particular international human rights, refugee, and humanitarian law.[13]

This resolution is an encouraging sign and signal and gives the United Nations a mandate to press for human rights observance in the fight against terrorism.

Notes

1. The views and opinions expressed in this paper are those of the author and do not necessarily reflect the official position of the United Nations where the author serves as senior crime prevention and criminal justice officer of the Terrorism Prevention Branch of the Office on Drugs and Crime in Vienna.

2. UN Ad Hoc Committee on Terrorism, Comprehensive Convention [draft], Article 2–A/C.6/56/L.9, annex I.B.

3. 'Coordinateur du Mardi Saint', Ramzi Ben Al-Shaiba promettait 'un Millier d'autres Operations de ce Type', *Le Monde* (16 Sep. 2001) p. 2 . F. Halliday observed in a similar vein: '11 September did not, nor was it designed to, destroy America as a power so much as to mobilize support against its Middle Eastern allies'. Fred Halliday, *Two Hours that Shock the World – September 11, 2001: Causes & Consequences* (London: Saqi Books 2002).

4. An example of this communication function (which is linked to intimidation) is a statement broadcasted by Al Jazeera in early October 2002 in which Aiman Al Zawahiri, the No. 2 in Al-Qaeda said, referring to the attack on German tourists in front of the Jewish synagogue in Djerba, Tunis, and to the attack on the French oil tanker *Limburg* off the coast of Yemen: 'The Mujahedeen youth has sent one message to Germany and another to France. Should the dose [of the message] not have been sufficient, we are ready – of course with the help of Allah – to increase the dose'. *Der Spiegel* 21 Oct. 2002. For an interpretation of terrorism along these lines, see A. P. Schmid, *Violence as Communication* (Beverly Hills: Sage 1982).

5. 'Remember. September 11 Changed the World. But Not Enough', *The Economist* (7 Sep. 2002) p.11. Osama bin Laden expressed the hope that 'these events [9/11] have divided the world into two camps, the camp of the faithful and the camp of infidels'. Bin Laden Statement, 7 October 2001: 'The Sword Fell', in John Prados (ed), *America Confronts Terrorism: Understanding the Danger and How to Think About It* (Chicago: Ivan R. Dee 2002), p.13.

6. Osama bin Laden has been explicit about his goal: 'We are seeking to incite the Islamic nation to rise up to liberate its land and to conduct a jihad for the sake of God'. Carl Conetta, *Dislocating Alcyoneus: How to Combat al-Qaeda and the New Terrorism* (New York: Columbia University Press 2002) p.2.

7. With regard to Al-Qaeda, Brian M. Jenkins hypothesized:' Al Qaeda's leadership probably anticipated that the attack would provoke a major military response, which it could then portray as an assault on Islam. This would inspire thousands of additional volunteers and could provoke the entire Islamic world to rise up against the West. Governments that opposed the people's wrath, quislings to western imperialism, would fall. The West would be destroyed'. Brian M. Jenkins, *Countering al Qaeda: An Appreciation of the Situation and Suggestions for Strategy* (St. Monica: RAND 2002) p.7.

8. For an elaboration of these two models, see Ronald D. Crelinsten, 'Analysing Terrorism and Counter-Terrorism: A Communication Model', *Terrorism and Political Violence* 14/2 (Summer 2002) pp.77–122.

9. Mary Robinson, 'Human Rights Are as Important as Ever', *International Herald Tribune* 21 June 2002. In another statement, Kofi Annan said: 'while the international community must be resolute in countering terrorism, it must be scrupulous in the ways in which this effort is pursued. The fight against terrorism should not lead to the adoption of measures that are incompatible with human rights standards. Such a development would hand a victory to those who so blatantly disregard human rights in their use of terror. Greater respect for human rights, accompanied by democracy and social justice, will in the long term prove effective measures against terror. The design and enforcement of means to fight terrorism should therefore be carried out in strict adherence with international human rights obligations'. Kofi

Annan, Message to the African Union's High Level Inter-Governmental Meeting on Terrorism, Algiers 11 Sep. 2002.

10. Sergio Vieira de Mello, Statement before the Counter Terrorism Committee of the Security Council, New York, 21 Oct. 2002.

11. Roger S. Clark, 'The United Nations Crime Prevention and Criminal Justice Program', *Formulation of Standards and Efforts at Their Implementation* (Philadelphia: University of Pennsylvania Press 1994) pp.95–125.

12. Annex to A/57/273–S/2002/875 Report of the Policy Working Group on the United Nations and Terrorism. General Assembly/Security Council (Provisional Agenda Item 162).

13. SC RES 1456 (2003).

4

The Security Council and Counterterrorism: Global and Regional Approaches to an Elusive Public Good

KENNEDY GRAHAM

United Nations University, Bruges, Belgium

This paper explores contemporary counterterrorism efforts as an instrument for attaining peace as a 'global public good'. It notes the lack of an agreed definition of terrorism, the distinction between freedom-fighting and terrorism, and the issue of 'excessive use of force' by the state. It assessed the extent to which US counter-terrorism policy has influenced policy in the UN Security Council, and the shortcomings in Council policy that require redress. The paper concludes that counterterrorism will be successful only when a 'global law enforcement' approach prevails over the national security-driven 'war-on-terror' and when genuine efforts are undertaken to address the root causes of terrorism, including the forward basing of US forces in the Arab world.

Defining the 'Good'

Global and Regional Public Goods

'Global Public Goods' and the 'Planetary Interest'

The concept of a 'public good' has been the purview of classical economists for centuries, if not millennia. The standard modern definition belongs to Samuelson: 'collective consumption goods ... which all enjoy in common in the sense that each individual's consumption of such a good leads to no subtraction from any other individual's consumption of that good'.[1]

The concept is often advanced in juxtaposition to the notion of a 'private good'. Thus:

> What is a public good? This question can best be answered by looking at the counterpart, a private good. Private goods are typically traded in markets. Buyers and sellers meet through the price mechanism. If they agree on a price, the ownership or use of the good (or service) can be transferred. Thus private goods tend to be excludable. They have clearly identified owners; and they tend to be rival. For example, others cannot enjoy a piece of cake, once consumed. Public goods have just the opposite qualities. They are non-excludable and non-rival in consumption. An example is a street sign. It will not wear out, even if large numbers of people are looking at it; and it would be extremely difficult, costly and

highly inefficient to limit its use to only one or a few persons and try to prevent others from looking at it, too. A traffic light or clean air is a further example.[2]

In recent decades the institutional and conceptual nature of the international community has transformed. In 1993 the UN secretary-general observed that the 'first truly global era has begun'.[3] This change is being increasingly reflected in a gradual metamorphosis in global policy-making. In 1999, UNDP published a path-breaking work by Inge Kaul et al., 'Global Public Goods', which extrapolated the concept of public goods from the national to the global level.[4] Global public goods were defined as:

> ... public goods whose benefits reach across borders, generations and population groups.[5]

A comparable conceptual approach to global policy analysis is the 'planetary interest'.[6] The planetary interest has been defined as:

> The interests of the planet, comprising (1) the survival and viability of humanity, contingent on maintenance of the physical integrity of Earth, and the protection of its ecological systems and biosphere from major anthropogenic change; and (2) the universal improvement in the human condition in terms of basic human needs and fundamental human rights.[7]

Thus the 'planetary interest' lies in the full realisation of all 'global public goods'. But what might these be? Global public goods, the UNDP study asserts, include the environment, health, culture and peace.[8]

Peace as a 'Global Public Good'

Peace, said the UNDP study, is an example of a global public good because 'when it exists, all citizens of a country can enjoy it; and its enjoyment by, say, rural populations does not distract from its benefits for urban populations'.[9] The concept of public goods is taken as a conceptual instrument for 'rethinking' traditional notions of defence and national security.[10] Thus, the UNDP study contends, the maintenance of global peace and security is the 'quintessential global public good, in both substance and form'. As with most public goods and goods with positive externalities, it is a function best carried out on a global scale by the international public sector, and in appropriate regional situations by regional public sectors. Governments acting in their national self-interest are 'not apt' to carry out this mandate.[11]

A Strategy for Peace: A 'Global Security System'?

Peace, however, is a human condition that, in a dangerous and divided world, cannot be purchased by wishful thinking. It can only be achieved by means of a workable global security strategy of some kind. Two fundamental issues are at stake: (1) the attainment of global governance of a kind acceptable to all of humanity and that underpins a legitimate authority structure; and (2) an optimal force capacity for enforcement responsibilities.

These twin goals of an enduring global security strategy – institutional legitimacy and enforcement capacity – are proving elusive to the emerging global community.

The absence of a universal consensus over economic equity, sources of sovereign authority and the projection of global power is breeding new dangers to the stability of the international community. The absence of a legitimate force level and authority structure is raising questions of how to react to these new dangers. Increasingly, the security agenda of the international community, traditionally the preserve of the nation-state, is being shaped by non-state entities – 'private groups'. The term 'terrorism' has, over the past several decades, taken centre-stage in the security debate. With the increasing prospect of weapons of mass destruction (WMD) slipping into the hands of such groups that pursue competing agendas to that of the 'global establishment', the stakes are becoming increasingly high.

The 'Bad' and the 'Good': Terrorism and Counterterrorism

Threats to international peace and security, including terrorism, are, in the lexicon of the UNDP study, to be seen as global 'public bads'. As the UNDP administrator has put it in the 2003 sequel:

> We are facing just one major challenge: how to rethink and reorient public policy-making to catch up with today's new realities of interdependence and globalisation. Many of the world's main crises – from climate change to terrorism – have characteristics of global public bads. They affect us all indiscriminately but hit those with the fewest assets more severely than those with private or national means to protect themselves against crises, risks and human insecurity.[12]

Terrorism in Warfare and Conflict

Terrorism, defined as causing a state of being 'greatly frightened; in dread or awe',[13] is as old as human conflict. Alaric's troops devoted seventy-two hours to sacking Rome in 410 CE and the civilian death toll was in the tens of thousands.[14] The crusaders Bohemund and Godfrey and their Christian troops slaughtered 70,000 Muslims in taking Jerusalem in 1099 and burned Jews alive in their synagogues before kneeling in the Holy Sepulchre to give thanks.[15] The Turkic-Mongol leader Timur built mounds of skulls from the dead in suppressing a Persian revolt to his rule in 1395, slew 100,000 fellow Muslim civilians in Delhi three years later[16] and an additional 20,000 civilians in Baghdad three years after that.[17] Terror as a political tactic for 'domestic' rule is also a time-honoured phenomenon – *vide* Spain's Inquisition (the fifteenth to eighteenth centuries), France's Reign of Terror (1790s), the USSR's Stalinist purges (1930s), Germany's Holocaust (1940s), Kampuchea's agrarian killing fields (1970s) and Iraq's Baathist rule (1980s/1990s).[18]

With the onset of the modern age, however, terrorism assumed even more destructive capacity in international warfare. Modern military terror between states, with articulated political rationales, includes the Allied incendiary bombings of Dresden and Tokyo (whose firestorms killed 235,000 civilians) and the American atomic bombings of Hiroshima and Nagasaki (that together killed some 250,000 civilians). That these actions were consciously designed to sow terror in the hearts and minds of the enemy was never in doubt and has never been disputed.[19] The stated rationale rested on a marriage of self-defence and revenge.[20] This was a time of total war, yet German and Japanese leaders were tried at the time for war crimes.

The latest military campaign by the same allied coalition against Iraq in 2003 rested on the same tactic – the 'shock-and-awe' blitzkrieg from American precision-guided missiles. That the aim was to instill terror in Iraq (both its military infrastructure and civilian psyche), for the purpose of political domination is made clear from prewar American strategic planning literature.[21]

The differentiation of 'terrorism' from the 'legitimate use of force' concerns the distinction between lawful combatants and civilians. Traditionally in the nation-state era, military conflict was mostly fought between two opposing armies in open fields located far from towns and villages, and in such circumstances it was rare for civilians to be caught up in the fighting. In modern times, however, military technology, especially that utilising aircraft and missiles, has brought cities within the direct target zone of military action. During World War I, 5 percent of casualties from the fighting were civilian; in World War II, some 50 percent; in the 1990s, some 90 percent.

Definition and Identification: The Legal-Moral Maze

Defining 'terrorism' and identifying a 'terrorist' is perhaps the most complex and highly charged issue of modern times. It has both legal and moral dimensions. Is the globally orchestrated campaign against terrorism a more easily understood, Manichean struggle between 'global good and evil', or is it a more culturally relative 'struggle between civilizations'? And is it a 'global war' with a military dimension or a 'global police operation' for law enforcement?

In reaching agreement on a definition of terrorism, two major issues stand out: the identification of 'private terrorist groups' and the inclusion or exclusion of 'state terrorism' by armed forces. Two related issues also arise. First is whether, in distinguishing military from civilian targets, 'infrastructural targets' (power plants, broadcasting stations, pipelines, transportation facilities) may be included as legitimate military targets. Secondly is the issue of whether a distinction between a political group and its 'military wing' can be credibly made.

'Private Terrorism'. During the main decolonisation era (from the 1960s through 1980s), many countries insisted on differentiating between terrorism on the one hand and the struggle against foreign occupation and for self-determination on the other hand. The policy distinction has been largely promoted by Arab and other Islamic countries, especially since the 1967 Israeli occupation of Palestinian territories.

Both doctrinally and empirically, it is difficult to identify which 'rebel forces' would be accepted, by international consensus, as comprising a force whose violent actions against government forces would be deemed not to constitute a terrorist action. Four kinds of forces can be identified for consideration, namely: national liberation movements, secessionist movements, regime change groups and superpower withdrawal groups.

National Liberation Movements. Those groups most likely to be exempt from the 'terrorism' charge are those struggling for national liberation against 'foreign occupation' of their own land. This originally involved decolonisation movements (SWAPO in Namibia, ZANU-ZAPU in Zimbabwe, Frelimo in Mozambique), but since that era the focus has fallen on Palestinian groups fighting Israeli occupation of Palestinian territory. In this respect, two distinctions need to be drawn.

- Groups aiming to 'exterminate' Israel (Hamas, Hizballah, PFLP) are culpable of aggression against a sovereign UN member state. Those that accept Israel's 'right to exist within secure borders' (Fatah, Al-Aqsa Martyrs Brigade) are not culpable of 'aggression'.
- Groups that hit Israeli military targets in Palestine alone would be seen as liberation movements. Those that hit Israeli civilian targets are terrorists.[22] The PFLP's killing of Israeli athletes at the 1972 Olympic Games, for example, was indisputably a terrorist act, as are the suicide bombings of Israeli civilians by Hamas and Al-Aqsa Martyrs Brigade today.

There is, however, an underlying element to the debate, involving the definition of a 'legitimate target'. Palestinian groups argue that by illegally occupying Palestinian land in Gaza and the West Bank, Israeli armed 'settler civilians' (many of them army reservists) align themselves with their military forces and thus no distinction can be made.

The question of the Palestinian National Authority (PNA), and in particular the PNA president, Yasser Arafat, is especially complex. In 1964 the Palestine Liberation Organization (PLO) was established during an Arab league summit as a quasi-governmental entity to support Palestinian interests, with political, cultural, fiscal and military departments. At that stage its avowed aim was to replace the state of Israel with a Palestinian state through military means, including guerrilla action. In the mid-1970s, however, it recognised Israel's right to exist and in the mid-1980s it renounced terrorism.[23] Officially the PNA remains opposed to 'terrorism' but the US and Israel, citing suspicions that Arafat is abetting terrorists or not doing enough to oppose them, has ceased dealing with him and will deal only with the Palestinian prime minister. Such a policy, however, disregards the collective responsibility the Palestinian cabinet carries under its president for all PNA policy.

The current situation in Iraq is problematic. Two views, diametrically opposed yet equally plausible, can be advanced:

- It can be contended that the coalition invasion was illegal, being conducted outside the UN Charter and with the Security Council declining to approve it. In such a situation, the Iraqi fighters bombing military targets would be seen as liberation forces defending occupied territory (which covers the attacks conducted against CPA targets – American, British, Italian and Polish).
- If, however, the Security Council's post-invasion acknowledgement of the CPA as 'occupying authority',[24] recognition of the Iraqi Governing Council (IGC) as a 'an important step to restoring Iraqi sovereignty',[25] and establishment of a 'multinational force' to police Iraq is taken to be *ex post facto* legitimisation of the invasion,[26] then the Iraqi irregular forces bombing military targets would be seen as terrorists (although even this can be contested).

It is, however, beyond contention that the bombing of the Jordanian embassy, the UN and International Committee of the Red Cross (ICRC) compounds and the Arab residential complex in 2003 must be regarded as terrorist acts. The anonymity of the attackers and the absence of any stated purpose for such acts precludes an informed judgement over the extent to which such actions are to be seen as a national liberation movement or a broader Islamic repudiation of a US military presence in the region. It is probable that both elements are involved.

Secessionist Movements. Groups in northern Spain, Northern Ireland, the southern Philippines and northern Sri Lanka are all fighting for self-determination.

If they confine themselves to Spanish, British, Filipino and Sri Lankan military targets, these would be deemed to be legal and not 'terrorist actions'. But if they hit civilian targets, they would be deemed to be terrorists. This raises, in turn, the definition of a 'liberation movement'. Can any group advocate secession from an established government and take up arms against its armed forces? How does this affect Quebec in Canada, Puerto Rico in the United States, Assam in India and Corsica in France? The Chechen *shahid* believe they are in a 'war of resistance' against Russia.[27]

The most complex situation of all concerns Kashmir: Whether the militants fighting India there are engaged in 'national liberation' or 'secession' depends on the starting assumption adopted concerning the absence of a plebiscite that was to have been held in the 1940s. Along with Palestine, it is the issue of Kashmir, with Pakistan's determination to preserve the 'rights' of 'liberation forces' there, that drives OIC policy on the terrorism issue.

Internal Regime Change Groups. Those groups fighting for internal regime change face the same doctrinal challenge: to convince the international community that a campaign of violence against the established national order is legitimate. The Shining Path in Peru demonstrably fails in this aim as do the FARC and ELN in Colombia. But the GIA and the Salafists in Algeria resorted to violence, initially against government and military targets, after the democratic electoral victory of the Islamic Salvation Front was annulled by the military with western support. The resistance to that electoral annulment would seem to be a legitimate struggle but, as with the Palestinian liberation movements, they become terrorist groups when civilian killings are undertaken.

In South Africa, the ANC dropped its policy of nonviolence in 1961, adopting instead a retaliatory policy of 'violence against violence'.[28] ANC leader Nelson Mandela was repeatedly offered freedom if his organization would renounce violence, an offer he repeatedly rejected. As a result the ANC was deemed by many western countries to have been a 'terrorist organization'. Yet within the United Nations the ANC was always regarded as a liberation movement legitimately fighting an internal oppressor.[29] With Mandela's release in February 1990 and his emergence as a presidential leader he became regarded as a global political icon by the same countries that had previously vilified him.[30] With the 'struggle' essentially won, the ANC announced in June 1990 that it was suspending all armed action with immediate effect.[31] The cycle of political dominance if not judicial impartiality was completed in late 2003 with two separate developments. White militant Afrikaner Resistance Movement leader Eugene Terre Blanche was convicted of terrorism for ordering bomb attacks during the 1994 elections that had brought about black majority rule.[32] Also, former black ANC 'saboteur', Robert McBride, who was once on 'death row' for a 1986 bombing that killed three women civilians in Durban, was appointed police chief of a district in Johannesburg.[33]

'Hegemonic Resistance' Groups
Al-Qaeda takes as its main goal the withdrawal of US forces from the Arabian Peninsula.[34] But it also advocates the overthrow of the Al-Saud monarchy in Saudi Arabia. Its bombings of US forces stationed around the world (the USS *Cole* in 2000) have been perceived in the 'Arab street' as operations against a legitimate target. But its attacks against New York's World Trade Centre (1993, 2001),

the US embassy attacks in Africa (1998) and the civilian complex in Saudi Arabia (2003) are indisputably acts of terrorism.

Al-Qaeda contends, however, in a similar manner to Hamas, that US civilians are legitimate targets because they are, through the democratic process, responsible for US aggression against them.[35] It perceives the situation between it and the US to be a state of war in which civilians are enemy targets. For its part, the US has declared a 'war on terror' in response to the World Islamic Front (WIF's) 1998 statement and especially its September 2001 attacks. Thus a state of declared war appears to exist between the two belligerent sides.

If this is the case, then there appears to be no moral difference between the Allied 'terror bombing' of German and Japanese cities in the 1940s, the killing of civilians by Islamic groups in the modern age and the aerial bombardment of Palestinian and Iraqi 'military targets' by Israeli and coalition aircraft in 2003 that are authorised by civilian leadership with a specific range of civilian deaths as 'collateral damage' estimated in advance.[36] A public petition signed by a group of twenty-seven Israeli pilots in September 2003 condemning such air strikes on moral grounds caused controversy in Israel and a swift rebuke by the government.[37]

The rationality of the motivation of terrorist groups has recently been explored in a Chicago University project involving a comprehensive global database of suicide bombings for the past decade (1988–2001). The study shows that such operations draw not from religious fundamentalism (which is seen as a rhetorical cloak) but rather to a secular 'strategic logic': to compel liberal democracies to withdraw their military forces from the perpetrators' territory.

Three general patterns emerge from the data analysis: (1) nearly all such attacks are part of an organized campaign; (2) liberal democracies are uniquely vulnerable; and (3) the objective of such campaigns is political self-determination. Finally, the study concludes, the strategies have mostly proven effective – forcing withdrawals (US and France from Lebanon, 1983; Israel from Lebanon, 1985; Israel from Gaza and the West Bank, 1994–95), and offers of autonomy (Turkey to its Kurdish region).[38]

Such a campaign has yet to succeed in Chechnya, but it has been partially successful in Sri Lanka. Above all, the Al-Qaeda attacks against the US (August 1998, November 2000, September 2001) have resulted in US withdrawal from Saudi Arabia – albeit at the cost of a temporary occupation of Iraq. The bombings have, of course, moved there.

The policy of eradicating terrorism, the study suggests, through a wholesale transformation of Muslim societies into democratic models ('draining the swamp' in Afghanistan, 'removing Saddam's thugs' in Iraq) rests thus on an erroneous premise.

'State Terrorism'. The international community remains divided also over global policy towards 'state terrorism', or indeed whether such a phenomenon is even acknowledged to exist.

Even setting aside the Allied bombings of World War II, it is difficult to conclude that states have not, in the modern age, engaged in tactics of terror from time to time. Indeed in 1984 the UN General Assembly expressed its 'profound concern' that 'state terrorism' was being practised 'ever more frequently'. The assembly condemned policies and the practice of terrorism in relations between states as a method of dealing with other states and peoples. It demanded that no action be aimed at military intervention and occupation of other states, the forcible change in or undermining of their socio-political systems, and the destabilization and overthrow of their governments. Member states were to initiate no military action to those ends.[39] And in 1986 the Security Council warned the 'racist regime of South Africa' against committing any 'acts of ... terrorism' against neighbouring states.[40]

The General Assembly's appeal is applicable to the coalition's invasion of Iraq nineteen years later, but other events are relevant as well. Only one year after the assembly's appeal, the Greenpeace vessel *Rainbow Warrior* was bombed in Auckland's Waitemata Harbour by French secret service agents, an action that killed one civilian and which was described by the New Zealand prime minister at the time as 'an act of state terrorism'. France's subsequent flouting of the UN secretary-general's ruling on the matter further underlined the propensity of the P5 to exempt themselves from international standards as they deem fit.[41] A similar charge has recently been made against the United States by Nigeria. In November 2003 Nigeria warned the United States not to try to capture former Liberian president Charles Taylor to whom it had granted exile as part of a political settlement underpinning the Sierra Leone peace accord. After having recognised Taylor as the legitimate president of Liberia for a number of years, the US placed a $2m bounty on his head for him to be turned over to the Special Sierra Leone Court for crimes against humanity. The US action has been condemned by Nigeria as 'close to state-sponsored terrorism'.[42]

The distinction between 'state terrorism' and the 'excessive use of force' has often been used, especially regarding Israeli reprisal attacks against Palestinians. These include missile attacks from helicopter gunships on civilian areas where the IDF suspects militants may be hiding, and also the demolition of the homes of families of suspected terrorists – actions that violate the laws of warfare. Immediately after the second Palestinian *intifada* commenced in October 2000, the Security Council condemned the 'excessive use of force against Palestinians' which resulted in over eighty civilian deaths and called upon Israel, the 'occupying power', to 'abide scrupulously by its legal obligations and its responsibilities' under the Fourth Geneva Convention on the protection of civilians in time of war.[43] The UN Commission on Human Rights affirmed this in its resolution the same month, condemning the 'disproportionate and indiscriminate use of force' by Israel against Palestinian civilians – actions it judged to constitute 'war crimes' and 'crimes against humanity'. In March 2003 the secretary-general deplored 'the use of disproportionate and excessive force' by the Israeli Army in the Jabalya refugee camp in Gaza that had led to eleven Palestinian civilian deaths. Such military actions in densely populated areas, he said, as well as the demolition of Palestinian homes, 'cannot be accepted as a legitimate means of self-defence' and were in violation of international humanitarian law.[44] In October 2003 Israeli forces destroyed some 200 buildings in Gaza leaving 2,000 Palestinian civilians homeless. The secretary-general 'strongly deplored' Israel's continuing demolition of Palestinian-owned buildings as illegal, especially the destruction of three thirteen-storey buildings. He reminded Israel that house demolitions amounted to 'collective punishment which is a clear violation of international humanitarian law'.[45] The UN special rapporteur for human rights advanced trenchant criticism of Israel's 'counter-terrorism' actions.[46] It is clear that Israel's 'excessive use of force' in its 'counter-terrorism' operations kill as many innocent civilians as do Palestinian terrorist operations.

For its part, the US has vetoed a number of draft resolutions in the Security Council that would condemn Israel for such actions. In December 2002, following the fatal shooting by Israeli forces of a British UN official inside the UN compound during civil disturbances, the US vetoed a Syrian draft resolution that would condemn the action, on the grounds that it appeared to be more intent on condemning Israeli occupation than on ensuring the safety of UN personnel.[47] In November 2003 the US undertook similar reprisal methods in the Iraqi town of Tikrit, including house demolitions of families of suspected fighters.

Counterterrorism: An Instrument for the Public Good?
Thus developing a global strategy to combat terrorism is, *prima facie*, to be counted as a global public good. This premise, however, masks a host of complexities and nuances that make the delivery of peace through counterterrorism a problematic issue, both intellectually and politically.

Delivering the 'Good'

The Global Counterterrorism Strategy

Legitimacy: The United Nations as Legitimising Factor
The closest thing to the 'conscience of the world's people' in the current age is the voice of the UN secretary-general. In the immediate aftermath of the September 2001 attacks, Secretary-general Kofi Annan was unequivocal on global terrorism. The attacks were, he said, 'vicious assaults on our common humanity' – a 'terrible evil' that had shocked the conscience of the entire world. And the struggle, he thought, was one on a global scale: 'Terrorism will be defeated if the international community summons the will to unite in a broad coalition, or it will not be defeated at all ... We are in a moral struggle to fight an evil that is anathema to all faiths. Every State and every people have a part to play. This was an attack on humanity, and humanity must respond to it as one'.[48]

Because of these two factors – the moral dimension and the global scale of the undertaking, the UN is 'uniquely placed' to lead the fight. 'The United Nations is uniquely positioned to serve as the forum for this coalition, and for the development of those steps governments must now take – separately and together – to fight terrorism on a global scale'.[49] There was a need to develop a long-term strategy to enable all states to undertake the hard steps needed to defeat terrorism. Legitimacy is the key: 'I believe they can only do so when the global struggle against terrorism is seen as necessary and legitimate by their peoples – and that such universal legitimacy is something the United Nations can do much to confer'.[50] After adopting resolution 1368 the day after the attacks, the secretary-general stated that terrorism was an 'international scourge': 'A terrorist attack on one country is an attack on humanity as a whole. All nations of the world must work together to identify the perpetrators and bring them to justice'.[51]

The UN's Counterterrorism Strategy: Prevention, Protection, and Prosecution
Prevention: Policy Prescription by the General Assembly. As the principal universal organ of the United Nations, the General Assembly is expected to give policy

direction for the international community on the issue of terrorism. In the 1960s the term was not used, the focus being on specific acts of violence such as those involving aircraft hijackings. The term 'international terrorism' first appeared in the assembly in December 1972 following the Munich Olympic Games hostage crisis. The debate in the General Assembly that year quickly unfolded along lines of opinion that have not diverged greatly since. Status quo countries were concerned about the suppression of terrorism while developing countries and other *demandeur* states were concerned about the causes of terrorism and the distinction between terrorism and freedom fighting.

Legitimacy became an issue from the outset of the international debate. The first General Assembly resolution in 1972 was an evenly balanced expression of these views.[52] The assembly was 'deeply perturbed' over acts of international terrorism which were occurring with increasing frequency and taking the toll of innocent lives. It invited states to take all appropriate measures at the national level for speedy and final elimination of the problem. But it also urged them to 'devote their immediate attention' to finding just and peaceful solutions to the 'underlying causes' of such acts. The assembly, moreover, reaffirmed the 'inalienable right to self-determination' of all peoples under 'colonial and racist regimes and other forms of alien domination', upheld the 'legitimacy of their struggle, in particular the struggle of national liberation movements', and condemned 'terrorist acts by colonial, racist and alien regimes'.

The assembly then set up an Ad Hoc Committee on International Terrorism to analyse the views of member states, study the underlying causes of terrorism and recommend practical measures to combat it.[53] In 1979 it recognized that the Security Council needed to 'pay special attention' to all situations that might give rise to international terrorism and endanger international peace and security.[54]

In 1994, following the World Trade Center bombing in New York, the assembly issued a major Declaration on International Terrorism. The worldwide persistence of such acts, said the assembly, could jeopardise the security of states and endanger the 'constitutional order'. Such acts were 'criminal and unjustifiable' and could threaten international peace and security, and their suppression was an 'essential element' for peace. The UN had to make 'every effort' to promote measures to combat and eliminate such acts. In its view:

> Criminal acts intended or calculated to provoke a state of terror in the
> general public, a group of persons or particular persons, for political pur-
> poses are in any circumstance unjustifiable, 'whatever the considerations
> of a political, philosophical, ideological, racial, ethnic, religious or any
> other nature that may be invoked to justify them.[55]

In 2001 the assembly condemned the 'heinous acts of terrorism' in New York, Washington DC and Pennsylvania. It urgently called for international cooperation to prevent and eradicate acts of terrorism, and stressed that those responsible for aiding or harbouring the perpetrators, organizers and sponsors of such acts would be held accountable.[56]

The assembly has provided the auspices for the conclusion of twelve counterterrorism conventions. Work is continuing on two further treaties: an international convention for the suppression of acts of nuclear terrorism, and a 'comprehensive convention on international terrorism'. The comprehensive convention is intended to fill in gaps left by the sectoral treaties.[57] Agreement has been reached on a draft treaty on all issues except two: the definition of 'terrorism' and its relation to liberation movements (Article 2); and possible exemptions to the treaty's scope, in particular the activities of the armed forces (Article 18). In April 2003 a working group was established to settle these issues. Rival texts by the group coordinator and the OIC remain on the table and progress, rapid in late 2001, has since slowed.[58] It is, in fact, increasingly being questioned now whether a comprehensive convention is possible, or even necessary.

In fact, an agreed definition was included in one of its multilateral legal instruments in April 2002. In the Financing of Terrorism Convention the UN defined terrorism as:

> Any... act intended to cause death or serious bodily injury to a civilian, or to any other person not taking an active part in the hostilities in a situation of armed conflict, when the purpose of such act, by its nature or context, is to intimidate a population, or to compel a government or an international organization to do or to abstain from doing any act.[59]

Protection: Enforcement Action by the Security Council. Acting within its primary responsibility for international peace and security, the Security Council has become the principal vehicle for enforcement of the global counterterrorism strategy. The UN does not yet maintain a 'global list' of 'terrorist organizations'. To date it has confined itself to a list, standing in late 2003 at 372, of individuals and groups associated with the Taliban and Al-Qaeda. Tight restrictions, maintained by the council's '1267 Committee', were imposed on these groups since 1999, two years before the 11 September attacks in the United States. These oblige member states to freeze assets, prevent entry or transit through member state territories and impose arms sanctions.[60] The list has been compiled largely from intelligence supplied to the 1267 Committee by the United States.[61]

The UN has also not compiled a list of 'terrorist states' from among its members. It has dealt directly with only two member states over alleged terrorism.[62]

- In the case of Libya, sanctions were applied (1992–2003) for its lack of cooperation in the criminal investigations over the Lockerbie/UTA bombings. They were lifted after Libya agreed to pay compensation to victims of both flights.
- In the case of Sudan, following the 'terrorist assassination attempt' of Egyptian President Mubarak in Khartoum in 1996, the council called upon the Sudanese government to 'desist from engaging in activities of assisting, supporting and facilitating terrorist activities, and from giving shelter and sanctuaries to terrorist elements'.[63] After three months of Sudanese noncompliance, the council imposed diplomatic and travel sanctions[64] and subsequently aviation sanctions.[65] These were lifted in September 2001, following an accord brokered by the Non-Aligned Arab League and OAU.[66]

Shortly after the September 2001 attacks, the Security Council adopted the seminal counterterrorism resolution (1373) which, *inter alia*, established the CounterTerrorism Committee (CTC). The CTC has become the mainstay of the UN's counterterrorism strategy, with a monitoring group to follow the implementation of the resolution by all states and a mandate to 'increase the capability of states to fight terrorism'.[67]

Resolution 1373 imposes binding obligations on all states, with the aim of combating terrorism 'in all its forms and manifestations'. The resolution requires member states to deny terrorists financial support; deny them safe haven, sustenance or support; share information on planned attacks; cooperate in investigation and prosecution; criminalize 'active and passive assistance' for terrorism in domestic law; and join all relevant international conventions.[68]

Thus this omnibus resolution imposes wide-ranging responsibilities on all member states to combat 'terrorism' and prosecute or extradite 'terrorists'. But so long as there is no 'global UN list' of terrorist organizations it remains quite opaque as to whom such activities are to be applied against beyond the 372 Taliban/Al-Qaeda elements. In practice, most countries are 'advised' by the United States on this, but such advice is not universally accepted, even by its allies, as was witnessed in their reluctance to accept US demands to extradite individual Iraqi civilians and close Iraqi embassies during the 2003 coalition invasion.

Prosecution: The Jurisdictional Competence of the International Criminal Court (ICC). The 1949 Geneva Convention on the Protection of Civilians applies legal constraints on inter-state combatants, and its two protocols in the 1970s feature similar laws for internal conflicts. The Fourth Geneva Convention requires noncombatants to be treated humanely and thus not be targeted.[69] These provisions comprise the mainstay of civilised behaviour towards civilians in situations of armed conflict. The problem that arises, however, is when such laws apply in situations in which formal 'war' is not declared – such as the current 'war on terror'.

Sanctions against countries, organizations or individuals go only a certain way in 'combating terrorism'. The judicial process (for arrest, prosecution and conviction) is also necessary. In this respect the main difficulty, both doctrinally and operationally, concerns the competing, and rival, powers of the Security Council as the 'executive branch' of global governance and the new ICC as the 'judicial branch'.

In the early 1990s, the Security Council, for the first and only time, judged it to be appropriate and feasible to issue arrest warrants for individuals for attacks on humanitarian and UN personnel. In June 1993, alarmed at the 'premeditated armed attacks' against UNUSOM II forces by forces 'apparently belonging to the United Somali Congress', it authorised the secretary-general to take 'all necessary measures' against them including their investigation, arrest and detention for prosecution, trial and punishment.[70] It was on the basis of this decision that the US sent in its 'elite troops' (Delta Force and Task Force Rangers) to effect the arrests on the secretary-general's behalf. Following the downing of the US helicopter gunships in October in which eighteen US troops were killed, the council did a *volte face* in its policy, stressing Somali responsibility for its own 'self-determination', and asking the secretary-general to suspend the arrest actions against 'those individuals who might be implicated but are not currently detained', and to 'make appropriate provision to deal with the situation of those already detained'.[71]

The resolution did not name individuals but the US had aimed to capture, arrest and prosecute United Small Congress leader Farah Aidid. The US Task Force Rangers never succeeded, capturing instead some fifty-five Somalis including two of his lieutenants. Detained for a month or so on an island off the Somali coast, they were subsequently released on the orders of the US president, in what was one of the more bizarre operations ever under Security Council authority.

The Security Council has established ad hoc international criminal tribunals to prosecute individuals for crimes committed in the former Yugoslavia and Rwanda. Defendants are prosecuted for war crimes and crimes against humanity. Former Yugoslav president Milosevic is currently on trial for individual criminal responsibility and superior criminal responsibility (under Article 7 of the tribunal's statute), one count of violations of the laws or customs of war (Article 3 [murder]), and four counts of crimes against humanity (Article 5 [deportation; murder, and persecutions on political, racial or religious grounds]).[72] Separately, an independent Special Court for Sierra Leone was established in August 2000 by agreement between the UN and that country. The court, described as a 'hybrid' involving both international and national lawyers, has jurisdiction granted by the council for war crimes, crimes against humanity and 'other serious violations of international humanitarian law'.[73] The chief prosecutor indicted seven people in 2001 including the rebel leader Foday Sankoh who died in custody. In June 2003 the prosecutor then indicted Liberian President Taylor in June 2003 while he was still in office.

In the past five years the international community has made great headway in the development of international criminal jurisdiction, most notably through the establishment of the ICC, in force since July 2002. Unlike the International Court of Justice (ICJ), which adjudicates disputes only between states, the ICC has jurisdiction to prosecute individuals for certain stipulated crimes.

The ICC has jurisdiction to prosecute individuals for genocide, crimes against humanity and war crimes. The crime of 'terrorism' is not included in the court's jurisdiction. The court may thus be able to prosecute terrorist acts only when they amount to any of the three stipulated crimes. All countries, however, have a duty to take all necessary steps to prevent the commission of terrorist acts and bring alleged terrorists to justice through the application of their national jurisdictional laws.

The ICC currently has ninety-two member states; of the Security Council's P5, only Britain and France are members. Russia voted for the adoption of the statute in 1998, signed the statute in September 2000, and is considering ratification. China voted against the statute but retains an 'open mind' about future membership of the court.[74] The US opposed the establishment of the ICC and has refused to join it, principally because it fears the ICC will 'undermine' the Security Council and 'threaten' US national sovereignty.[75] It has negotiated bilateral agreements with some states in which the latter undertake not to prosecute US armed forces personnel. When the ICC came into force, the UN Security Council adopted a resolution under binding authority, upon US urging, that if a case arises involving personnel in a UN peacekeeping operation, the ICC will not commence proceedings unless the Security Council decides otherwise.[76] This accords the council authority over the court in UN peacekeeping matters.

Regional Counterterrorism Strategies

Are there any differences between the global counterterrorism strategy and regional strategies? The 1999 UNDP study referred to the regional dimension of global public goods. The latter, it said, 'form part of the broader group of international public goods which include as another sub-group, regional public goods'.[77]

Regional peace, in turn, is a global public good in that it is 'an element – a building-block – of world order'.[78] There is, today, a growing recognition that multilateral action to that end can be carried out by regional as well as global multilateral institutions.

Until the 1980s 'terrorism' had been largely confined to areas of regional tension, mainly the Middle East, the most notable attack being the October 1983 attack against US barracks in Lebanon (which killed 262 personnel) and the French military base (which killed 58), occasioning a US/French withdrawal.[79] In 1993, however, following the Gulf War, the ensuing sanctions against Iraq and the US military presence in Saudi Arabia and Kuwait, terrorism became 'global', striking at the United States through the bombing of the World Trade Centre which killed 6 civilians, and again in 2001 which killed some 2,900.

The regional approach to terrorism can be seen as two-fold: reflecting a 'global consensus' over the network of facilitating instruments for strengthening prevention, protection and prosecution of terrorism, and a 'global dispute' over which groups those instruments are to be applied against.

Thus, in developing the facilitating instruments, all major regions have committed themselves to opposing and suppressing terrorism through regional binding conventions – the Americas in 1971, Europe in 1977, South Asia in 1987, the 'Arab Nation' in 1998, and Africa and the former Soviet CIS in 1999.

The 'global dispute' reflects disagreement between an American-European policy and an Arab-African-Asian policy. The division turns on the two issues disputed in the UN negotiations over the Comprehensive Convention identified earlier: the definition of terrorism and the inclusion or exclusion of armed forces from liability. The former group perceives terrorism in broadly similar manner (largely agreeing on which groups are 'terrorist') although the European counterterrorism strategy has discernible differences from the American. The latter group disputes the two issues with the American-European group.

The Arab World

The Arab world reflects the region carrying the greatest sensitivity on issues of 'terrorism'. In 1998 the Arab League adopted its regional convention. The league desired to promote mutual cooperation in the suppression of terrorist offences, since they posed a 'threat to the security and stability of the Arab Nation' and endangered its vital interests. Arab states were committed to the 'highest moral and religious principles' and, in particular, to the tenets of the Islamic *sharia*, as well as to the humanitarian heritage of an Arab Nation that rejects all forms of violence and terrorism and advocates the protection of human rights. Such Islamic precepts, it said, conformed with the principles of international law.

At the same time, the league affirmed the right of peoples 'to combat foreign occupation and aggression by whatever means, including armed struggle, in order to liberate their territories and secure their right to self-determination, and independence'. They could do this in such a manner as to preserve the territorial integrity of each Arab country. This, too, was in accordance with the purposes and principles of the charter and all UN resolutions.

The league was not afraid to offer a definition of terrorism:

> Any act or threat of violence, whatever its motives or purposes, that occurs in the advancement of an individual or collective criminal agenda and seeking to sow panic among people, causing fear by harming them, or placing their lives, liberty or security in danger, or seeking to cause

damage to the environment or to public or private installations or property or to occupying or seizing them, or seeking to jeopardize national
resources.[80]

Asia

The South Asian countries completed a convention in 1987 that focused principally
on extradition. It offered a rather quixotic definition of terrorism, *viz.*:

> ... conduct shall be regarded as terroristic and for the purposes of extra-
> dition shall not be regarded as political offence, or as an offence connec-
> ted with a political offence, or as an offence inspired by political motives
>   murder, manslaughter, assault causing bodily harm, kidnapping and
> hostage-taking;
>   offences relating to firearms, weapons, explosives and dangerous
> substances, when used as a means to perpetrate indiscriminate violence
> involving death or serious bodily injury to persons or serious damage
> to property;
>   offences covered under the treaties on aircraft hijacking, aviation
> safety and internationally-protected persons;
>   an offence under any South Asian regional treaty that obliges mem-
> ber states to extradite.

This extraordinarily broad definition of terrorist offences has done little to mitigate
mutual Indo-Pakistani recrimination over alleged terrorism by Muslim Kashmiri
separatists operating against Indian sovereignty in its part of Kashmir.

Africa

The OAU defined terrorism in its 1999 convention clearly:

> 'Terrorist act' means any act which is a violation of the criminal laws of a
> State Party and which may endanger the life, physical integrity or freedom
> of, or cause serious injury or death to, any person, any number or group
> of persons or causes or may cause damage to public or private property,
> natural resources, environmental or cultural heritage and is calculated or
> intended to:
>
> (i) intimidate, put in fear, force, coerce or induce any government, body,
>   institution, the general public or any segment thereof, to do or
>   abstain from doing any act, or to adopt or abandon a particular
>   standpoint, or to act according to certain principles; or
> (ii) disrupt any public service, the delivery of any essential service to the
>   public or to create a public emergency; or
> (iii) create general insurrection in a State.

America

The OAS completed in 1971 a convention to prevent and punish acts of terrorism.
It was, however, seen as allowing 'enormous gaps' and a new Inter-American
Convention against Terrorism was floated in the mid-1990s, galvanised by the Sep-
tember 2001 attacks and completed in June 2002. This, however, speaks only of

cooperative measures to implement on a regional scale all international legislation on the subject. In effect, the US pursues its own national counterterrorist strategy, and expects the OAS to reflect its concerns. The OAS is the only regional body, of which the US is a member, in which a regional country (Cuba) is on the US list of 'state sponsors of terrorism'. The US is resisting calls from a number of other OAS countries for Cuba's readmission to the regional body.[81]

Europe

In 1977 the Council of Europe concluded a similar facilitating treaty. In December 2001 the EU adopted a 'Common Position', essentially transposing the Resolution 1373 requirements into its regional mechanism for counterterrorism. The EU maintains a list of eighteen 'terrorist organizations'. The list extends beyond the UN's Al-Qaeda/Taliban list, including Egypt's Al-Gama'a al-Islamiyya, Turkey's PKK and DHKP/C, and Peru's Shining Path. The EU and US are coordinating their group identification increasingly closely – the latter joined the EU in moving against the Basque group ETA.

A National Counterterrorism Strategy (The United States)

The US has developed a more far-reaching counterterroism strategy than the United Nations has been prepared to accept for itself. The US is driving the UN's counterterrorism strategy, conflating the UN's responsibility for determining 'threats to international peace' with its own national security concerns.

The US has its own national definitions of 'terrorism' and related concepts. Thus:

'Terrorism' is:
   'premeditated, politically motivated violence perpetrated against non-combatant targets by sub-national groups or clandestine agents, usually intended to influence an audience'.
'International terrorism' is:
   'terrorism involving citizens or the territory of more than one country'.
A 'terrorist group' is:
   'any group practicing, or which has significant subgroups which practice, international terrorism'.[82]

Unlike the UN and regional organizations, the US maintains two lists: of 'state sponsors of terrorism' and 'foreign terrorist organizations' (FTOs). These were commenced in 1997 as a method of tracking and taking action against terrorist groups around the world. FTOs are

> groups that either engage in or have the capacity or intent to carry out terrorist activity that threatens U.S. nationals or U.S. national security, including efforts to disrupt national defense, foreign relations, or U.S. economic interests.

The list provides the United States with the legal basis to prosecute people within its jurisdiction for aiding, through money or other resources, any designated FTO. The United States also has the authority to compel US financial institutions to freeze any assets linked to an FTO, and report them to the US Department of the Treasury.

The US currently identifies thirty-four organizations as 'foreign terrorist organizations', located in nineteen countries (see Appendix). They include:

- eight secessionist groups (in Britain, Spain, France, Turkey, Pakistan (for Kashmir), Sri Lanka and the Philippines);
- twelve groups working to overthrow their government and set up an alternative regime, either an Islamic state (in Algeria, Egypt, Lebanon and Uzbekistan), a Marxist state (in Colombia and the Philippines), a secular state (in Iran) or a biblical state (in Israel);
- one anti-insurgency group (in Colombia) which fights the rebels and their supporters;
- eight groups which seek the termination of the state of Israel and, usually, establish an Islamist state in its place;
- four groups which seek the withdrawal of US forces (and in some cases NATO forces and the EU) from their national territory or region;
- one millenarian cult (Japan).

These groups differ enormously in membership, wealth and destructive potential – ranging from Al-Qaeda, seen by the US as the major national security threat, to small or near-defunct cells without potent destructive capacity.

The US definition exempts governments from inclusion in the definition of any 'terrorist act'. It does, however, maintain an official list of 'state sponsors of terrorism' and in 2003 the list included seven countries: Cuba, Libya, Iran, Iraq, North Korea, Sudan and Syria. These countries face various US embargoes and have their assets frozen in the US.[83]

Within the US, 'domestic terrorism' is defined as 'the unlawful use, or threatened use, of force or violence by a group or individual based and operating entirely within the US or its territories, without foreign direction, committed against persons or property to intimidate or coerce a government, the civilian population, or any segment thereof, in furtherance of political or social objectives'.[84] The USA Patriot Act (PL 107–56, 26 October 2001) provides expanded US law enforcement powers to enhance the administration's efforts 'to detect and deter acts of terrorism in the US or against US interests abroad'. It is this act that has given rise to serious criticism of alleged curtailment of civil liberties of US nationals and violations of the human rights of foreign nationals under international law.

Since September 2001 the US has created a new category that remains unrecognised in international law – that of 'enemy combatant'. Individuals whom the US has captured in Afghanistan and indeed elsewhere are not perceived as 'prisoners of war', notwithstanding its declaration of a 'war on terror', and as a result the individuals are not accorded prisoner-of-war status. The 600 foreign nationals detained at Guantanamo Bay are thus accorded no legal rights under US law or under international law, but are simply detained indefinitely, without trial or legal representation. These include allied nationals such as Australians and Britons.

The US reaction to the September 2001 attacks has been a hybrid. The campaign against the Taliban and Al-Qaeda in Afghanistan had clear international support. The US campaign since then, including especially the invasion of Iraq, has not.

Recent US policy developments have caused concern, both internationally and domestically, as a recent critique by former presidential adviser, Zbigniew Brzezinski, makes clear.[85]

Measuring the Good

Conclusions and Recommendations

As this paper has shown, the issue of terrorism and counterterrorism is the most complex security dilemma that the international community faces. This is because it adds, to the traditional challenges of statecraft, the more emotive issues directly affecting humanity as a whole. The following conclusions and recommendations are advanced from the foregoing.

Conclusions

Defining the Good: Peace as a 'Public Good' and Counterterrorism as Its Instrument
Conclusion 1. The reality of peace as a 'public good' is more complex than first appears. A city's traffic light can indeed be 'enjoyed by all', but only provided the community has an adequate supply of the nation's electricity which depends on the world's fuel resources. This in turn raises complex questions of global sustainability and distributive justice. Similarly, a communal enjoyment of a secure and peaceful environment depends ultimately on a near-identical set of national and global public goods – sustainability and distributive justice. Such a challenge is weakening the recognisable architecture of global security. As the secretary-general observed, 'we seem no longer to agree on what the main threats are, or on how to deal with them'.[86]

Above all, he warns, we must be 'intensely aware' of the changes in the security environment: It is 'vitally important' not to allow recent differences to persist and to find a unity of purpose based on a 'common security agenda' with a global consensus on, and response to, the major threats.[87] Such a common security agenda will need to reflect equally the security threats faced by the South (*inter alia*, poverty alleviation and epidemic disease) as much as those faced by the North (primarily terrorism and WMD proliferation – all under the emerging concept of 'human security'.

The true 'public good' is a 'positive peace' in which the international community develops a rational way of utilising the planet's resources on a sustainable basis, agrees on territorial rights among societies and evinces mutual respect for traditional belief patterns. Terrorism is the manifestation of global ill-health and should be seen as a disease of the global body politic. As long as it is seen in Manichean terms of global 'good' versus 'evil' and something whose symptoms must be 'suppressed' rather than causes removed the international community will invite, through undue retaliatory violence from the establishment, more of the same. As the UN secretary-general has put it, we must proceed with our minds rather than our hearts.[88]

Conclusion 2. As a corollary, a true counterterrorism strategy is not a 'war on terror' which can never be 'won' because it has no identifiable foe or value-based objective, but rather a focus on the 'dialogue among civilizations' proposed by the president of Iran in 1998, and the interfaith dialogue that is under way.[89]

Delivering the Good: Global and Regional Counterterrorism Strategies
Conclusion 3. The UN is the only 'legitimising instrument' in defining 'terrorism'. Any regional or national definition will reflect an undue bias in security perception. Progress in global counterterrorism will not be significant until and unless agreement is reached on a definition that can be applied objectively and dispassionately to all groups engaging in violent actions. Failing that, the major powers, and particularly the US, will continue to prosecute counterterrorism operations that reflect their own national security perceptions.

Conclusion 4. The involvement of the UN, however, does not *ipso facto* result in total policy consistency. Its unstinting support for African liberation movements resulted in its overlooking attacks that were perpetrated against civilians which would, today, encounter criticism and opposition as acts of 'terrorism'.

Conclusion 5. The biggest problem, partly because of the definitional shortcoming, is the lack of a comprehensive list of terrorist organizations maintained by the UN. The US list cannot suffice. As a result, all UN member states are expected to develop the comprehensive policies for counterterrorism without having clear guidance as to whom these are to be applied against (apart from the Taliban/Al-Qaeda groups).

Conclusion 6. The regional agencies have taken the lead from the UN Security Council in developing legal instruments for coordinated counterterrorism action. Yet it is one thing to agree on coordinated legal provisions for action against 'terrorism', and quite another to agree on which groups are 'terrorists'. Although there is little difference between the American and European regional approaches in identifying terrorists, significant political differences are currently discernible over the propensity to intervene (the US adopting a unilateralist approach and the EU opting for an 'effective multilateralism' and 'constructive engagement'). Greater differences of view are evident between Asian, African and Arab regional views of identification of terrorists, thwarting the global consensus that is necessary to effective long-term action.

Measuring the Good
Conclusion 7. Because of these shortcomings, an effective global counterterrorism strategy is proving elusive. Currently the international community is failing to speak with one voice on terrorism, the UN General Assembly's policy prescriptions and the Security Council's enforcement actions not being totally compatible. The council's policy reflects the undue influence of US national security perceptions and policies, and does not accurately reflect the overall views of the international community. A more effective counterterrorism strategy is therefore required that reflects a more balanced global view.

Recommendations
Recommendation 1. It may be a more promising route to relate the concept of 'terrorism' to that of crimes currently covered by the newlye stablished International Criminal Court which would then have jurisdictional competence. This would not be 'genocide' but could be either 'war crimes' or 'crimes against humanity'.[90] While this would incur the current opposition of the United States, it is within the competence of the state parties to the ICC to determine which crimes are to be covered by the court.

Recommendation 2. The international community will only proceed properly against terrorism when a 'global list' of terrorist organizations is agreed upon by the United Nations. A mechanism for this needs to be established, beyond the present 1267 Committee (involving perhaps a revision of that committee). But this will depend upon agreement on a definition as a *sine qua non* of proceeding.

Notes

1. Paul A. Samuelson, 'The Pure Theory of Public Expenditure', *Review of Economics and Statistics* 36 (Nov. 1954) pp.387–9.
2. Inge Kaul, *Le Monde Diplomatique* (June 2000).
3. *UN Chronicle* 30/1(March 1993) cover.
4. Inge Kaul, Isabelle Grunberb and Marc Stern (eds), *Global Public Goods: International Co-operation in the 21stCentury* (UP 1999).
5. Kaul (note 2).
6. 'The "planetary interest" is the kind of forward-looking concept we need, as the world goes through a period of profound transformation'. Kofi Annan, 'Foreword', in Kennedy Graham (ed), *The Planetary Interest* (Rutgers University, New Brunswick, New Jersey and UCL Press, Taylor and Francis, London, 1999).
7. Ibid, p.7.
8. Kaul (note 4) p.x. This is echoed in the 'planetary interest' study: 'The three vital planetary interests politically recognised by the international community in the 1990s are global strategic security, global environmental security, and global sustainability. Avoiding self-destruction, protecting Earth and meeting humanity's basic human needs on an enduring, inter-generational basis rank as the three global priority issues of our age ... These three need to be treated separately from all others – *sui generis* – in terms of how nation-states determine their national policies and how humanity constructs global powers of policy-making and enforcement'. Also see Graham (note 6) p.10.
9. Kaul (note 4) p.4.
10. 'World history is largely a history of wars. All have been fought in a world without governance – where national 'defence', regional military alliances, balance of power and hegemonic imperialism have been the prevailing regimes. There is a manifest need for a system under universal auspices for maintaining global peace and security. The notion of a global public good is a logical starting point for considering how such a system would operate ... Defence has traditionally been held up as a pure public good in the domestic sphere ... In contrast, peace meets the substantive (that is, welfare) as well as formal criteria of a public good ... It is the best state of society for human survival ... At the international level, global peace benefits all, much like the pubic good of law and order at the domestic level'. Kaul (note 4) pp.382, 388.
11. Kaul (note 4) p.404.
12. Mark Malloch Brown, 'Foreword', in *Providing Global Pubic Goods: Managing Globalization*, (Oxford: OUP 2003) p.xvi.
13. *Shorter Oxford English Dictionary*, 3rd edn. (Oxford: OUP 1965) p.2155.
14. Will Durant, *The Story of Civilization*, vol. 4 (New York: Simon & Schuster 1950) p.36.
15. Ibid, p.592.
16. Durant (note 1.1), vol. 1 p.463.
17. *Encyclopaedia Britannica*, vol. 11 p.784.
18. China's great famine that killed 30m civilians (1959–61) is not included, being the product of incompetence deriving from ideological delusion rather than the use of terror for political repression.
19. 'It seems to me that the moment has come when the question of bombing of German cities simply for the sake of increasing the terror should be reviewed. Otherwise we shall come into control of an utterly ruined land ... I feel the need for more precise concentrations upon military objectives ... rather than on mere acts of terror and wanton destruction'. This sentiment was voiced by prime minister Winston Churchill in March 1945. see Murray Williamson, *War in the Air*, (London: Cassell 1999).

20. 'Having found the bomb we have to use it. We have used it against those who attacked us at Pearl Harbour, against those who have starved and beaten and executed American prisoners of war, against those who have abandoned all pretence of obeying international laws of warfare. We have used it in order to shorten the agony of war, in order to save thousands and thousands of young Americans'. Harry Truman, Address to the Nation, 9 Aug. 1945.

21. 'Since before Sun Tzu and the earliest chroniclers of war recorded their observations, strategists and generals have been tantalized and confounded by the elusive goal of destroying the adversary's will to resist before, during, and after battle. Today, we believe that an unusual opportunity exists to determine whether or not this long-sought strategic goal of affecting the will, understanding, and perception of an adversary can be brought closer to fruition ... Perhaps for the first time in years, the confluence of strategy, technology, and the genuine quest for innovation has the potential for revolutionary change. We envisage Rapid Dominance as the possible military expression, vanguard, and extension of this potential for revolutionary change. The strategic centers of gravity on which Rapid Dominance concentrates, modified by the uniquely American ability to integrate all this, are these junctures of strategy, technology, and innovation which are focused on the goal of affecting and shaping the will of the adversary. The goal of Rapid Dominance will be to destroy or so confound the will to resist that an adversary will have no alternative except to accept our strategic aims and military objectives ... To affect the will of the adversary, Rapid Dominance will apply a variety of approaches and techniques to achieve the necessary level of Shock and Awe at the appropriate strategic and military leverage points. This means that psychological and intangible, as well as physical and concrete effects beyond the destruction of enemy forces and supporting military infrastructure, will have to be achieved. It is in this broader and deeper strategic application that Rapid Dominance perhaps most fundamentally differentiates itself from current doctrine and offers revolutionary application'. see Harlan K. Ullman and James P. Wade *et al.* (eds), *Shock and Awe: Achieving Rapid Dominance'*, (National Defense University Press 1996).

22. The Al-Aqsa Martyrs Brigade, for example, initially vowed to target only Israeli soldiers and settlers in the West Bank and Gaza, but in early 2002 it launched attacks against civilians in Israeli cities, and in March after a suicide bombing in Jerusalem, the US added it to its FTO list.

23. In June 1974 the PLO called for the creation of a 'national authority' in the West Bank and Gaza, implying tacit recognition of Israel. It also 'condemned all outside operations and forms of terrorism'. In December 1976 it called for the establishment of an independent state of Palestine on the same two territories which was seen as confirmation of Israel's right to exist. In 1985 Arafat issued the Cairo Declaration stating that 'the PLO denounces and condemns all terrorist acts, whether those involving countries or by persons or groups, against unarmed innocent civilians in any place'. He undertook to take 'all punitive measures against violators'. In June 1988 the league endorsed the first *intifada* and reaffirmed the PLO's role as the 'sole legitimate representative of the Palestinian people'. On 14 Dec. 1988, speaking on behalf of the PLO Executive Committee, Arafat announced a change in PLO policy, accepting: '... the right of all parties concerned in the Middle East conflict to exist in peace and security, and as I have mentioned, including the state of Palestine, Israel and other neighbours, according to the resolution 242 and 338 ... We totally and absolutely renounce all forms of terrorism, including individual, group and state terrorism'. In September 1993 following the secret talks with Israeli prime minister Rabin, Arafat affirmed in writing that the PLO recognised Israel's right to exist, and renounced 'the use of terrorism and other acts of violence' in exchange for Israeli recognition. All PLO covenant statements to the contrary were 'inoperative and no longer valid'. In April 1996 the PNC voted (by 504–54) that all clauses in the covenant which contradicted recent PLO pledges were to be annulled. A new charter was to be drawn up to formalise this, but in February 1998 the PLO Executive Committee deferred this action. *Political Handbook 1999* (CSA, Binghamton, NY, 1999) pp.1110–1.

24. S/RES/1483-22 May 2003.

25. S/RES/1500-14 August 2003.

26. S/RES/1511-16 October 2003.

27. 'It [the Moscow theatre siege] happens due to the war. The main reason is the war and the will of the Chechen nation to keep the resistance going. Now it cannot ever be broken ... I think it is principally impossible to condemn the people, who sacrificed their lives for the free-

dom and independence of their own nation. As for the statements made by the Western countries, where they call upon condemning and punishing the Chechen Mujaheddins, I think it is just a case of hypocrisy and crime against the Chechen nation. I completely agree with the opinion that none of the countries has a moral right to demand the Chechens to refrain from applying this or that method against the Russian aggression ... A bloody and terrible war is fought in Chechnya, and it got initiated by the Kremlin in order to eliminate the whole Chechens ethnos. The nation offers as hard a resistance as it can. No one has the right to forbid the nation, which fights to defend its own rights for existence, to choose the methods and means for defending their own lives'. Statement of Movladi Udugov, head of the Chechen Defence Committee Information Politics. Quoted in the *Georgian Times*. http://www.kafkas. org.tr/english/Ajans/2002/aralik/31.12.2002_Why_Do_Chechen_Mujaheddins.htm

28. 'In 1961, when for the last time, the oppressed people, led by the ANC, made a call for a national convention in place of a whites-only Republic, the fascist regime replied with the most unprecedented mobilisation of the oppressor army in an attempt to crush the national stoppage of work which we called in reply to the enemy's refusal to summon a national convention. Our call was answered with the ruthless forms of legalised, police and military terrorism. Political organisations were banned; the leaders of the people were arrested, tortured and restricted. The white minority regime declared open war against an unarmed people. This marked the close of a chapter in the history of our struggle for freedom and justice. The peaceful avenues of struggle were closed, and severe penalties, up to the death sentence, were imposed. In these circumstances, the African National Congress was compelled to lead the oppressed people in a violent offensive against a violent repression. Armed repression could only be met by armed revolt'. Statement by the ANC, 4 Oct. 1971. Quoted in Aquino de Braganca and Immanuel Wallerstein, *The African Reader*, vol. 3 pp.108–9. Also see http://www.anc.org.za/ancdocs/pr/1970s/pr711004.html

29. As early as 1960 following the Sharpeville incident, the Security Council had deplored the *apartheid* government's policies (S/RES/134-1 April 1960). They were 'abhorrent to the conscience of mankind' and a 'crime against humanity' (S/RES/182-4 Dec. 1963, S/RES/392-19 June 1976, S/RES/556-23 Oct. 1984). In 1964 it appealed to Pretoria to renounce the execution of any persons for their opposition to *apartheid* (S/RES/191-18 June 1964). In the 1970s it recognised the 'legitimate struggle' of the 'oppressed people of South Africa' (S/RES/282-23 July 1970, S/RES/311-4 Feb. 1972, S/RES/417-31 Oct. 1977). In 1980 it called upon the 'South African regime' to release Nelson Mandela and 'all other black leaders with whom it must deal in any meaningful discussion of the future of the country' (S/RES/473-13 June 1980).

30. 'Terrorism' has been famously described by Nelson Mandela as a relative concept: 'Those people who [referred] to many of us as terrorists are now dealing with us as members of responsible governments, and therefore terrorism is a relative term. Those people who did not agree with your activities will label you a terrorist. But when you succeed, the same people are prepared to accept you and have dealings with you as a head of state'. Former president Nelson Mandela while visiting UN headquarters, One News, 16 Nov. 2001. Two leaders of liberation movements, formerly branded as 'terrorists' in some quarters, were subsequently awarded the Nobel Peace Prize (Mandela, 1993; Arafat, 1994). http://onenews.nzoom.com/ onenews_detail/0,1227,67105-1-9,00.html

31. 'The ANC announces that it is suspending all armed action with immediate effect. As a result of this, no further armed action or related activities by the ANC or its military wing, Umkhonto we Sizswe, will take place'. Pretoria minutes between South African Government and ANC, 6 June 1990.

32. *International Herald Tribune*, 13 Nov. 2003. Terre Blanche, already serving a sentence for assault in 1996, was given a suspended six-year sentence under a plea bargain.

33. *International Herald Tribune*, 27 Nov. 2003.

34. 'The Arabian Peninsula has never ... been stormed by any forces like the crusader armies spreading in it like locusts, eating its riches and wiping out its plantations ... In the light of the grave situation and the lack of support, we and you are obliged to discuss current events, and we should all agree on how to settle the matter. First, for over seven years the United States has been occupying the lands of Islam in the holiest of places, the Arabian Peninsula, plundering its riches, dictating to its rulers, humiliating its people, terrorising its neighbours, and turning its bases into a spearhead through which to fight the neighbouring

Muslim peoples ... Second, despite the great devastation inflicted on the Iraqi people by the crusader-Zionist alliance ... the Americans are once again trying to repeat these horrible massacres ... Third, if the Americans' aims behind these wars are religious and economic, the aim is also to serve the Jew's petty state and divert attention from its occupation of Jerusalem and murder of Muslims there ... All these crimes and sins committed by the Americans are a clear declaration of war on Allah ... The ruling to kill all Americans and their allies – civilians and military – is an individual duty for every Muslim who can do it in any country in which it is possible to do it, in order to liberate the al-Aqsa Mosque and the holy mosque [Mecca] from their grip, and in order for their armies to move out of all the lands of Islam, defeated and unable to threaten any Muslim'. World Islamic Front Statement signed by Shaykh Usama bin-Muhammad Bib-Laden, 23 Feb. 1998. http://www.fas.org/irp/world/para/docs/980223-fatwa.htm

35. 'Why are we fighting and opposing you? The answer is very simple: because you attacked us and continue to attack us. You attacked us in Palestine ... You attacked us in Somalia. You supported the Russian atrocities against us in Chechnya, the Indian oppression against us in Kashmir, and the Jewish aggression against us in Lebanon. Under your supervision, consent and orders, the governments of our countries which act as your agents, attack us on a daily basis ... Your forces occupy our countries; you spread your military bases throughout them; you corrupt our lands, and you besiege our sanctuaries, to protect the security of the Jews and to ensure the continuity of your pillage of our treasures. You have starved the Muslims of Iraq ... You may dispute that all the above does not justify aggression against civilians, for crimes they did not commit and offences in which they did not partake. This argument contradicts your continuous repetition that America is the land of freedom and its leaders in this world. Therefore, the American people are the ones who choose their government by way of their own free will; a choice which stems from their agreement to its policies ... The American people are the ones who employ both their men and their women in the American forces which attack us ... America does not understand the language of manners and principles, so we are addressing it using the language it understands'. Osama bin Laden, 'Letter to America', *Observer Worldwide* 24 Nov. 2002. http://www.observer.co.uk/worldview/story/0,11581,845725,00.html

36. 'Among the disclosures provided in the internal briefing and in a later interview [with Lt. Gen. Michael Mosely, chief allied war commander]: ... Air war commanders were required to obtain the approval of Defense secretary Donald Rumsfeld if any planned airstrike was thought likely to result in deaths of more than 30 civilians. More than 50 such strikes were proposed and all of them were approved". Michael Gordon, *International Herald Tribune* 21 July 2003.

37. 'We, veteran and active pilots ... are opposed to carrying out the illegal and immoral attack orders of the sort that Israel carries out in the territories ... We are refusing to continue to attack innocent civilians'. The Israeli prime minister said the protesting pilots would be dealt with swiftly. The pilots' protest came after some 500 Israeli reserve soldiers chose prison over military service in the Palestinian territories, claiming that Israel's occupation of the West Bank and Gaza was illegal. *USA Today* 25 Sep. 2003.

38. Robert A. Pape, *International Herald Tribune*, (23 Sep. 2003).

39. A/RES/39/159-17 Dec. 1984.

40. S/RES/581-13 Feb. 1986.

41. Two of the seven French agents were arrested before fleeing the country after the attack, accused of murder and sentenced under a plea bargain to ten years for manslaughter. Under intense retaliatory economic pressure from France, New Zealand appealed to the UN for arbitration. The secretary-general's ruling elicited from France an apology plus reparations, with the two agents being transferred to a French military atoll in the Pacific to serve the remainder of their sentences. Both were subsequently released by the French government in violation of the arbitration and repatriated to Paris where they were given state honours.

42. Nigeria 'would not be harassed by anyone' into handing Taylor over to the court Oluremi Oyo, spokesperson in the Nigerian presidential office, *International Herald Tribune*, (10 Nov. 2003). Such a venture would violate Nigeria's territorial integrity – violating 'not only international law but also all the norms of civilized behaviour' (*National Post* (Canada) 11 Nov. 2003 and *Washington Times* 11 Nov. 2003). The US bounty was 'a little

bit close to what many of us would describe as state-sponsored terrorism' (Nigerian presidential spokesman Femi Fane Kayode). http://news.bbc.co.uk/2/hi/africa/3253113.stm

43. S/RES/1322-7 Oct. 2000 (adopted 14-0-1; US abstaining).

44. *UN Information Centre*, 7 March 2003. A similar condemnation was made in April following an Israeli air raid in Gaza.

45. *UN News Centre*, 27 Oct. 2003.

46. 'The Special Rapporteur finds it difficult to accept that the excessive use of force that disregards the distinction between civilians and combatants, the creation of a humanitarian crisis by restrictions on the mobility of goods and people, the killing and inhuman treatment of children, the widespread destruction of property and, now, territorial expansion can be justified as a proportionate response to the violence and threats of violence to which Israel is subjected ... On occasion, Israel's action in the OPT is so remote from the interests of security that it assumes the character of punishment, humiliation and conquest. Some limit must be placed on the violation of human rights in the name of counterterrorism. A balance must be struck between respect for human rights and the interests of security'. UN Special Rapporteur of the Commission on Human Rights for the OPT, John Dugard, *UN News Centre*, 30 Sep. 2003.

47. Explanation of vote by US representative to the UN, 20 Dec. 2002, http://www.un.int/usa/02_220.htm

48. UN doc. SM/SG/7977-1 Oct. 2001.

49. Ibid.

50. UN doc. SG/SM/8105-18 Jan. 2002.

51. UN Security Council press release, SC/7143-12 Sep. 2001.

52. General Assembly Resolution 3034 (XXVII), 18 Dec. 1972.

53. See also A/RES/31/102 (1976) and 32/147 (1977).

54. A/RES/35/145-17 Dec. 1979.

55. Declaration on Measures to Eliminate International Terrorism A/RES/49/60-9 Dec. 1994.

56. A/RES/56/1-18 Sep. 2001.

57. This work is done under the auspices of the General Assembly's Ad Hoc Committee on Measures to Eliminate International Terrorism; see the supplement to the 1994 declaration A/RES/51/210-17 Dec. 1996.

58. Current draft Article 2 provides for armed 'acts of self-determination by states and peoples' to be exempt from terrorist actions provided they are not directed at civilians. The dispute over draft Article 18 revolves around whether acts already covered by humanitarian law are not relevant to the terrorism convention: whether such acts are to be 'governed by' humanitarian law (the western preference) or 'in conformity with' such law (the OIC preference).

59. International Convention for the Suppression of the Financing of Terrorism, annexed to UN General Assembly Resolution Article 2.1(b).

60. S/RES 1267 (1999), S/RES 1333 (2000), S/RES 1390 (2002) and S/RES 1455 (2003).

61. http://usinfo.state.gov/topical/pol/terror/01111206.htm

62. In the case of Afghanistan, because the Taliban was never recognized at the UN as a legitimate government, the council sanctions against it were never seen as applying against Afghanistan as a member state.

63. S/RES/1044-31 Jan. 1996.

64. S/RES/1054-26 April 1996.

65. S/RES/1070-16 Aug. 1996.

66. S/RES/1372-28 Sep. 2001.

67. The council aspires to keep the international community strictly in line. In October it noted with concern that forty-eight states 'are late' in submitting their reports to the monitoring group. S/PRST/2003/17-17 Oct. 2002.

68. S/RES 1373, op. para. 3d.

69. 'In the case of armed conflict not of an international character occurring in the territory of one of the High Contracting Parties, each Party to the conflict shall be bound to apply, as a minimum, the following provisions: (1) Persons taking no active part in the hostilities, including members of armed forces who have laid down their arms and those placed hors de combat by sickness, wounds, detention, or any other cause, shall in all circumstances be

treated humanely, without any adverse distinction founded on race, colour, religion or faith, sex, birth or wealth, or any other similar criteria. To this end the following acts are and shall remain prohibited at any time and in any place whatsoever with respect to the above-mentioned persons: (a) violence to life and person, in particular murder of all kinds, mutilation, cruel treatment and torture; (b) taking of hostages; (c) outrages upon personal dignity, in particular humiliating and degrading treatment; (d) the passing of sentences and the carrying out of executions without previous judgment pronounced by a regularly constituted court, affording all the judicial guarantees which are recognized as indispensable by civilized peoples'. Convention (IV) Relative to the Protection of Civilian Persons in Time of War, Article 3.

70. S/RES/837-6 June 1993.

71. S/RES/885-16 Nov. 1993.

72. UN Case Information Sheet, http://www.un.org/icty/glance/milosevic.htm

73. S/RES/1316-14 Aug. 2000.

74. 'Chinese government considers that the operation of the Court must strictly adhere to the relevant principles underpinning the establishment of the Court. To begin with, the principle of complementarity: one of the important roles of the ICC is to promote countries to refine their respective domestic judicial systems so as to ensure the jurisdiction of countries over those perpetrators of heinous crimes by way of domestic judicial systems. Second, the Court should confine itself only to those most heinous international crimes as prescribed by the Statute. Third, activities of the Court cannot be at odds with the provisions of the UN Charter, in particular when it comes to the crime of aggression. They should be in line with those provisions. Fourth, the Court must be objective and fair in performing its functions, do its best to avoid political bias so as to prevent the Court from relegating to a place of indiscriminate political lawsuits ... As regards the accession to the Statute, China keeps an open mind. The practical performance of the Court will be one of the factors for consideration by China, and we do not rule out the possibility of joining the Statute at a time China deems appropriate". PRC Ministry of Foreign Affairs, Beijing. http://www.fmprc.gov.cn/eng/gjwt/tyfl/2626/2627/t15473.htm

75. 'We have concluded that the ICC does not advance these principles [justice and the promotion of law]. Here is why: We believe the ICC undermines the role of the UN Security Council in maintaining international peace and security. We believe in checks and balances. The Rome Statute creates a prosecutorial system that is an unchecked power. We believe that, in order to be bound by a treaty, a state must be party to that treaty. The ICC asserts jurisdiction over citizens of states that have not ratified that treaty. This threatens US sovereignty. We believe that the ICC is built on a flawed foundation. These flaws leave it open for exploitation and politically motivated prosecutions'. US State Department 6 May 2002. http://www.state.gov/p/9949.htm

76. S/RES/1422-12 July 2002.

77. Kaul (note 4).

78. Ibid., p.389.

79. As already noted, many in the Arab-African-Asian world contend that these were military targets in a national liberation operation.

80. Arab Convention for the Suppression of Terrorism, Article 2.

81. Strictly, Cuba remains a member of the OAS but has had its participation suspended since 1962 on the grounds that its political system did not 'conform with the hemisphere's principles'.

82. US Code, Title 22, Section 2656D, Used by the US State Department and the CIA. http://www.armscontrolcenter.org/terrorism/101/definitions.html

83. US Public Law 102-138, Section 304 This requires the administration to provide annual reports to Congress concerning the nature and extent of assets held in the US by 'terrorist countries and organizations engaged in international terrorism'. See US State Department, Patterns of Global Terrorism 2002, in http://www.globalsecurity.org/security/library/report/2003/dos-pgt2002.htm. State sponsors of terrorism are those countries designated by the secretary of state under Section 40D of the Arms Export Control Act, Title 22, US Code Section 2780D. Such assets frozen in the US as of May 1993 totalled US$2.4b (Cuba, $111m; Iran, $22m; Iraq, $1,108m.; Libya, 903m.; North Korea, $3m.; Syria, 249m). http://www.fas.org/irp/congress/1993_cr/h930503-terror.htm

84. Arms Control Centre website (see note 28).

85. 'Paradoxically, American power worldwide is at its historic zenith while its global political standing is at its nadir. Why? Since the tragedy of Sept. 11, which understandably shocked and outraged every American, the US has increasingly embraced, at the highest official level, what can fairly be called a paranoiac view of the world. This is summarised in a phrase repeatedly used at the highest level: "He who is not with us is against us" ... There are two troubling conditions that accompany this mindset. First, making the "war on terrorism" the central preoccupation of the US in the world today reflects a rather narrow and extremist vision of foreign policy of the world's primary superpower, of a great democracy, with genuinely idealistic traditions. The second troubling condition which contributes to the crisis of credibility and to the isolation in which the US finds itself today, is the absence of a clear, sharply defined perception about what is actually happening abroad. This kind of blindness is of particular concern regarding the spread of weapons of mass destruction. It is terribly important not to plunge headlong into the tempting notion that America will unilaterally take preemptive action on suspicion that a country possesses WMD, which is what the doctrine right now amounts to. Without a revitalised American intelligence service the US simply does not know enough to be able to pre-empt with confidence. All of this calls for a serious debate about America's role in the world. Can a world power provide global leadership on the basis of fear and anxiety? Can the US mobilise support, particularly the support of friends, when it tells them, "you are against us if you are not with us!"? The need for such a serious debate cannot be satisfied by theologising the challenge as "terrorism", which is used by "people who hate things" while we are "people who love things", as America's highest spokesman has put it. Terrorism is a technique for killing people. That can't be an enemy. It's as if we said that World War II was not against the Nazis but against blitzkrieg. We need to ask who the enemy is, and what springs him or her to action against us? ... Today, for the first time, America's commitment to idealism worldwide is challenged by a sense of vulnerability. The US has to be very careful in that setting not to become self-centred, pre-occupied only with itself and subordinating everything else in the world to an exaggerated sense of vulnerability'. Zbigniew Brzezinski, 'To Lead, US Must Give Up Paranoid Policies', *International Herald Tribune*, (16 Nov. 2003).

86. *UN News Centre*, 8 Sep. 2003.

87. A/58/323.

88. 'While terrorism is an evil with which there can be no compromise, we must use our heads, not our hearts, in deciding our response. The rage we feel at terrorist attacks must not remove our ability to reason. If we are to defeat terrorism, it is our duty, and indeed in our interest, to try to understand this deadly phenomenon, and carefully to examine what works, and what does not, in fighting it ... The fact that a few wicked men and women commit murder in its name does not make a cause any less just. Nor does it relieve us of the obligation to deal with legitimate grievance. On the contrary, terrorism will only be defeated if we act to solve the political disputes and long-standing conflicts which generate support for it. If we do not, we shall find ourselves acting as a recruiting sergeant for the very terrorists we seek to suppress ... Upholding human rights is not at odds with battling terrorism: on the contrary, the moral vision of human rights ... is among our most powerful weapons against it ... We have to win hearts and minds. To do this we should act to resolve political disputes, articulate and work towards a vision of peace and development and promote human rights ... If these ideas guide us in shaping our response to terrorism, our moral position in the fight against it will be assured'. Kofi Annan, Address to International Peace Academy Seminar, New York, 22 Sep. 2003.

89. '... over the years your ministry has tirelessly stressed that inter-religious dialogue should exist side by side with intra-Christian unity. In our part of the world, where Christianity, Islam and Judaism are integral parts of the fabric of society, this need is not a simple commodity. It is a living and witnessing reality ... We share your belief that the future of humanity is bound up with the reconciliatory efforts of the ecumenical movement as much as those of inter-religious dialogue. In this regard, it was most thoughtful of Your Holiness to express the apology of the Holy See for the Crusades and the Inquisition. This significant step certainly helps to eradicate scars of past wounds as much as it will contribute to a promotion of a peace culture, based in part, on the courage to utilise the lessons of the past for building a more peaceful future. Today, at the cusp of a new millennium, the narrow and self-isolating con-

cepts of insular religions or nation states can only lead to chauvinism, jingoism and possibly even war'. Letter from HRH Prince Hassan bin Talal to His Holiness Pope John Paul II, 20 March 2000, http://www.princehassan.gov.jo/main/recent/archive/2000/March/20-3.htm

90. It has been suggested that consideration might be given to taking the existing consensus on 'war crimes' as a point of departure. The core elements of war crimes are three-fold: deliberate attacks on civilians, hostage-taking and the killing of prisoners. If this concept were extended to peacetime, acts of terrorism could be defined as 'peacetime equivalents of war crimes'. A. Schmid, Report to the UN Office on Drugs & Crime, http://www.unodc.org/unodc/terrorism_definitions.html

Appendix

US List of Foreign Terrorist Organizations

Movement	Organization	Country	Stated Goal
Secession	2. Abu Sayyaf	Philippines	Islamist state for southern Philippines
	7. Basque ETA	Spain/France	Independent homeland for Basques
	10. HUM	Pakistan	Kashmiri independence
	13. JEM	Pakistan	Kashmiri independence
	16. PKK	Turkey	Establish independent, democratic Kurdish state in Middle East
	17. Army of the Righteous	Pakistan	Kashmiri independence
	18. Tamil Tigers	Sri Lanka	Independent state for northern Sri Lanka
	26. Real IRA	UK	Secession of Northern Ireland from UK
Internal	4. GIA	Algeria	Overthrow govt; set up Islamic state
Regime Change	5. Asbat al-Ansar	Lebanon	Overthrow govt; remove US influence
	8. Islamic Group	Egypt	Overthrow govt; set up Islamic state
	12. IMU	Uzbekistan	Overthrow govt; set up Islamic state
	14. Al-Jihad	Egypt	Overthrow govt; set up Islamic state
	15. Kahane Chai	Israel	Set up biblical state in Israel; expel Arabs
	19. Khalq	Iran	Overthrow govt; set up secular state

Category	Group	Location	Objective
	20. ELN	Colombia	Overthrow govt; set up Marxist state
	27. FARC	Colombia	Overthrow govt; set up Marxist state
	31. Salafist Group	Algeria	Overthrow govt; set up Islamic state
	32. Shining Path	Peru	Overthrow govt; set up Marxist state
	34. NPA	Philippines	Overthrow govt; set up Marxist state
Anti-Insurgent National Liberation	33. AUC	Colombia	Thwart ELN/FARC insurgency
	3. Al-Aqsa Martyrs Brigade	Palestine	Expel Israel from Palestinian Authority territory; set up Palestinian state
Termination of Israel	1. Abu Nidal	Palestine	Set up Islamic state in place of Israel
	9. HAMAS	Palestine	Set up Islamic state in place of Israel
	11. Hezbollah	Lebanon	Set up Islamic state in place of Israel
	21. PIJ	Palestine (Gaza)	Set up Islamic state in place of Israel
	22. PLF	Iraq/Lebanon	Set up Islamic state in place of Israel
	23. PFLP	Syria/Lebanon	Set up Islamic state in place of Israel
	24. PFLP-GC		Set up Islamic state in place of Israel
US Force Withdrawal	25. Al-Qaeda	Afghanistan/Asia	Withdrawal of US/western forces from Arabian peninsula; end US support of Israel
	28. Revolutionary Nuclei	Greece	Withdrawal of US/NATO/EU from Greece
	29. 17 November	Greece	Withdrawal of US/NATO/EU from Greece
	30. DHKP/C	Turkey	Withdrawal of US/NATO/EU from Turkey
Cults	6. Aum Shinrikyo	Japan	Take over Japan, then the world

Balancing Security
and
Civil Liberties Since 9/11

5

Security and Freedom on the Fulcrum

LAURA K. DONOHUE

Center for International Security and Cooperation,
Stanford University, Stanford, California, USA

Counterterrorist arguments that justify the erosion of individual rights frequently depend on the claim a balance can—and should—be struck between security and freedom. But this analogy, under both consequentialist and rights-based analysis, is at best misleading and at worst structurally wrong. Calculations from utility resting on the immediate dangers posed by terrorism do not give appropriate weight to (a) the long-term effects of inroads into individual rights, (such as individual harm, blocked political, social, and legal mechanisms), and (b) precedent-setting in a tightly-interwoven structure of individual rights and state power. Constitutive rules further delimit the types of measures that can be introduced, regardless of the "tradeoffs" considered in balancing security and freedom. In the rights-based realm, arguments related to expanded state powers, distributive justice, and practical effect undermine the analogy.

Introduction

Counterterrorist debates frequently revolve upon the idea that a balance must be struck between security and freedom. Those who defend measures that erode individual rights argue that in order to be safe, citizens within the state must be willing to sacrifice some degree of liberty. Many who object to counterterrorist provisions agree that the metaphor is *à propos* – the issue centers on where the fulcrum should be aligned in the weighing of the two extremes.

This general claim is not new. Thomas Hobbes argued in *Leviathan* that in order to gain security individuals enter into society, giving up in the process some of the freedom inherent in an, albeit objectionable, state of nature. Nicolo Machiavelli's *raison d'État* is rooted in the assumption that individuals are willing to cede certain powers to the state in order to effect personal security. The Prince introduces what measures may be found necessary to preserve the state, even if this means severely curtailing the freedoms of individual citizens. The continuation of the state protects their best interests. The concept of this balance continues to pervade contemporary discussions – particularly those related to counterterrorism. Transcripts from debates on legislation introduced into Britain's Houses of Parliament, Ireland's Dail

Éireann, Israel's Knesset, Turkey's Büyük Millet Meclisi and the United States' Congress are filled with references to the need to weigh liberty against the threat posed by terrorism.

For those who take this balance between security and freedom as their basic framework in evaluating constitutional limits on the state in the aftermath of a terrorist attack, two schools of thought dominate: At one extreme, the claim is made by those defending incursive counterterrorist measures that liberal democracy itself stands as the enemy, and the very mechanisms that protect the individual from excessive state power appear to hamper the state's ability to respond effectively to the threat. Lawrence Tribe, Floyd Abrams, Richard Posner, Jonathan Alter and others, in the rush to respond to the challenge posed by Al-Qaeda on 11 September 2001, quote the final phrase of United States' Supreme Court Justice Robert Jackson's words from *Terminiello v. City of Chicago* (1949): 'There is danger that, if the court does not temper its doctrinaire logic with a little practical wisdom, it will convert the constitutional Bill of Rights into a suicide pact'.[1] Addressing respectively whether to allow indefinite detention, racial profiling, concentration camps and torture, the sentiments expressed by these commentators make the claim that the American Constitution, which protects individual rights, is not meant for times of national danger.[2]

At the other extreme individuals assert that it is *particularly* for times of crisis that individuals enter into the social compact, as a guarantee that the state adheres to its basic principles when the expansionist/limitation tension within liberal democracies stands in danger of giving way to the exigencies of the moment. As Benjamin Franklin exhorted, 'They who would give up an essential liberty for temporary security, deserve neither liberty or security'.[3]

Wherever one falls along the spectrum, at or between these two extremes, there is a certain logic in, following a terrorist event, applying the balance between security and freedom as a mode of analysis. Non-state terrorism directed against a liberal, democratic regime does call into question the security of individuals within the state. It undercuts the current regime's capacity and, more broadly, the state's ability to protect the life and property of the citizens. Counterterrorism is thus perceived as a *response* to the actual and potential challenge and as a necessary constituent of the current regime and state upholding their contractual obligation to the citizens.

What is lost in the focus subsequently placed on the specific nature of the threat facing the state is that counterterrorism is *more* than just one regime's response to a specific act or threat. And so to focus on the balance that must be struck between security and freedom in addressing terrorism in some sense misses the larger picture. Counterterrorism is inextricably linked to a broader and ongoing liberal, democratic dialogue within and between states. It is imbedded in both past and future challenges to state legitimacy that transcend the immediate threat posed by the individuals or organizations involved. It affects the degree to which the regime and state can draw on additional resources to counter the immediate challenge. Counterterrorism impacts the regime's and state's ability to pursue its domestic and foreign policy agenda in other areas. And, as state power rapidly expands, it has the potential to unravel the domestic social, political and legal fabric of increasingly multiethnic, heterogeneous societies.

The balance metaphor also assumes that security is, in fact, *gained* through sacrificing freedom. But is this the case? How effective *are* the measures introduced under the guise of balancing security and freedom?[4] Clearly, some provisions do not help to address security concerns yet carry no serious inroads into individual rights concerns – such as the suspension of curbside check-in at the airports or the use of plastic silverware on flights. Other provisions seem somewhat counterproductive – in that they actually *increase* the security risk but bear no other, immediate, rights effects (e.g., the rapid expansion in 'security' services without extensive knowledge of the new hires). Still others may be counterproductive and bear with them a significant effect on fundamental rights, such as free speech, due process and the presumption of innocence. While the first two categories are not unimportant, it is measures in this last category that, under the balance framework, present the hard cases. And these are the provisions of import to the current discussion. Examples might include expanded surveillance, powers of arrest, restricted movement, judicial alteration, free speech strictures, house and village demolition, assassination, torture, disappearances and military aggression.

In this paper I examine the assumed trade-off between security and freedom that is used to justify this third category: measures that may be counterproductive and that significantly affect important individual rights. I consider first, consequentialist, and second, rights-based theories, that are marshaled to support the introduction of new measures in adopting and calibrating the balance between security and freedom. In the first realm, consequentialism, I begin with a hard case: possible terrorist use of nuclear or biological weapons. I then examine the calculations from utility that mark the justification of incursive counterterrorist measures to protect against the possible terrorist use of these weapons. Such calculations, though, do *not* afford appropriate importance to the long-term effects of the inroads into individual rights. Here, three aspects of the effect of such measures are relevant: individual harm, blocked political, administrative and social channels, and the establishment of precedent. In this first section I also consider whether consequentialist claims are appropriate for cases involving civil liberties, or whether certain Wittgensteinian constitutive rules delimit the types of measures that can be introduced. In the second, rights-based realm, I argue that three areas are of particular importance: expanded state powers, issues of distributive justice and the practical effect of counterterrorist measures with a significant impact on individual rights. I conclude by suggesting that both the consequentialist arguments that dominate the counterterrorist discourse and the rights arguments that counterterrorist provisions evoke argue against using the concept of a balance between security and freedom as a way to think about counterterrorism. A better metaphor would see counterterrorism as a constellation of long- and short-term trade offs linking the risks incurred in the suspension of (interconnected) rights.

Consequentialist Arguments

I begin by presenting the strongest case for thinking about security and freedom in terms of a balance. What if a terrorist organization or network had the capability of developing or acquiring and detonating a nuclear weapon and the desire to use it against a vulnerable target? Alternatively, what if an organization had sophisticated knowledge of and access to biological weapons and was able to disseminate smallpox against an unprotected population? In the United Kingdom and the United States as of late public debate and, indeed, national security strategies afford particular priority to the latter scenario. Setting aside whether or not specific individuals or states have the capability of launching this type of attack, general concerns regarding acquisition and dissemination of biological weapons appear warranted: The material can be obtained and produced, infection can be either through a spray or direct physical contact, organisms can be made stable and resistant to medication, and the modern urban environment is characterized by a high concentration of people, who then become proxy weapons carriers.[5] Either type of attack would have enormous physical, social, economic and political consequences, placing the state itself on the precipice of destruction.

At first consideration these scenarios appear to differ substantially from one in which a group or individual gains access to a cache of conventional weapons and plastic explosives. Indeed, the balance assumption would suggest that the types of measures introduced to counter the threats in the first instance would involve greater restrictions on liberty than those introduced to address the lesser one. Certainly an actual event would bring this assumption into sharp relief and may increase the intensity of the measures introduced. What might have been unacceptable limitations on freedom on 10 September 2001 became broadly accepted for inclusion into the United States' counterterrorist arsenal on 12 September 2001. The more aggressive the attack compared with previous experience, perhaps the more significant the alteration following the event. Jeremy Waldron suggests that the mechanism for this alteration resides in a concept of risk: Terrorist events force individuals to reevaluate the maximum risk one is 'prepared to bear as a result of people's liberty'.[6] When the circumstances appear to exceed this maximum risk, a recalculation and consequent constriction of such liberties ensues. Waldron points out that this calculation could just as easily be turned around: That is to say, if one emphasizes the minimum liberty one is prepared to accept, then the recalculation following a terrorist incident, or string of terrorist incidents, may well be to fortify one's courage to accept greater risk.[7] And he suggests that in reality, the manner in which the calculus is conducted blends the two approaches.

With this in mind, the chief concern in an era of nuclear, radiological, biological and chemical weapons is whether the threat posed by dissident states, networks, groups and individuals is of sufficient magnitude to warrant a recalculation of the risk and, consequently, the liberties to be afforded to citizens. Actors can take advantage of the strengths of an open society, such as mobility, communications, security, democratic legal systems, easy access to arms and the vulnerability of targets.[8] What happens when groups capable of severe devastation, trained to take advantage of a liberal, democratic state and seeking to destroy the state or society emerge? How should the target state respond?

Utility Calculus and the Long-Term Effect of Blocked Rights

The utility calculus that currently dominates the American national discourse suggests that the state not only may, but in fact must, constrict freedoms in order to take account of these (assumedly new) risks and ensure the security of the citizens. The argument is that the United States faces a threat unlike any other either it or any other country has faced. Technology has rapidly advanced, increasing the possible lethality of future attacks. And so the greatest good for the greatest number of people is to restrict individual liberties in order to ensure the safety of the people. The problem with this assertion is that this calculus, borne of deep concern about the possibility of terrorist use of weapons of mass destruction (WMD) – such as nuclear or biological weapons – is a distortion of the argument from utility on which it relies for validity. The contemporary calculus either ignores the long-term costs of restrictions on freedoms, or considers the long-term costs, but places inadequate emphasis on the weighing of individual rights within a structure of interconnected rights and restrictions on state power.

Individual Harm

We begin with a basic question: what motivates terrorists to engage in violence? While the terrorist literature goes into great detail on the psychological aspects of individual engagement, two themes dominate: the role of personal grievances and the lack of alternative routes of expression and change. Resultantly, sufficient representation of a sub- or alternative-state challenge depends on looking at state actions not in their intent, but in their normative quality and substantive impact on individuals. The decision *to become involved* in violence grows out of personal experience. An understanding of actions with direct, personal effect therefore becomes vital to being able to diminish the threat of violence towards the state and its citizens.

Active members of non-state terrorist movements frequently hearken back to intensely personal experiences of injustice perpetrated by the state or other non-state actors against themselves and their communities.[9] A calculus that ignores the long-term effect of measures that impact individual rights, such as house demolition, torture, assassination and arbitrary detention, fails to consider significant long-term security issues. What might seem to be an expedient route to head off immediate violence may generate grievances reaped in the form of stronger support for future violence. In this case, the suggestion that a simple dichotomy exists – security or freedom – falls short. It is precisely because of limits in freedom that the security of the citizens may be negatively affected.

Blocked Political, Social and Legal Mechanisms

The limitations placed on freedoms also have a chilling effect on the social and political mechanisms for change. What underscores the inappropriate nature of the balance analogy is that, as Luigi Bonanate has suggested, terrorism itself is 'symptomatic of a blocked society'. Individuals may argue over the extent of social cleavage, but the preconditions and precipitant events, as Martha Crenshaw puts it, lead to 'the disaffection of a fragment of the elite, who may take it upon themselves to act on the behalf of a majority unaware of its plight, unwilling to take action to remedy grievances, or unable to express dissent'.[10] If terrorism can thus be seen, at least in part, as an *effect* – not a cause – then the mechanism via which security best can be guaranteed shifts. If the majority of suicide bombers are, as experts on the subject claim, drawn from particularly vulnerable communities and manipulated by 'handlers' in the movements, then it becomes critical to ensure that society does not become so blocked that hope for change is lost. If these groups perceive that there is no other possibility for change, then there is nothing to lose.[11] My goal in ascribing causality here is *not* to point the finger of blame to one party or another, but rather to determine *the best point* at which a state can institute change to increase security. In this context, the question with which we are confronted is: If part of the reason for the violence in the first place is related to constricted liberty, *will further restricting freedoms* (in order to obtain more security) *have the desired effect*? For multiple reasons, the answer falls short of a resounding endorsement.

First, measures that block political, social and legal outlets increase the desire for political change (the object ostensibly at the heart of the terrorist challenge).

Simultaneously, such measures decrease nonviolent alternatives. There is considerable historical evidence to suggest that in the past, when individual rights have been constricted (ostensibly to increase the security of the population), it has actually undermined safety as personal injustices increase and channels for expressing discontent and altering the political, legal and social structures close.

Second, such measures impede authorities' attempts to prevent terrorism by creating concerns in parties that might have information that they will be implicated in the terrorist violence should they try to step forward. Returning to the WMD argument, the development and use of such weapons is, at this point in our technological development, relatively difficult to plan and execute.[12] The public's role in such an event may be particularly important, making the curtailment of liberties that may result in alienating the population an unwise course of action. In Japan, the public alerted police to the smells emerging from buildings where Aum Shinrikyo was building weapons. What if the citizens had feared that they would be harassed or interned for coming forward? This effect may become exaggerated as measures intended to target 'guilty' terrorists end up being applied not to those engaged in violence but to communities the state can ill afford to alienate in attempting to apprehend those responsible. (I will return to this point later in the paper.)

Third, such measures undermine the restrictions of conscience, which seem to play a role in the ability of terrorist organizations to wage violence. Members of Aum Shinrikyo decided in the final event not to release sarin on two previous occasions because of crises of conscience related to the loss of innocent lives. The wife of a member of the Patriots' Council, concerned about the use of the weapons being developed, brought a jar of ricin to the Federal Bureau of Investigation (FBI).[13] Two members of the Covenant, the Sword, and the Arm of the Lord made admissions about chemical weapons development to the FBI.[14] The issue of conscience and internal security causes apprehension within organizations wielding terror as a weapon. In an effort to stifle dissenting opinions within the Kurdish tribes, for three decades the Partiya Karkeren Kurdistan (PKK) directed significantly more violence towards Kurds than Turks. The IRA instituted punishment shootings, such as knee-capping and the iron cross, for those suspected of passing information to the state – whether motivated by conscience or otherwise. Concern at the role that might be played by conscience in the commission of the 11 September Al-Qaeda attacks may have been the basis on which the true nature of the mission was masked from those involved in the hijacking itself. And recent evidence suggests that Palestinian suicide bombings in Israel are accompanied by remote activation devices in case individuals undertaking the action change their minds.[15] By acting in a manner that avoids new grievances and ensures open channels of communication, states may be more likely to be recipients of vital information that contributes to heightened long-term security.

Fourth, aside from the practical issues of acquiring, assembling and using WMDs, there is a cultural force working against terrorist organizations. If they use such weapons, their political viability dramatically decreases.[16] Terrorist organizations with a long-term interest in survival cannot afford this loss. While the terrorist literature often underscores the strengths of terrorist organizations, it frequently misses the weaknesses. Like states, terrorist organizations need constituents to survive.

Fifth, the very question assumes that the proper aim of counterterrorism is to end terrorism. This means that the state can take the offensive and progress down a path of increasingly stringent measures until the desired security is obtained.

Yet states will never be able to get around the defensive component of being the object of a terrorist attack. Following the Brighton bombing, the Provisional IRA issued a telling statement to the Thatcher government, '[R]emember[,] we only have to be lucky once. You have to be lucky always'.[17] When states have adopted this steady progression, they have at times blatantly failed: For instance, postcolonial movements succeeded in pushing the French from Algeria, and Britain from Aden, Cyprus, Dublin, Palestine and the United States. In these and other circumstances, the harsher the measures that were introduced, the more resistant the movements became. Further, while the terrorism literature frequently parrots the idea that terrorism cannot exist in a totalitarian regime (aside from that levied by the regime itself), counterexamples readily proliferate. Franco's Spain introduced extremely harsh measures against ETA that were remarkably unsuccessful in ending the movement. The various underground movements in the former USSR existed despite extensive state intelligence and punishment capabilities. Although Peru introduced drastic measures and harsh military rule, the state did not manage to end Sendero Luminoso's campaign. And Israel has been under attack since its inception. The character of the occupied territories reflects a Hobbesian world, with air attacks, shelling of border settlements and refugee camps, revenge raids, suicide bombing, house demolition and sniper attacks. It has become a war of attrition. Despite the extent to which these states were willing to suspend the liberty of those within their borders, the countermeasures proved remarkably unsuccessful in eliminating the terrorist threat. This at least calls into question the underlying assumption that such measures necessarily increase security.

Sixth, the type of threat posed by the worst-case scenario comprises a minute percentage of the actual range of terrorist threats faced by the state. It does *not* logically follow, though, from the existence of *a* threat that *all* cases of possible terrorism be treated in a manner that may actually increase the risk of further attack. For the highly unlikely WMD scenario, in order to successfully levy an attack, an organization needs the technical *capability* to develop and execute the operation and the *intent* to use such weapons against a population. Moreover, the target must be *vulnerable* to attack. These factors limit the number of individuals or organizations that are able to engage in this behavior. Nevertheless, the measures introduced to address the possibility of this threat are significantly more Draconian than what otherwise would be followed. Yet very serious threats have been posed to states by groups drawing on conventional means, such as the Provisional IRA, ETA, the Soviet resistance organizations, Sendero Luminoso and Hamas – and their splinter organizations. If measures that restrict freedoms end up creating less stable conditions, and other organizations and groups to whom the measures are applied become targets of the extraordinary measures, the security risk overall to the state may increase.

Seventh, many commentators justify the assumption of the balance with the assertion that it is not citizens' liberties that must be balanced with security, but the rights of noncitizens located either inside or outside the geographic bounds of the state. But, what happens to the metaphorical balance between security and freedom if the rights conferred by citizenship are removed from the equation? Consider an individual or group external to the state with believed access to WMD and, by all indications, the intent to use it against a state's population. What does the consequentialist calculus look like for security and freedom?

One feature of this calculation is in relation to non-state actors located outside the target state, the near absence of legal precedent. Domestic and international structures regulate state-to-state interaction and to govern the relationship of the state to an individual within the state, but no legal corpus regulates the relationship between a state and an individual noncitizen external to the state. Such cases are considered to be in the realm of state sovereignty and thus subject to the rules governing state-to-state interaction.[18]

Attempts have been made to address this scenario through the concept of discriminate force. What if, instead of declaring war on terrorism, the United States had declared war on Al-Qaeda, or more extraordinarily, war on Osama bin Laden? This might be possible theoretically, but in the real world it is impracticable. The nature of a dispersed, international network would bring the United States into direct confrontation with other states. And so, instead, we find the staccato use of such sovereignty-infringements as rendition, assassination and missile attacks, with attempts to justify outright state war on traditional, state-specific grounds. The Bush administration's preemption doctrine introduced post-9/11 thus resides in both the relatively developed area of state-to-state relations and the more nebulous realm of state-to-nonstate-actor relations.[19] But here, the same arguments that dog domestic consideration of security and liberty arise: The failure of the calculus to give sufficient weight to individual rights obscures the long-term security effects of the curtailment of individual freedoms and the blockage of political, legal and social mechanisms that regulate change. The United Kingdom's use of the five techniques later deemed to be 'inhuman and degrading' by the European Court of Human Rights incensed the Republic of Ireland, which then refused to help Britain in its counterterrorist efforts. Large swaths of land decimated by the American bombardment of Afghanistan have already proven fertile recruitment grounds for more converts to Al-Qaeda. What will be the price in European-American relations of the bellicosity of the current administration? States have limited resources. The distribution of funds and foci of attention are subject to political sensitivities. Punitive international measures may have a considerable and lasting effect on the security of a state and its people.

Precedent Setting in the Interwoven Structure of Rights and Power
One final relevant omission in the consequentialist calculus between security and freedom is the role played by precedent and the complex nature of rights. The argument turns on the assumption that if the risk is great enough, then (specific) liberties can be restricted. In reality, liberties are far more inter-connected than this model assumes. Take for instance the case of free speech and due process. On the surface, these would seem to be two entirely different aspects of a liberal, democratic state, and different counterterrorist measures would point to a downgrading of liberties in each area. Censorship, for example, would affect the first, while indefinite interment without charge would more appropriately be seen to impact the second. Yet if a state were to maintain free speech but lift its adherence to due process, an individual might be detained arbitrarily on the basis of public communication – thus rendering the retention of free speech meaningless. Similarly, if due process remained unchanged and free speech, instead, were affected by new measures, then lapses in the manner in which due process was conducted would go unreported. Changes to one right may have a snowball effect on the ability of citizens to claim – and to act upon – other rights.

Does it make sense to establish a precedent where the executive, if the threat posed is sufficiently grave, is presented with the authority to restrict one or more freedoms? The interconnected nature of the rights, and the subsequent power this might generate for the executive, might encourage rather than discourage the presentation of similar threats of sufficient magnitude to restrict rights. The cost is borne in the realm of personal freedom, without requisite impact on security concerns.

Constitutive Rules

The second central consideration in relation to consequentialist arguments relates not to the weight of individual rights afforded in the long-term calculation of balancing security and freedom, but rather whether it even makes sense to apply consequentialist arguments to justify appeal to the trade-off. Here the claim is that certain aspects of liberal, democratic states act as what Ludwig Wittgenstein would refer to as 'constitutive' rules. The question is thus: Are there, as there appear to be in chess, certain rules in according to which liberal democracy must act, such that to alter them would be akin to changing the game? For instance, if I decided to use dice or began to leapfrog my bishop over other pieces, would I still be playing chess? Perhaps there are rules that do not relate to how efficiently (or inefficiently) I obtain my goal. They simply set the parameters within which I seek the prize. It would make little sense, in other words, for me request that I be allowed to sacrifice my king in order to win.[20]

At the heart of the discussion is the currency of the rights dialogue. Liberal democratic states depend on the protection of individual rights for their survival. When the state suspends its protection of certain rights, while *a state structure* may continue to exist, it seems at least theoretically possible to claim that at some point the state has fundamentally altered and therefore lost its liberal claim. One could concede that it may be difficult to determine at what point this claim is lost. So, on a case-by-case basis, specific gains may be seen to trump rights. Indeed, the battle between individual rights and utility that rages within the liberal discourse underscores that liberalism incorporates both individual and group rights and, in the weighing of these, differences of opinion lead individuals to be willing to forego or determined to maintain contrary rights and freedoms.[21]

This is particularly true when threats to the *politas* are touted as justification for the new measures and a national security dialogue takes hold. National security bears with it a Machivellian justification that those in command of state power may introduce such measures as determined necessary to protect the political structures. Deprived of the intimate knowledge assumedly available to government ministers, the population must trust that the threat faced by the state indeed is of sufficient magnitude to justify the curtailment of individual freedom – and that the measures adopted by the state will, indeed, address the threat level. And so a new treaty replaces the social compact – an agreement forged largely on the strength of the argument that the balance between freedom and security must be recalculated in light of recent terrorist atrocities. Inasmuch as such states want to maintain the claim to being a liberal state, though, their legitimate assertion of this claim would seem to at least depend on the protection of a set of rights wherein individual freedom is maximized within a stable political order.

Even with these considerations in mind, however, I would suggest that it does *not* make sense to think about liberal, democratic states in this almost definitional sense. Chess, for instance, *was* at one time played with dice, and until the sixteenth century, the bishop *could* jump other pieces.[22] In fact, the history of chess is littered with significant rule changes. In the fifteenth century two families catapulted the queen into the strongest piece on the chessboard and changed the object of the game from eliminating the opponents' pieces to placing the king in check.[23] It was not until 1929 that the standard rules via which we play today entered into effect.[24] Yet throughout this period, the game 'chess' existed. Granted, during this time the pieces and board were not altogether eliminated and replaced with, for instance, a horse with a rider carrying a stick and trying to whack a ball through goalposts. Such a radical transformation might not have been seen as contiguous with the previous state of affairs and thus a departure from the traditional game of chess.

So too would it seem with the argument for constitutive limitations on liberal, democratic states. To speak about each counterterrorist measure and consequent limitation on freedom as somehow affecting the actual constituent rules governing liberal democracy seems to be a linguistic trick that does not accomplish much. Yet it would seem clear that we could think of certain changes akin to the horse and goalposts. Although Adolph Hitler came to power through democratic means, one would hardly consider the Third Reich to be a liberal, democratic entity. So how useful is the idea of constitutive rules for evaluating the relevance of the trade-off between security and freedom?

Here I would suggest that a definitional consideration is different from an ideal type, and it is in relation to an ideal type, and to justifications for it, that we see exceedingly strong arguments against considering the restriction of freedoms in relation to increasing security. Perhaps a better way to think about security and freedom is in terms of a certain disconnect. If I buy tickets to see *Tristan und Isolde* and invite my friend to spend the evening with me at the opera house, in one clear sense it does not matter if, on my way out the door I see it is raining and realize that I would far prefer to sit by the fire and read a good book. Moreover, my silk gown may well be damaged by the water. It may be the only dress that I own that would be suitable for the opera. I may thus want to take protective measures—such as putting on a coat, but the possibility that it still may be damaged—and my preference for sitting by the fire—do not affect my financial and fiduciary obligations.[25]

Philosophers and intellectuals have written extensively and persuasively about the moral, *a priori* and practical reasons for protecting individual rights.[26] Some of these are grounded in human nature, others in natural law and still others in consequential terms. It is not my intent in this paper to readdress what other writers have already eloquently examined. I find the justifications underlying the protection of individual rights and therefore according them privilege in a liberal, democratic state to be utterly convincing. To these, however, I will add an additional consideration specifically related to counterterrorism: the possibility that in some areas it is *only* through freedom that the security of civilians in a state can be obtained.

I have already argued this case in relation to the first consequentialist concern – that grievances and ease of expression and change enter into the risk incurred by a state in the introduction of new restrictive measures. This can be thought of as liberty in a negative sense: The avoidance of the creation of grievances and abnegation of the blockage of the political, legal and social structures increases long-term security. I will here argue for liberty in a positive sense: It is through *acting on liberties afforded* (rather than refraining from creating grievances) that increased security can be obtained.

Consider, for instance, powers of surveillance. David Brin notes that since the late 1980s, in the United Kingdom and the United States, there has been a significant increase in the number of cameras monitoring public areas.[27] The mere presence of the cameras in public areas does not impact individual freedom; rather, it is the placement of the cameras and the manner in which information gleaned from such sources is distributed and used that privileges one portion of society over another. Brin asks a telling question: What would happen if the images captured by public cameras were widely accessible to the public? Should a crime be committed, the possibility would exist that numerous individuals who happened to be watching that particular street corner would bear witness. Similarly, if a state official, such as a police officer, were to be derelict in their duties or abusive in their actions toward a civilian, this too would be monitored by society. And what if the cameras were present not just in the city blocks but in the municipal and civic buildings? Would this not provide an efficient civilian check on public programs and the use of public funds? Perhaps it is *through* ensuring free access that security in its deepest sense – both from dissident members of society *and* from governmental agencies – can be guaranteed.

With this said, obtaining security through freedom is not the only reason to protect the individual entitlements of the citizenry. There are strong moral and political reasons related to human rights that provide a check on state authority.

Arguments from Rights

I turn now to arguments from rights which shed light on the assumed balance between security and freedom. For purposes of the discussion, I refer to individual rights, civil rights and civil liberties. While the terms overlap, I distinguish them in the following manner: Rights can be thought of in a Hohfeldian sense as a claim that places a duty on some entity in relation to the right-holder.[28] An individual holding the right may depend upon the state to ensure the exercise of the entitlement, but I do not require the entitlement to be that which one has a legal claim to at the time it is held, for I consider an individual right to exist prior to legal structures. Rights can be distinguished from privilege, power and immunity, which do not place a correlative duty against the right. As Hohfeld writes, 'A right is one's affirmative claim against another, and a privilege is one's freedom from the right or claim of another. Similarly, a power is one's affirmative "control" over a given legal relation as against another; whereas an immunity is one's freedom from the legal power or "control" of another as regards some legal relation".[29]

These rights and liberties translate into the framework of the domestic civic arena in the following manner: Civil rights are understood to represent individuals' abilities to engage freely and equally in political affairs to promote a particular agenda either directly or through representation. They are thus linked to the democratic nature of the state. Protection of the right to vote and political participation, the right to equality under the law, the right to health and freedom of person and thought, and the rights to life and property become some of the necessary constituents of participation in political affairs. In contrast, civil liberties refer more directly to the protection of the individual's right to articulate preferences or convictions and to act freely upon them in the private sphere without undue or intrusive interference by the government. They are thus connected more intimately with the liberal nature of the regime. Freedoms thus enumerated relate to the press, movement and association, expression, religion, undue surveillance, communication, education and economic pursuit.

Counterterrorist measures often infringe on one or more of these civil rights and liberties. For instance, land redistribution, house and village demolition, the interruption of vital services, the confiscation of property and the freezing of assets affect the right to property. Liberty suffers directly from wider powers of arrest, stricter sentencing, the use of internment or detention, extradition, exclusion, kidnapping and travel strictures. Proscription, banning meetings, preventing the use of facilities, the use of martial law or curfew, restriction and travel bans, quarantine and the use of identity cards affect freedom of movement and association. And censorship and interference with the management of the media affect freedom of speech. In each of these violations, considerably more is at stake than the immediate effect intended by the measure. Censorship provides a good example: The cost of suspending free speech is borne by citizens' ability to participate in the basic democratic structures of the state. How can one vote without access to free information? How can one branch provide a check on another? How can government policy be subjected to the debate and scrutiny necessary to form a strong policy that benefits the citizenry as a whole? Such measures serve to paralyze the political life of an entity that depends on that life for its own existence and evolution. The protection of these rights strengthens equality and justice within the political order.

Expanded State Power

State power, in and of itself, has neither positive nor negative connotations. It would be easy to think of circumstances under which state power might not just be innocuous, but desirable. If I lived in a grasslands area with a high danger of wildfire, I would probably prefer that the state have the ability to assemble and use firefighting capabilities. But when increased state power is specifically linked to the loss of important individual rights, the resulting redistribution of power is of consequence.

Here, the already naturally expansive tendencies of the state are relevant: Despite the liberal claim, and even outside of the specific challenge posed by terrorism, it is the nature of the state to increase power and to erode the individual rights of citizens. Freedom, the culture of equality and the rights of dissent and resistance central to a liberal state carry with them a high price: the possibility of the overthrow of the state. Accordingly, in seeking to protect individuals from others acting to assume power or to dissolve the political structure, states constantly evolve new measures to increase knowledge of affairs in the state and to ensure that the administrative and judicial structures obviate potential threats. Thus measures designed to monitor public and private information, judicial alteration and extrajudicial measures steal their way into state action.[30]

The state's natural drive to expansion, however, is not without limitation. It was in response to the extraordinary powers assumed by the monarch that the liberal discourse began. The 1688 Glorious Revolution in England was glorious precisely because it created limits on what the king or queen could – and could not – do. It also secured for the aristocracy a position of power and influence independent of the monarch. Locke's *Second Treatise* laid out the rights to be protected from the advance of the sovereign. These rights, and the entitlements developed through subsequent liberal discourse, became the cornerstone of constitutionally limited orders. The right of rebellion is rooted in the state's obligation to respect these entitlements.

Not only, then, does the rapid expansion in state power feed into a latent dynamic traditionally kept in check by the possibility of violence from the citizenry, thus destabilizing the relationships between citizens and the state, but relations within the different branches of the state itself also shift. The growth in domestic state power that results from new counterterrorist provisions is not evenly distributed. This effect is particularly pronounced under the national security model. The executive, freed from traditional checks and balances, assumes central importance and gains a significant amount of autonomy. Where the balance falls is not decided by the legislative bodies but by the executive, often on the basis of privileged information. And so to say that it is specifically freedom and the liberties of the population that are to be traded for the supposed security of the state and citizens within it is somewhat of a misnomer. What also is traded for the supposed security are the checks and balances placed on the distribution of power within the state.

Distributive Justice

In some ways the counterterrorist discourse is a perversion of the liberal dialogue: It is about establishing the legitimacy of the state to erode its liberal institutions in order to ensure the security of citizens, persons and property – which is what those liberal institutions were meant to protect. It is equally about delegitimating the challenge being posed to the ruling strata. And it is in the manner in which this counterterrorist discourse unfolds in a liberal, democratic regime that tension between liberalism and democracy can be seen: Majoritarian demands made under the guise of national security concerns often conflict with individualist, liberal tenets of the rights dialogue. What makes the majoritarian character of particular consequence is that the counterterrorist measures subsequently applied do not impact the rights of most citizens. States, in fact, frequently justify counterterrorist measures on the grounds that they are applied only to 'terrorists'. As the pig, Napoleon, put it in George Orwell's *Animal Farm*, 'All animals are equal, but some animals are more equal than others'. Individuals who place themselves in a state of war towards the *politas* are considered to have stripped themselves of their rights.

But the assumption that a citizen has become an 'enemy of the state' means that ordinary due process is bypassed. Individuals have been deemed guilty prior to guilt being demonstrated through judicial structures. Moreover, in the emotional atmosphere that surrounds the commission of an act of terrorism, even standard judicial procedures net improper results. Altering or suspending them and stripping citizens accused, but not tried, of rights accorded to them by nature of their participation in the state, sets a dangerous precedent and one directly antithetical to the principles of liberal, democratic government.

What is important here is that it isn't everyone who is subjected to such treatment. As a result, significant issues of distributive inequities symptomatic of counterterrorist provisions enter into the equation. Returning then to the claimed balance, it is well and good to say that there exists a trade-off between security and freedom – but, as Waldron notes, a more accurate statement would be that the freedoms of *some portion* of the population, often identifiable via race, gender, age and religion, are sacrificed for the perceived security of another group in society.[31] So on the grounds of undistributed (in)justice, in essence, the claimed balance misleads. These measures create a precedent for a cultural double standard. Britain's treatment of the minority Irish Catholic community in Northern Ireland, Turkey's inequitable use of extraordinary powers against Kurds in the southeastern region and the United States' discriminatory actions against people of Arabic decent since 11 September 2001 establish precedents that wrench the fabric of multiethnic, democratic states.

Practical Effect

The application of liberty restrictions to the group most closely identified as perpetrators of terrorist action often underscores the claims being made by those engaged in violence in the first place. That is to say it reinforces the claims to injustice at the heart of the terrorist challenge. This risks increased support for the movement from individuals not yet involved in violence but perhaps sympathetic to the claims of the disgruntled organization and subject to extraordinary powers. These measures, in essence, backfire. A good example of this phenomenon is in the realm of extended detention.

Terrorist organizations depend upon stealth and the ability to avoid or mitigate state countermeasures in order to survive. One could view the organizations that emerge as significant threats in a Darwinian sense: These are the nominal 'winners'.[32] When the state answers violence by introducing certain measures, such as extended detention or internment without trial, one could make the reasonable assumption that such a move would have been contemplated and avoided by the organization. Indeed, groups often 'go to ground' immediately before an actual attack. Intelligence agencies recognize this and look for a sudden drop in the 'noise' level as an indication of an impending operation. This means that broad state powers are then directed not against those involved in the violence – but against those perhaps once removed from the violence. Yet this is the most important target group to court – not alienate. Again, this counters the claim that security and freedom must be weighed against each other, with the presumption that limitations on freedoms will, indeed, have the desired effect.

As was previously discussed, while states have an obligation to protect their citizens' rights, what is less clear are the obligations incurred towards noncitizens present within domestic bounds and noncitizens external to the geographic region encompassed by the state. For those noncitizens overseas, the state tends to trump their individual rights with the protection of rights and freedoms of its own population. The omission of noncitizen's individual rights from the calculus of national security, however, carries the risk of fomenting further violence against the state in a realm not readily amenable to state influence and power.

Embedded in the concept of counterterrorism is the idea that, by enacting these measures, the state regains control. The *duty* to take the lead in responding to terrorism, moreover, lies in the state realm. Here it is different from, for example, car accidents, where the state sets a broad perimeter within which individual agency influences the risk borne when an individual gets behind the wheel. Perhaps *because of* the indiscriminate nature of terrorist attacks, and the ubiquitous nature of the threat, responsibility rests with the state to protect, broadly, society as a whole. What responsibilities, then, do citizens bear to the state? In other words, what rights does the state hold against the citizenry? As terrorism becomes increasingly seen as a national security issue, issues relating to the collective responsibilities of society rise to the fore. Is it, then, the *duty* of the citizen within the state to forego certain rights – either as a member of the society that benefits from the state or as a representative of the state itself – in order to maintain the existence of the state?

If we are to respond to this question with the long-term security interests of the state in mind, then it would appear that there is more than one duty that the individual bears toward the polity. For instance, the duty to challenge the growth of state power to diminish increasing security threats posed by other dissident groups is directly affected by the closure of social and political structures. As has already been argued, many measures that erode individual rights are simply not effective over the long term. Moreover, they have a deleterious effect on the citizen's ability to fulfill his or her other obligations to the state and to society more broadly.

Conclusion: Reevaluating the Calculus

The central theme that weaves its way through the previous consequentialist and rights-based arguments is that a certain class of counterterrorist measures impacts the state's short- and long-term domestic and international interests, and that this effect matters. Three particular forms of political legitimacy are implicated: first, that of the legal structures and the distribution of power within the state. Here the emphasis is on the manner in which legal rules develop, how they are altered and the manner in which they are applied, according to a set of developed legal criteria.[33] Second, the ideal conditions under which a state might be said to be legitimate.[34] Third, I include the degree to which the state acts in accordance with the beliefs held by observers and participants in the state structure, thus reinforcing its claim to moral authority.[35]

This theme, and the three approaches to state political legitimacy, are not without controversy.[36] I nevertheless consider the legal, political, theoretical and social-scientific approaches to illuminate the consequences of decisions made in the name of the 'balance' between security and freedom. Terrorist movements frequently seek to undermine the legitimacy of the states in which they operate. By calling a regime's authority into question, such non-state organizations directly challenge the right of the state to wield power. If effective, this challenge cannot be ignored – particularly when, as in a liberal, democratic state, the goals of those in power depend on the cooperation of the populace. The degree to which the state can exert its power relies on the extent to which it is viewed as the legitimate political authority. In a liberal, democratic state, this is intimately tied to the protection of individual rights.

In seeking then to determine what is a legitimate course of action, we return to the argument most frequently put forward to justify these measures: that a balance must be obtained between security and freedom. But, all too frequently, consequentialist and seemingly utilitarian arguments applied to this argument, which emphasize the greatest good for the greatest number of people as measured by the outcome of a state's actions, fail to give sufficient weight to the place and complexity of individual rights. This carries with it legal, normative, and empirical consequences for ascertaining state political legitimacy. Unfortunately, particularly after the devastation caused by 11 September 2001, the fulcrum analogy dominates the public discourse. A national security orientation influences the placement of the fulcrum. And the American administration defines national security as state security, not as the security of the people within the state, which would make issues of human and individual rights central to the discussion. Contemporary arguments invoke reasons of state in justification for ever-broader provisions and a narrowing of constitutional rights. They mark,specifically, discussions related to 'catastrophic terrorism', where the possible terrorist use of WMD, seems to create a new set of rules via which states can respond.

Perhaps a better way to think about counterterrorism is in terms of a constellation of short- and long-term trade offs that consider the risks imposed on the state by the suspension—and maintenance—of complex and interconnected rights. Such an approach would force a more nuanced and accurate evaluation of the impact of new measures on both liberty and security. The consequences are borne in the three realms of political legitimacy.

Open societies exhibit a level of privacy and ease of transfer within which individuals dedicated to attacking and even overthrowing the state can operate. But in the many senses discussed in this paper, it is only through liberty that security can be obtained. Rights create a shield within which individuals can maximize their freedom. They confer dignity and respect upon individuals that do not have access to power – a dignity and respect contested in the very act of terrorism. Giving economic, social and political rights to individuals supposedly represented by the groups engaged in violence often undermines the claims of the groups themselves. And operating according to liberal, democratic standards ensures the support of other countries versed in the liberal, democratic discourse.

Notes

1. Jacob Levich, 'Justice for Robert Jackson: The War on Terror is not a Suicide Pact', CommonDreams.org 20 June 2002, http://www.commondreams.org/views02/0620-06.htm
2. Ibid.
3. http://www.wisdomquotes.com/000958.html and http://www.brainyquote.com/quotes/quotes/b/benjaminfr110256.html
4. Jeremy Waldron,'Security and Liberty: The Image of Balance', *Journal of Political Philosophy* 11/3 (2003) pp.191–210. Waldron discusses this point at some length, suggesting that potential payoffs provide insufficient reasons to support the immediate, deleterious effect on 'suspects and dissidents'. He writes, '. . . given the record of the bumbling incompetence and in-fighting of American intelligence and law-enforcement agencies wielding the already very considerable powers that they had in the weeks leading up to September 11, there is no particular reason to suppose that giving them more power will make them more effective in this desperately difficult task. But it might make them more effective in the somewhat easier task of acting oppressively towards vulnerable political opponents at home' (p.209).
5. Clive Walker noted these on 14 July 2003.
6. Waldron, note 4, pp.191–210.
7. See note 4.
8. Frank Bolz Jr., Kenneth J. Dudonis, and David P. Shulz, *The Counterterrorism Handbook*. (Boca Raton, FL: CRC Press 2002). Authors write of the democratic liability, 'The laws of a country and its systems and procedures for safeguarding the rights of its citizens are perverted by terrorists in order to help them achieve success in undermining that country . . . Civil rights guarantees and procedures make for long, drawn out, and costly trials'.
9. Interviews conducted by author in Northern Ireland, South Africa and Turkey as part of doctoral research, 1993–1998.
10. Martha Crenshaw, ed., 'Introduction', *Terrorism in Context* (University Park, PA: Pennsylvania State University Press 1995).
11. Garth Whitty, *op cit*. Bonanate reminds us that while a blocked society may be unable to alter in response to citizen demands, it nevertheless may be 'capable of preserving and reproducing itself'. Alberto Oldani, Luigi Migliorino, Luigi Bonanate, *Political Violence in the Contemporary World*. (Milano: F. Angeli, 1979), p.205. Terrorism may become a feature of an otherwise stable social or political structure.
12. Outside of a state-sponsored realm, efforts to develop and deploy biological weapons have met with little success. For instance, despite extensive funding and highly educated

scientists, Aum Shinrikyo's various attempts to launch a biological attack met with minimal success. For further discussion of efforts to use and obtain biological weapons see generally J. B. Tucker, ed., *Toxic Terror: Assessing Terrorist Use of Chemical and Biological Weapons.* (Cambridge, MA: MIT Press 2000).

13. 'Next Dominant Domestic Terrorism Fear: Biochemical Weapons', *Gannett News Service* 28 March 1997.

14. Jessica Stern, 'Apocalypse Never, But the Threat Is Real', *Survival* 40/4 (Winter 1998–99) p.178.

15. Garth Whitty, (2003), '*Terrorism and Human Rights*', CSTPV International Conference: July 14, St. Andrew's Bay, Scotland.

16. Here international norms against using such weapons are of utmost importance, as are state attempts to continue to place their use beyond the pale. This norm provides a high level of protection to the state. While on the one hand the more spectacular the attack, the more attention is generated to a cause, on the other hand, the more spectacular, the less discriminate, and the less discriminate the greater the loss of legitimacy.

17. http://news.bbc.co.uk/1/hi/uk/1201738.htm

18. Tom Heller raised this point in a panel on post-9/11 measures held at Kresge Auditorium, Stanford University, 3 October 2001. What is perhaps ironic is that the precedents for violating state sovereignty in order to establish a relationship with an individual located in another state derive from the field of human rights. Efforts of organizations, such as the United Nations Human Rights Commission, to address the ill treatment of individuals located in one of the member states, when their actions contradict the state's wishes, represent a violation of sovereignty. But the question with which we are confronted is whether a perceived threat provides a justifiable reason. Does the breach of sovereignty introduced by the human rights dialogue open the door to violations of individual rights? In other words, what if a state's actions are not to protect an individual, but rather to restrict their freedoms or end their lives? Does a state then have a right to restrict the rights of noncitizens located outside the state's borders?

19. US National Security Council National Security Strategy of the United States, http://www.whitehouse.gov/nsc/nss.pdf

20. Waldron also uses the chess example, but in relation to Nozickian side-constraints. He suggests that the defense 'It would really make a difference to my game' – in order to justify placing one's king into check, is irrelevant in chess'. (Waldron, note 4, p.196). See Robert Nozick, *Anarchy, State and Utopia* (Oxford: Blackwell 1974) p.28.

21. Indeed, as Waldron notes, debates in political theory relating to competing rights are only now beginning to come into their own (Waldron, note 4, p.196).

22. See generally Harry Golombek, *A History of Chess* (Routledge & Kegan Paul, London 1976) and Ron Hassner, (2002), 'Conflict, Identity and Change: A Short History of Chess', International Studies Association Annual Conference: March 24–27, New Orleans, Louisiana.

23. Ricardo Calvo and Egbert Meissenburg, 'Valencia und die Geburt des Neuen Schachs', in Strouhal (ed), *Vom Wesir zur Dame: Kulturelle Regeln, ihr Zwang und Bruechigkeit. Ueber Kulturelle Transformationen am Beispiel des Schachspiels* (Vienna: 1995). Cited in Hassner, above.

24. For the rules as sanctioned by the World Chess Federation and the United States Chess Federation see Martin Morrison (ed), *Official Rules of Chess* (New York: David McKay Company 1978).

25. Waldron addresses this point with an analogy to promise-keeping. He argues against a simple cumulative view of reasons to – or not to – protect individual rights and suggests, 'Maybe – like promises – [civil liberties] too are not supposed to be sensitive to changes in the scale of social costs' (note 4, p.196).

26. See for instance Ronald Dworkin, *Taking Rights Seriously* (Cambridge, MA: Harvard University Press 1978); Jeremy Waldron, *Liberal Rights: Collected Papers* (Cambridge: Cambridge University Press 1993); Joseph Raz, *The Morality of Freedom* (Oxford: Clarendon Press 1986); Lon Fuller, *The Morality of Law* (New Haven: Yale University Press 1964); Matthew Kramer, *A Question of Rights;* Quentin Skinner, 'The State', John Locke, *Second Treatise of Government* ed. by Thomas P. Peardon (Upper Saddle River, NJ: Prentice Hall 1997); H. L. A. Hart, 'Are There Any Natural Rights?', *Philosophical Review* 65/2 (April 1955); John Rawls, *A Theory of Justice* (Cambridge, MA: Harvard University Press 1971).

27. David Brin, *The Transparent Society: Will Technology Force Us to Choose Between Privacy and Freedom?* (Reading, MA.: Addison-Wesley 1998.)

28. Wesley Newcomb Hohfeld, *Fundamental Legal Conceptions as Applied in Judicial Reasoning* (New Haven: Yale University Press 1964).

29. Ibid., p.60. Human rights I understand to be claims held by individuals and prior to legal structures, which place a correlative duty on both states and other individuals in relation to the entitlement. More substantively, I specifically draw in my discussion from the Universal Declaration of Human Rights, adopted by the United Nations General Assembly in 1948. The declaration recognized the right to equality; the right not to be discriminated against based on race, color, gender, religion, property or birth; the right to life, liberty and security; and the right not to be enslaved. Further articles addressed the right not to be subjected to cruel, inhuman or degrading treatment or punishment; to equal protection under the law; and to an effective remedy by the competent national tribunals for violations of rights granted by the state. The document specified the right not to be subjected to arbitrary arrest, detention or exile. Protections extended to a fair and public hearing by an independent and impartial tribunal, the right to presumption of innocence and the guarantee of provisions necessary for one's defense. The declaration also stated that everyone has a right to a nationality. The document recognized a number of freedoms as well: freedom of movement, freedom from undue or arbitrary interference, freedom of thought, conscience and religion; freedom of opinion and expression; and freedom of peaceful assembly and association. The document stated that individuals hold a right to be granted such freedoms. Two instruments of international law gave the declaration binding force: the International Covenant on Economic, Social and Cultural Rights and the International Covenant on Civil and Political Rights. The five regions considered in this tract ratified these instruments, with Israel and the United Kingdom entering derogations consistent with Article 4 and under the claim of terrorist activity actions against the state.

30. Herein lies the apparent dilemma: The more intrusive the measures that are introduced, the more effective (assumedly) the state will be in accomplishing its objective of protecting the life and property of the citizens, even at the expense of individual rights. It is easy to conceive of situations where one would willingly waive basic rights. At the end of my block there is a corner store. Should a robbery occur and, with the police in hot pursuit, the culprit were to run down the street and enter my home, I would have no difficulty agreeing that a search warrant would not be required for the police officers to enter my premises. One could think of other cases in which the threat of crime might be enough to convince some, but not all, to abrogate rights they otherwise might prefer to maintain. The woman who lives in fear of rape may forego the opportunity to live alone and in circumstances of freedom and instead chose to reside behind iron gates or in a group living situation in which a guard notes dates and times of egress and ingress. A man taking his two-year-old to the fair may more easily submit to being frisked for weapons as he enters the gates to the fairground. And a city where previously electronic public surveillance was limited to police stations may silently acquiesce to the placement of cameras at every intersection.

31. See particularly Waldron, note 4, pp.200–4.

32. On the Darwinian concept of terrorist organizations see Daniel Byman, (2002), paper presented at the Social Science Seminar Center for International Security and Cooperation, Stanford University, Stanford, CA.

33. This is the realm of jurisprudence, which tends to focus on the nature, location and source of sovereignty, itself absolute and indivisible. In constitutional theory, 'sovereignty' is broadly defined as the right to make commands which cannot be contradicted. Rodney S. Barker, *Political Legitimacy and the State* (New York: Oxford University Press 1990) p.10. Discussion revolves around individuals, not around existence or the order of obedience, with the identification of sovereignty arising from courts and legislatures. Legal theories are not overly interested in either the consequences of erosions in legitimacy, or in the conditions under which sovereignty is effective or breaks down. Of central importance are legal disputes about power, and the interpretation of legal rules: how they are initiated, revised and reinforced. David Beetham, *The Legitimation of Power* (Basingstoke: Macmillan Education 1991) p.4. As Dworkin puts it, 'A State is legitimate if its constitutional structure and practices are such that its citizens have a general obligation to obey political decisions that purport to impose duties on them'. Ronald M. Dworkin, *Law's Empire* (Cambridge, MA: Bellknap

Press 1986) p.191. Under legal interpretation, legitimacy represents legal validity, where the exercise of power is conducted in accordance with the law. Whether the law itself is justifiable or conforms to political or moral principles becomes one of various positions on what the law ought to prescribe. The understanding of legitimacy as it relates to law tends to derive from within the society in question. In other words, it assumes a legitimacy to the established legal order. Sub state, anti state or nationalist terrorist groups may or may not call the legal order into question. Their contention may be primarily with the manner in which law is applied and the ethnic identity of those deciding the 'validity' of legal statutes, where alternate-state options are preferred in which a similar order is espoused. Such inquiry varies by case study and is particular to each historical context.

34. Derived from the considerations of political theory, this normative approach considers the conditions for consent and the extent to which moral obligation can be levied. This strand considers the empirical consequences of power relations and consequent erosions in state power.

35. Lacking to some extent an ideal form of legitimacy, established by some normative criteria independent of experience, this approach tends to focus on the beliefs of a particular society under question: Here enters Max Weber's equation of legitimacy with belief in legitimacy as demonstrated by individual members of society. This approach suggests that acknowledging a government's right to govern is what makes it an observable event in human history. In this view, 'Legitimacy is precisely the belief in the rightfulness of the state, in its authority to issue commands, so that those commands are obeyed ... because they are believed in some sense to have moral authority'. Barker, (1990) note 33 p.11. As Barker also notes, the historical approach seems to assume that observable conduct somehow carries with it a validity independent of the observer's assessments and preferences. Because of the focus on the relationship between the state and those it governs, within social science the various ways in which this relationship is described further distinguish approaches to the question of legitimacy.

36. Social and economic reductionists, for example, argue that the extent to which legitimacy is conferred by individuals within a state is inextricably linked to a complex set of social and economic values, within which government plays a subordinate role. It is thus asserted that a specifically political form of legitimacy – as a matter of observed relations between government and governed – cannot be isolated. Until such a time as the state is inseparable from those within it, however – a point I would argue we have not reached – to talk of political legitimacy is to discuss the relationship between the state and those with whom it has a relationship.

6

Disregard for Security: The Human Rights Movement and 9/11

BERTIL DUNÉR

Swedish Institute of International Affairs, Stockholm, Sweden

International human rights NGOs have warned that human rights have been threatened since September 11. However, the matter is complicated since what is involved is in reality a relationship between two concepts: human rights and security against terrorism. This article demonstrates that there is a tendency for international human rights NGOs to brush aside questions on security against terrorism. NGOs have stipulated that human rights values should be superior, or they have maintained, but failed to show, that there is no goal conflict between security and human rights—even that human rights fulfil a considerable instrumental function with respect to freedom from terrorism.

Introduction

Traditional realist thinking holds that human rights are not one of the most important goals on the foreign policy agenda. In his now classic article on human rights in foreign policy, R. John Vincent argues that this is in the nature of things, since diplomats have an interest in maintaining good relations with each other – not just relations – and that free trade and security are given priority. In these circumstances, he concludes, we might expect the issue of human rights to surface in foreign policy only in two kinds of situations: 'when it plainly serves the interest of the state' and 'when attention to it endangers no other interest of the state.'[1]

It is a *locus communis* that human rights concerns, not to mention human rights rhetoric, have gained in salience over the past decades, in international forums as well as in bilateral politics. The conflict between the goals of human rights and of security may thus have been somewhat mitigated over the years. However, there are no reasons to believe that foreign-policy makers have ever started to accord them equal importance. On the contrary, the attacks on the US of 11 September 2001 may have changed the balance or tipped the scales to the detriment of human rights.

The 11 September attacks meant a drastic increase in the prominence of security thinking, now in the garb of counterterrorism. This is manifested in national thinking and in positions taken by the United Nations, including the powerfully worded Resolution 1373 (28 September 2001), of which Article 2 calls for antiterrorist action in a number of ways, including the modification of domestic laws where necessary so that the financing, planning, preparation for or perpetration of terrorist acts or support for terrorist acts are 'established as serious criminal offences' in domestic laws and regulations, and so that any person who participates in such actions is brought to justice.[2]

This development implies a considerable risk for human rights, regardless of the fact that the Security Council has also expressed its view that the fight against terrorism must be based on the principles of the charter of the United Nations and the norms of international law, including respect for international humanitarian law and human rights (UN Security Council, Resolution 1269, 19 October 1999, reaffirmed by Resolution 1373).

Civil society claims to be the driving force in the human rights movement, and international human rights nongovernmental organizations (NGOs) have, in accordance with their mandates, warned that human rights have been threatened since 11 September. Their endeavours are certainly widely appreciated. However, the matter is complicated since what is involved here is a relationship between two concepts. There is a certain tendency among leading human rights NGOs to take the other side of the relationship – security against terrorism – rather lightly. This attitude and the problems involved are the subject of this article.

NGOs' Positions

NGOs of course recognize that states have the responsibility for the security of their citizens, but they do not necessarily see a conflict between the goal of security and that of human rights. Amnesty International has stated before the UN Commission on Human Rights: 'The Commission must send a clear message that there is no contradiction between human rights and security'[3] and a leading article in *Human Rights Monitor*, published by a meta-NGO which services NGOs at the UN human rights headquarters in Vienna, states: 'States are under the obligation to investigate crimes, to apprehend the guilty, to condemn them after a fair trial, and to compensate the victims. There is no reason that this should change, even in the wake of the frightful massacre of 11 September'.[4]

The denial that there is a goal conflict would imply that antiterrorism measures can be taken without any harm being done to human rights. An Open Statement to the 2002 Commission on Human Rights by five leading international human rights organizations did in fact state that: 'Effective action against terrorism can be taken without violating human rights'.[5] Moreover, not only is there an obligation to protect human rights, but human rights also have an instrumental function. The open statement says: 'Indeed, one of the best weapons to combat the root causes of terrorism is the full observance of human rights'. According to *Human Rights Monitor*: 'In order to be effective, the commitment to fight against terrorism should take the form of a concerted effort by the international community, and remain within the legal framework and mindful of human rights norms, regardless of who the aggressors and the victims may be, and without various political, economic and geo-strategic interests coming to the fore'.[6] In the wake of 11 September, a statement was prepared by Civicus, an international alliance for the support of civil society throughout the world, and endorsed by a considerable number of internationally active NGOs, including Amnesty International, Oxfam International and OneWorld International. This 'Joint Civil Society Statement on the Tragedy in the United States' said: 'We do not underestimate the difficulty or the urgency of the task facing political leaders. But we are convinced that a safer world for all can only be achieved by the extension of human rights and the rule of law. As they act to prevent such attacks in the future, we urge governments to uphold the fundamental civil liberties that underpin democratic participation'.[7]

As we can see, these ideas boil down to two theses, on the one hand concerning the question of a *trade-off* between security and human rights, and, on the other, concerning the *instrumentality* of human rights for security. Both are analysed below.

In the author's view, these ideas meet with the approval of a considerable part of the international NGO community, although, of course, is it impossible to establish how representative they are. In reality NGOs' positions can vary a good deal. An open letter of October 2001 from NGOs, directed to the UN General Assembly, expressed profound concern about Security Council Resolution 1373. These organizations, including the Women's Caucus for Gender Justice and many others said to represent the rights and needs of women, state that: 'The response to such threats as represented by September 11 must give primacy to the rule of law and be vested in an international body such as the United Nations and not in individual nations or collectivities of nations'.[8] A similar statement has been made by another constellation of NGOs with some degree of peace orientation.[9] These statements are not empirically testable: They are simple stipulations of the supremacy of human rights. They command less interest since they dodge the issue of the relationship between human rights and security, which many people perceive as a rather complicated matter.

Instrumentality

The statements on instrumentality cited above seem to mean that human rights are a necessary condition for security, and tend to be a sufficient condition.

With respect to the first aspect it is easy to produce counterexamples. There are certainly a number of countries which have not paid due respect to human rights – authoritarian states – but which have encountered little terrorism or none. The Soviet Union and its East European vassals could be cited as historical examples. In today's world we have, for instance, Cuba and, of course, North Korea – even China (which has experienced relatively little terrorism in view of its mosaic of populations and wide geographical extension).

However, it has been maintained that building a stronger human rights culture is necessary, *in the long run*, if terrorism is to be defeated.[10] This seems to be pure conjecture, of course, informed by pious hopes for the values of the western world, which gave birth to the idea of universal human rights. Other conjectures (of no less weight) may point in other directions. For instance, given the widespread and manifold misery in our world, we might assume that many people would tend to accept a certain degree of authoritarianism (whether religious or not) as long as they live in a secure environment and socioeconomic standards are improving.

Human rights have been held to be one of the best weapons for combating the root causes of terrorism. Arguments for this thesis seem to be primarily theoretical. Using the examples of some recent developments in the Middle East and North Africa, Human Rights Watch (HRW) seeks to underscore the value of human rights and democratization. A process of liberalization has begun 'without empowering extremists'. 'Morocco and Jordan have become more open societies, while Qatar and Bahrain have begun to loosen political restraints and have promised to hold elections. Kuwait already has an elected parliament'. HRW concludes that: 'These experiences suggest that the appeal of violent and intolerant movements diminishes as people are given the chance to participate meaningfully in politics and to select from a range of political parties and perspectives'.[11] However, these examples may not be wholly to the point since there is no clear line drawn between violence and terrorism.

If human rights and democracy are important protective devices, then of course we would expect that relatively few democracies would be hit by terrorism. Which countries we can suggest as examples in this connection and how many instances of terrorist action we can adduce will, of course, depend on the definition of terrorism we apply. As is well known, no internationally recognized definition has been agreed upon. Here we will apply a concept of terrorism that is widely used – violence against civilians perpetrated by non-state groups for political purposes. Looking at recent decades we find examples of traditional democracies which have been hit by terrorism, as well as examples of countries with less stable democratic regimes (generally considered to be democracies, although not necessarily perfect ones) which have seen terrorism. A list would include Angola, Argentina, Bosnia, Canada, Colombia, Ecuador, France, Greece, India, Indonesia, Israel, Italy, Japan, Kenya, Mexico, Peru, the Philippines, Russia, South Africa, South Korea, Spain, Sri Lanka, Turkey, Uganda, the United Kingdom and the US.[12]

It should be noted that some countries may have seen terrorist deeds on their soil not in spite of being democracies but rather because they were democracies or wanted to perfect their democratic system. This logic can be explained by the fact that democracy for some extremist groups may represent a lax and contemptible way of life. This seems to have played a role in Bali in 2002.

All of this gives us reasons to be doubtful about the concept of democracy as an important, even one of the best, weapons for rooting out terrorism. We should bear in mind that the list of countries above is certainly not complete.

It should be stressed that the thesis under discussion cannot be grounded in terrorism research. We have no theory of terrorism that explains the phenomenon in a general way or provides trustworthy recipes for ways of eradicating it. In particular, there is no support for the idea, frequently voiced, that some factors are key factors, frequently called root causes – be it poverty, inequality, deprivation, oppression, globalization, energy, fundamentalism or any other.[13] It seems that the overall picture is too complex to be captured within a general formula, or, as Walter Laqueur has stated: 'Society faces not one terrorism but many terrorisms'.[14] In fact, an expert panel of the US National Research Council states that, since the factors influencing contemporary terrorism are a blend of so many different things, 'the logic of cause-followed-by-effect is inappropriate to the understanding of origins and contexts of terrorism'.[15]

This is not to say that we are unable to find correlations of varying strength between background conditions and terrorist actions. Whether there is a strong correlation with human rights can be questioned. After 11 September, many observers may of course be inclined to regard Islamic fundamentalism as a very salient (background) factor. In contrast to this view it should be observed that, with respect to the US, there is one particular factor which was in focus long before 11 September and seems to have gained in relevance thereafter. Many deeds in other countries have *de facto* had the US as a target or co-target – for instance, the Iran hostage crisis in 1979. This means that the US as a democracy is relatively hard-hit by terrorism. Yet there is no simmering civil strife or violent uprising going on within the country – in contrast to Spain or the United Kingdom, for instance – which might give rise to terrorist action. On the basis of an extensive review of terrorist acts directed against the US, Ivan Eland has suggested that there is a strong correlation between US activism overseas and anti-American attacks.[16]

Trade-Off

International NGOs have usually tended to focus on authoritarian states, which is logical since these states are the principal violators of human rights. However, with regard to the human rights – security/antiterrorism nexus democratic states, primarily the US, have come to the fore in an unusually strong way, with the NGOs blending their condemnation of them with express disappointment.

According to *Human Rights Monitor*, 'For human rights defenders in many countries, the wake of 11 September has been marked by the resurgence of a State discourse that was formerly only heard from dictatorial regimes. All measures seem justified in the fight against "subversion" and the maintenance of public order, etc. This tendency is very disturbing'.[17] The general secretary of Amnesty International says: 'The readiness of governments to trade human rights in the interest of security is nothing new. The doctrine of national security has been used frequently in the past to deny human rights. The difference this time lay in the uneasy realisation that it was not autocratic regimes but established democracies that took the lead in introducing draconian laws to restrict civil liberties in the name of public security'.[18]

Disappointment with the democracies is particularly strong with respect to some particular issues, including US treatment of suspected terrorists after 11 September. They will be tried either before general criminal courts or before special military commissions. A Presidential Order on Detention, Treatment, and Trial of Certain Non-Citizens in the War Against Terrorism (13 November 2001) authorized the trial by military commission of any individual who was not a US citizen and who had links to Al-Qaeda or international terrorism against the United States.[19] No details of the criteria to be applied in the identification and selection of such individuals were given. Human Rights Watch characterizes the Presidential Order as a 'flagrant ... affront to international fair-trial standards'.[20] Global Exchange states:

> Today in the United States some 20 million people are living under martial law. They are the permanent legal residents and undocumented immigrants who could be tried, convicted without right to appeal, and sentenced to death by the military tribunals President Bush established in November.
>
> The proposed military tribunals *are the most shocking* element of a rollback of civil liberties that affects citizens and non-citizens alike.[21]

The US policy was officially explained with reference to several factors. The Presidential Order declared that 'an extraordinary emerg-ency' exists, and the president stated that 'it is not practicable to apply in military commissions under this order the principles of law and the rules of evidence generally recognized in the trial of criminal cases in the United States district courts'.[22] The vice president stated in a television interview: 'Here, we've got the opportunity, using these military tribunals, giving people full and fair trials, and represented by counsel to proceed to bring them to justice and, at the same time safeguard those very important elements of national security information'.[23] The military commissions were allegedly important from a security point of view:

> We have to be very aggressive if we're going to intercept, if we're going to disrupt, if we're going to prevent future attacks against the United States. We also need to be able to protect and preserve sources of intelligence. One of the prime reasons for doing this is that it will allow us to use intelligence information that we couldn't use in a regular court proceeding in order to bring these people to justice and, at the same time, be able to protect the sources of information.[24]

Criticism has also been voiced about the handling of US prisoners abroad, notably those held in Guantanamo Bay, the US base in Cuba. Human rights groups and others have accused President George W. Bush of ignoring the Guantanamo Bay prisoners' fundamental rights to trial by due process and of holding them in inhumane conditions. It is maintained furthermore that the US is flouting international law, since the prisoners are denied protection as prisoners of war (POWs) in the meaning of the Geneva Conventions on the law of wars, in particular No. III on prisoners of war. This disregard for international law, concludes the Washington–based Center for Constitutional Rights, can only serve to encourage other nations to act likewise, thereby undermining the very 'war on terrorism' it seeks to fight.[25]

The US government has maintained that the detainees are treated humanely and that the US is acting in accordance with international law. Some of the prisoners are Taliban; others belong to Al-Qaeda. Being a foreign terrorist group, Al-Qaeda is not a party to the Geneva Convention and, accordingly, its members are not entitled to POW status. Afghanistan is a party to the convention and the Taliban are covered by the convention, but under the terms of the Geneva Convention the Taliban detainees do not qualify as POWs. However, even though neither the Taliban nor the Al-Qaeda detainees are entitled to POW status, they will be given many POW privileges as a matter of policy.[26]

These prisoners are believed to pose a continuing threat to the United States and its interests. The vice-president has declared: 'These are bad people. I mean, they've already been screened before they get to Guantanamo. They may will [*sic*] have information about future terrorist attacks against the United States. We need that information, we need to be able to interrogate them and extract from them whatever information they have'.[27]

The US has also been criticized in strong terms for its attitude to new developments in emerging international law, and particularly the establishment of the International Criminal Court (ICC). The US has withdrawn its support and tried to reduce the risk of US citizens being brought before the ICC by concluding bilateral agreements with individual countries. The crime of terrorism is not under the jurisdiction of the ICC but could possibly be included in the ICC list of crimes later by way of a Review Conference.[28] US policy in this case is frequently seen by international NGOs as related to antiterrorism. The International Federation for Human Rights (Federation International des Droits de l'Homme, or FIDH) says: 'If one analyses it globally, this arsenal [against the ICC] cannot be separated from the means the American [*sic*] have implemented in order to fight terrorism. American actions are aimed at giving carte blanche to American military and civilian leaders involved in counter terrorism and other military operations abroad . . . '[29]

Criticism of the US policy on the ICC, as exemplified in the lines quoted, is wide-spread, in particular criticism of the bilateral agreements. An example is a policy document of the Coalition for the International Criminal Court (CICC), which describes itself as a network of well over 1,000 NGOs advocating for a fair, effective and independent International Criminal Court: 'It is clear that the US is only concerned with preventing the ICC from fulfilling its mandate. That the US should seek to aggressively undermine the court is not a surprise'.[30]

The US maintains that the ICC undermines the role of the UN Security Council, creates a prosecutorial system that is unaccountable, and asserts jurisdiction over citizens of states that have not ratified the treaty (notably the US itself). These flaws, it is maintained, open up the way for the court to be exploited for politically motivated prosecutions.[31] The US permanent representative to the UN has maintained that: 'We are especially concerned that Americans sent overseas as soldiers, risking their lives to keep the peace or to protect us all from terrorism and other threats, be themselves protected from unjust or politically motivated charges' and 'we know that prosecutors who are responsible to no one constitute a danger, and we will not expose our citizens to such a danger. We cannot accept a structure that may transform the political criticism of America's world role into the basis for criminal trials of Americans who have put their lives on the line for freedom'.[32]

Not only the US among the western democracies has drawn sharp criticism; so has the United Kingdom, which adopted a law in December 2001 as a consequence of the 11 September attacks – the Anti-terrorism, Crime and Security Act (ATCSA). The most controversial aspect relates to immigration and asylum: For instance, the law was intended to speed up the asylum process for suspected terrorists; and substantive consideration of asylum claims was to be waived where the secretary of state certifies that a person's removal from the country would be conducive to the public good. Amnesty International has stated that it is 'deeply concerned about serious human rights violations that have taken place as a consequence of the United Kingdom (UK) authorities' response to the 11 September 2001 attacks'.[33] Liberty, one of the UK's major human rights and civil liberties organizations, has maintained:

> In the aftermath of September 11th, we needed reassurance that we would be protected against terrorism. But in its determination to be seen to be doing something, the Government rushed not to make us safer, but to cut our freedoms. Rather than ensure our security services were making best use of their powers and had the resources to do so, the Government reached again for the statute book – less justified and effective, but far more headline-making . . . The Government has used our fear of possible terrorism as an excuse for sweeping restrictions on the lives and liberties of every innocent person in the UK.[34]

In connection with the ATCSA the British government sought derogation from the European Convention of Human Rights in respect to the powers of detention in the act. This derogation has been severely criticized. For instance, Liberty stated:

> So significant is this measure that the government, only one year after enshrining the European Convention on Human Rights into our law, is having to opt out or 'derogate' from one of its fundamental provisions, the prohibition on arbitrary detention. Such derogations are supposed

to be reserved for 'war or other public emergencies threatening the life of the nation'. There is no imminent threat of the complete breakdown of civil society in the UK. We have not reached this point as yet and although there are threats, the nation itself is not in jeopardy.[35]

In response to criticism both within and outside Parliament, the government has maintained that the law is not in contradiction to international law. With respect to the powers of detention, the government can refer to the Court of Appeal, which determined that these powers are appropriate.[36] Before the act was sent to Parliament an extensive review of existing legislation was carried out to ensure that the UK had the necessary powers to protect the safety of its citizens at home and abroad. The ATCSA was intended to expand on powers already established to take account of the changed situation after 11 September.[37]

In sum, the US and the UK have been engaged in legal defences of their policies – which is obviously needed, since both have drawn criticism on legal grounds. But there is no doubt about their rationales: they are security concerns. It is quite natural, of course, that the US, being a true world power, has security interests which far exceed the UK perspective.

What does the NGOs' denial that there is a trade-off dilemma mean in the context of these issues? Since NGOs claim that action to counter terrorism is possible without prejudicing human rights, it seems that they should in fact make an effort to:

- make an assessment of the security benefit of these US and British policies; and
- make it believable that there exist alternative policies which are not to the detriment of human rights and which would be equally (or preferably more) effective.

They tend to do neither. For instance, in a written statement to the UN Commission on Human Rights the International Federation for Human Rights makes a general assessment of 'human rights and the fight against terrorism'.[38] This document is essentially on the 'exigencies of law' and, although the antiterrorist effort is severely criticized, its goals and policies are not discussed. In an extensive report on the UK, entitled 'Rights Denied: The UK's Response to 11 September 2001', Amnesty International discusses the ATCSA, although without addressing the government's conflict of goals. A footnote states laconically: 'Amnesty International has strongly condemned the attacks of 11 September 2001 in the USA and has called for those allegedly responsible to be brought to justice. However, the organization believes that this must be done in accordance with international human rights and humanitarian law'.[39]

In its 'World Report 2002', Human Rights Watch severely criticizes the US for undermining the ICC and finds that 'Washington has opposed the court because it theoretically could be used to scrutinize the conduct of US armed forces'.[40] This brief comment is not a fair description of the US position, much less, of course, is it an analysis of it. However, in a journal article the HRW chairman discusses the US position fairly extensively, and in so doing says: 'We have to recognize that the U.S. have many enemies who might initiate unjustified legal action'.[41] Still, the US concerns are not taken seriously. The HRW report states that the risks for the US are 'theoretical', thus suggesting that they are nil, and the article cited says that the US position is meaningless ('*tiene poco sentido*') since there are so many 'safeguards'. In fact, the article maintains that when US 'excuses' and 'rationalizations' are rebutted there is only one explication left: the US government is intoxicated by its power in the world and following international norms does not serve its interests. It is much better off if no limits are set to its freedom of action. Needless to say, no alternative US policy is suggested which would accommodate US security concerns.

Deeply concerned by the US worldwide campaign to get bilateral agreements to ensure that US personnel will not be surrendered to the ICC, Amnesty International has engaged in a campaign seeking to prevent states from entering into such impunity agreements. In an elaborate report it presents a wide array of arguments against the US efforts.[42] These are purely legal arguments focusing on the Rome Statute of the ICC, Status of Forces Agreements (SOFAs) and so on, whereas US security concerns are not addressed, not even in the section on 'The Typical US Impunity Agreement'.

Admittedly, it may not be an easy task for human rights NGOs to analyse strategies for security against terrorism since they lack information and expertise in the field. That begs the question. Since the relationship between security and human rights is in focus, they need to broaden their competence.

Not only do NGOs fail to spell out alternative security policies, they seem clearly to scorn the security policies followed after 11 September. The International Federation for Human Rights (FIDH), in the document referred to above, writes:

> However, these periods of security troubles are precisely the moments when it is necessary to fight for the application of civil and political freedoms. History teaches us that the moments of hysteria, war or instability are times when no new laws should be promulgated when they restrict liberties and give even greater powers to the State and its repressive bodies. In the fight against terror, law should not forget its essence. Opportunism and haste must give way to a pertinent reaction.[43]

Since no particular state is named in the document, and no distinction is made between democratic and authoritarian states, it is apparent that states of all kinds are being criticized in this paragraph, primarily, perhaps, the US. According to Amnesty, states which have agreed to conclude bilateral agreements with the US (in the context of the ICC) have, 'caved in to US pressure' or 'succumbed to US pressure', and some states are 'known to be under threat' or 'under particular threat' from the US.[44]

Regime Change and Human Rights

There is, evidently, a tendency for international human rights NGOs to brush aside questions on security against terrorism, sometimes with a touch of arrogance. NGOs have stipulated that human rights values should be superior or they have maintained, but failed to show, that there is in reality no goal conflict between security and human rights – even that human rights fulfil a considerable instrumental function with respect to freedom from terrorism.

It seems, therefore, that they are out of step with popular opinion in large parts of the world. While the war against terrorism is heavily criticized by NGOs, there is a broad popular support for the US goal of combating terrorism, the most notable exception being conflict-ridden Muslim countries.[45]

Moreover, many people probably believe that there is a conflict between security and personal liberty – and would be willing to sacrifice some of the latter on the altar of the former when they think this is warranted. Such thinking was clearly manifested in the US both before and after the 11 September attacks.[46] A willingness to see some reduction in personal liberties does not appear strange at all, given the traditional understanding of the state as primordially a *Nachtwachter* state. Turkey provides an illustration of this which is as striking as it is surprising. Turkey has routinely been harshly criticized abroad for its poor compliance with human rights and an excessively powerful security apparatus. Yet the Turks have shown stronger trust in the military than in most other social institutions in the country.[47]

Do not opinions of this kind deserve to be taken seriously?

More importantly, there are intellectual figures who are certainly no less qualified to analyse than prominent NGOs – rather the contrary – and who come to different conclusions. For instance, professor of law Ruth Wedgwood has commented on the debates on the ICC and post–11 September reactions, and finds many misperceptions about military law and inadequate criticism of US policy. She makes the point that the law of armed conflict is in several respects less than well determined, and actions that the US finds both effective and lawful are being questioned without consideration of the difficulties involved in striking balances between law and effectiveness. She also argues against the notion that military commissions usurp civilian jurisdiction, since a military commission is a time-honoured legal recourse for prosecuting war crimes and the US certainly is at war. It offers the advantage of safeguarding sensitive information which cannot reasonably be made public since it is important for a country's own protection, and furthermore has the advantage of permitting new types of evidence that would not be admitted in a civilian court.[48]

Those who are influenced by such points of view and recognize the intellectual problems involved here may feel that there is a great need for an intellectual debate about the conditions under which security concerns could be allowed to dominate over human rights. However, one gets the impression that the NGO community would be a less than enthusiastic discussion partner.

The 11 September attacks quite naturally have let loose debate on a change of the constituent elements of international security orders. This debate has been carried out in terms of concepts such as imminent threat, the right to self-defence, preventive war and unilateral action. This study suggests the need for similar unprejudiced debate on human rights fundamentals, notably the relationship between human rights and security, including the rules for the handling of terrorist fighters and their supporters, the adequacy of existing judicial systems in new threat situations, and derogation from human rights obligations.

With regard to the last point, discussion is all the more important as the need for it existed a long time before 11 September. Fundamental human rights instruments, including the International Covenant of Civil and Political Rights (ICCPR) of 1966, give the parties the lawful possibility of pushing citizens' rights aside in dire situations. The ICCPR allows this 'in time of public emergency which threatens the life of the nation', although only 'to the extent strictly required by the exigencies of the situation' (Article 4:1). In such cases states have the duty to inform the UN about derogations made and the reasons for doing so (Article 4:3). However, this recourse has frequently been misused, particularly during an 'institutional epidemic' of states of emergency from the 1970s onwards, when authoritarian regimes tended to use it as legal device to legitimize their abuses.[49]

Although there have been positive changes, a strong case could be made for revising the institution of derogation. The control function under the ICCPR is weak and the embedded principle of notification is not widely respected.[50] The circumstances in which derogation is allowed are broadly formulated and open to interpretation.[51] A revision of this institution could specify terrorism situations as legitimate grounds for derogation; in the terms of the analysis above, a line needs to be drawn between legitimate and illegitimate trade-offs between security and human rights.[52]

If terrorism is what we are talking about, then it is essential to define the term, even if this is a sensitive matter. It is certainly symptomatic that the UN has not been able to produce a workable definition, not even in specific contexts where its own policy is under discussion.[53]

However, there are more sensitive matters. Although human rights regimes rest on agreements between states, they are intended to serve individuals. So can we then say that the degree of popular support for a derogation decision would be an irrelevant factor? Or should we rather maintain that derogation presupposes a high degree of popular support? The least complicated way of operationalizing popular support would be by way of listening to the voice of genuine popular representations. For all practical purposes this would mean that derogation is for democracies only, not for authoritarian regimes.

This brings up a sore point in the UN human rights system – the presence of so many authoritarian regimes. The virulence of the NGOs against western antiterrorism policies is to a great extent due to the alleged indirect effects of those policies. It has frequently been maintained that the US-led coalition against terrorism has inspired less democratic countries to more repression and makes it easier to get away with human rights violations now that the western moral influence has been eroded.

Interestingly, warnings have sometimes been put forward in rather unexpected terms. For instance, a spokesman for Global Exchange states:

> The status quo has created a vast distrust of the US. Until we embrace policies that truly reflect our values, we won't be able to disarm that distrust. If we want the world to work with us to isolate terrorism, then we will have to work with the rest of the world. For too long parochial self-interest has driven our national policies. Now more than ever we need foreign policies informed by enlightened self-interest. The requisite for global security is global justice.[54]

In moral philosophy the rights of individuals, such as human rights, would typically be seen as being at odds with *consequentialism*, as in the example given here.

The risk of the world campaign against terrorism being exploited by authoritarian regimes can certainly not be brushed aside. But is it enough, or is it even an adequate reaction, to condemn the antiterrorism campaign for this reason? Is it not more useful to start seriously discussing the role of authoritarian states within the global human rights regime since their violations in the wake of the 'war against terrorism' would tend to be of an incremental nature? In her analysis of the workings of the global human rights order, professor of law Anne Bayefsky concludes that the supervision system does not work, 'at bottom, because it presupposes democratic impulses on the part of states parties that in reality are not shared'.[55] This conclusion would certainly be widely supported by human rights expertise.

The strong presence of authoritarian states is a serious concern in many areas of UN activity. It certainly impinges on the debates on the relevance of the world organization in building security. The question involved has been formulated as follows by Count Otto Lambsdorff, honorary European chairman of the Trilateral Commission: 'Should the United Nations be the sole venue for decision because, however imperfect it may be, "we only have one UN"? Or should we prefer as "legitimizers" for intervention such groups of genuine democratic nations as NATO and the European Union, rather than the United Nations, "home to so many tyrannies"?'[56] The UN's legitimacy may run the risk of being questioned also with respect to human rights matters. Bayefsky's is certainly not a lone voice. 'The membership of such states in the treaty regime saps its integrity'.[57]

It seems that discussions about fundamentals of this kind could profit immensely from NGO participation. But NGOs need to take care not to be narrow-minded lest they undermine the confidence in them that has built up over decades and renew the risk of being tarred with the 'brush of amateurism'.[58]

References

'After September 11th', *Human Rights Monitor* 55, 2001, pp.1–2.

Amnesty International, 2002 (a). 'UN Commission on Human Rights: No Dichotomy between Human Rights and Security', *AI Index*: IOR 41/009/2002, 22 March 2002.

———, 2002 (b). 'International Criminal Court: US Efforts to Obtain Impunity for Genocide, Crimes against Humanity and War Crimes', *AI Index*: IOR 40/025/2002, August.

———, 2002 (c). 'United Kingdom: Rights Denied: The UK's Response to 11 September 2001', *AI Index*: EUR 45/016/2002, 5 Sep. 2002 http://web.amnesty.org/aidoc/aidoc_pdf.nsf/index/EUR450162002ENGLISH/$File/EUR4501602.pdf

———, Cairo Institute for Human Rights Studies, Federation International des Ligues des Droits de l'Homme, Human Rights Watch and International Commission of Jurists, 2002. Open Statement to the 2002 Commission on Human Rights, available on the homepage of Amnesty International, *AI Index*: IOR 41/007/2002, 22 March 2002.

Bayefsky, Anne F., 1994. 'Making the Human Rights Treaties Work', in Henkin, Louis and John Lawrence Hargrove (eds), *Human Rights: An Agenda for the Next Century*. Studies in Transnational Legal Policy 26. Washington DC: American Society of International Law.

British Home Office, 2002. 'Counterterrorist Action since September 2002' (Statement by the Home Secretary, David Blunkett), http://www.homeoffice.gov.uk/atoz/counter_terrorism.pdf

———, (undated). 'Anti-terrorism, Crime and Security Act 2001: Summary', http://www.homeoffice.gov.uk/oicd/antiterrorism/atcsa.htm

Center for Constitutional Rights, 2002. 'The State of Civil Liberties: One Year Later. Erosion of Civil Liberties in the Post 9/11 Era', http://www.ccr-ny.org/v2/reports/docs/Civil_Liberities.pdf

Crimes of War Project, 2001. 'Prosecuting Al Qaeda: September 11 and its Aftermath', 7 December, http://www.crimesofwar.org/expert/al-wedgwood.html

Derechos Human Rights, 2002 (a). 'The US Under Secretary for Political Affairs, Marc Grossman, Announces That the US Will Not Ratify, Nor Cooperate with, the International Criminal Court', 6 May http://www.derechos.org/nizkor/icc/grossman.html

———, 2002 (b). 'John D. Negroponte, US Permanent Representative to the United Nations, Welcomes SC Resolution Granting One-Year Exemption from ICC for Peacekeepers', 12 July http://www.derechos.org/nizkor/icc/negroponteicc.html

Dunér, Bertil and Hanna Geurtsen, 2002. 'The Death Penalty and War', *International Journal of Human Rights* 6(4), 1–28.

Eland, Ivan, 1998. 'Does US Intervention Overseas Breed Terrorism? The Historical Record', *Cato Foreign Policy Briefing* (Cato Institute, Washington DC) 50 (17 December).

Emergency Response and Research Institute (ERRI), *ERRI CounterTerrorism Archive*, available at http://www.emergency.com/cntrterr.htm

Fitzpatrick, Joan, 1994. 'Protection against Abuse of the Concept of "Emergency"', in Henkin, Louis and John Lawrence Hargrove (eds), *Human Rights: An Agenda for the Next Century*, Studies in Transnational Legal Policy 26. Washington DC: American Society of International Law.

Global Exchange Newsletter, 2002. 'The Threats to Liberty', spring, available at, http://www.globalexchange.org/september11/2002/nlSpr02_Liberty.html

Human Rights Watch, 2002. *World Report 2002*, Internet edition available at http://www.hrw.org/wr2k2

Khan, Irene (Secretary General of Amnesty International), 2002. 'Foreword: Security and Human Rights', *Amnesty International Report*, June, available at http: amnesty.org

International Federation for Human Rights (undated). 'No to American Exception: Cover of War against Terrorism, A Destruction Offensive against the ICC', http://www.iccno-www.iccnow.org/html/fidh200209english.doc

Lambsdorff, Otto (Count), 2002. 'Europe as a Valuable Peacemaker', *International Herald Tribune*, 28 November.

Lewis, Ted, 2001. 'The Virtue of Vulnerability', 8 October http://www.alternet.org/story.html?StoryID = 11672

Liberty (National Council for Civil Liberties), (undated). 'Terrorism', http://www.liberty-human-rights.org.uk/issues/terrorism.shtml

————, 2001. 'Briefing on Anti-terrorism, Crime and Security Bill 2001', November, http://www.liberty-human-rights.org.uk/resources/policy-papers/policy-papers-2001/pdf-documents/nov.pdf

Laqueur, Walter, 1996. 'Postmodern Terrorism', *Foreign Affairs* 75(5): 24–36.

NGO Coalition for the International Criminal Court, 2002. 'CICC Memo', 23 August, http://www.iccnow.org/html/ciccart98memo20020823.pdf

'Open Letter from NGOs to the United Nations General Assembly Concerning the Terrorism Debate', 1–2 October 2001, United Nations, available from the homepage of the Women's Caucus for Gender Justice, http://www.iccwomen.org/news/openltrga911.htm

Oraá, Jaime, 1982. *Human Rights in States of Emergency in International Law*. Oxford: Clarendon Press.

Pew Research Center for the People and the Press, Pew Global Attitudes Project, 2002. *What the World Thinks in 2002*. Washington DC: Pew Research Center.

Roth, Kenneth, 2002 (a). 'A Dangerous Security', *Worldlink (Magazine of the World Economic Forum)* January/February.

————, 2002 (b). 'El rechazo de EEUU al Tribunal Penal Internacional' [translation into English], *Papeles* (Madrid) 79.

Smelser, Neil J. and Faith Mitchell, (eds), 2002. *Terrorism: Perspectives from the Behavioral and Social Sciences*. Washington DC: National Academies Press for the National Research Council, Committee on Science and Technology for Countering Terrorism, Panel on Behavioral, Social and Institional Issues, pp.127–135.

Turkmen, Fusun, (updated). 'The Military Establishment in Turkey', Galatasaray University, http://www.bsos.umd.edu/ius/IUS/Turkmen.pdf

Vincent, R. John, 1989. 'Human Rights in Foreign Policy', in Dilys M. Hill, (ed), *Human Rights and Foreign Policy: Principles and Practice*. Houndmills and London: Macmillan.

United Nations, 1997. 'Report by the UN Special Rapporteur, Mr Leandro Despouy, on the Question of Human Rights and States of Emergency', UN document E/CN.4/Sub.2/1997/19, 23 June.

————, 1998. 'Final Act of the United Nations Diplomatic Conference of Plenipotentiaries on the Establishment of an International Criminal Court', UN document A/CONF.183/10, 17 July 1998, Annex, I:E (Resolutions Adopted by the United Nations Diplomatic Conference of Plenipotentiaries on the Establishment of an International Criminal Court).

————, 1999. Security Council Resolution 1269, S/RES/1269, 19 October 1999.

————, 2001. Security Council Resolution 1373, S/RES/1373, 28 September 2001.

————, 2002 (a). 'Written Statement Submitted by the International Federation for Human Rights (FIDH)', UN document E/CN.4/2002/NGO/170, 20 February.

————, 2002 (b). 'Report of the Policy Working Group on the United Nations and Terrorism', Annex to UN document A/57/273-S/2002/875, 6 August.

————, Office of the High Commissioner for Human Rights, 2002. 'NGO Joint Statement on the Violations of Human Rights in the "War Against Terror"', March 2002, 58th Session of the Commission on Human Rights, Agenda Item 11: Civil and Political Rights, available on the Internet site of Global Policy Forum, http://www.globalpolicy.org/wtc/liberties/2002/0418ngos.htm

United States Department of State, Bureau of Public Affairs, Office of the Historian, 2001. 'Significant Terrorist Incidents, 1961–2001: A Brief Chronology', http://www.state.gov/r/pa/ho/pubs/fs/5902.htm

United States White House, 2001 (a). 'President Issues Military Order', 13 November, http://www.whitehouse.gov/news/releases/2001/11/20011113–27.html

————, 2001 (b). 'Interview of Vice President Cheney with Diane Sawyer of ABC', 29 November, http://www.whitehouse.gov/vicepresident/news-speeches/speeches/vp20011129.html

————, 2002 (a). 'The Vice President Appears on ABC', 27 January http://www.whitehouse.gov/vicepresident/news-speeches/speeches/vp20020127.html

————, 2002 (b). Office of the Press Secretary, 2002. 'Fact Sheet, Status of Detainees at Guantanamo, United States Policy', 7 February http://www.whitehouse.gov/news/releases/2002/02/20020207–13.html

Wedgwood, Ruth, 2002. 'World Criminal Court a Slippery Slope For US', *Boston Globe*, 10 August.

Notes

1. John Vincent, 'Human Rights in Foriegn Policy', in Dilys M. Hill (ed), *Human Rights and Foriegn Policy: Principle's and Practice* (London: Macmillan 1989) p. 57ff.

2. Pursuant to the resolution, the Security Council furthermore set up a counterterrorism committee. 'UnCommission on Human Rights', *AI Index* IOR *41/009/2002*

3. Amnesty International, (22 March 2002).

4. 'After September 11th', *Human Righs Monitor*, No. 55 (2001) p.2.

5. Amnesty International, Cairo Institute for Human Rights Studies, Federation International des Ligues des Droits de l'Homme, Human Rights Watch and International Commission of Jurists, 'Open Statement to the 2002 Commission on Human Rights', *AI Index* IOR 41/007/2002 (22 March 2002).

6. 'After September 11th' (note 4).

7. The statement is available on the Civicus homepage, http://www.civicus.org

8. Open Letter from NGOs to the United Nations General Assembly Concerning the Terrorism Debate, http://www.iccwomen.org/news/openltrga911.htm

9. Report of the Policy Working Group on the United Nations and Terrorism: Annex UN doc. A/57/273-5/2002/875 = 6 Aug. 2002.

10. Kenneth Roth, 'A Dangerous Security', *Worldlink* (Jan./Feb. 2002).

11. Human Rights Watch, *World Report 2002*, http://www.hrw.org/wr2K2

12. Among easily accessible lists of terrorist acts is Emergency Response and Research Institute (ERRI), *ERRI Counter terrorism Archive*, http://www.emergency.com/cntrterr.htm; and US Department of State, Bureau of Public Affairs, *World Report 2002*, Office of the Historian *Significant Terrorist Incidents 1981–2001: A Brief Chronology*, http://www.state.gov/r/pa/ho/pubs/fs/5902.htm

13. Neil J. Smelser and Faith Mitchell (eds), *Terrorism Perspectives from the Behavioural and Social Sciences* (Washington DC: National Academics Press 2002) p.18.

14. Walter Laqueur, 'Postmodern Terrorism', *Foreign Affairs* 75, 5 (1996) pp.24–36.

15. Smelser and Mitchell (note 13) p.18.

16. Ivan Eland, 'Does US Intervention Overseas Breed Terrorism? The Historical Record: in *Cato Foreign Policy Briefing* (Washington DC: Cato Institute 1998).

17. 'After September 11th' (note 4).

18. Irene Khan, 'Foreword: Security and Human Rights', in *Amnesty International Report* (Amnesty International 2002), http://www.web.amnesty.org/weh/ar2002.nsf/FOREpart2/FOREpart2?OpenDocument

19. President Issues Military Order, http://www.whitehouse.gov/news/releases/2001/11/20011113. 27.html

20. Human Rights Watch, 2002.

21. Global Exchange describes itself as 'a human rights organization dedicated to promoting environmental, political, and social justice around the world. Since our founding in 1988, we have been striving to increase global awareness among the US public while building international partnerships around the world'. See http://www.globalexchange.org

22. States White House, (note 19).

23. United States White House, Interview of Vice President Cheney with Diane Sawyer of ABC, http://www.whitehouse.gov/vicepresident/news-speeches/speeches/vp20011129.html

24. Ibid.

25. Center for Constitutional Rights, The State of Civil Liberties: One Year Later. Erosion of Civil Liberties in the *Post 9/11 Era*, http://www.ccr-ny.org/v2/reports/docs/Civil_Liberties.pdf

26. White House Fact Sheet, Status of Detainees at Guantanamo, United States Policy, http://www.whitehouse.gov/news/releases/2002/02/20020207–13.html

27. White House The Vice President Appears on ABC, http://www.whitehouse.gov/vicepresident/news-speeches/speeches/vp20020127.html

28. Find Act of the United Nations Diplomatic Conference of Penipotentiaries on the Establishment of an International Criminal Court UN doc. A/CONF. 183/10-17 July 1998.

29. International Federation for Human Rights, No To American Exception: Cover of war against Terrorism A Destruction offensive against the ICC, http://www.iccnow.org/html/fidh200209english.doc

30. NGO Coalition for the International Criminal Court, *CICC memo*, http://www.iccnow.org/html/ciccart98memo200206823.pdf

31. Derechos Human Rights, The US Under Secretary for Political Affairs, Marc Grossman, Announces that the US Will Not Ratify, Nor Cooperate with the International Criminal Court, http://www.derechos.org/nizkor/icc/grossman.html

32. Derechos Human Rights, John D. Negroponce, US Permanent Representative to the United Nations, Welcomes SC Resolution Granting One-Year Exemption from ICC for Peacekeepers, http://www.derechos.org/nizkor/icc/negroponteicc.html

33. Amnesty International, 'United Kingdom: Rights Denied: The UK's Response to 11 September 2001', *AI Index* EUR 45/016/2002 (5 Sep. 2002) http://web.amnesty.ort/aidoc/aidoc-pdf.nsf/index/EUR450162002ENGLISH/$File$/EUR4501602.pdf

34. Liberty, (National Council for Civil Liberties), Terrorism, http://www.liberty.human-rights.org.uk/issues/terrorism.shtml

35. Liberty, (National Council for Civil Liberties), Briefing on Anti terrorism Crime and Security Bill 2001, http://liberty-human-rights.org.uk/resources/policy-papers/policy/papers-2001/pdf documents/nov.pdf

36. British Home Office, Counter terrorist Action Since September 2002, http://www.homeoffice.gov.uk/atoz/counter_terrorism.pdf

37. British Home Office, Anti-Terrorism Crime and Security Act 2001-Summary, http://www.homeoffice.gov.uk/oicd/antiterrorism/atcsa.htm

38. Written Statement Submitted by the International Federation for Human Rights (FIDH) UN doc. E/CN4/2002/NGO/170-20 Feb. 2002.

39. Amnesty International (note 33).

40. Human Rights Watch, (note 11).

41. Kenneth Roth, 'EI Rechazo de EEUU al Tribunal Penal Internacional, [English trans.], Papeles 79 (2002) p.128.

42. Amnesty International, 'International Criminal Court: US Efforts to Obtain Impunity for Genocide, Crimes against Humanity and War Crimes', AI Index IOR 40/025/2002.

43. United Nations, (note 38).

44. Amnesty International (note 42) p.33, 35.

45. Interestingly, there is also a strong consensus that the US foreign policy disregards the views of others. Pew *What the World thinks in 2002* (Washington DC: Pew Research Center 2002) p.53ff.

46. Bertil Dunér and Hanna Geurtsen, 'The Death Penalty and War', *International Journal of Human Rights* 6/4 (2002), pp.1–28.

47. Fusun Turkmen (Galatasaray University), The Military Establishment in Turkey, http://www.bsos.und.edu/ius/IUS/Turkmen.pdf

48. Ruth Wedgwood, 'World Criminal Court a Slippery Slope For US', *Boston Globe*, 10 Aug. 2002. Also see Crimes of War Project, Prosecuting Al Qaeda: September 11 and its Aftermath, http://www.crimes of war.org/expert/at wedgwood.html

49. Report by the UN Special Rapporteur, Mr. Leandro Despouy, on the Question of Human Rights and States of Emergency UN doc. E/CN.4/Sub.2/1997/19-23 June 1997.

50. Jame Oraa, *Human rights in States of Emergency in International Law.* (Oxford: Clarendon Press 1982) p.85ff.

51. Compilation of General Comments and General Recommendations Adopted by Human Rights Treaty Bodies: Addendum UN doc. HRI/GEN/1/Rev.5/Add.1-18 April 2002. Professor of law Joan Fitzpatrick holds that the principle of a threshold of severity is 'underdeveloped'. Joan Fitzpatrick, 'Protection against Abuse of the Concept of "Emergency"', in Louis Henkin and John L. Hargrove, (eds), *Human Rights: An Agenda for the Next Century*, (Washington DC: American Society of International Law 1994) Chapter 9, pp.203–227.

52. Needless to say, this does not mean that the question of minimum standards in derogation situations is any less urgent – rather the contrary.

53. Report of the Policy Working Group on the United Nations and Terrorism: Annex UN doc. A/57/273-S/2002/875-6 Aug. 2002.

54. Ted Lewis, The Virtue of Vulnerability, http://www.alternet.org/story.html?Story lD-11672

55. Anne F. Bayefsky, 'Making the Human Rights Treaties Work', in Louis Henkin and John L. Hargrove (eds), *Human Rights: An Agenda for the Next Century* (Washington DC: American Society of International Law 1994) p.263ff.

56. Otto Lambsdorff, 'Europe as a Valuable Peacemaker', *International Herald Tribune*, 28 Nov. 2002.

57. Bayevsky, (note 55) p.264.

58. Vincent (note 1).

7

The Eu's Response to 9/11: A Case Study of Institutional Roles and Policy Processes with Special Reference to Issues of Accountability and Human Rights

FRANK GREGORY

Politics and International Relations Division,
University of Southampton, Southampton, United Kingdom

The challenges of 9/11 required a wide ranging response across all three of the broad divisions of EU policymaking competence: the economic and monetary union, common foreign and security policy and internal security. These policy divisions make up the 'three pillars' of the EU's political architecture. This article reviews general issues of accountability and human rights protection in the EU's policymaking and implementation process, the evolution of the EU's response to terrorism, and the general response to 9/11. It then considers, in detail, the implications of the various response measures adopted under each 'pillar'. The article demonstrates the emphasis that the Member States have placed on security measures and the wider concerns that their content and speed of adoption left little scope for other views to be heard. The article lays stress upon the fact that the effectiveness of the response measures are crucially dependent on the variable implementation capacity of the Member States. The article concludes by noting how the 2004 EU Constitution [Article I-42] requires Member States to '...act jointly in a spirit of solidarity if a Member State is a victim of a terrorist attack....'

Introduction

In addressing issues related to terrorism, the European Union possesses a wide range of competencies under the union treaties, especially under the 1992 Treaty of European Union (TEU/Maastricht) and through the amendments under the 1997 Amsterdam Treaty. These treaty-based competencies, in areas related to counterterrorism, were based upon nearly two decades of intergovernmental and interagency cooperation through the internal security (TREVI) dimension of the European Community's political cooperation process.

However, it is important to understand at the outset that the EU possesses a very limited amount of its 'own resources' in terms of personnel, budget and physical assets. For example, the European Union Police Office (Europol) had[†] 242 staff in 2002 (pre-9/11 only 7 were in its counterterrorism section), has a current budget of €57.66m euros and no actual operational powers. Therefore nearly all EU response measures have to rely upon member states for their implementation, either through changes in laws and procedures, through the secondment of experts to the EU or by the enhancement of national capabilities. The national capability enhancements can take time to achieve as shown by the UK National Audit Office report of November 2002 which described the UK National Health Service's readiness to respond to NRBC incidents as 'unsatisfactory'.[1]

Even producing a single definitive EU terrorism threat assessment to help set response parameters has yet to be achieved. However, the various forms of EU response can be very influential in both shaping national responses and in producing a more harmonised approach throughout the EU. Moreover, this influence also extends to the accession states and even to other states with formal links to the EU such as the Ukraine.

This case study also provides an opportunity to reflect upon the 'realities' of the EU's 'deliverables' in terms of policy outcomes. In the foreign policy area the issue of a 'capabilities-expectations' 'gap' has long been recognised.[2] Identifying more than legislative or organisational implementation 'outcomes' from internal security initiatives is also difficult. For example, with respect to Europol, its annual report data on case or operational involvements has no qualitative or quantitative context to provide a basis for assessing significance. With respect to economic and social policy making Hix notes that the outputs of the EU system are 'regulatory rather than redistributive'[3] and if we expand 'regulatory' to include 'parameter' setting then this is a reasonable description of both the EU's regulatory and internal-security policy responses to 9/11. In general terms the EU's response to 9/11 clearly fits into the 'governance' mode, and this point is well discussed by Elaine Kamarck in 'Applying 21st-Century Government to the Challenge of Homeland Security'.[4] The case study also offers the chance to explore, in this policy area, the longstanding concerns about the 'democratic deficit' in EU policy-making with respect to accountability and human rights issues.

This paper commences with an examination of the general issues of accountability and protection of human rights within the EU's policy-making and implementation processes. It considers next the pre-9/11 Economic Community(EC)/EU involvement with counterterrorism and then proceeds to consider the Common Foriegn and Security Policy(CFSP) (external security) response in detail, the Justice and Home Affairs (JHA) (internal security) response with emphasis on Europol and finally the EC response. The conclusions address 'implementation/outcomes' issues, institutional roles and the use of cooperative mechanisms by member states' counterterrorist agencies outside the EU system (notwithstanding Council decisions to prioritise Europol's role) and human rights and democratic accountability issues.

Accountability and Human Rights Protection within the Eu Policy-Making and Implementation Processes

In order to understand these issues it is necessary to give a brief overview of the EU as a political system. The EU has been well described by Helen Wallace as a hybrid institution because it is a mixture of supranational processes, powers and laws and intergovernmental processes and powers.[5] For example, money-laundering is the subject of EC directives (i.e., EC supranational law) with direct effect in member states, whereas the legal basis for the establishment of Europol is by a treaty under international law binding upon its signatories, i.e., the EU member states. To confuse the issue further, key responses to 9/11 have used the 'third pillar' (JHA) instrument of a Framework Decision (binding on member states as to outcome) which is not an instrument of 'first pillar' European Economic Community law but a 'harder version' of 'third pillar' 'soft law', which is based on the assumption that member states will comply with treaty obligations.

Why do we talk about 'pillars'? Because that is how the EU describes its policy-making areas and their associated processes from the Treaty of European Union (Maastricht) onwards. The pillars start with the 'first', or European Economic Community, covering all aspects of economic policy, societal protection and monetary union. This pillar is governed by EC law, the European Commission is the formal initiator of policy proposals, and policy-making powers are the shared responsibility of the Council of Ministers and the directly elected European Parliament. However, the degree of parliamentary power is a variable factor and most significant in those policy areas under the co-decision procedures. Also in some key policy areas member states retain national vetoes under the unanimity provisions, although an increasing number of policy areas are coming under qualified majority voting (QMV) procedures. Within the 'first pillar' the Court of Justice exercises powers akin to those of the US Supreme Court over the actions of both the EU and member states in respect of community law.

The 'second pillar', or Common Foreign and Security Policy 'pillar', deals with matters in the traditional area of foreign policy including defence, but only in respect of the 'Petersberg' roles for the EU's embryonic Rapid Reaction Force. In these areas the European Commission and the European Parliament play lesser roles and greater power resides with the member states in the council and the bureaucracy of the Council Secretariat. To complicate matters further, 'external relations' necessary to the functioning of the Economic Community come under the 'first pillar'. This is why, as will be shown later, the Commission becomes involved when US Customs seek to exercise frontier control provisions on the territories of member states notwithstanding the fact that member states may have agreed on bilateral measures with the US. Policy-making for CFSP is dominated by the consensus mode and nothing can stop individual member states from taking unilateral, bilateral or even multilateral decisions on foreign policy that do not involve or even command the tacit support of noninvolved member states. The UK position on the Iraq War is, so far, the most prominent example of national autonomy in this common policy area.

The 'third pillar' deals with what are generally regarded as 'internal security' matters and is known from its Maastricht era as the 'Justice and Home Affairs' or JHA 'pillar'. Although formally under the Amsterdam Treaty it was re-titled 'Police and Judicial Cooperation in Criminal Matters'. Under this 'pillar' policies are developed under a mixture of regional international law, for example the EU Mutual

Legal Assistance Convention, Framework Decisions (such as that on terrorism, which are binding as to outcome) and 'soft' law instruments such as Action Plans. This 'pillar' is heavily dominated by intergovernmental processes, and the Court of Justice has no involvement and the Parliament is limited to a consultation and advisory role.

With regard to issues of democratic accountability, therefore, parliamentary and judicial accountability is much greater in the first pillar than in pillars two and three because of the powers assigned to these institutions by the treaties. However, it must also be remembered that the parliaments of the member states can, and do to varying degrees, seek to hold their governments to account for policy proposals and policy decisions made at the EU level. But, of course, in areas of policy such as foreign policy and internal security policy this has always been a more difficult exercise than in less sensitive areas. One basic problem that has arisen, in respect of accountability for post-9/11 decisions, has been the question of access to Council of Ministers documents. At one point it looked as if the ludicrous situation was going to arise where the US Congress would be able to debate an EU-US 9/11-response measure but not some EU parliaments! Rather gloomily, two political scientists, Dobson and Weale, consider that developments in the democratic legitimacy of EU governance must tackle the 'overriding task' which is to secure 'greater clarification of the democratic values its citizens want to secure, and the balances they are willing to strike between those values'.[6]

Systems of accountability have been considered at some length because they provide important means of protecting human rights in respect of official policies and policy instruments. At the very basic level all EU members are signatories to the Council of Europe's European Convention on Human Rights (ECHR). However, individual EU member states can exercise their rights under that convention to implement derogations. The TEU refers to human rights in two articles, Article 6(1) of the TEU refers to the EU respecting and upholding the principles of freedom, democracy, human rights, basic freedoms and the rule of law. Article 6(2) of the TEU refers to fundamental rights, the ECHR and the protections afforded by the constitutions of member states. Fifty fundamental rights have been separately set out in the EU Charter of 2000, however, this is only a declaratory document and not a legal instrument because the member states did not agree to incorporate it into the Nice Treaty. However, the Charter of Fundamental Rights of the EU has been incorporated in Part II of the 2004 EU constitution. An assumption also seems to be that, in general, because all the EU member states are democracies operating under the rule of law, human rights and civil liberties are somehow 'naturally' protected. Of course, policies can and sometimes do infringe upon civil liberties or human rights but these can be challenged through the courts, as the UK home secretary knows only too well. In some instances the EU Court of Justice may well become involved, as in case C-285/98, Judgement, 1 November 2000, where the court agreed that Article 12a of the German Constitution constituted 'direct discrimination'.[7]

A detailed discussion of 'Practices in Relation to Human Rights' by Curtin and Dekker is to be found in Craig and De Burca's *The Evolution of EU Law*, and the following paragraphs draw upon this work. Curtin and Dekker argue that 'it does not take much reflection to appreciate the potential effect of Union activity in the field of justice and home affairs on the . . . rights and interests of individuals'. For Curtin and Dekker, a key point is the degree of jurisdiction available to the Court of Justice. Moreover, they draw attention to the gap between references to human rights in preambles and texts, as in the case of the Europol Convention (OJ C316/1, 1995) and the Joint Action on organised crime (OJ L 344/7, 1997) and the fact that 'jurisdictional avenues for potentially affected individuals.' are not always created.[8] Curtin has particularly argued that entities such as Europol and the executive committees established under the terms of, for example, the Schengen Implementing Convention and the External Borders Convention 'exist formally in a type of constitutional and institutional limbo outside the remit of any effective judicial or parliamentary control'. Referring to the ECHR, Curtin and Dekker note, with reference to Europol, 'As the ECHR is currently worded and interpreted it does not seem likely that complaints against a collectivity of states concerning decisions of organizations established by these states would be declared admissible'.[9]

As for the role of the Court of Justice, the TEU only provides for optional jurisdiction in respect of the Europol Convention for those member states who wish to use such provisions. However, they do suggest that the Court of Justice might be tempted to take on an interventionary role regarding JHA matters and the protection of human rights, as the protection of fundamental human rights is now a general principle of EU law.

In respect of the EU's response to 9/11 the above considerations have to be related to the EU's aims within the Amsterdam Treaty of ensuring that the EU was 'an area of freedom, security and justice'. In this aim we can identify the potential for the classic freedom/security dilemma in response to 9/11. Within the paper, this dilemma will be explored in respect of a number of responses across the three pillars. In general, it sometimes appears as if EU member states' governments have tended to place more emphasis on 'security' factors than 'freedom' factors. Therefore most of the human rights and civil liberties challenges have come from a few national parliaments, the European Parliament and interest groups working in those areas such as Statewatch, Human Rights Watch, migrants' rights activists, European Digital Rights (EDRI, on data protection issues) and the CFR-CDF (the EU network of independent experts in fundamental rights). This last body just produced its first annual report in May 2003, which includes a thematic report on freedom and security and responses to terrorist threats and which expresses a number of major concerns around issues such as proportionality and redress in cases of abuse of power. The aims of the US to be treated as if it was an EU member state in respect of some measures causes particular concerns about issues of reciprocity and very different legal regimes, for example, in respect of data protection and controls on the powers of US law enforcement agencies.

Ec/eu Counterterrorism Background

During the TREVI Period (1975–1992, where member states met in political cooperation outside the EC Rome Treaty framework), the then EC states were able to utilise, in a rather opaque intergovernmental mode, the counterterrorist support services available from three sources. Firstly, from the output from the information exchange remit of TREVI Working Group I, which focused on terrorism. TREVI I was able to arrange for a secure communications network (Bureau d'Liaison, BdL) to link participating security and intelligence agencies of the EC states. TREVI I also provided terrorism threat analysis to the EC's General Affairs Council. Secondly, the EC states could draw upon the network of European security and intelligence agencies participating in the Club of Berne. Thirdly, the EC states gave support to the practitioner initiative which produced the wider-membership Police Working Group on Terrorism (PWGT has a current membership of the EU states, Poland, Hungary, the Czech Republic, Slovakia, Slovenia, Norway and Switzerland PWGT is a Non-EU body). PWGT also has a secure communications system linking bodies like the French UCLAT (Unite de Coordination de la Lutte Anti-Terroriste) and the European Liaison Section of the UK's Metropolitan Police Special Branch. These counterterrorism interagency linkages continued to be active alongside the new TEU initiatives and the establishment of Europol.

The EU's current response to terrorism takes place within the parameters set by its international obligations in the twelve counterterrorism conventions, the 1996 G8 Action Programme (Lyon) and the work of the Financial Action Task Force. The EU's response is also within the parameters of the 1995 La Gomera Declaration of EU JHA ministers that referred to terrorism as a threat to democracy, the free exercise of human rights and economic and social development. Most recently, and importantly, there are the obligations laid upon all states by the UN Security Council Resolution 1373 of 28 December 2001.

The response to 9/11 drew upon the obligations, policy-making systems and policy instruments established by the TEU. The TEU provided for three policy areas or 'pillars', as discussed in detail earlier. The European Economic Community is the supranational 'first pillar' and there are the two intergovernmental pillars, which are the Common Foreign and Security Policy (CFSP) 'second pillar' and the Justice and Home Affairs (JHA) 'third pillar'. In the 'first pillar', obligations may be laid upon member states under community law, which has supremacy over the laws of member states. Under the 'second and third pillars', such obligations arise out of a mixture of treaty law provisions and their associated policy instruments such as Joint Actions and Framework Decisions. The latter are binding upon member states as to the outcome but allow flexibility in the way that outcome is to be achieved.

Under the TEU, as amended by the Amsterdam Treaty, terrorism is defined as both a matter of 'common interest' (Article 29) and as a threat to the achievement of making the EU an 'area of freedom, security and justice' (Article 2). Moreover, the European Union Police Office (Europol) had its counterterrorism coordinating role activated in 1999. Between Maastricht in 1992 and September 2001 the EU and member states had available a number of what might be termed post-TEU 'building block' counterterrorism measures. There was the Police Working Group on Terrorism (PWGT non-EU) which has a now expanded network of Counter-Terrorist Liaison Officers (CTLOs) reporting back to their sending states, the 'second pillar' Counter-Terrorism Working Party (COTER) and the JHA Terrorism Working Group. Moreover, in October 1996 a JHA Joint Action had required the creation and maintenance of a 'Directory of Specialised Counter-terrorist Competencies, Skills and Expertise in the Member States'.[10]

When the particularly sensitive area of counterterrorism was included in Europol's mandate in 1999, it was put in under very controlled conditions. A five-task initial priorities programme was agreed on in relation to tackling terrorism, with further tasks to follow. However, progression to fresh tasks required JHA Council approval and was only to be undertaken when the previous tasks were implemented. The potential contribution of Europol became more visible, following the activation of its Terrorism Mandate and was set out in Europol's first 'counterterrorism report' to the JHA Ministerial Council.[11] This report referred to the establishment of the Europol Counter-terrorism Unit (now called SC5 [Serious Crime]) within a secure physical area in the Europol Organised (Serious) Crime Department. The unit's initial five tasks were:

- Encouraging the exchange of information among member states counterterrorism authorities.
- Creating an initial series of Analytical Work Files (AWFs) on counterterrorism.
- Creating a store of counterterrorism and related legislation.
- Assuming responsibility for the administration of the EU Directory of Counter-terrorism Competencies.
- Creating a glossary of terrorist groups.

These were followed by the identification of three more priority tasks:

- Creating a directory about the division of counterterrorist responsibilities at the national level.
- Producing a digest of relevant open source information.
- Producing situation/trend reports.

All of the above are facilitative and supportive in nature and not really closely operationally related or intrusive, in terms of national laws and systems.

The EU 'Terrorism Trends Report' covering September 2000 to September 2001 provided a useful general contextual overview of how the EU sees its vulnerability in respect to terrorism. The report identifies three forms to terrorism impacting on the EU:[12]

- 'Traditional' terrorism (including Islamic)
- Ecoterrorism
- Anarchist terrorism

It notes that although there has been a small decrease in the number of terrorist incidents, there has been a rise in their importance and impact. The EU not only sees itself as a target area but also recognises that the EU area is used by terrorist groups for preparatory and logistics purposes. The report concludes that whilst Islamic extremist terrorism could be regarded as ' the main threat' many European terrorist groups still remain significantly active. The 2002 report reports arrests of clusters or cells with Al-Qaeda or GSPC (Salafist Group for Collaboration and Combat–Algerian terrorist group) links in Italy, Germany, the Netherlands, Belgium and the UK relating to activities ranging from financing and docment, forgery to a poss-ible chemical attack on the Rome water supply. The report also refers to the 'new tendency' of the diverse groups/cells towards 'co–laborating and providing mutual assistance'.[13]

The Response to 9/11

The response to 9/11 necessarily drew on the competencies and resources of all three EU 'pillars' and, in some policy areas, reflected the inherent interdependency between the 'pillars'. Indeed Den Boer and Monar argue that '11 September must be regarded as the first truly 'cross-pillar' test of the Union's role as a security actor'.[14] For example, response linkages with the US are a common feature in all three 'pillars'. The overall picture of the EU's response was set out in the 'Table of Measures', derived from the EU Council presidency 'road map' note of December 2001.[15] From this document the following general points can be drawn out. Under the European Community 'first pillar', the EU has the competence necessary to contribute to addressing social and economic issues, in terms of development aid, in states where terrorist groups may have bases. It also has the competence to address issues relating to terrorist finances and money-laundering. Other powers in this 'pillar' can be used in relation to people-movement controls, safety and security relating to transportation systems and general measures in the field of civil protection.

The CFSP 'second pillar' has not been able to play such an active role in the EU response because of the problems of achieving consensus on European security and defence policy operational matters and the very proactive national policies of a few key member states, especially the UK, over the operations in Afghanistan. However, under this 'pillar', the EU has addressed issues relating to cooperation between external intelligence agencies and, in a more longer-term, area matters relating to nonproliferation, arms control and common approaches in military antiterrorism roles via a military staff one-star post.[16] A common response item across all three 'pillars' has been the interaction with the US through the need to address the forty counterterrorism response priorities set out in President Bush's letter of 16 October 2001 to European Commission President Romano Prodi.

In addition, under this pillar the EU has extended its use of 'conditionality' in relations with third states. Recently, the EU had begun to insert into agreements with countries in areas such as the Middle East and Africa conditions relating to the granting of trading preferences or development aid from the EU. These initially covered requirements to promote democracy and the rule of law, but recently conditions were inserted concerning obligations to try to control illegal immigration and human trafficking post-9/11.

The EU's response to the threat from terrorism in its relations with states other than the EU accession states is a mixture of the declaratory level of policy, the use of the CFSP or 'first' pillar external relations instruments and the encouragement of bilateral or multilateral initiatives by member states. This response sees economic or economic-related responses being drawn up by the European Commission under its 'first' pillar powers while the more political matters, such as human rights and counterterrorism, come under the 'second' pillar. As a general foundation the EU Council agreed to a declaration in June 2002 which proposed, in paragraph 4, that antiterrorism clauses should be included in EU agreements with third countries. This was amplified in paragraph 7, which listed as an EU priority 'deepening political dialogue with third countries to promote the fight against terrorism, including by the promotion of human rights and democracy as well as non-proliferation and arms control, and providing them with appropriate international assistance'.[17]

Typical of the declaratory responses are the statements from the second EU-Latin America and Caribbean Summit (EU-LAC) of 17 May 2002 and the fourth Asia-Europe Meeting (ASEM) of 23–24 September 2002. The EU-LAC statement condemns all forms of terrorism and adds in paragraph 17, 'We reaffirm our full conviction that 'the fight against terrorism must respect human rights and fundamental freedoms and the rule of law'.[18] The ASEM statement noted the progress in EU-ASEAN (Association of South East Asian Nations) cooperation against terrorism and reaffirmed, in paragraph 2, that 'the fight against terrorism must be based upon the principles of the UN Charter and basic norms of international law'.[19]

A good example of the carrot-and-stick approach to counterterrorism relations with third countries is that of the EU with Iran. A potential form of influence for the

EU is the fact that the EU is Iran's biggest trading partner (in 2001 EU-Iran trade was in excess of €13 bn euros). In June 2002 the EU Foreign Ministers Council agreed the directives for a Trade and Cooperation Agreement (TAC) with Iran, to be negotiated by the European Commission, and for instruments on political dialogue and antiterrorism to be negotiated in parallel by the EU presidency. These parallel negotiations were duly launched in December 2002. Currently the EU is backing international pressure on Iran with respect to its nuclear programme and threatening to withhold trade-deal concessions.[20]

Some EU–third country relations in respect of counterterrorism very clearly pose dilemmas in the form of conflicting objectives in regard to respect of human rights and the rule of law. In the aftermath of the Bali bombing the European Commission announced that, if the Indonesian government agreed, the EU would provide help by financing a team of experts, through the Rapid Reaction Mechanism (RAM), to address the problems of money-laundering and terrorist financing.[21] However, whilst the EU may well be correct in supporting the Indonesian efforts to implement measures in conformity with Security Council Resolution 1373, the EU should take account of the Indonesian government's very poor record in human rights and respect for the rule of law in the management of its internal affairs.

Responses under the 'Third Pillar'—With Special Reference to Europol

Not surprisingly, the majority of measures come under the auspices of the internal security JHA 'third pillar'. These include the use of Framework Decisions on Combating Terrorism [in this Framework Decision the terrorism definition and range of offenses were seen by the civil liberties groups as perhaps threatening legitimate public protest activity], asset freezing, fast-track extradition (the European Arrest Warrant), the prevention of crime via electronic means and Joint Investigation Teams.[22]

Two particular concerns have been raised concerning the EU Framework Decision on Combating Terrorism of 13 June 2002. The first is that the definition used is too imprecise. The EU civil rights network CFR-CDF has argued that since qualifying an offence as 'terrorist' justifies the use of special methods of inquiry that entail major interference in private life, the distinction between 'terrorist' offences and other offences must be sufficiently precise to meet the condition of lawfulness to which the legitimacy of this interference is subject. This is not the case when the distinction between the two offences is described exclusively by the gravity of their consequences and the objective of the perpetrator.[23]

Secondly, long-standing concerns have been raised relating to linkages that some member states are making between counterterrorism, as in this Framework Decision, and the potential applicability of the decision to offences committed in major public disorders such as the Genoa summit protests. The Spanish presidency of the EU has suggested that Article 1 of the Framework Decision on Combating Terrorism was meant to include 'violence and criminal damage orchestrated by radical extremist groups, clearly terrorising society'.[24] It has suggested that on this reading of the Framework Decision a further Framework Decision could be agreed on that standardised information exchanges on incidents caused by radical groups with terrorist links. Countries such as the Netherlands opposed this initiative, so the Spanish presidency has downgraded the initiative to a Draft Council Recommendation referring to standardised information exchanges where there 'might be a risk that terrorist organisations will use larger international events for carrying out terrorist offences as defined in Article 1 of the Framework Decision on combating terrorism'.[25]

With reference to problems of democratic accountability, the fourth revised draft on 11 April 2003 was the first one to reach the UK House of Commons European Scrutiny Committee. The accompanying Home Office memo from junior minister, Bob Ainsworth suggested that there were no major policy implications for the government. The committee was less happy with the proposal and said that they shared the concerns of the Netherlands government and were concerned about what would prevent the form being used for 'persons who exercise their constitutional rights set out in Article 6 TEU'.[26] The Commons European Scrutiny Committee and the House of Lords EU Select Committee have both maintained scrutiny reserves on these measures. That is to say they have not given their approval and ministers are supposed to endeavour not to agree to such measures before receiving Parliamentary approval, though of course they do in some cases.

The member states are supposed to implement the Framework Decision on the European Arrest Warrant by January 2004. This measure contains three controversial but important and innovative developments in the area of extradition. Firstly, the principle of double criminal liability is abolished for a list of thirty-two offences including terrorism – the offence will only have to exist in the requesting state. Secondly, 'political offence' will no longer be cited as a reason to refuse extradition. Thirdly, nationals cannot be exempted from extradition requests. A cluster of responses are related to the expansion of the role of Europol. Before examining some of these measures in detail, it is important to note that a number were in the policy proposal pipeline before 9/11, for example the European Arrest Warrant and Joint Investigation Teams (JITs), but as Boer and Monar noted, after 9/11 they 'sailed through on a political window of opportunity'[27] and civil liberties groups have raised concerns about inroads into human rights provisions and democratic accountability.

Is all this terrorist-related pre- and post-9/11 activity just a programme of intent or has it actually achieved concrete results? This analysis will focus on Europol, the Police Chiefs Operational Task Force (PCOTF), cooperation with the US, civil protection and aviation security. Europol's engagement with Islamic terrorist activity was evident from 2000 when it opened an Analytical Work File (AWF) on extremist Islamic terrorism. However, the pre-9/11 Europol only had seven counter-terrorist specialists. By 15 October 2001, a team of around thirty-five nationally seconded counterterrorist specialists, the Counter Terrorist Task Force [CTTF], (for details see the 'Europol Annual Report 2001')[28], were working in Europol as a direct consequence of the enhanced post-9/11 counterterrorism remit given to Europol by the JHA Council. They had a three-part remit:

- Collection of all relevant information and intelligence on the current threat.
- Providing operational and strategic analyses.
- Drafting threat assessments.

These secondments are not permanent but on a six-month renewable basis and are ended in December 2002. Among its activities the CTTF produced an EU 'Threat Assessment Document on Islamic Extremist Terrorism' and procured 'an Arabic-to-English translation system for the evaluation of the large amount of intelligence in Arabic transmitted by Member States to Europol'.[29]

Europol has asked for budgetary allocations sufficient to support an enhancement of its permanent SC5 staff numbers to twenty-five. In this area the Commission has tried to bring Europol into a reporting relationship to the Commission by recommending using funds proposed in the EU budget by the European Parliament for Europol anti-terrorism work.[30] However, the UK government particularly feels that this is unacceptable, as it is not in line with the intergovernmental approach to Europol funding. The House of Commons-European Scrutiny Committee (ESC) found the Commission proposal 'astonishing' and the Home Office under secretary of state Ainsworth shared the ESC's surprise and stressed that member states determined Europol's level of funding via the Europol Management Board.[31]

Overall guidance and support to Europol (SC5) and member states 9/11 responses in JHA law enforcement areas is supposed to flow through the JHA 'pillar' Terrorism Working Group (interior ministry, police etc.) and the meetings of EU security and intelligence service heads (Club of Berne) in the new post-9/11 Counter-Terrorism Group. Europol also has brought into being a 'high level expert group' (with representatives from member states key bodies such as the UK Metropolitan Police Special Branch) which is chaired by a Europol deputy director. However, the achievements of all these groups and collective activity is not yet readily identifiable from information in the public domain. An audit of Europol's post-9/11 counterterrorism achievements has concluded that it has fulfilled its remit within the limitations produced by the varying levels of actual input from the member states. The audit has concluded that, after the withdrawal of the temporary nationally seconded Counterterrorism personnel, there should be some expansion in the size of SC5.

The high level expert group has suggested that the remaining CTTF tasks of strategic analysis/threat assessment and operational analysis (AWF 99/008) be transferred to Europol SC5. The group also took account of the Danish presidency's proposal for a project on terrorist profiling within a range of possible additional tasks and proposals to 'freeze' certain, now lower-priority, ongoing tasks. High priority is to be assigned to monthly assessments of the Islamic terrorism threat and terrorist finances, with medium priority assigned to a project on the use of false/forged ID papers. SC5's pre-9/11 work on a bomb database is also to be continued.[32] These kinds of tasks seem to be commensurate with Europol's capabilities and the probable level of staff enhancement of SC5.

Europol has also been enhancing its US links by, for example, secondments to the FBI and, more controversially, sending information files to the US before the establishment of any formal data exchange agreement. However, there are still significant differences in mutual legal assistance requirements and practices between the EU and the US with respect to issues such as data protection regimes and the presence of the death penalty in the US.[33] These sorts of issues have meant that the FBI agent seconded to Europol only stayed for six months and law enforcement personnel from the EU working in the US have faced restrictions on their access to information in US law enforcement agency files. However, positive results *may* follow the establishment, in August 2002, of a Europol liaison office (the first one) in Washington DC.

Moreover, the expansion of Europol's role has to be set alongside questions of preference in terms of channels of information and intelligence sharing and the enhancement of other groups' roles. Many member states continue to prefer to use established bilateral or multilateral interagency channels for the sharing of sensitive information. Also there seems to be some potential for overlap between Europol and the PCOTF. The latter has been asked to compile an inventory of national measures and alert plans and to propose ways of strengthening external border controls. However, to date PCOTF has only held subgroup meetings and has yet to produce any major input into the EU response. In particularly sensitive areas of information and intelligence exchange both Europol and PCOTF may be overshadowed by what are called the 'senior group' meetings of top officials from EU internal security and external intelligence agencies.[34] A further reinforcement of intergovernmental channels of communication and action is provided by the meetings, since May 2003, of the self-styled 'G5' group of EU interior ministers from France, Italy, Spain, Germany and the UK. They are seeking to develop EU-wide response measures in areas such as counterterrorism by initiating a series of bilateral agreements.

The issue of Europol's Draft Agreement on exchange of personal data and related information with the US continues to be a contested issue with civil liberties and parliamentary bodies. At the end of 2002 the Commons ESC was still insisting on maintaining its scrutiny reserve on these proposals. However, Home Office parliamentary under secretary Lord Filkin said 'This is an important agreement both in terms of its substance and symbolism of the joint commitment between the EU and USA to work together to fight terrorism. . . . It has been in negotiation for some time and it is urgent to implement it . . . I have therefore reluctantly decided that I have to over-ride parliamentary scrutiny'.[35] The EU Council approved the agreement at the end of the Danish presidency.

However, controversy still surrounded the proposals for EU-US agreements on mutual legal assistance and extradition and the EU Council, despite saying in April 2002 that 'the interests of protecting the Council's objectives outweighs the interest in democratic control'[36] was forced by parliamentary and civil society interest group pressure to release the drafts in April 2003. Concerns were expressed in the following areas: that the crime scope was wider than terrorism, that too broad a scope was allowed to JITs and on suspect surveillance. Tony Bunyan of Statewatch commented in April 2003 that 'the lack of scrutiny, accountability and data protection in the draft agreements means they have no place in a democratic society'.[36]

The European Parliament's Committee on Citizens' Freedoms and Rights, Justice and Home Affairs reported on 12th May 2003 to the council regarding the above proposed EU-US agreements. The Committee report, whilst broadly endorsing the expected benefits as a 'significant political step forward. . .with respect to the efficacy of the fight against international crime'[37] noted important concerns over human rights protections and data protection. Significantly, the report also highlighted key issues relating to accountability in the EU. Firstly, the report viewed the proposals as constituting a 'basic choice'.[38] In CFSP, the Council is required to consult the European Parliament (EP) under the provisions of Articles 21, 34(2)(c) and 39(1) (TEU), and not just merely inform the EP as happened in this case. Secondly, the report argued that the initial attempts to exclude the EP and national parliaments from the process of concluding these agreements was 'a flagrant breach of the democratic principle on which the Union claims to be founded' (see Article 6(1) TEU).[39]

In addition to these important issues and the opportunity for only rather belated parliamentary scrutiny, of further concern is the fact that some member states seem ready to 'fast-track' bilateral agreements with the US in these areas. On 31 march 2003 home secretary David Blunkett and US attorney general John Ashcroft signed a new bilateral extradition treaty, based upon the draft EU-US agreement, which the home secretary said removed 'layer on layer of judicial blockage'.[40] Yet, as Susan

Alegre of Justice said, 'It is hard to see how such a reduction in safeguards is justifiable in the current climate. Recent high profile cases such as that of Lofti Raissi, the Algerian pilot, released after several months in prison on a extradition request from the USA when no evidence was forthcoming raise serious concerns about the government's decision to remove the requirement for prima facie evidence in extradition cases to the US'.[41]

9/11 Responses under 'Pillar One'

Whilst the EU has the competence to be involved in 9/11 response management areas such as civil protection and security, its involvement is necessarily limited. The involvement is limited firstly by the principles of 'subsidiarity' and 'proportionality', which restricts the EU, in terms of new measures, to those which are best achieved, in whole or in part, by a collective response. Secondly, the EU is limited by budgetary constraints on the funding that may be available for new initiatives. A third limitation on the EU's response capability is that it has to rely on experts from member states to supplement its own relatively small body of officials and experts (the term 'commitology' is applied to this form of working).

The civil protection measures are well set out in a communication from the Commission to the Council of June 2002.[42] These measures are all derived from an EU Council request for work to be done 'to improve co-operation between the Member States in preparedness, detection and intervention to reduce the consequences of [NRBC] threats to society'. In response, the Commission's aim is to identify and link the various national services for civil protection, health protection and research expertise to form 'a common platform to co-ordinate the EU's optimum response'. Under this platform, there are five priority initiatives:

● Providing teams of experts from member states for coordinating intervention.
● Carrying out a stocktaking exercise to identify expertise and resources, for example, inventories of serums and vaccines.
● Providing training and exercise for intervention teams.
● Providing a dedicated EU-wide emergency communication and information system.
● The establishment of the Monitoring Information Centre. This has more than doubled its staff since April 2002, with support from seconded experts from member states. The center's function is to facilitate the provision of any extra personnel and resources needed by a participating state. (The centre's membership covers the EU states, Norway and six accession states.)

In a number of the above areas, the EU has been able to build upon existing networks, such as the European Community Urgent Radiological Information Exchange (ECURIE) and upon its own existing initiatives, such as the network for epidemiological surveillance and control of communicable diseases in the EU. The latter was established in 1998, following an EU Council and Parliament Initiative.[43] The network has now been expanded to include pathogenic agents that might be used in bioterrorist attacks. As with measures for civil aviation security, the EU actions in the health protection area are coordinated with the other fora, to which the EU belongs. These include the Global Health Security Action Group set up after the November 2001 G7 meeting and the WHO's work on bioterrorism. The first EU civil protection exercise was held in the Var region of France in October 2002. Euratox 2002 was an exercise simulating radiological and chemical fallout as a result of a terrorist attack. The aim was to test aid control channels in member states and the flows of aid to the state in which the attack has taken place.

Post-9/11, civil aviation security has been addressed by an ad hoc group set up by the EU Transport Minister's Council on 14 September 2001.[44] This group comprises officials from member states, aviation security and JHA departments, plus representatives from the European Civil Aviation Conference (ECAC), the International Civil Aviation Organisation (ICAO), Eurocontrol and the Joint Aviation Authorities (JAA). This group is assisted by a 'stakeholders group' drawn from airlines, airports, aircrew, ground staff, business aviation and aircraft manufacturers. The ad hoc group's remit, set by the Transport Council, is to:

- Examine EU cooperation and coordination needs to guarantee consistency of security measures.
- Consider legislative initiatives under EC law, which might guarantee efficient and uniform implementation.
- Ensure that EU measures are also consistent with US requirements.

As mentioned in other areas, the EU response is also based upon existing external obligations. Aviation security is based upon Annex 17 of the Chicago Convention and Decision 30 of ECAC. Three weak security areas within the EU were identified prior to 9/11. These are:

- The uneven implementation achievements of member states.
- Security standards not being applied to domestic flights.
- Deficiencies in staff training (especially poor quality security staff).

In its communication on the work of the ad hoc group, the Commission noted that any EU response must work alongside international cooperation, otherwise 'any measures adopted at European level will have a limited effect'.[45]

With reference to what the communication calls 'new measures able to prevent kamikaze terrorists (getting) onboard aircraft',[46] ECAC has proposed the following measures to enhance airport security:

- New working measures and improved cooperation between airports, intelligence services, police and airport security staff. For the latter, enhancement of status and training has been noted as a priority.
- Enhancement of passenger control methods, for example, the use of profiling techniques.
- Restrictions on 'hand' luggage.
- More controls and vetting of aircrew trainees.

In terms of actual aircraft security, ECAC and JAA are examining:

- Cockpit isolation.
- Transponder inviolability.
- The carrying of 'sky marshals'.

All of these measures are being contemplated in the context of the problem of how 'to prevent an act, where the terrorist has no negotiation aim'.[47]

In this area of transportation security the EU and member states have also found themselves, perhaps surprisingly, to be raising by their responses to 9/11, and in particular to US demands, questions concerning democratic accountability and human rights. These issues have been raised in respect of US Customs checks on container freight in EU ports and the advance provision of passenger manifest lists. In the autumn of 2002 the US Customs had issued a 'Container Security Instrument' (CSI) under which the US required all ships carrying containers to the US to give cargo details. This was to allow US Customs to analyse the information and if necessary be enabled to screen high-risk containers at EU ports. The US announced that the instrument would come into effect in sixty days from 30 October 2002.[48] In response, Germany, France, the Netherlands, Belgium, Spain, Italy and the UK signed bilateral agreements with the US to permit US Customs CSI searches at designated ports in their countries, for example, Felixstowe, Antwerp and Le Havre. The EU transport commissioner then challenged the legality of the actions of these member states on the grounds that under EC law it was the commission's responsibility to negotiate trade and customs agreements on behalf of the EU. Note the commission was not against the move *perse*, it was only protesting at the method used. Additionally the commission said it would be negotiating with the US and be stressing the need for 'reciprocity' in such measures. A point of general concern is that no details of the bilateral agreements have been made public other than the ports involved.

On passenger information requirements, the US Immigration and Naturalization Service of the Justice Department published on 4 January 2002 a new rule on manifest requirements under Section 231 of the Enhanced Border Security and Visa Entry Act of 2002, which required 'the submission of arrival and departure manifests electronically in advance of an aircraft or vessel's arrival in or departure from the United States'.[49] A fine of $1,000 per violation may be levied on a carrier for any person for whom such data is not submitted. A major concern is that the US would allow other agencies than the just the US Customs access to this data, which would be contrary to the 1995 EC directive on data protection. It should be noted that the US now has a unified border control agency, the Bureau of Customs and Border Protection (BCBP), which combines the inspections service of US Customs, the border patrol and inspections service of Immigration and Naturalization Service (INS) and the animal and plant inspections service of the Department of Agriculture. On 5 March 2003 the European Commission signed an agreement with US Customs to give them access to European travelers' Passenger Name Records (PNRS) for all flights to, from or through the US. Statewatch commented that this was 'due to political and economic pressures by the US government'.[50] As of July 2003, the European air carriers' data warehousing company, Amadeus Systems, was supplying the full forty data fields per passenger to US Customs. This data, under US law, can be held and accessed for up to seven years. The European Parliament and the pressure group European Digital Rights is protesting strongly about the legality of this agreement. One of their complaints, apart from the data protection issues, is that this agreement, like the proposed EU-US Mutual Legal Assistance (MLA) agreement, has a far wider scope than the original counterterrorism justification as the agreement just mentions that the data can be used 'for enforcement purposes'. Internal market commissioner Bolkestein is trying to resolve what even he admits is a 'situation of doubtful legality'.[51]

Conclusions

Reviewing the range of response measures proposed by the EU, it is obvious that there are no 'quick fix' solutions. Different interests have to be reconciled, a wide range of states are involved, there are resource (both human and physical) availability issues and budgetary constraints. In some instances, it is necessary for agreements at EU level to be followed up by national implementation measures, which can be subject to delays. For example, the UK is not yet in a position to formally implement the running of Joint Investigation Teams (JITs) because the necessary enabling legislation, the Police Reform Bill, is still going through Parliament. In some cases procedural corners may be 'cut', as in the case of data exchanges with US law enforcement authorities. The 'umbrella' response, the Framework Decision on Terrorism, came into force 23 June 2002, and under TEU Article 11.1 all member states are supposed to comply with the measures, in terms of outcomes to be achieved, by 31 December 2002. The EU has moved quite swiftly to impose restrictive measures on suspected terrorists and terrorist organisations. This was initially done by Article 2 (3) of Regulation (EC) No. 2580/2001 of 27 December 2001 and this listing is regularly updated by EC Council Decisions.

However, in what might be considered some really key areas, the EU is still clearly struggling to reach common positions and identifiable outcomes. For example, it was only at the July 2002 Meeting of the General Affairs Council that the EU agreed the need to develop 'a common evaluation of [the] terrorist threat against the Member States'.[52] Moreover, under the Spanish presidency in April 2002, it was still necessary for Spain to put forward an 'Initiative' for a Council Decision to implement specific measures for police and judicial cooperation as set out in Article 4 of EU Council Common Position 2001/931/CFSP. For example, in the Initiative (Article 4), member states are still being enjoined to 'fully exploit the possibilities and advantages of joint investigation teams, in order to investigate and prosecute terrorist offences involving any of the listed persons, groups or entities'.[53]

Not surprisingly, responding to 9/11 has been significantly under the intergovernmental 'pillars' of the EU and thus has reinforced the role of the Council of Ministers, Council Secretariat and the supporting networks on national officials. However, the Commission is clearly using its rights and powers wherever possible and the 'pillar one' responses seem to be entirely realistic and appropriate (receiving endorsement in the latest UK Cabinet Office 9/11 response update of 9 November 2002). Unity in 'pillar two' responses has been particularly problematic in the context of actual or anticipated military operations. Even in the 'third pillar' issues relating to the sharing of classified information and the bureaucratic strengths of security/intelligence agencies have starkly shown an 'implementation' 'gap' between ministerial agreements in Council in respect of information-sharing with Europol and what security/intelligence agencies will actually share and how they will share, the emphasis being on bilateral or multilateral 'practitioner created' links or structures like the Police Working Group on Terrorism (PWGT).

Looking to the future role of the EU reference can be made to the provisions of the 'Draft Treaty establishing a Constitution for Europe'.[54] In Part I is to be found, partly, a restatement of previous TEU provisions regarding continued commitment to an area of freedom, security and justice (Article I-3[2]) as a shared commitment with member states (Article I-13[20]) and member states retaining primary responsibility for domestic policing, (Article I-5[1]). However, Part I also contains an important new common commitment, the 'Solidarity clause' (Article I-42). This provides that 'the Union and its Member states shall act jointly in a spirit of solidarity if a Member State is the victim of a terrorist attack or natural or manmade disaster [and] the Union shall mobilise all the resources at its disposal, including the military resources made available to it by the Member States'.[55] The means of implementing the 'solidarity clause' are set out in Part II, Article III-226.

The new Draft Treaty highlighted rights in Part II, 'The Charter of Fundamental Rights' and the treaty also continues to deal, additionally and specifically, with matters such as the Protection of Personal Data, Article I-50. Thus we see attempts to balance security concerns and human rights. Accountability issues are also further addressed by proposals to give greater visibility to the roles of national parliaments in the legislative process. In the final version of the constitution, as accepted at the EU Summit in June 2004, the counterterrorism commitment has been reaffirmed, although Britain entered a reservation about protecting, if necessary, its approach to criminal law. However, whilst the Charter of Fundamental Rights remains part of the Constitution, as accepted in June 2004, Britain has also entered reservations about the extent of its coverage so, here, a divisibility on fundamental rights has crept in, which is somewhat unfortunate. Whether the new Constitution will be finally ratified, of course, depends on a number of national procedures, including a British referendum!

Overall, the response to 9/11 in the EU has seen, not surprisingly because of the perception of high threat levels, a concerted use of intergovernmental procedures and processes. This, coupled with the usual information restrictions in respect of counterterrorism measures and pressures from the US, have led to attempts to push through measures which appear to overemphasise 'security' and make compromises with human rights and civil liberties. Is this justified? If it is how will the EU citizens know? In the light of the debate around the rationale for the Iraq War, finding adequate 'proof' of necessity for certain policies and instruments seems to be a problematic matter.

Notes

1. National Audit Office, *Facing the Challenge: NHS Emergency Planning in England* (HC36, London, HMSO, November 2002), conclusion 10.

2. C. Hill, 'The Capabilities-Expectations Gap, or Conceptualizing Europe's International Role', *Journal of Common Market Studies* 31/3 1993, pp. 305–28, and see also W. Wagner, 'Why the EU's CFSP Will Remain Intergovernmentalist', *European Public Policy* 10/4 2003, pp. 576–95.

3. S. Hix, *The Political System of the European Union* (Basingstoke: Macmillan 1999) p.364.

4. E. Kamarck, 'Applying 21st Century Government to the Challenge of Homeland Security', in *New Ways to Manage Series* (2000) and see also RAND, *Quick Scan of Post 9/11 National Counterterrorist Policy Making and Implementation in Selected European Countries*, RAND-Europe Paper No. MR-1950 (RAND-Europe: 2002).

5. H. Wallace and W. Wallace (eds), *Policy Making in the European Union* (Oxford: OUP 2002).

6. L. Dobson and A. Weale, 'Governance and Legitimacy' in E. Bomberg and A. Stubbs (eds), *The European Union: How Does It Work?* (Oxford: OUP 2003) p.172.

7. A. Wiener, 'Citizenship', in M. Cini (ed), *European Union Politics* (Oxford: OUP 2003) p.407.

8. D. Curtin and I. Dekker, 'The EU as a "Layered" International Organization: Institutional Unity in Disguise', in P. Craig and G. De Burca (eds), *The Evolution of EU Law* (Oxford: OUP 1999) p.127.

9. Ibid, pp.128–9.

10. EU Justice and Home Affairs Ministerial Council, *Joint Action to Create a Directory of Specialised Counterterrorist Competencies, Skills and Expertise in Member States*, EU Council Doc. 96/610/JHA (Brussels: European Union 1996).

11. Europol, *Counterterrorism Report to the JHA Ministerial Council*, EU Council Doc. 7514/1/99 (Brussels: European Union 1999).

12. EU Justice and Home Affairs Ministerial Council, *Terrorism Trends Report September 2000 to September 2001*, EU Council Doc. 5759/02 (Brussels: European Union 2002).

13. Ibid.

14. M. Den Boer and J. Monar, '11 September and the Challenge of Global Terrorism to the EU as a Security Actor', *Journal of Common Market Studies* 40 (2002) p.11.

15. EU Council, *Road Map Note*, EU Council Doc. 14925/01 (Brussels: European Union 2001).

16. Interview UK MoD(Army) One Star Officer, 14 January 2003.

17. EU Council Declaration, Bulletin European Union EU-6 (Brussels: 2002).

18. Statement from the EU-Latin America and Caribbean Summit (EU-LAC) of 17 May 2002 (Brussels: European Union EU-LAC 2002) para.17.

19. Statement from the 4th Asia-Europe Meeting (ASEM) of 23–24 Sep. 2002 (Brussels: ASEM 2002) para.2.

20. *The Times* (20 June 2003).

21. European Commission press statement, IP702/10/02 (Brussels: European Commission 2002).

22. On JITs see T. Schalken and M. Pronk, 'On Joint Investigation Teams, Europol and Supervision of Their Joint Actions', *European Journal of Crime, Criminal Law and Criminal Justice* 10/1 (2002) pp.70–82.

23. http://www.statewatch.org/news/index/html

24. Ibid.

25. Ibid.

26. House of Commons European Scrutiny Committee (2002–03) xxth Report.

27. Boer and Monar, op. cit., p.21.

28. Europol, *Europol Annual Report* 2001, EU Council Doc. 8381/02 (Brussels: European Union 2002).

29. Ibid.

30. European Parliament, EU Budget Proposals, OJ No. L29, Art. B5–822, and see also *Defense News* 17/36, (Sep. 2002).

31. House of Commons European Scrutiny Committee (2002–03) Fifth Report, HC63-v (London: HMSO 2003) referring to European Commission document 11702/02COM (02) 439.

32. Europol, *High Level Expert Group Recommendations*, Europol File No. 1-2546-233 (The Hague: Europol 2002).

33. See further D. Dubois, 'The Attacks of 11 September: EU-US Cooperation against Terrorism in the Field of Justice and Home Affairs', *European Foreign Affairs Review* 7 (2002) pp.317–35.

34. Boer and Monar, op. cit., p.23.

35. House of Commons European Scrutiny Committee, (note 31) (note 14) op. cit., referring to EU Doc. 13689/02 + ADD and EUD. 13966/02.

36. EU Council, EU Doc. 8296/1/REV1 (Brussels: European Council 2003) and see http://www.statewatch.org/news/index/html

37. European Parliament, Committee on Citizens' Freedoms and Rights, Justice and Home Affairs, *Report Containing a Proposal for a European Parliament Recommendation to the Council on the EU-USA Agreements on Judicial Cooperation on Criminal Matters and Extradition*, EP Doc. FINAL A5-0172/2003 (Strasbourg: European Parliament 2003).

38. Ibid.

39. Ibid.

40. http://www.statewatch.org/news/index/html

41. Ibid.

42. *Civil Protection–Progress Made in Implementing the Programme for Preparedness for Possible Emergencies*, COM (02) 302, final.

43. European Council, *Decision on the Network for Epidemiological Surveillance and Control of Communicable Diseases*, Decision 2119/98/EC (Brussels: European Council 1998).

44. Report to the EU Transport Ministers' Council of the Ad Hoc Group on Civil Aviation, (Brussels: European Council 2002).

45. Ibid.

46. Ibid.

47. Ibid.

48. Richard M. Stone, Testimony before the Subcommittee on Homeland Security, House of Representatives, Washington DC 16 June 2003.

49. Ibid.

50. http://www.statewatch.org/news/index/html

51. Ibid. see also http://www.statewatch.org/news/2003/oct/17eppnr.htm

52. EU General Affairs Council, *Conclusions* (Brussels, European Council 2002).

53. Spanish Presidency, *Initiative*, EU Council Doc. 7756/02 (29th Brussels: European Union 2002).

54. European Convention Secretariat, *Draft Treaty Establishing a Constitution for Europe*. Doc CONV 820/03 and Doc. CONV 725/03 (Brussels: European Convention Secretariat 2003).

55. Ibid.

8

Terrorism and Human Rights: A Defence Lawyer's Perspective

EDWARD B. MACMAHON, JR.

Attorney, Middleburg, Virginia, USA

The author of this article is one of the attorneys appointed to represent Zacarias Mous-saoui in the United States. Mr. Moussaoui is the only person facing criminal charges for alleged involvement in the September 11 plot. The author describes the system of government in the United States with a specific emphasis on several terrorism cases pending in the United States. He seeks to assure the readers that the rule of law is para-mount in the United States. Recent decisions of the Supreme Court—in the Hamdi and Guantanamo cases—that confirm the constitutional rights of even the most dedicated enemies of the United States, which decisions post-date this submission, only affirm the writer's theme.

In December of 2001, I was appointed to represent Zacarias Moussaoui at the Uni-ted States District Court for the Eastern District of Virginia. Moussaoui is facing the death penalty for charges of conspiracy related to the 11 September attacks in the United States. I have also been appointed twice by the Fourth Circuit Court of Appeals to represent Moussaoui and have twice argued on his behalf in the court.

When the conference organisers asked me to contribute my views on the subject of terrorism and human rights, my initial reaction was to say that I was struck by the skeptical perceptions of American policy that I heard at the conference voiced by some of the participants. Americans love their freedom and believe, from early in their lives, that they live in a land that is blessed with freedom. Our Constitution guarantees us many liberties and those freedoms are cherished by all Americans. All of our leaders–politicians, policemen and judges–swear an oath of allegiance to protect and defend the Constitution. Countless Americans have died all over the globe fighting for freedom.

Thus it is quite shocking, especially in the aftermath of the 11 September attacks in which so many innocents were slaughtered, to hear insinuations that Americans are the enemies of freedom and not its protectors. This belief, I submit, arises from a fundamental misunderstanding of the rule of law that supports our constitutional system of government. An attendee at the conference might have believed that the president of the United States controls the government without limitation, that he can, by waving his hand, arrest citizens, wage war, detain foreign nationals and otherwise subvert liberty at will. This belief, however, is entirely unfounded as there is an ongoing debate in the United States about the proper balance between fighting the war on terrorism and the constitutional rights we all enjoy. That debate is steeped in history, which is traditional and appropriate. And, contrary to the views espoused by many at the conference, the president is enjoying only mixed results in his efforts to expand the parameters of the constitutional power to wage war as he faces a judiciary equally jealous of its constitutional prerogative to decide what is and is not constitutional. I will try to explain this debate with reference to three cases of which I am familiar and with a short explanation of the constitutional issues that frame the debate.

First, the form of government established by the United States Constitution entails three separate but coequal branches of government. No one of the three branches of government created by the Constitution possesses any power that is not allocated to it by the Constitution. With respect to the issue of war and human rights, the powers in this area are divided among and between the three branches of government as follows. First, the Congress, which includes the House of Representatives and the Senate, possesses the power to 'provide for the common defense' and to 'declare war' (Article 1 § 8). Second, the president, under the Constitution, is the commander in chief of the army and the navy of the United States (Article 2 § 2). Also, the president is constitutionally required 'to carry into effect all laws passed by the Congress for the conduct of war'. Finally, the judicial branch, created under Article 3 of the Constitution, is charged with interpreting the constitutionality of the laws passed by the Congress.[1] One of the earliest cases decided by the Supreme Court established the precedent that the Supreme Court was the only branch of government that could rule on the constitutionality of the acts of either executive or elected branches of government. By devolving these responsibilities to the three branches of government, the founders of the United States sought to create a system of checks and balances that would preserve the rights of the people as guaranteed by the Constitution and the Bill of Rights.[2]

The current legal disputes now raging in the United States about the collision between the president's power to wage war and the protections guaranteed by the Bill of Rights are in keeping with the traditions of our government and courts and should not be viewed as an aberration. In times of war, presidents have repeatedly sought to expand their powers by citing the constitutional obligation to protect the American people as a basis to infringe upon or otherwise curtail individual liberties. For example, President Lincoln sought to try Americans captured in the North in military tribunals, citing the need to protect national security. In *Ex Parte Milligan*, (1866) 71 US 2, the Supreme Court rejected that effort ruling that the president's power to wage war could never justify infringing upon a citizen's right to a fair trial. Thus, even in America's darkest hour–the Civil War–the Supreme Court refused to allow the rule of law to be replaced by a rule that vested absolute power in the executive branch. That opinion, it should be noted, cites the many outrages common to the British monarchs as examples of the abuses that our Constitution will not allow. This is one of the great opinions of American jurisprudence. During both world wars, attorneys for German nationals who were subject to deportation complained that the president could not order them to be deported. In *Ludecke v. Watkins*, (1948) 335 US 160 the Supreme Court disagreed, finding that the president had the authority to detain and deport alien enemies during war. Also, Germans detained in China before the end of the World War II sought but received no review of the legality of their subsequent detention as seen in *Johnson v. Eisentrager*, (1950) 339 US 763. Finally, In *Ex Parte Quirin*, (1942) 317 US 1, the Supreme Court allowed the president, acting through the secretary of defense, to detain and execute German spies and saboteurs who were arrested in the United States. Significantly, one of the *Quirin* defendants was an American citizen[3] who was executed by the military without enjoying the constitutional protections that would have otherwise guaranteed him a fair trial in a civilian court.

The conflict between the holdings in *Milligan* and *Quirin*, at least as it relates to the United States citizen, is clear. Milligan was freed by the Supreme Court because there was a civilian court that could have heard his case and thus the military could not try him. Milligan was facing charges that could have been addressed in a civilian court. Yet the Supreme Court allowed the execution of the American defendant in *Quirin* after a military tribunal, when the civilian courts were similarly open and operating. To the Supreme Court, the difference was that Milligan was charged with a statutory offense while the *Quirin* defendant was charged with a violation of the rules of war for which no defendant enjoyed constitutional protections.[4] What is critical for my submission, however, is the fact that all of these cases were litigated all the way to the Supreme Court of the United States which then had the final say. There was no unilateral action taken by the president that was not subject to judicial review. While scholars have – as they will–debated the effectiveness or fairness of the review accorded, all of these defendants were given a day in court.

With this historical background in mind, there are three cases now pending in the United States that address the collision between individual liberties and the president's power to wage war.

The case of *United States v. Zacarias Moussaoui*, in which I have been appointed counsel, involves a French citizen arrested in the United States before the 11 September attacks. That case is now before the Fourth Circuit Court of Appeals on a government appeal. At issue is the trial judge's determination that the government was obligated to produce witnesses to the defense that would be able, the trial court found, to exculpate the defendant from the charges or the death penalty. Of course, I am not at liberty to discuss the factual details of the case at this time. However, the issue in this case is the clash between the defendant's constitutional right to confront the evidence against him and to call witnesses on his behalf and the president's right to detain prisoners. For purposes of the appeal, the court assumed that the witnesses at issue were in the custody of the United States. The dispute was precipitated by the president's refusal, on grounds of national security, to allow the defendant to have access to the disputed witnesses on the grounds that allowing the defendant, an admitted Al-Qaeda member, to have contact with other alleged Al-Qaeda members, would interfere with the war and intelligence gathering. The district court refused to allow a 'national security' exception to the Bill of Rights and dismissed the death penalty and awarded other relief. That order is now on appeal at the Fourth Circuit Court of Appeals. So far, this case has not been a win for the president, though no one would predict the outcome of any appeals.

In the case of *Hamdi v. Rumsfeld*, Hamdi, who is an American citizen by birth, was allegedly detained by the United States Army while he was fighting for the Taliban against the Northern Alliance in Afghanistan in the late fall of 2001. Interestingly, Hamdi was detained along with John Walker Lindh, also known as the 'American Taliban'. Upon learning that Hamdi was born in Louisiana, the military transferred Hamdi from the Guantanamo Bay Naval Base[5] in Cuba to the Navy Brig in Norfolk, Virginia. The federal public defender in Virginia, a government official, filed a suit challenging the detention of Hamdi without charges. The government responded saying that it had the right to detain enemy combatants detained overseas without charges and without access to an attorney. The district court ordered that Hamdi be allowed to meet with the federal public defender and ordered the government to prove that Hamdi was an enemy combatant. On appeal, the Fourth Circuit ruled that Hamdi had stated no basis upon which to contest his detention thus giving the president a victory. The United States Supreme Court has taken Hamdi's appeal and that case will be argued in the spring of this year.

In the case of *Padilla v. Rumsfeld*, Padilla, who is an American citizen by birth and an alleged Al-Qaeda member, was arrested in Chicago after flying from Pakistan to the United States. In Chicago, he was arrested as a material witness in the 9/11 investigation and sent to New York. In New York, he was given an attorney at government expense–just like all of the defendants identified herein–and he was allowed to meet with the attorney. Thereafter, the president declared Padilla an enemy combatant and ordered him transferred to the Navy Brig in Charleston, South Carolina. Media reports indicate that the government learned that Padilla was a member of Al-Qaeda and was planning to explode a 'dirty bomb' somewhere in the United States. Like in *Hamdi*, Padilla's attorney filed a civil action to contest his detention without charges and to contest the government's refusal to let that attorney meet with Padilla. The trial court ruled that Padilla did have the right to meet with his counsel despite the government claim that such a meeting would endanger national security. The government appealed and the Second Circuit Court of Appeals, sitting almost a block from the site of the World Trade Center, ruled for Padilla. The court ordered the government to allow Padilla to meet with his attorneys and ordered Padilla's release in the event he, like Milligan, did not face charges in a civilian court. This ruling represented a stinging rebuke to the president. The Supreme Court has agreed to hear this case as well and has set arguments for the same date that the Hamdi case will be heard.

Conclusion

In the United States there is an ongoing profound debate as to the important issues that were raised at the conference. As I detailed above, these issues are being fought diligently in various federal trial and appellate courts including the Supreme Court itself. The Supreme Court will have resolved the Hamdi and Padilla cases before this submission is published and in doing so will issue opinions as constitutionally significant as those issued in *Milligan*, *Eisentrager* and *Quirin*. The commitment to human rights, as expressed in the Constitution and Bill of Rights, is of critical importance to each and every American and that commitment is often displayed in vigorous and often difficult litigation. The judges in these cases have consistently interpreted the law in accordance with their oath to support and defend the Constitution of the United States. Criminal defense attorneys of all political stripes are arguing to the best of their abilities to support the rights of unpopular defendants without reproach because of the great respect that exists for the rule of law. Finally, the president is acting consistently with historical precedent in seeking all powers he believes are needed necessary to defend the United States. But it is the judiciary and not any politician or military officer that will have the final say in these matters and those judges are notoriously independent. As judge Wilkins of the Fourth Circuit wrote in rejecting the government's claim of national security in the *Moussaoui* case:

> My colleague would apparently have us simply rule in favor of the government in cases like this one ... Siding with the government in all cases where national security concerns are asserted would entail

surrender of the independence of the judicial branch and aband(
our sworn commitment to uphold the rule of law.

In closing, I would stress to you that most Americans are confid
of law will prevail even in time of war because we believe in the sy
ment that was created by the Constitution. That system provides the best protection
for the individual liberties guaranteed to all Americans.

Notes

1. In response to a notorious English practice of delaying or denying pay to judges to obtain results favorable to the Crown, federal judges in the United States are appointed for life and their pay can never, as a matter of constitutional law, be reduced or delayed.

2. The Bill of Rights sets forth individual rights and liberties that cannot be infringed upon by the government. Those rights generally include freedom of speech, freedom of religion, the right to bear arms, the right to trial by jury, the right to confront evidence and to call witnesses in a criminal case, the right to use the process of the court to obtain witnesses and evidence, and the right to be free from cruel and unusual punishment.

3. One of the *Quirin* defendants was from Chicago as is Padilla.

4. Modern criminal statutes, such as the terrorism statute under which Moussaoui is charged, certainly blur this line. It can clearly be argued that the offenses that Moussaoui is charged with violate both the law of war and federal law. The Supreme Court has never had to decide whether there is an exclusive forum to hear claims of violations of the law of war.

5. Despite all of the protest about the detention of prisoners at Guantanamo Bay, this practice is in accordance with the law of war dealing with unlawful combatants as well. I certainly believe that some due process should be granted these detainees, but the president plainly has the power to detain unlawful combatants. *Quirin* regardless, there are two cases before the Supreme Court on this issue as well.

9

Derogating from International Human Rights Obligations in the 'War Against Terrorism'? — A British–Australian Perspective

CHRISTOPHER MICHAELSEN

Strategic & Defence Studies Centre, The Australian National University, Canberra, Australia

This article examines the United Kingdom's Anti-terrorism, Crime and Security Act 2001 and the Australian Security Intelligence Organisation Legislation Amendment (Terrorism) Act 2002 (Cth) from an international human rights law perspective. It argues that both pieces of legislation raise serious concerns in relation to international legal obligations under the European Convention on Human Rights and the International Covenant on Civil and Political Rights. Both international treaties allow for 'derogation' from certain provisions in times of 'public emergency'. While the United Kingdom has officially derogated from some of its treaty obligations, Australia has yet to submit a similar notification. This article argues, however, that the United Kingdom's derogation is unlawful. Likewise, current circumstances in Australia would not permit lawful derogation from the ICCPR.

Introduction

The tragic events of 11 September 2001 have led to a dramatic change in the perception of international terrorism. The unthinkable turned into reality and it soon became clear that the so-called 'war on terrorism' was to be one of the defining conflicts of the early twenty-first century. Proclaiming that the attacks on New York City and Washington DC were a threat to international peace and security, the United Nations (UN) Security Council, acting under Chapter VII of the UN Charter, called on all states to redouble their efforts to prevent and suppress the commission of terrorist attacks, including denying safe haven to those who finance, plan or support terrorist acts.[1] Governments around the world answered the United Nations call by enacting new legislation as part of their campaign to combat international terrorism. Unfortunately, many of these new antiterrorism laws curtail civil liberties and human rights. While it cannot be denied that it was (and still is) sensible and necessary to reassess existing laws in the light of the 9/11 attacks, doubts arise as to whether the fight against international terrorism can be won ultimately by introducing new repressive laws.

The difficult question of how to respond to terrorism has not only arisen with the attacks of 9/11. For more than thirty-five years, policy makers, academics and lawyers have been preoccupied with developing efficient counterterrorism models. While they were unable to develop a foolproof blueprint for effective and democratically acceptable countermeasures, most terrorism experts agreed that any campaign against terrorism, if were to be successful, had to adhere strictly to liberal democratic princi-ples and the rule of law.[2] As the British pioneer of terrorism studies, Paul Wilkinson, pointed out, 'the primary objective of any counter-terrorist strategy must be the pro-tection and maintenance of liberal democracy'. He concluded that 'it cannot be suffi-ciently stressed that this aim overrides in importance even the objective of eliminating terrorism and political violence as such'.[3] The maintenance of democracy requires, most of all, unfailing respect for three of liberal society's fundamental values: the rule of law, civil liberties and human rights. In the context of human rights it is essential to comply with fundamental legal principles established in important international treat-ies, such as the UN International Covenant on Civil and Political Rights (ICCPR) and the European Convention for the Protection of Human Rights and Fundamental Freedoms (ECHR). As confirmed by the UN General Assembly in Resolution 54/164, 'all measures to counter terrorism must be in strict conformity with the rel-evant provisions of international law, *including international human rights standards*'.[4] Liberal democratic countries such as the United Kingdom and Australia, which have played a significant role in the development of human rights standards, bear a parti-cular burden to uphold these rights even during the gravest of emergencies.

This essay assesses British and Australian legal responses to the events of 9/11 from an international human rights–law perspective. It examines the United King-dom's Anti-terrorism, Crime and Security Act 2001 (hereinafter 'ATCSA') and the Australian Security Intelligence Organisation Legislation Amendment (Terrorism) Act 2002 (Cth) (hereinafter 'ASIO Act'). Central to this analysis is the question whether or not British and Australian antiterrorism laws are consistent with their international legal commitments, specifically with provisions of the ECHR and the ICCPR. It is argued that several passages of the ATCSA and the ASIO Act raise ser-ious concerns with regard to obligations under the international instruments. In a subsequent section, attention is drawn to circumstances in which breaches of inter-national human rights law may be legally justifiable. Both the ECHR and the ICCPR allow for so-called 'derogation' from treaty obligations in times of 'public emergency threatening the life of the nation'. Yet the validity of any derogation depends on the fulfilment of strict legal requirements set forth in the treaties and further developed by relevant jurisprudence of the international monitoring organs. While the United Kingdom has officially derogated from Article 5 ECHR and Arti-cle 9 ICCPR due to threats from international terrorism in late 2001, Australia has yet to submit a notice of derogation. However, it might be asked, is the British proclamation legally valid? Answering this question requires analysis in two stages. First, it is examined whether and to what extent 'international terrorism' can qualify as 'time of public emergency threatening the life of the nation'. Second, the question is whether or not the United Kingdom has fully complied with the requirements for lawful derogation. Finally, the analysis focuses on whether current circumstances would permit an Australian derogation from the ICCPR.

Recent Antiterrorism Legislation and International Human Rights Law

United Kingdom

The Anti-terrorism, Crime and Security Act 2001
Antiterrorism legislation in the United Kingdom is, of course, nothing new. Con-fronted with terrorism and political violence in both Northern Ireland and on the

*n*land for decades, the United Kingdom had a wide range of legislative *m*sures in place even before 9/11.[5] The centrepiece of this legislative frame-*
the Terrorism Act 2000, which placed many of the (temporary) emergency
powers of the 1970s and 1980s on a permanent footing. Nevertheless, in the light
of *9/*11 attacks existing antiterrorism laws were found to be insufficient and the
British government introduced the Anti-terrorism, Crime and Security Act (ATCSA)
into Parliament on 12 November 2001.[6] The ATCSA is a lengthy piece of legislation
consisting of 129 sections and eight schedules and is portrayed by some observers as
the 'most draconian legislation Parliament has passed in peacetime in over a century'.[7]
While the ATCSA contains a number of reasonable provisions dealing with important
security safeguards (i.e., powers to freeze 'terrorist' assets or reinforcing powers concerning security in the nuclear industry), the central and most controversial part (Part 4)
introduces powers to detain 'suspected international terrorists' indefinitely, and
without trial.[8]

Indefinite Detention of 'Suspected International Terrorists'
According to s. 21(1) ATCSA, the secretary of state may issue a certificate in respect
of a person if he reasonably believes that the person's presence in the United Kingdom is a risk to national security and that the person is a terrorist. For the purposes
of this section 'terrorist' is defined as 'a person who (a) is or has been concerned in the
commission, preparation or instigation of acts of international terrorism, (b) is a
member of or belongs to an international terrorist group, or (c) has links with an
international terrorist group' (s. 21(2)).[9] 'Terrorism' has the meaning given by s. 1
of the Terrorism Act 2000.[10] The core of the ATCSA is to be found in s. 23(1). It provides that a 'suspected international terrorist', upon certification, may be detained
indefinitely if either a 'point of law' or a 'practical consideration' prevents his removal
from the United Kingdom.[11] The provision applies to persons subject to immigration
control under the Immigration Act 1971, and therefore does not apply to British
citizens.

The detention of foreign nationals under s. 23 ATCSA is incompatible with Article 5 ECHR.[12] Article 5 ECHR guarantees the right to liberty and security and principally seeks to prevent arbitrary interference by a public authority with an
individual's personal liberty. Nevertheless, the European Convention permits deprivation of liberty on condition that deprivation measures are 'in accordance with a
procedure prescribed by law'. Of particular relevance in the present context is Article
5(1)(f), which allows for 'lawful arrest or detention of a person to prevent his effecting an unauthorized entry into the country or of a person against whom action is
being taken with a view to deportation or extradition'. The purpose of s. 23 ATCSA
is to detain suspected international terrorists that cannot be removed from the
United Kingdom due to a point of law, in this case Article 3 ECHR.[13] Hence, detainees under s. 23 ATCSA are persons against whom action is *not* being taken with a
view to deportation. S. 23 ATCSA therefore is in breach of Article 5(1) ECHR and
does not fall under the exception of Article 5(1)(f)[14] or any other paragraph of Article 5(1).[15] Because of the incompatibility of s. 23 ATCSA with Article 5(1) ECHR
some conservative members of Parliament wanted home secretary Blunkett to consider withdrawing from the European Convention altogether.[16] The British government, however, preferred to derogate formally from Article 5(1) ECHR and issued
an order in accordance with Article 15(3) ECHR.[17] No derogations were notified
in relation to any other obligation under the ECHR.[18]

Limited Access to Judicial Review

According to s. 25(1) ATCSA, a 'suspected international terrorist' cannot appeal to a British court of law against his certification under s. 21 ATCSA. Appeal is only available to the Special Immigration Appeals Commission (SIAC),[19] which has the power to cancel the certificate if it believes that it should not have been issued in the first place.[20] This limited access to judicial review is in breach with Article 5(4) ECHR. Article 5(4) ECHR states that 'everyone who is deprived of his liberty by arrest or detention shall be entitled to take proceedings by which the lawfulness of his detention shall be decided speedily by a court and his release ordered if the detention is not lawful'.

SIAC is not a typical court of law integrated in the standard British court system. However, in *X v. United Kingdom*, the European Court of Human Rights held that in the context of Article 5(4) ECHR 'the word "court" is not necessarily to be understood as signifying a court of law of the classic kind, integrated within the standard judicial machinery of the country'. The term rather serves to denote 'bodies which exhibit not only common fundamental features of which the most important is independence of the executive and of the parties of the case … but also the guarantees of a judicial procedure'.[21] While SIAC has been established as an impartial and independent tribunal with the same status as the high court and thus undoubtedly provides some degree of control, serious doubts arise as to whether proceedings before it offer sufficient guarantees of judicial procedure.

The European Court of Human Rights found it essential that the person concerned be present at an oral hearing, where he/she has the opportunity to be heard either in person or through a lawyer, and the possibility of calling and questioning witnesses.[22] In *Bouamar v. Belgium*, for instance, the court held that hearings before a juvenile court – undoubtedly a 'court' from the organizational point of view – conducted in the absence of the applicant's lawyers did not satisfy the requirements of Article 5(4) ECHR.[23] Also required is the benefit of an adversarial procedure ensuring equality of arms.[24]

Proceedings before SIAC may be held in absence of the appellant and/or his/her counsel. The detainee and his/her legal representatives will not be entitled to see all the evidence and will not be informed in detail about the reasons for the decisions that have been made in respect to him/her. Furthermore, the appellant's legal representatives will be chosen for him/her by the attorney general and will not be responsible to the appellant.[25] Proceedings before SIAC therefore do not offer sufficient guarantees of judicial procedure and cannot be considered a 'court' within the meaning of Article 5(4) ECHR.

Australia

New Antiterrorism Legislation

In contrast to the United Kingdom, Australia has had little or no experience of terrorism, and before 9/11 there were no Australian laws dealing with terrorism specifically.[26] A first package of antiterrorism legislation, comprising five bills, was introduced into the Federal Parliament on 12 March 2002.[27] The most important bill of this first package was the controversial Security Legislation Amendment (Terrorism) Bill 2002, which passed Parliament and the Senate only after it had been amended substantially to include recommendations by the Senate Legal and Constitutional Legislation Committee.[28] The second cornerstone of Australia's new antiterrorism laws is meant to be the Australian Security Intelligence Organisation Legislation Amendment (Terrorism) Act 2002 (Cth). Its main purpose was to authorize the detention by ASIO of persons for questioning in relation to terrorism offences, as well as the creation of new offences in respect to withholding of information regarding terrorism. The ASIO Bill was first introduced into Parliament on 21 March 2002 and was likewise subject to heated discussion.[29] While attorney general Daryl Williams was convinced that the new legislation would enable ASIO 'to engage in an *appropriate* form of interrogation'[30] to gather relevant information for the prevention of terrorist attacks, critics argued that the bill is 'rotten to the core' and would establish 'part of the apparatus of a police state'.[31] After contentious debate in the Senate, the bill was referred to the Senate Legal and Constitutional Affairs References Committee for a public inquiry and report. Still, the Senate rejected it on 13 December 2002. The bill was reintroduced into Parliament in late March 2003, subject to a number of minor amendments. After intense negotiations between the government and the opposition, the revised bill finally passed the Senate on 26 June 2003.[32]

Arbitrary Detention of Non-Suspects

The ASIO Act authorizes ASIO to seek a warrant to detain and question people for up to forty-eight hours. The person detained does not need to be suspected of any offence. People can be taken into custody without charges being laid or even the possibility that they might be laid at a later stage. According to s. 34D(1) it is sufficient that the 'issuing authority' has 'reasonable grounds for believing that the warrant will substantially assist the collection of intelligence that is important in relation to a terrorism offence'. An 'issuing authority' is defined as a person, appointed by the minister, who is a federal magistrate or judge, or a member of another class of people nominated in regulations (s. 34AB) and therefore lacks sufficient independence from the executive. The warrant either requires a person to appear before a 'prescribed authority' to provide information or produce records or things or authorizes a police officer to take the person into custody and bring him or her before a 'prescribed authority' for such purposes.[33] While a single warrant must not exceed forty-eight hours, it is possible to extend detention by requesting successive warrants. In total, the successive extensions may not result in a continuous period of detention of more than 168 hours (seven days) from the time the person first appeared before any 'prescribed authority' for questioning under an earlier warrant (s. 34F(4)(aa)).

The detention of non-suspects authorized by a nonjudicial body for the mere purpose of questioning is incompatible with Australia's international human rights commitments, specifically obligations under the ICCPR.[34] Article 9(1) ICCPR states that 'everyone has the right to liberty and security of person. No one shall be subjected to arbitrary arrest or detention'. Referring to the ICCPR's *travaux preparatoires*, Manfred Nowak pointed out that the term 'arbitrary' is not to be equated with 'against the law' but includes elements of injustice, unpredictability, unreasonableness, capriciousness and unproportionality.[35] Confirming this interpretation, the Human Rights Committee stated in *Van Alphen v. The Netherlands* that detention 'must not only be lawful but *reasonable* in all the circumstances' and 'must be *necessary* in all the circumstances, for example to prevent flight, interference with evidence, or the recurrence of a crime'.[36] It is difficult to see how the detention of non-suspects for the purpose of questioning and intelligence gathering can be regarded as 'necessary and reasonable in all the circumstances'.

First, ASIO confirmed in April 2002 that 'there is no known specific terrorist threat to Australia at present'.[37] Although Australia was a possible target, there were 'a series of other countries more at risk of attack', among them the United States and the United Kingdom.[38] Nonetheless, neither the United States nor the United Kingdom have felt compelled to introduce legislation that facilitates the detention of non-suspects for mere questioning purposes.

Second, even in circumstances where detention for questioning purposes is considered to be indispensable, there is no clear reason why such detention should not be strictly confined to those reasonably suspected of being terrorists or being involved in terrorist activities.

Third, the ASIO Act falls short of providing sufficient safeguards. Comparable legislation in Canada, for example, requires that a regular judge – independent from the executive – must make out the orders for so-called investigative hearings.[39] In the absence of similar provisions the Australian proposals lack any necessity, reasonableness and proportionality in 'all the circumstances', specifically as a response to a possible terrorist threat. In consequence, detention powers under the ASIO Act constitute arbitrary interference with the individual's right to liberty and security as protected by Article 9(1) ICCPR.

Limited Access to Judicial Review
The detention of non-suspects is not only unnecessary and disproportionate but also breaches Article 9(3) ICCPR. Article 9(3) requires that 'anyone arrested or detained on a criminal charge shall be brought promptly before a judge or other officer authorized by law to exercise judicial power and shall be entitled to trial within a reasonable time or to release'. Under the ASIO Act, persons are not detained on criminal charges, but for questioning purposes. However, it would be inconsistent with the ICCPR's underlying principles if it granted greater rights to persons officially arrested on criminal charges than to those who are compulsorily detained for questioning in relation to terrorism offences. Article 9(3) therefore is also applicable to administrative detention for questioning purposes. As the Human Rights Committee stated in its General Comment 8, prompt appearance before a judge or other officer authorized by law to exercise judicial power requires that the period before appearance 'must not exceed a few days'.[40] In *Freemantle v. Jamaica*, a four-day delay in bringing the detainee before a judge was found to violate Article 9(3) ICCPR.[41] Similarly, the European Court of Human Rights held in *Brogan v. United Kingdom* that four days and six hours was too long to satisfy the requirement of 'promptness'.[42] ASIO Act provisions allow for detention for up to 168 hours (seven days) without judicial oversight at all. These arrangements constitute a serious breach of Article 9(3) ICCPR.

A further point of concern is that a 'prescribed authority' oversees the detention of persons for questioning purposes.[43] Regarding Articles 9(3) and 9(4) ICCPR and Articles 5(3) and 6 ECHR, both the Human Rights Committee and the European Court have confirmed that the functions prescribed therein can only be carried out by a judicial body and not by quasi-judicial substitutes.[44] The 'prescribed authority', however, is either a federal magistrate or a member of the Administrative Appeals Tribunal (AAT). AAT members (other than presidential members) are appointed for fixed periods and dependent on the favour of the executive if they wish to be reappointed. As an administrative body it is even 'less' judicial than the British SIAC. Rather it is similar to a British nonjudicial body known as the 'three wise men'. The 'three wise men' acted as a review of the home secretary's decisions to remove aliens from the United Kingdom whose presence was deemed to be 'not conducive to the public good' for reasons of national security. The European Court held in *Chahal v. United Kingdom* that the system of the 'three wise men' contravened the European Convention and that the national authorities could not be 'free from effective control by the domestic courts whenever they choose to assert that national security and terrorism are involved'.[45] In consequence, the 'prescribed authority' as established in the ASIO Act can not be considered a 'court' or 'officer authorized by law to exercise judicial power' within the meaning of Articles 9(3) and 9(4) ICCPR.[46]

Privilege Against Self-Incrimination and the Detention of Children
S. 34G of the ASIO Act contains offences (five years imprisonment) for failing to give the information, record or thing requested in accordance with the warrant. 'Strict liability' attaches to this offence and the detainee bears the burden of proof to establish that he/she does not have the information sought.[47] In effect, these provisions remove the right to silence and reverse the onus of proof. Moreover, while the act protects the detainee against *direct* use of answers in criminal proceedings against him/her (except in proceedings for an offence against s. 34G), it does not provide protection from *derivative* use of any answers in future proceedings. This means, for example, that if the police forces find evidence based on the person's answers during questioning (e.g., by later finding incriminating material at the person's premises), this evidence may be used against the person in criminal proceedings. These provisions breach the non-derogable right to be presumed innocent until proved guilty enshrined in Article 14(2) ICCPR and also recognized in Article 11 of the Universal Declaration of Human Rights and Article 6 ECHR. Article 14(3)(g) ICCPR further clarifies that the accused has the right 'not to be compelled to testify against himself or to confess guilt'. In *Saunders v. United Kingdom* the European Court of Human Rights found that the right of any person charged to remain silent and the privilege against self-incrimination are generally recognized international standards which lie at the heart of the notion of a fair procedure. The rationale of both rights lies, *inter alia*, in 'protecting the person charged against improper compulsion by the authorities and thereby contributing to the avoidance of miscarriages of justice and to the fulfilment of the aims of Article 6 ECHR (right to a fair trial)'. In consequence, the court held that it was a violation of Article 6 ECHR to admit evidence during a criminal trial which had been obtained at an earlier administrative hearing during which the accused had been compelled by statute to answer questions and adduce evidence of a self-incriminatory nature.[48] Similarly, the Human Rights Committee pointed out in its General Comment 13 that 'in order to compel the accused to confess or to testify against himself, frequently methods which violate these provisions (Article 14 ICCPR) are used. The law should require that evidence provided by means of such methods or any other form of compulsion is *wholly* unacceptable'.[49] The fact that the Human Rights Committee specifically used the term 'wholly' indicates that Article 14 ICCPR does not only prohibit *use immunity* but also *derivative use immunity*. S. 34G of the ASIO Act is therefore in breach of Article 14 ICCPR.

Finally, and most disturbing, the ASIO Act also permits the detention of children. S. 34NA provides that a person between the ages of sixteen and eighteen can be detained for questioning purposes if it is likely that this person 'will commit, is committing or has committed a terrorism offence'. While these powers raise the utmost ethical concerns, they also violate essential provisions of the UN Convention on the Rights of the Child to which Australia became a party in 1991. In particular, it breaches Article 37 which provides that no child should be deprived of his or her liberty arbitrarily and that any detention should be used only as a *measure of last resort* and for the *shortest appropriate period of time*.[50] Furthermore, any child is to be presumed innocent until proven guilty.[51]

Derogation from International Human Rights Obligations

The International Rules on Derogation

In addition to several limitation clauses governing certain individual rights, both the ECHR and ICCPR contain a derogation clause with specific standards for emergencies.[52] While the state parties may not derogate from the entire treaty, they may legally suspend their obligation to respect and enforce specific rights contained in the convention during times of 'war or other public emergency threatening the life of the nation'.[53] In other words, not all rights enshrined in the covenant/conventions ntions are absolute. In exceptional circumstances, state parties are permitted to take measures that interfere with the enjoyment of rights otherwise protected by these instruments. Yet even during the gravest of emergencies, a number of rights are strictly 'non-derogable' on the grounds that they are too fundamental and too precious to be dispensed with. The ICCPR's and ECHR's derogation articles' purpose is, thus, to balance the most vital needs of the state in times of crisis with the strongest protection of human rights possible. The derogation's validity depends on the fulfilment of several legal requirements. First, the derogating government must establish the existence of a 'public emergency threatening the life of the nation'. Second, the 'public emergency' must be officially proclaimed and relevant treaty organs must be notified. Third, the measures which derogate from any obligation under the treaty must only be to the extent strictly required by the exigencies of the situation. Finally, these measures must neither be inconsistent with other obligations under international law nor discriminatory.

Requirements for Derogation

The Existence of a 'Public Emergency'
The ICCPR and ECHR both lack a specific definition of 'time of public emergency threatening the life of the nation'. Nevertheless, the international monitoring organs established under the treaties, notably the European Court and Commission, have extensively interpreted the term and provided jurisprudence valuable for determining its meaning and scope. As the Strasbourg authorities tend to examine Article 15 in its natural and common sense and due to the fact that many provisions in the ICCPR and ECHR are similar, the derogation clauses in particular, European decisions and findings are easily applicable to ICCPR cases.

The first substantive interpretation of Article 15 ECHR was made in *Lawless v. Ireland*.[54] Confirming the European Commission's determination that Article 15 should be interpreted in the light of its 'natural and customary' meaning, the European Court of Human Rights defined 'time of public emergency' as 'an exceptional situation of crisis or emergency which afflicts the whole population and constitutes a threat to the organized life of the community of which the community is composed'.[55] The definition was further developed and clarified in the *Greek* case.[56] Reaffirming the basic elements of the court's approach in *Lawless v. Ireland*, the commission emphasized that the emergency must be actual or at least 'imminent', a notion that is present in the merits judgment in French (authentic version) but not in the English version.[57] In order to constitute an Article 15 emergency the Commission held that a 'public emergency' must have the following four characteristics:[58]

1. It must be actual or imminent.
2. Its effects must involve the whole nation.
3. The continuance of the organized life of the community must be threatened.[59]
4. The crisis or danger must be exceptional, in that the normal measures or restrictions permitted by convention for the maintenance of public safety, health and order, are plainly inadequate.[60]

As stated by the European Commission in the *Greek* case, and by the Human Rights Committee in its General Comment 29, the state parties bear the burden of proof to establish the existence of a 'public emergency'.[61] However, in assessing whether a 'public emergency' exists and what steps are necessary to address it, states are granted a so-called margin of appreciation. The doctrine of margin of appreciation thus illustrates the general approach of the international organs to the difficult task of balancing the sovereignty of contracting parties with their obligations under the convention.[62] In the context of derogation in times of 'public emergency threatening the life of the nation', the margin of appreciation represents the discretion left to a state in ascertaining the necessity and scope of measures of derogation from protected rights in the circumstances prevailing within its jurisdiction.[63] In *Ireland v. United Kingdom*, the European Court held that 'it falls in the first place to each contracting state, with its responsibility for "the life of [its] nation", to determine whether that life is threatened by a "public emergency" and, if so, how far it is necessary to go in attempting to overcome the emergency. By reason of their direct and continuous contact with the pressing needs of the moment, the national authorities are in principle in a better position than the international judge to decide both on the presence of such an emergency and on the scope of derogations necessary to avert it. In this matter Article 15(1) leaves the authorities a *wide* margin of appreciation'.[64] Yet, the court stressed that states do not enjoy an unlimited margin of appreciation. The discretion of the state is 'accompanied by a European supervision'.[65] The Strasbourg court generally seems prepared to grant a much *wider* margin of appreciation than the monitoring organ of the ICCPR, the Human Rights Committee. In *Landinelli Silva v. Uruguay*, for instance, the committee found that 'the State Party is duty-bound to give a sufficiently detailed account of the relevant facts when it invokes Article 4(1)' and that it is the committee's function 'to see to it that States Parties live up to their commitments under the Covenant'.[66]

The Requirements of Proclamation and Notification
Article 4(1) ICCPR requires that the existence of public emergency be 'officially proclaimed'. As explained by the Human Rights Committee in its General Comment 29, states 'must act within their constitutional and other provisions of law that govern

such proclamation and the exercise of emergency powers'.[67] Failure to comply with this requirement constitutes a violation of international law. This legal effect distinguishes the proclamation from the international duty to notify under Article 4(3) and Article 15(3). As Manfred Nowak observed, the latter is not a necessary condition of the lawfulness of emergency measures, but serves only the purpose of supervision by the international monitoring organs.[68] Surprisingly, the requirement of official proclamation does not appear expressly in the ECHR. Indeed the European Court in *Lawless* found that Article 15 'does not oblige the State concerned to promulgate the notice of derogation within the framework of its municipal law'.[69] However, Article 15 also provides that any derogation measure must be consistent with other obligations under international law. As a consequence, it appears that states party to both the ECHR and the ICCPR would still have to fulfil the requirement of 'official proclamation'. Among others, this issue arose in *Brannigan and McBride v. United Kingdom*. Intervening NGOs challenged the United Kingdom's declaration of a state of emergency on the grounds that it was not 'officially proclaimed'. However, the European Court was satisfied that the detailed explanation by the home secretary in the House of Commons was sufficient to comply with the proclamation requirement. In any case, declarations of 'public emergency' must be made in good faith. Although not explicitly expressed in the derogation clauses themselves, the good faith principle can be derived from certain other provisions of the two treaties, which provide that no state may perform any act aimed at the destruction or undue limitation of rights and freedoms protected by the instruments.[70] It is also recognized in Siracusa Principle 62, which states that any proclamation of a public emergency not made in good faith constitutes a violation of international law.[71]

The Proportionality of Measures: 'To the Extent Strictly Required'

A fundamental requirement for any measures derogating from the ECHR or the ICCPR is that such measures are limited 'to the extent strictly required by the exigencies of the situation'.[72] In other words, derogation measures must be strictly proportionate. The principle of proportionality constitutes a general principle of international law and includes elements of severity, duration and scope.[73] It is equally applied by the Strasbourg authorities and the Human Rights Committee, yet with slightly different nuances.[74] Any derogation measure must fulfil the following five basic requirements:

1. The measures must be necessary, i.e., actions taken under ordinary laws and in conformity with international human rights obligations are not sufficient to meet the threat.
2. The measures must be connected to the emergency, i.e., they must *prima facie* be suitable to reduce the threat or crisis.
3. The measures must be used only as long as they are necessary, i.e., there must be a temporal limit.
4. The degree to which the measures deviate from international human rights standards must be in proportion to the severity of the threat, i.e., the more important and fundamental the right which is being compromised, the closer and stricter the scrutiny.
5. Effective safeguards must be implemented to avoid the abuse of emergency powers. Where measures involve administrative detention, safeguards may include regular

review by independent national organs, in particular by the legislative and judicial branches.

In determining whether derogation measures are strictly required by the exigencies of the situation a certain 'margin of error' must be granted to the national authorities. In other words, the doctrine of margin of appreciation is applicable not only in the process of assessing the existence of a 'public emergency' but also in the context of proportionality. The European Court held in *Ireland v. United Kingdom* that it falls to the contracting party to determine 'how far it is necessary to go in attempting to overcome the emergency'.[75] Again, Strasbourg seems to grant a substantial amount of discretion to national governments. On the other hand, the Siracusa Principles explicitly state that the principle of strict necessity shall be applied in an 'objective manner' and, moreover, that 'the judgment of the national authorities cannot be accepted as conclusive'.[76]

The Principles of Consistency and Nondiscrimination

Article 4(1) ICCPR furthermore states that derogation measures may not be inconsistent with other obligations under international law. Furthermore, they may not involve discrimination 'solely on the ground of race, colour, sex, language, religion or social origin'. The ICCPR's *travaux preparatoires* indicate that some delegations suggested extending the nondiscrimination clause to include the criteria of national origin. The proposal, however, was rejected on the grounds that disparate treatment of enemy aliens would be necessary during wartime. While the principle of consistency also appears in Article 15 ECHR, the nondiscrimination passage is missing in the European derogation clause. Nevertheless, the absence of the nondiscrimination principle in Article 15 ECHR effectively has no major consequences, as discriminatory application of derogation measures is in most cases incompatible with the general nondiscriminatory provision of Article 14 ECHR.[77] Moreover, arbitrary discrimination against disfavoured groups of various types would be usually difficult to justify as being 'strictly required by the exigencies of the situation'. In contrast to Article 4(1) ICCPR, Article 14 ECHR also prohibits discrimination on the basis of national origin.

Derogation in the Face of International Terrorism

The Phenomenon of International Terrorism

Circumstances which can provoke the proclamation of a 'public emergency', were originally considered to involve war, internal unrest, natural disasters or economic crises.[78] The phenomenon of terrorism was not contemplated when the European Convention and the International Covenant were drafted in the aftermath of World War II. Yet all cases that have reached the European Court of Human Rights on Article 15 have concerned threats to internal security arising from acts of terrorism. In *Lawless*, *Ireland v. United Kingdom* and *Brannigan and McBride*, the governments' declarations of 'public emergency' were triggered by terror campaigns of the Irish Republican Army (IRA) and their Unionist counterparts. Both Catholic and Protestant terrorist organizations were operating in Northern Ireland and, to a lesser extent, in England. Unlike these traditional forms of terrorism, however, the threat from Islamic extremism is not limited by geography. Terrorism today is a complex and global problem, not necessarily a localised and domestic one. As the US coordinator for counterterrorism, ambassador Francis X. Taylor pointed out, 'small cells of terrorists have become *true transnational threats* – thriving around the world without any single state sponsor or homebase'.[79] Moreover, unlike its previous manifestations, contemporary terrorism is hardly attributable to a confined number of terrorist organizations, even though it has been mainly associated with Al-Qaeda.[80] In other words, the threat scenario is much more diffuse and abstract. Most experts therefore expect the 'war on terror' to last for many years, with Islamic fundamentalist terrorism remaining a menace of profound concern. An important question that now has to be asked is: What implications do these findings have for the interpretation of international human rights treaties, specifically in the context of derogations due to threats from international terrorism?

In most circumstances the existence of a 'public emergency threatening the life of the nation' is or will be claimed in relation to a threat. In consequence, there has to be an assessment of the risk of the execution of the threat, as well as its seriousness. This assessment has to be conducted on a case-by-case basis. Because the terrorist threat is usually 'international' and nonspecific, the government's burden of justification in respect of the existence of a 'public emergency' is particularly high. In addition, the margin of appreciation granted to individual states in assessing the existence of a 'public emergency' and the proportionality of response-measures need to be reconsidered and adjusted. The more global and nonspecific the threat, the lesser the amount of discretion left to the state. As the threat of international terrorism is global, national authorities are not necessarily in a better position to decide on the imminence of a 'public emergency'. Quite the opposite, other countries might even have superior intelligence on specific terrorist threats. Consequently, reactions and perceptions of other states have also to be taken into account. As far as the threat level in European countries is concerned, it is significant that an overwhelming majority of Council of Europe states have not regarded the actual terrorist threat to be of sufficient gravity to meet the 'public emergency' criteria and found enough flexibility in the convention standards to accommodate any special provisions for counterterrorist purposes. Besides, in its Resolution 1271 (2002), the Parliamentary Assembly of the Council of Europe called upon all member states '*not* to provide for any derogation to the European Convention of Human Rights' and to 'refrain from using its Article 15 to limit rights and liberties guaranteed under its Article 5 (right to liberty and security)'.[81] This can be seen as an indication that, at present, the threat from international terrorism in Europe should not be considered constituting an Article 15 emergency.

United Kingdom

The Existence of a 'Public Emergency'
At the time of writing there have been no terrorist incidents directly attributed to Islamic extremism in the United Kingdom or anywhere else in Europe.[82] Terrorist attacks believed to have been conducted by Al-Qaeda took place in Kenya, Tanzania, Yemen, Saudi Arabia, Tunisia, and, on 11 September 2001, in the United States. In consequence, the current situation is completely different to the United Kingdom's position in Northern Ireland, which the European Court of Human Rights found to constitute an Article 15 ECHR 'public emergency'. Between 1972 and 1992, over 40,000 terrorist incidents related to the Northern Ireland conflict caused approximately 3,000 deaths and injured thousands more.[83] This level of atrocity is clearly

on a much greater scale than the international terrorism which has afflicted the United Kingdom since 9/11. Terrorism at that time was occurring on a regular basis over a long period of time directly affecting the day-to-day lives of British citizens and creating a certain kind of general panic. Although it may be said that there is real concern among the population regarding acts of international terrorism, the level of public anxiety is in no way comparable to the fear caused by Northern Ireland–related terrorist incidents. Moreover, those terrorist activities were directly connected to the affairs of the British government. In contrast, Islamic extremist terrorism, for the most part, finds its roots in the Israeli-Palestinian conflict and American military presence in the Arab world.[84] Apparently recognizing these fundamental differences, the United Kingdom's claim of the existence of an Article 15 ECHR emergency is not based on the actual existence of a 'public emergency' but rather on imminent threats from international terrorism. As the 'public emergency' is being claimed in relation to a threat, the United Kingdom bears a heavy burden to establish that it is facing the risk of an immediate execution of this threat. Yet, home secretary David Blunkett and several other government officials stated repeatedly on a number of occasions that there was 'no immediate intelligence pointing to a specific threat to the United Kingdom'.[85] If the threat is neither immediate nor specific, then how can there be a 'public emergency threatening the life of the nation'?

The British claim of the existence of a 'public emergency' rests mainly on the assumption that as a result of its strong support for the United States and Israel – even before the war in Iraq – the United Kingdom has become a potential target. However, in its submission to the Council of Europe, the United Kingdom did not explain why it should be more affected than other major European countries, which are also close allies of the United States. Given the exceptionality of measures, and the fundamental importance of Article 5 ECHR (right of liberty and security), such clarification would have been necessary. In the absence of sufficient explanation, it remains questionable whether there is a 'public emergency' within the terms of Article 15 ECHR existing at this time. It is also significant that the Human Rights Committee, in its concluding observations dated 2 November 2001 following the examination of the United Kingdom's fifth periodic report on the implementation of the ICCPR, expressed 'concern' about the British government's proposals to derogate.[86]

Nonetheless, in *A and others v. Secretary of State for the Home Department*, SIAC held on 30 July 2002 that the United Kingdom government was 'entitled to form the view that there was and still is a public emergency threatening the life of the nation and that the detention of those reasonably suspected to be international terrorists involved with or with organisations linked to Al Qa'ida is strictly required by the exigencies of the situation'.[87] On this issue, the Court of Appeal upheld the judgment on 25 October 2002. However, apart from the general finding that 'no other European nation is threatened in quite the same way' neither SIAC nor the Court of Appeal explained why the United Kingdom should be distinguished from its neighbours.

The Proclamation of a 'Public Emergency'
A state party derogating from the convention or covenant must issue the proclamation of 'public emergency' in good faith.[88] Equally, restoration of a state of normalcy where full respect for the international instruments can again be secured must be the predominant objective of derogation.[89] On 12 November 2001, home

secretary David Blunkett publicly declared a 'state of emergency'. At the same time, Blunkett told the *Guardian* that the declaration was *not* a response to any imminent terrorist threat, but rather a 'legal technicality', necessary to ensure that certain anti-terrorism measures that contravene the ECHR could be implemented.[90] Moreover, in a statement to Parliament on 15 October 2001, Blunkett said that there was 'no immediate intelligence pointing to a specific threat to the United Kingdom'. The home secretary's public pronouncements therefore raise grave concerns that the United Kingdom sought to derogate from its international human rights obligations in the absence of conditions qualifying as a *bona fide* state of emergency.[91]

Proportionality: 'To the Extent Strictly Required'
Doubts also arise as to whether British measures are 'strictly required by the exigencies of the situation'.[92] First, it is generally questionable whether powers contained in sections 21–23 ATCSA are strictly necessary. In *Aksoy v. Turkey* the European Court of Human Rights found that not even the undoubted 'public emergency' in southeast Turkey could justify the detention of the applicant for fourteen days, without sufficient judicial control, on suspicion of involvement in terrorist offences.[93] In the light of the *Aksoy* decision it is difficult to ascertain how *indefinite* detention of suspected international terrorists can be 'strictly required', even in circumstances that amount to an Article 15 emergency. Moreover, the United Kingdom government has not established why actions taken under existing laws and in conformity with international human rights obligations are not sufficient to meet the terrorist threat. The Terrorism Act 2000, for instance, provides extensive powers for the arrest and prosecution of those reasonably suspected of being involved in terrorism. In particular, s. 41(1) of the Terrorism Act states that 'a constable may arrest without a warrant a person whom he reasonably suspects to be a terrorist'.

Second, the principle of proportionality requires the government to demonstrate that the measures impair the right at issue, in this case, the right to liberty and security, as little as reasonably possible in order to achieve the legislative objective. The ATCSA's purpose is to protect the United Kingdom from acts of international terrorism. Central to the introduction of the act is the assumption that the United Kingdom could be subject to an attack of the magnitude of the 9/11 atrocities. The 9/11 attacks on the United States are believed to have been carried out by Al-Qaeda, the only international terrorist organisation at the time considered to be capable of conducting large-scale terrorist operations. Indeed, the British government found that 'no other organisation has both the motivation and the capability to carry out attacks like those of the 11 September – only the Al Qaida network under Osama bin Laden'.[94] The claim of the existence of a 'public emergency' is consequently dependant on the threat posed by the Al-Qaeda network. However, sections 21–23 ATCSA do not only apply to suspected terrorists associated with the Al-Qaeda group, but to all international terrorists, whether they threaten national security of the United Kingdom or other states altogether.[95] In other words, ATCSA provisions facilitate, for instance, indefinite detention of suspected Tamil Tigers or operatives from the Kurdish PKK and covers even persons that only have 'links' to the aforementioned organisations.[96] The scope of detention powers therefore goes well beyond what could be reasonably considered as 'strictly required by the exigencies of the situation'.

Third, as only the Al-Qaeda network has the 'motivation and capability' to pose a threat to the security of the United Kingdom which is constituting an Article 15 emergency, the government bears the burden to establish evidence for the continuing operational effectiveness of the terrorist organisation. A failure to do so would result in current measures being no longer strictly required by the exigencies of the situation. After an allegedly successful military campaign in Afghanistan, the detention of several Al-Qaeda fighters in Guantanamo Bay and the capture of the suspected mastermind of the 9/11 attacks in Pakistan in February 2003, Cofer Black, a long-time CIA terrorism official and now head of the State Department's counterterrrorism office, described the Al-Qaeda leadership's losses as 'catastrophic' and pointed out that the broader network 'has been unable to withstand the global onslaught' of counterterrorism operations.[97] President George W. Bush, in a speech on 1 May 2003, noted that 'about half of all the top Al-Qaeda operatives are either jailed or dead' and that 'in either case, they're not a problem anymore'.[98] The president's judgment might be overly optimistic, as it cannot be ruled out that terrorists associated with the Al-Qaeda network will conduct further attacks in the future. However, in the light of these statements and the allegedly successful counterterrorism operations, it seems questionable whether Al-Qaeda can nonetheless pose a threat to the United Kingdom which is so potentially serious that it requires extraordinary powers as set forth in ATCSA.[99]

Fourth, the ATCSA measures are disproportionate in the sense that they do not provide sufficient safeguards to avoid abuse of emergency powers. Detention orders are subject only to an appeal to SIAC rather than to a regular court of law. SIAC was originally instituted to hear appeals against immigration and deportation decisions that have been taken on national security grounds. It is not designed to deal with issues of indefinite detention.[100] Furthermore, SIAC proceedings lack fundamental guarantees of judicial procedure.[101] Given the fundamental importance of the right to liberty and security (Article 5 ECHR/Article 9 ICCPR), it is not strictly required by a public emergency allegedly caused by threats from international terrorism to deny suspected international terrorists basic judicial principles, such as the right to a fair hearing or trial.

Both the Court of Appeal and, to a lesser extent, SIAC were reluctant to exercise close scrutiny as to whether measures under the ATCSA were 'strictly required by the exigencies of the situation'. Referring to *Home Secretary v. Rehmann*[102] and *Brown v. Stott*,[103] the Court of Appeal held that 'decisions as to what is required in the interest of national security are self-evidently within the category of decisions in relation to which the court is required to show considerable deference to the Secretary of State because he is better qualified to make an assessment as to what action is called for'.[104] While it appears that the court uses the deference to the home secretary's decision as substitute for coherent legal analysis of the issues at stake, this finding is also inconsistent with European case law. Although granting a certain margin of appreciation to governments, the European Court of Human Rights expressly stated that this does not mean that national authorities could be 'free from effective control by the domestic courts whenever they choose to assert that national security and terrorism are involved'.[105] This implies that the amount of discretion, which is left to the executive by a domestic court, is much lesser than the discretion that is granted by the European Court.

Consistency and Nondiscrimination
As indicated, derogation measures must fulfil the requirements of consistency and nondiscrimination. The United Kingdom has derogated from Article 5(1) ECHR

and Article 9(1) ICCPR only. However, as British derogation measures also breach Article 5(4) ECHR,[106] they lack required consistency with other obligations under international law.

Furthermore, the derogation measures do not fulfil the requirement of nondiscrimination. Sections 21–23 ATCSA apply only to persons subject to immigration control under the Immigration Act 1971. They do not apply to British citizens. These arrangements may be inconsistent with the requirement of nondiscrimination as set forth in Article 14 ECHR and Article 4(1) ICCPR. While not explicitly mentioned in Article 4(1) ICCPR or Article 15(1), it has long been recognized in the international law of human rights that, in the absence of war, disparate treatment on the grounds of national origin may be incompatible with the nondiscrimination provisions.[107]

Not all differences of treatment are considered to be discriminatory. In *Belgian Linguistics* the European Court of Human Rights held that only those differences in treatment are discriminatory for which the state could not give a 'reasonable and objective' justification.[108] Nonetheless, the burden of justification is particularly high if certain grounds of discrimination are relied upon such as race, sex, nationality and illegitimacy. This was confirmed in *Gaygusuz v. Austria*, where the court held that differences in treatment on the grounds of nationality require very weighty justification.[109] In the present case, the United Kingdom government needs to establish that treating British nationals differently from aliens is reasonably and objectively justified. A distinction would be reasonably and objectively justified if the terrorist threat to the United Kingdom exclusively originates from the alien section of the population. However, the threat is not so confined. Hundreds of British nationals attended Al-Qaeda training camps in Afghanistan.[110] Indeed, would-be shoe bomber Richard Reid holds British citizenship.[111] In these circumstances it is difficult to ascertain how the United Kingdom derogation can be regarded as other than discriminatory on the grounds of national origin.

While the violation of the principle of nondiscrimination was confirmed by the SIAC judgment in *A and others v. Secretary of State for the Home Department*, the Court of Appeal has reached a different conclusion on the basis that British nationals are not in an analogous situation to foreign nationals who currently cannot be deported because of fears for their safety.[112] 'Such foreign nationals do not have the right to remain in the United Kingdom but only a right not to be removed'. However, this difference in legal status is neither relevant nor reasonably justifiable as the threat from acts of international terrorism stems from British nationals and aliens alike. Given that the threat is neutral as to nationality, the legal distinction between the statuses of the two groups bears no connection to the justification for detention. In consequence, the difference in legal status is not sufficient to meet the requirement of 'very weighty justification'.

Summing up, the United Kingdom's derogation from the ECHR and ICCPR is unlawful. The existence of a 'public emergency' remains questionable and its proclamation was not made in good faith. Moreover, the derogation measures lack any proportionality, and do not fulfil the requirements of consistency and nondiscrimination.

Australia

The Existence of a 'Public Emergency'
Much of what has been said in relation to the existence of a 'public emergency' in the United Kingdom is applicable to the situation in Australia. To this date there has not

been any terrorist incident on Australian soil. Nor, indeed, has Al-Qaeda even been identified unambiguously as the perpetrator of the attacks on the United States. Responding to a series of questions from members of the Senate's Legal and Constitutional Legislation Committee, ASIO confirmed in April 2002 that there was 'no known specific terrorist threat to Australia at present' and that there were a 'series of other countries more at risk of attack'.[113] Since April 2002, Canberra's unconditional support of American foreign policy and Australian involvement in the war on Iraq has undoubtedly increased Australia's profile as a terrorist target. Besides, the federal government's advice on 'how to spot a terrorist' and freely dispatched fridgemagnets containing emergency instructions for terrorist attacks are likely to have heightened public anxiety. Nevertheless, while Australia may be in a state of alert, the actuality or imminence of a 'public emergency' remains strongly questionable. In particular, it is hard to see why Australia should be more affected by international terrorism than major European countries such as the United Kingdom, Germany, France or Italy.[114]

Other Requirements for Derogation

At the time of writing, Australia has neither proclaimed the existence of a 'public emergency' nor notified the UN secretary-general about its intention to do so. According to ASIO there is currently 'no known specific terrorist threat to Australia'.[115] It is therefore doubtful whether any proclamation could be regarded as made in good faith. In addition, even if it is assumed that the present threat to Australia constitutes an Article 4 ICCPR 'public emergency', it is highly unlikely that the detention of non-suspects, authorized by a nonjudicial body for the mere purposes of intelligence gathering, is justifiable as 'strictly required by the exigencies of the situation'.

First, it is generally debatable whether the detention of non-suspects is essential in order to gather intelligence on terrorist activities. The government must demonstrate that the legislative objective of the ASIO Act, i.e., collecting intelligence that assists in the investigation of terrorism offences, cannot be achieved sufficiently by other means. To this date, Canberra has not established evidence that the collection of relevant intelligence is not achievable through other, less repressive, courses of action.

Second, as indicated, the ASIO Act allows for detention of non-suspects on the basis that such detention 'substantially assists the collection of intelligence material that is important to a terrorism offence'. The intelligence information sought does in no way have to have any connection to the terrorist activities and possible threats by the Al-Qaeda network. However, as the existence of the 'public emergency' is likely to be claimed on the grounds of imminent threats by Islamic fundamentalist terrorism, a specific reference to it would be indispensable. In consequence the scope of ASIO Act provisions is not strictly required by the exigencies of the situation.

Third, measures as introduced by the ASIO Act are disproportionate since they do not provide sufficient safeguards to avoid abuse of emergency powers. The detention of non-suspects is overseen by a nonjudicial body lacking necessary independence from the executive. The ASIO Act does not allow for adequate judicial review of measures that seriously curtail the fundamental right to liberty and security.

Finally, any Australian derogation from the ICCPR would lack consistency with other obligations under international law. As indicated, the ASIO Act provides for powers to detain children. These arrangements contravene essential provisions of the

UN Convention on the Rights of the Child.[116] In the light of these factors, Australia is not lawfully entitled to derogate from its international human rights obligations under the ICCPR.

Conclusion

One of America's founding fathers, Benjamin Franklin, warned in 1759 that 'they that can give up essential liberty to obtain a little temporary safety neither deserve liberty nor safety'.[117] Ironically, the United Kingdom and Australia gave up essential liberty without being able to obtain even temporary safety. It has been no part of the argument presented in this article that governments should be denied powers they genuinely need to defend our liberal democratic way of life against the scourge of international terrorism. But these powers need to strike a proper balance between the vital needs of the state and the liberty of its citizens, between national security necessities and international human rights obligations.

The British Anit-terrorism, Crime and Security Act 2001 and the Australian Security Intelligence Organisation Legislation Amendment (Terrorism) Act 2002 (Cth) have not come close to accomplishing this delicate task. In particular, various provisions of both pieces of legislation raise serious concerns in relation to the United Kingdom's and Australia's legal commitments under the European Convention on Human Rights and the International Covenant on Civil and Political Rights respectively. As a consequence, the British government submitted derogation from both treaties. However, for a number of reasons the legal validity of this derogation remains problematic. First, even granted a wide margin of appreciation, the United Kingdom has not sufficiently established that it faces a 'public emergency threatening the life of the nation' within the meaning of Article 15(1) ECHR and Article 4(1) ICCPR. Second, serious doubts arise as to whether the proclamation of the 'public emergency' has been made in good faith. Third, indefinite detention of suspected international terrorists regardless of whether or not they have links with the Al-Qaeda network could hardly be regarded as strictly required by the exigencies of the situation–in particular, as persons detained under ATCSA provisions do not have access to regular judicial review. Finally, measures as introduced by the legislation violate the principle of nondiscrimination. The United Kingdom government has failed to give a reasonable and objective justification for differently treating British nationals and aliens.

In contrast to the United Kingdom, Australia has not officially proclaimed derogation yet, and, indeed, it is highly doubtful that current circumstances would allow for derogation from the ICCPR. First, it is difficult to see how there can be a 'public emergency' in the terms of Article 4(1) ICCPR existing in Australia at this time. Second, proposed measures arguably fail to fulfil the further requirements of lawful derogation. The detention of non-suspects authorized by a nonjudicial body for the mere purpose of questioning goes well beyond what is strictly required to defend Australia from acts of international terrorism. In addition, several passages of the ASIO Act are not only inconsistent with ICCPR provisions but also with Australia's other obligations under international law, specifically with the UN Convention on the Rights of the Child.

Speaking to the Australian Law Council one month after the 9/11 attacks, Australian high court justice Michael Kirby rightly warned that 'every erosion of liberty must be thoroughly justified. Sometimes it is wise to pause. Always it is wise to keep our sense of proportion and to remember our civic traditions as the High Court Justices did in the *Communist Party Case* of 1951'.[118] Such restraint at the height of the Cold War and in the 'golden age'[119] of Soviet espionage should have served as an example today, both in the United Kingdom and Australia.

Notes

1. UNSC Res. 1368, 12 Sept. 2001, UN Doc. S/Res/1368 (2001) and UNSC Res. 1373, 28 Sept. 2001, UN Doc. S/Res/1373 (2001).
2. Paul Wilkinson, *Terrorism and the Liberal State* (New York: New York University Press, 1986) p.125–36; Grant Wardlaw, *Political Terrorism: Theory, Tactics, and Counter-measures* (Cambridge: Cambridge University Press, 1982) p.63–75; Peter Chalk, 'The Response to Terrorism as a Threat to Liberal Democracy,' *Australian Journal of Politics and History* Vol.44, No.3 (1998) p.373–77.
3. Wilkinson, (note 2) p.125. Moreover, several scholars argued that an ability to deal with terrorism in a way that is widely held to be in conformity with established political and judicial principles will, in actuality, strengthen the commitment to uphold democratic institutions and, thus, further isolate and weaken those who seek to destroy them. See e.g., Peter Chalk, 'The Liberal Democratic Response to Terrorism,' *Terrorism and Political Violence* vol. 7, No. 4 (winter 1995) p.10.
4. UN GA Res. 54/164 'Human Rights and Terrorism' 17 Dec. 1999, UN Doc. A/RES/54/164 (1999) (emphasis added).
5. Relevant legislation includes the Terrorism Act 2000, the Immigration Act 1971, the Extradition Act 1989, the Taking of Hostages Act 1982, the Customs and Exercise Management Act 1979 and the Export of Goods (Control) Order 1994.
6. The act received royal assent on 14 Dec. 2001. The full text version and other related information can be found at http://www.hmso.gov.uk/acts/acts2001/20010024.htm
7. Adam Tomkins, 'Legislating against Terror: The Anti-terrorism, Crime and Security Act 2001', *Public Law* (Summer 2002) p.205. See also Rhiannon Talbot, 'The Balancing Act: Counterterrorism and Civil Liberties in British Anti-terrorism Law', in John Strawson (ed), *Law After Ground Zero* (2002) p.123–32. Talbot, however, examines British counterterrorism legislation from a civil liberties angle rather than from the international human rights perspective.
8. For a good summary of the principal changes made by the act, see http://www.homeoffice.gov.uk/oicd/antiterrorism/atcsa.htm.
9. According to s. 21 (3) a group is an international terrorist group for the purposes of subsection (2)(b) and (c) if: (a) it is subject to the control or influence of persons outside the United Kingdom, and (b) the secretary of state suspects that it is concerned in the commission, preparation or instigation of acts of international terrorism. S. 21 (4) states that for the purposes of subsection (2)(c) a person has links with an international terrorist group only if he supports or assists it.
10. For the Terrorism Act 2000, see http://www.hmso.gov.uk/acts/acts2000/20000011.htm. Section 1 reads:

1. In this Act 'terrorism' means the use or threat of action where:

   (a) the action falls within subsection (2),
   (b) the use or threat is designed to influence the government or to intimidate the public or a section of the public, and
   (c) the use or threat is made for the purpose of advancing a political, religious or ideological cause.

2. Action falls within this subsection if it:

   (a) involves serious violence against a person,
   (b) involves serious damage to property,
   (c) endangers a person's life, other than that of the person committing the action,

(d) creates a serious risk to the health or safety of the public or a section of the public, or

(e) is designed seriously to interfere with or seriously to disrupt an electronic system.

3. The use or threat of action falling within subsection (2) which involves the use of firearms or explosives is terrorism whether or not subsection (1)(b) is satisfied.

4. In this section:

(a) 'action' includes action outside the United Kingdom,

(b) a reference to any person or to property is a reference to any person, or to property, wherever situated,

(c) a reference to the public includes a reference to the public of a country other than the United Kingdom, and

(d) 'the government' means the government of the United Kingdom, of a Part of the United Kingdom or of a country other than the United Kingdom.

5. In this Act a reference to action taken for the purposes of terrorism includes a reference to action taken for the benefit of a proscribed organisation.

11. Examples for a 'point of law' preventing removal include other international obligations such as Article 3 ECHR (see note 13). An example for 'practical consideration' would be the absence of relevant travel documents.

12. The author acknowledges that the ATCSA provisions also breach obligations under the ICCPR, specifically Article 9(4). Although there are slight differences in the wording of Article 5 ECHR and Article 9 ICCPR, the provisions are similar. As Article 9(4) ICCPR will be subject to an in-depth analysis in the Australian context, focus here is on Article 5 ECHR only.

13. The paradigm example for removal from the United Kingdom being prevented by a 'point of law' is the case where such removal would expose the person to the risk of torture, or of inhuman or degrading treatment (Article 3 EHCR). See *Chahal v. United Kingdom*, (1996) 23 EHCR 413.

14. In *Chahal v. United Kingdom* the European Court of Human Rights held that 'any deprivation of liberty under Article 5 (1)(f) will be justified only for as long as deportation proceedings are in progress. If such proceedings are not prosecuted with due diligence, the detention will cease to be permissible'. *Chahal v. United Kingdom*, (1996) 23 EHHR 413 para.113.

15. In particular, s. 23 ATCSA does not fall under the exeption of Article 5(1)(c) ECHR.

16. Patrick Wintour, 'Blunkett Rejects "Airy Fairy" fears', *The Guardian* 12 Nov. 2001.

17. Human Rights Act 1998, (Designated Derogation) Order 2001, No. 3644. The relevant passage reads: 'There exists a terrorist threat to the United Kingdom from persons suspected of involvement in international terrorism. In particular, there are foreign nationals present in the United Kingdom who are suspected of being concerned in the commission, preparation or instigation of acts of international terrorism, of being members of organizations or groups which are so concerned or having links with members of such organizations or groups, and who are a threat to the national security of the United Kingdom. As a result, a public emergency, within the meaning of Article 15 (1) of the Convention, exists in the United Kingdom'.

18. The United Kingdom also notified the UN secretary-general of its Article 4(1) ICCPR derogation from Article 9(1) ICCPR.

19. SIAC was established by the Special Immigration Appeals Commission Act 1997 to hear appeals against immigration and deportation decisions that have been taken on national security grounds.

20. It seems worthy to note, however, that a cancellation does not prevent the secretary of state from issuing a new certificate, 'whether on the grounds of a change of circumstance or otherwise' (s. 27(9)).

21. X *v. United Kingdom*, (1981) ECHR Applic. No. 7215/75 para.53.

22. See e.g., *Singh v. United Kingdom, Hussain v. United Kingdom*, (1996) 22 EHRR 1.

23. *Bouamar v. Belgium*, (1987) 11 EHRR 1.

24. *Sanchez-Reisse v. Switzerland*, (1986) 9 EHRR 71; *Lamy v. Belgium*, (1989) 15 EHRR 529. See also *Toth v. Austria*, (1991) 14 EHRR 551; *Kampanis v. Greece*, (1995) 21 EHRR 43.

25. Special Immigration Appeals Commission Act 1997, s. 6.

26. Except in the Northern Territory, see Criminal Code Act (NT), Part III Div. 2.

27. These five bills include the Security Legislation Amendment (Terrorism) Bill 2002 (No. 2), Suppression of the Financing of Terrorism Bill 2002, Criminal Code Amendment (Suppression of Terrorist Bombings) Bill 2002, Border Security Legislation Amendment Bill 2002, Telecommunications Interception Legislation Amendment Bill 2002.

28. The bill introduced a definition of 'terrorist act' into federal law and contains criminal sanctions for involvement with a terrorist organisation, including for providing support or funding, recruiting members, directing its activities or being a member. According to s. 102.1 a terrorist organisation is 'an organisation that is directly or indirectly engaged in preparing, planning, assisting in or fostering the doing of a terrorist act (whether or not the terrorist act occurs)'.

29. The ASIO Bill, as read a third time, is available at http://zem.squidly.org/cache/asio-11100200.pdf. For the bill, as read a first time, see http://www.aph.gov.au/house/committee/pjcaad/TerrorBill2002/terrorism2002.pdf. For the revised version of 20 March 2003, see http://parlinfoweb.aph.gov.au/piweb/Repository/Legis/Bills/Linked/17040301.pdf.

30. General Daryl Williams, quoted in Mark Forbes, 'Deadlock on ASIO Bill', *The Age* 13 Dec. 2002. See also Daryl Williams, 'How the Anti-Terrorism Laws Assure Security and Freedom', *The Age* 11 June 2002 (emphasis added).

31. George Williams, 'Why the ASIO Bill is Rotten to the Core', *The Age* 27 Aug. 2002. For a critical examination of Australian antiterrorism legislation see also George Williams, 'One Year On – Australia's Legal Response to September 11', *Alternative Law Journal* vol. 27, No. 5 (2002) p.212; Joo-Cheong Tham, 'ASIO and the Rule of Law', *Alternative Law Journal*, vol. 27, No. 5 (2002) p.216.

32. Attorney-General, Stronger Tools for ASIO to Combat Terrorism, http://national security.ag.gov.au

33. According to Section 34B of the ASIO Act, the 'prescribed authority' is either the deputy president or a senior member or member of the Administrative Appeals Tribunal (AAT) who has been enrolled as a legal practitioner for at least five years.

34. Australia signed the ICCPR on 18 Dec. 1972 and ratified it on 13 Aug. 1980.

35. Manfred Nowak, UN Covenant on Civil and Political Rights: Commentary (Kehl, N.P. Engel, 1993), p.178.

36. *Van Alphen v. The Netherlands*, (1990) HRC Comm. No. 305/1988, UN Doc. A/45/40 para.5.8 (emphasis added). See also *A v. Australia*, (1997) HRC Comm. No. 560/1993 para9.2.

37. 'Australia Will Be Terrorist Target for Years: ASIO', *The Age* 19 April 2002.

38. Ibid.

39. C-36 (An Act to Amend the Criminal Code, the Official Secrets Act, the Canada Evidence Act, the Proceeds of Crime (Money Laundering) Act and Other Acts, and to Enact Measures Respecting the Registration of Charities, in Order to Combat Terrorism), s. 83.28 (1) and s. 83.28 (11). Available at http://www.parl.gc.ca/37/1/parlbus/chambus/house/bills/government/C-36/C-36_4/C-36TOCE.html

40. HRC General Comment 8 (1982) para.2.

41. *Freemantle v. Jamaica*, (1998) HRC Comm. No. 625/1995.

42. *Brogan v. United Kingdom*, (1988) ECHR Applic. No. 11209/84.

43. See above note 33 and accompanying text.

44. See above notes 20–25 and accompanying text.

45. *Chahal v. United Kingdom*, (1996) 23 EHRR 413 para.131.

46. The ASIO Bill may also violate Article 17(1) ICCPR which provides that 'no one shall be subject to arbitrary or unlawful interference with his privacy, family, home or correspondence, nor to unlawful attacks on his honour and reputation'. In *McVeigh, O'Neill and Evans v. United Kingdom* the European Commission of Human Rights found that the detention of suspected terrorists for forty five hours without access to their wives breached Article 8 ECHR, the equivalent to Article 17 ICCPR in the European Convention. *McVeigh, O'Neill and Evans v. United Kingdom*, (1980) 5 EHRR 71.

47. For 'strict liability', see s. 6.1 of the Criminal Code.

48. *Saunders v. United Kingdom*, (1996) 23 EHRR 313.

49. HRC General Comment 13 (1984) para.14 (emphasis added).

50. Emphasis added. The UN Convention on the Rights of the Child (CROC) is available at http://www.unicef.org/crc/crc.htm

51. The bill may also breach Articles 2(2), 3(1) and 19(1) CROC. Article 2(2) provides that a child must not be discriminated against on the basis of the expressed opinions of their parents. Article 3 (1)1 provides that in all actions concerning children the best interests of the child shall be a primary consideration. Article 19(1) provides that the state must take all appropriate measures to protect the child from all forms of injury or abuse.

52. Accounts on emergency derogations in general include Rosalyn Higgins, 'Derogations under Human Rights Treaties', *British Yearbook of International Law* 48 (1976–77) p.281; Thomas Buergenthal, 'To Respect and Ensure: State Obligations and Permissible Derogations', in Louis Henkin (ed), *The International Bill of Rights: The Covenant on Civil and Political Rights* (New York: Columbia University Press, 1981) p.72–91; Joan F. Hartman, 'Working Paper for the Committee of Experts on the Article 4 Derogation Provision' *Human Rights Quarterly* vol. 7, No.1 (1985) p.89; David J. Harris, Michael O'Boyle and Chris Warbrick, *Law of the European Convention on Human Rights* (London: Butterwoth 1995) pp.489–507; Anna-Lena Svensson-McCarthy, *The International Law of Human Rights and States of Exception* (The Hague: M. Nijoff, 1998).

53. Article 15 ECHR reads:

1. In time of war or other public emergency threatening the life of the nation any High Contracting Party may take measures derogating from its obligations under this Convention to the extent strictly required by the exigencies of the situation, provided that such measures are not inconsistent with other obligations under international law.

2. No derogations from Article 2, except in respect of deaths resulting from lawful acts of war, or from Articles 3, 4 (paragraph 1) and 7 shall be made under this provision.

3. Any High Contracting Party availing itself of this right of derogation shall keep the Secretary General of the Council of Europe fully informed of the measures which it has taken and the reasons therefor. It shall also inform the Secretary General of the Council of Europe when such measures have ceased to operate and the provisions of the Convention are again being fully executed.

Article 4 ICCPR reads:

1. In time of public emergency which threatens the life of the nation and the existence of which is officially proclaimed, the States Parties to the present Convention may take measures derogating from their obligations under the present Covenant to the extent strictly required by the exigencies of the situation, provided that such measures are not inconsistent with their other obligations under international law and do not involve discrimination solely on the ground of race, colour, sex, language, religion or social origin.

2. No derogation from Articles 6, 7, 8 (paragraphs 1 and 2), 11, 15, 16 and 18 may be made under this provision.

3. Any State Party to the present Covenant availing itself of the right of derogation shall immediately inform the other State Parties to the present Covenant, through the intermediary of the Secretary-General of the United Nations, of the provisions from which it has derogated and of the reasons by which it was actuated. A further communication shall be made, through the same intermediary, on the date on which it terminates such derogation.

54. *Lawless v. Ireland*, *(No.3)* (1961) IEHRR 15.

55. Ibid. p.31.

56. *Greek* Case (1969) 12 *Yearbook* ECHR 1.

57. The relevant part reads: 'Une situation de crise ou de danger public exceptionnelle et *imminente* ... ' (emphasis added).

58. *Greek* Case (note 56) para.153.

59. Some members of the commission argued that when the organs of the state are functioning normally, there is no grave threat to the life of the nation, and therefore emergency measures are not legitimate. However, the majority in the commission did not follow this reasoning. In practice, both criteria (2) and (3) are generally applied in a rather relaxed way.

60. Evidence of these requirements being recognised as general legal standards in the process of determining the meaning of 'public emergency' can also be found in the Siracusa Principles on the Limitation and Derogation Provisions in the ICCPR, reproduced in *Human Rights Quarterly* vol. 7, No. 1 (1985) p.3. The Siracusa Principles were drafted by a group of thirty one distinguished experts in international law convened by a number of well-respected organisations such as the International Commission of Jurists. The conference was held in Siracusa, Italy in the Spring of 1984. In addition, these criteria are expressed in the International Law Association's (ILA) work on the issue, the Paris Minimum Standards of Human Rights Norms in a State of Emergency. For the ILA Paris Minimum Standards, see *American Journal of International Law* vol. 79, No. 4 (1985) p.1072.

61. HRC General Comment 29 (2001) para.154.

62. As Ronald St. J. Macdonald observed, it is the doctrine of margin of appreciation which allows the court to escape the dilemma of 'how to remain true to its responsibility to develop a reasonably comprehensive set of review principles appropriate for application across the entire Convention, while at the same time recognizing the diversity of political, economic, cultural and social situations in the societies of the Contracting Parties'. See Ronald St. J. Macdonald, 'The Margin of Appreciation', in Ronald St. J. Macdonald *et al.* (eds), *The European System for the Protection of Human Rights* (The Hague: M. Nijoff, 1993) pp.83–124.

63. See e.g., Daniel O'Donnell, 'The Margin of Appreciation Doctrine: Standards in the Jurisprudence of the European Court of Human Rights', *Human Rights Quarterly* 4 (1982) p.474.

64. *Ireland v. United Kingdom*, Series A No. 35 (1978) para.207 (emphasis added).

65. Ibid.

66. *Landinelli Silva v. Uruguay*, (1981) HRC Comm. No. 34/1978.

67. HRC General Comment 29, (2001) para.2. This requirement mainly seeks to reduce the incidence of the *de facto* states of emergency by obliging states to declare the emergency following the procedures of municipal law.

68. Nowak (note 35) p.80.

69. *Lawless v. Ireland*, (note 55) paras. 44–5.

70. Joan Fitzpatrick, *Human Rights in Crisis: The International System for Protecting Rights During States of Emergency* (Philadelphia: University of Pennsylvania Press, 1994) p.59.

71. A reference to a *bona fide* proclamation is also made in Siracusa Principle 66.

72. See Article 15(1) ECHR and Article 4(1) ICCPR.

73. See e.g., Marc-Andre Eissen, 'The Principle of Proportionality in the Case-Law of the European Court of Human Rights', in Ronald St. J. Macdonald *et al.* (eds), *The European System for the Protection of Human Rights* (1993) pp.125–37.

74. Ibid.

75. *Ireland v. United Kingdom* (note 64) para.207.

76. See Siracusa Principles 54 and 57.

77. See e.g., Jaime Oraa, *Human Rights in States of Emergency in International Law* (Oxford: Clarendon Press, 1992) p.178.

78. Ibid. pp.30–1.

79. Francis X. Taylor, Address to the Institute for National Strategic Studies, National Defense University, Washington DC, 23 Oct. 2002. Also available at http://www.state.gov/s/ct/rls/rm/14570pf.htm. (emphasis added).

80. The list of Islamic extremist terror organisations is both a long and an open one. It is also noteworthy that although the 9/11 attacks are considered to be initiated by Osama bin Laden, to this date neither Al-Qaeda nor any other terrorist group has officially claimed responsibility.

81. Parliamentary Assembly of the Council of Europe, 'Combating Terrorism and Respect for Human Rights', Res. 1271 (2002), paras. 9, 12. Also available at http://assembly.coe.int/Documents/AdoptedText/ta02/ERES1271.htm. (emphasis added).

82. The author acknowledges that European countries, particularly France, Germany (e.g., Munich Olympics, 1972) and the United Kingdom (e.g., Lockerbie crash of Pan Am 103, 1988) have been subject to attacks from terrorist groups with links to the Middle East. However, to this day, there have not been any attacks in Europe from Islamic fundamentalist terrorists commonly associated with Al-Qaeda.

83. Figures quoted by Adam Tomkins, 'Legislating against Terror: The Anti-terrorism, Crime and Security Act 2001', *Public Law* 205 (2002) pp.215–6.

84. See e.g., Rohan Gunaratna, *Inside Al Qaeda–Global Network of Terror* (New York: Columbia University Press, 2002); Yonah Alexander and Michael S. Swetnam, *Osama bin Laden's al-Qaida: Profile of a Terrorist Network* (Ardley, NJ: Transnational Publishers, 2001); Bruce Hoffman, *Inside Terrorism* (New York: Columbia University Press, 1998).

85. Wintour. The (note 16).

86. 'The Committee notes with concern that the State Party, in seeking inter alia to give effect to its obligations to combat terrorist activities pursuant to Resolution 1373 of the Security Council, is considering the adoption of legislative measures which may have potentially far-reaching effects on rights guaranteed in the Covenant, and which, in the State Party's view, may require derogations from human rights obligations. The State Party should ensure that any measures it undertakes in this regard are in full compliance with the provisions of the Covenant, including, when applicable, the provisions on derogation contained in Article 4 of the Covenant'.

87. SIAC judgment in *A and Others v. Secretary of State for the Home Department*, 30 July 2002, Appeal No. SC/1-7/2002.

88. See above notes 67–71 and accompanying text. As the British government notified the Council of Europe and the UN secretary-general about the derogation from the ECHR and ICCPR, the requirement of notification has been fulfilled and is not discussed here any futher.

89. HRC General Comment 29 (2001) para.1.

90. Wintour, (note 16).

91. Well-respected human rights lawyer David Pannick QC, in an opinion prepared for the National Council for Civil Liberties (Liberty), made the additional point that the derogation from Article 5(1) is prompted by concern about an inability to remove foreign nationals from the United Kingdom because of Article 3 ECHR. He was 'very doubtful' that it is a valid use of Article 15(1) to impose detriments on persons because they seek to take advantage of rights conferred by Article 3, especially when Article 15(2) prohibits any derogation from Article 3 itself because of its fundamental nature. For Pannick, it is strongly arguable that the home secretary is not seeking to derogate from Article 5(1) because of a public emergency threatening the life of the nation, but because Article 3 prevents him removing from the United Kingdom asylum-seekers who may face persecution abroad. See Joint Committee on Human Rights (2001–02) Fifth Report, HL 51, HC 420 (London: HMSO 2002) Appendix 5, para.6(5). Available at http://www.publications.parliament.uk/pa/jt200102/jtselect/jtrights/51/5102.htm.

92. It is significant to note that some of the measures, as a former home secretary admitted in the House of Lords, have been 'hanging around in the Home Office for a long time' waiting for a suitable legislative opportunity to arise. Quoted by A Tomkins (note 83) p.220.

93. *Aksoy v. Turkey*, (1996) ECHR Applic. No. 21987/93.

94. Quoted in Joint Committee on Human Rights (note 91) Appendix 3, para.10.

95. In *Home Secretary v. Rehman*, (2001) 3 WLR 877, it was held that 'action against a foreign state may be capable indirectly of affecting the security of the United Kingdom' and that 'the promotion of terrorism in a foreign country by a United Kingdom resident would be contrary to the interests of national security', at 884E and 894H.

96. For the Tamil Tiger example, see David Anderson QC and Jemima Stratford, Opinion Prepared for JUSTICE, Joint Committee on Human Rights (note 91) Appendix 3, para. 21–2.

97. Walter Pincus and Dana Priest, 'Spy Agencies' Optimism on Al Qaeda Is Growing', *Washington Post* 6 May 2003.

98. George W. Bush, quoted in Mark Hosenball and Michael Isikoff, 'Al Qaeda Strikes', *Newsweek*, 20 May 2003.

99. Terrorism experts believe that recent terrorist attacks in Riyadh and Morocco were 'probably not orchestrated by al Qaeda' and have 'little or no connection to Osama bin Laden'. The attacks are rather believed to have been carried out by local groups with antimonarchist motivations. See e.g., William O. Beeman, 'Saudi-Bombing – A Calculated Act With a Political Message', *Pacific News Service* 14 May 2003.

100. It is not without significance that a number of British MPs rejected extending SIAC powers to rule on appeals of detention orders. Replying to the home secretary's argument that MPs did not object to the creation of SIAC in 1997, one member of parliament pointed out that 'had MPs known that SIAC – a star chamber of an organisation, with draconian powers over evidence – was to be used as an appeals procedure, not for deportation but for the indefinite incarceration of people without charge or trial, MPs would not have voted for it'.See Bob Marshall-Andrews MP, A Fundamental Attack on Liberty Which Must Be Stopped, http://www.poptel.org.uk/scgn/articles/0112/page6d.htm

101. See above notes 20–25 and accompanying text.

102. *Home Secretary v. Rehman*, [2001] 3 WLR 877 at 897–7 (Lord Hoffman).

103. *Brown v. Stott*, [2001] 2 WLR 817 at 834–5 (Lord Bingham of Cornhill).

104. *A and Others v. Secretary of State for the Home Department*, [2002] EWCA Civ 1502 para.40 (Lord Woolf CJ).

105. *Chahal v. United Kingdom*, (1996) 23 EHRR 413 para.131.

106. See above notes 20–25 and accompanying text.

107. 'The Paris Minimum Standards of Human Rights Norms in a State of Emergency', *AJIL* 79 (1985) p. 1072, section B 2(d). As Colin Warbrick observed correctly, the list of prohibited grounds of discrimination is both a long one and an open one. Colin Warbrick, 'The Principles of the European Convention on Human Rights and the Response of States to Terrorism' *European Human Rights Law Review* vol. 3, No.3 (2002) p. 313–4.

108. *Belgian Linguistics, Case (No. 2)* (1962) 1 EHRR 252.

109. *Gaygusuz v. Austria*, (1997) 23 EHRR 365 para.42.

110. Peter Beaumont, 'Briton Held in US Camp as Al-Qaeda Prisoner', *Observer* 13 Jan. 2002. In addition, nine British citizens allegedly involved in terrorist activities were detained as a consequence of allied military action in Afghanistan. One of these detainees was recruited by a British preacher from a London mosque. See e.g., Richard Willing, 'London Mosque Called Central to Al-Qaeda Efforts', *USA Today* 30 Aug. 2002.

111. Richard Reid tried to blow up a transatlantic flight from Paris to Miami on 22 Dec. 2001 using explosives hidden in his sports shoes. See e.g., Gary Younge and Duncan Campbell, 'Shoe-Bomber Sentenced to Life in Prison', The *Guardian* 31 Jan. 2003.

112. *A and Others v. Secretary of State for the Home Department*, (2002 EWCA Civ 1502 paras. 45–56.

113. 'Australia Will Be Terrorist Target for Years: ASIO' (note 37).

114. An audiotaped message from Osama bin Laden in November 2002 warned of further terrorist attacks on countries 'allying themselves with America'. Although bin Laden referred to Australia as potential future target, Australia was mentioned only after Britain, France, Italy, Canada and Germany. See 'Official: Voice on Tape Is Bin Laden's', CNN News 13 Nov. 2002 http://www.cnn.com/2002/WORLD/meast/11/12/binladen.statement

115. see note 113.

116. See above notes 50–51 and accompanying text.

117. Benjamin Franklin, quoted in Emily Morrison Beck (ed), *Bartlett's Familiar Quotations: A Collection of Passages, Phrases, and Proverbs Traced to their Sources in Ancient and Modern Literature,* 15th edn., 125th edn., (London: McMillan, 1980) p.348.

118. Michael Kirby, Speech to the Law Council of Australia, Thirty-second Australian Legal Convention, 11 Oct. 2001. Available at http://www.hcourt.gov.au/speeches/kirbyj/kirbyj_after11sep01.htm.

10

Interesting Times for International Humanitarian Law: Challenges from the 'War on Terror'*

GABOR RONA

International Committee of the Red Cross

'May you live in interesting times' is reputed to be an old Chinese curse. To call a curse what at first blush appears to be a blessing is to emphasize the risks over the opportunities inherent in living in interesting times. These are, indeed, interesting times for international humanitarian law, otherwise known as the law of armed conflict.[1] Whether history will reward the pessimist or the optimist is, of course, uncertain. Still, there are some indications of how the pressures being brought to bear on humanitarian law by the war on terror will resolve. The aim of this article is to explore some of those indications and, if it is not too ambitious, to possibly influence the debate.

These are interesting times not only for humanitarian law, but also for international law in general. Recent events have generated renewed debate on the long-standing question: 'Is international law really law?' The unique position of the United States in world affairs today, coupled with its apparently unique positions on so many current issues affecting international law, has been cited as proof that power is, indeed, the constitution of international law.[2] The purpose of this observation is not to open debate on that loaded question, but only to point out that with regard to living in interesting times, humanitarian law is in good company.

The Accusation Against Humanitarian Law and the Reply

The question has been posed: Is humanitarian law passe, or at least stale and in need of revision – inadequate to deal with the demands of modern day terrorism and the efforts to combat it? Several analysts have attempted to make this case, attributing specific shortcomings to the law of armed conflict. Some of the criticisms merely misrepresent or misapply humanitarian law, while others correctly state its substance but fail to grasp the ramifications of suggested changes. The section of this article entitled 'In Defense of Humanitarian Law' addresses some of the most significant of these allegations and observations. The response to them requires familiarity not only with the substance, but also with the scope of application of humanitarian law in relation to other branches of relevant domestic and international law. The section of this article entitled 'The scope of Application of Humanitarian Law' addresses the scope of application criteria.

As concerns the scope of application, it must first be understood:

- that humanitarian law applies only in armed conflict;
- that other legal regimes such as domestic and international criminal and human rights law also apply, but only to a limited extent, during armed conflict;[3]
- that terrorism and the war on terror are sometimes manifested in armed conflict, other times not; and
- that there are good reasons involving the global balance between state and personal security, human rights and civil liberties for this division of legal labor between humanitarian law and other laws.

As for substance, the criticism of humanitarian law seems to come in two forms that are at once related and contradictory: that applicable law is lacking and that applicable law exists but is a hindrance. First, there is the complaint that humanitarian law has failed to keep up with the changing nature of armed conflict, always fighting the last war rather than the next one. Indeed, though the first Geneva Convention dates from 1864,[4] it was only in response to World War I, in which massive numbers of prisoners were subjected to unspeakable abuse, that the Geneva Convention for the protection of prisoners of war came into being. Likewise, there was no Geneva Convention for the protection of civilians in armed conflict until after World War II, in which civilians were the main victims and were subjected to mass extermination, indiscriminate attack, deportation and hostage-taking.

We may concede these facts. We may even concede that humanitarian law, as most recently codified in the Geneva Conventions of 1949[5] and their Additional Protocols of 1977,[6] does not *anticipate* armed conflict in the context of modern terrorism (that is, between a state and one or more transnational armed groups). But to conclude that humanitarian law cannot *accommodate* terrorism and the efforts to combat it when these phenomena amount to armed conflict (the very circumstance that humanitarian law is meant to address) would be wrong.

A second criticism suggests that existing law is a hindrance and proposes that when law and material reality collide, it is law that must give way.[7] This attractive observation must be parsed. It implies that existing law has been 'overtaken' by facts on the ground and, therefore, must be revoked or ignored. But law does not give way only because it is overwhelmed by the frequency or intractability of violations. Were that the case, everything from illicit drug use to tax evasion to (some might argue) murder would be decriminalized. Rather, it is the shift from opprobrium to acceptance that places prohibitions at risk. Violations may be frequent – even rampant – but the burden remains on those who challenge the wisdom and sufficiency of existing norms to prove their obsolescence.

Let us also bear in mind that the 'collision course' between law and material reality takes place on a two-way street. Law can be said to give way either when it is moving from prohibition to permission, or vice versa. To fill a legal void when conduct shifts from tolerated to intolerable (whether it is reducing the blood-alcohol level at which driving becomes a crime or defining the crime of genocide) is also a form of collision.

While there has been plenty of rhetoric suggesting the inadequacies of humanitarian law in the context of terrorism, I hope to show that existing norms of humanitarian law are appropriate and sufficient when the war on terror amounts to armed conflict and that the material reality of the war on terror has not collided with humanitarian law.

Returning to the scope of application question, I hope also to show that it is both correct and good that humanitarian law does not accommodate terrorism and the war on terror when those phenomena *do not* amount to armed conflict. Why is this a good thing? The reasons for respecting the existing limits of application of humanitarian law become clear upon a closer look at its function and substance.

The aims of humanitarian law are humanitarian, namely, to minimize unnecessary suffering by regulating the conduct of hostilities and the treatment of persons in the power of the enemy. But humanitarian law is a compromise. In return for these protections, humanitarian law elevates the essence of war – killing and detaining people without trial – into a right, if only for persons designated as 'privileged combatants', such as soldiers in an army. Those who take part in hostilities without such a privilege are criminals subject to prosecution and punishment, but they do not thereby forfeit whatever rights they may enjoy under humanitarian, human rights or criminal law. Therefore, fiddling with the boundaries or, more accurately, with the overlap between humanitarian law and other legal regimes can have profound, long-term and decidedly 'un-humanitarian' consequences on the delicate balance between state and personal security, human rights and civil liberties.[8]

In short, humanitarian law is quite at home with the war on terror when it amounts to armed conflict. When the war on terror does not meet the criteria for armed conflict, it is not that humanitarian law is inadequate, but rather that its application is inappropriate.

The Scope of Application of Humanitarian Law

What is the scope of application of humanitarian law to the war on terror? There is no evidence of any *lex specialis*[9] for wars on terror within the *lex specialis* of humanitarian law. That is, no rule of conventional (i.e., treaty based) or customary international law addresses the conditions of application of humanitarian law, especially with respect to the war on terror. Humanitarian law applies, as a general matter, when the Geneva Conventions (GCs) and their Additional Protocols (APs) say it applies, namely, in the event of armed conflict.[10] The conventions and protocols cover and distinguish between two categories of armed conflict: international armed conflict and internal, or non-international, armed conflict.[11]

The International Humanitarian Law of International Armed Conflict

The rules of humanitarian law applicable to international armed conflict are contained in the four Geneva Conventions (GCs I-IV) of 1949 and their Additional Protocol I (AP I) of 1977. The scope of application of these rules is found in Common Article 2 (CA 2) to the four GCs.[12] The International Committee of the Red Cross (ICRC) Commentary[13] to CA 2 further clarifies that 'any difference arising between two States and leading to the intervention of armed forces ... is an armed conflict within the meaning of Article 2, even if one of the Parties denies the existence of a state of war. It makes no difference how long the conflict lasts, or how much slaughter takes place'.[14]

An international armed conflict is one in which two or more states are parties to the conflict. Armed conflicts that fall outside of this category are those in which a state is engaged in conflict with a transnational armed group whose actions cannot be attributed to a state. To avoid confusion with a term whose use connotes state action, it would be better to speak of this type of armed conflict as 'interstate' or 'transnational' rather than 'international'.

The International Humanitarian Law of Non-International Armed Conflict

Non-international armed conflict has historically been thought of as involving rebels within a state against the state or against other rebels. The rules applicable to non-international armed conflict are found in Common Article 3 (CA 3)[15] to the GCs and in AP II. The scope of application of these rules is also found in CA 3 and in Article 1 of AP II.[16] The ICRC Commentary to Article 3 provides the following negotiating history of criteria to determine the scope of application. These were rejected from the final text, but are deemed by the Commentary to remain relevant to determining the existence of a non-international armed conflict:

> What is meant by 'armed conflict not of an international character'? . . . It was suggested that the term 'conflict' should be defined or, which would come to the same thing, that a certain number of conditions for the application of the Convention should be enumerated. The idea was finally abandoned – wisely, we think. Nevertheless, these different conditions, although in no way obligatory, constitute convenient criteria, and we therefore think it well to give a list of those contained in the various amendments discussed; they are as follows:

1. That the Party in revolt against the de jure Government possesses an organized military force, an authority responsible for its acts, acting within a determinate territory and having the means of respecting and ensuring respect for the Convention.
2. That the legal Government is obliged to have recourse to the regular military forces against insurgents organized as military and in possession of a part of the national territory.
3. (a) That the de jure Government has recognized the insurgents as belligerents; or
   (b) that it has claimed for itself the rights of a belligerent; or
   (c) that it has accorded the insurgents recognition as belligerents for the purpose only of the present Convention; or
   (d) that the dispute has been admitted to the agenda of the Security Council or the General Assembly of the United Nations as being a threat to international peace, a breach of the peace, or an act of aggression.
4. (a) That the insurgents have an organization purporting to have the characteristics of a State.
   (b) that the insurgent civil authority exercises de facto authority over persons within determinate territory.
   (c) that the armed forces act under the direction of the organized civil authority and are prepared to observe the ordinary laws of war.   (d) that the insurgent civil authority agrees to be bound by the provisions of the Convention.

> The above criteria are useful as a means of distinguishing a genuine armed conflict from a mere act of banditry or an unorganized and short-lived insurrection. Does this mean that Article 3 is not applicable

in cases where armed strife breaks out in a country, but does not fulfill any of the above conditions (which are not obligatory and are only mentioned as an indication)? We do not subscribe to this view.[17]

While application of the international humanitarian law of non-international armed conflict to the war on terror cannot be ruled out, it is, admittedly, not an elegant fit. We can dismiss AP II from having any bearing on terrorist acts or on the war on terror because its application requires control of the high contracting party's territory by an organized armed group (Article 1.1). If the state that is a party to the conflict is not a party to AP II (for example, the United States), or if the organized armed group controls no territory, then AP II does not apply.

Application of CA 3, on the other hand, does not require territorial control. What is more, the GCs enjoy virtually universal adherence. Still, humanitarian law cannot be applied to any situation until the following criteria are addressed.

Specific Criteria Applicable to Non-International Armed Conflict

The following criteria apply to all determinations of armed conflict, but are described below with specific reference to the law of non-international armed conflict.

Identification of Parties (Ratione Personae)

The essential humanitarian function of humanitarian law is carried out through the parties to the conflict. They have rights and responsibilities. There can be no humanitarian law conflict without identifiable parties.

'Terror' or 'terrorism' cannot be a party to the conflict. As a result, a war on terror cannot be a humanitarian law event. It has been suggested that wars against proper nouns (e.g., Germany and Japan) have advantages over those against common nouns (e.g., crime, poverty, terrorism), since proper nouns can surrender and promise not to do it again. Humanitarian law is not concerned with the entitlement to engage in hostilities or the promise not to do so again (the '*jus ad bellum*'). Rather, it concerns the conduct of hostilities and the treatment of persons in the power of the enemy (the '*jus in bello*'). But there is still a strong connection to humanitarian law in this observation. The concept of a 'party' suggests a minimum level of organization required to enable the entity to carry out the obligations of law.[18] There can be no assessment of rights and responsibilities under humanitarian law in a war without identifiable parties.

A terrorist group can conceivably be a party to an armed conflict and a subject of humanitarian law, but the lack of commonly accepted definitions is a hurdle. What exactly is terrorism? What is a terrorist act? Does terrorism include state actors? How is terrorism distinguished from 'mere' criminality? How has the international community's reaction to terrorism differed from its treatment of mere criminality; from its traditional treatment of international and non-international armed conflict?

There are numerous conventions and other authorities that treat these questions, but none provides a definition of 'terrorism' or 'terrorist acts'.[19] Negotiations on a Comprehensive Convention on International Terrorism[20] are proceeding, but with considerable difficulty, in no small part due to an inability to reach agreement on the definition of terrorism. Terrorism is not a legal notion.[21] This very fact indicates the difficulty, if not impossibility, of determining how terrorism and responses to it may be identified historically or defined within a legal regime. For example, when the United States in 1998 was still engaged in the negotiations to establish a permanent International Criminal Court in Rome, it took a position against inclusion of terrorism in the court's statute on the ground that a definition was not achievable. Without international consensus on these questions, how can one determine, for purposes of assigning legal consequences, who are the parties to the war on terror and which branch, if either, of humanitarian law should apply?[22]

We are all now familiar with the refrain that one man's terrorist is another man's freedom fighter. The need for criteria to distinguish terrorists from freedom fighters is more than rhetorical. It may be critical to the determination of whether humanitarian law can apply, and if so, whether it is the rules of international armed conflict or those of non-international armed conflict that will govern. The reason is simply that hostilities directed against a government and undertaken by a belligerent group seeking self-determination may qualify as an international armed conflict under AP I, while the same conduct of a group with different aims will not.[23]

This does not, of course, mean that humanitarian law cannot apply to the conduct of persons responsible for the 11 September attacks.[24] On the other hand, the attacks do not, *per force*, amount to armed conflict which would trigger the application of humanitarian law. In addition to other criteria mentioned below, the non-state participants must qualify as belligerents or insurgents – a status of doubtful applicability to a group not associated with any specific territory.[25] One commentator has suggested that armed attacks by Al-Qaeda, which is neither a state, nation, belligerent, nor insurgent group (as those terms are understood in international law), can trigger a right of selective and proportionate self-defense under the UN Charter against those directly involved in such armed attacks. However, neither these attacks nor the use of military force by a state against such attackers can create a state of war under international law.[26] Another commentator has asked: 'Should the events of September 11 be considered an "act of war"? It depends on whether a government was involved'.[27]

Identification of Territory (Ratione Ioci)

While CA 3 does not require territorial control by the non-state party, the conflict must still occur 'in the territory' of a high contracting party. Some analysts construe this requirement to mean that the conflict must be limited to the territory of a high contracting party.[28] For this element alone, terrorist attacks on civilian targets in New York may suffice, but retaliation against alleged terrorists in Yemen, for example, may not.[29] This is not because Yemen is not a party to the GCs. It is. Rather, it is because CA 3 is of questionable application to an isolated, targeted killing of persons outside of US territory.

Relationship of Events to an Identified Conflict (Ratione Materiae)

The strike in Yemen on 4 November 2002 highlights another element. 'Acts of war' is an understandable, perhaps inevitable, description of the 11 September attacks. However, this rhetorical reaction does not answer the question of whether or not those attacks and the response to them are part of an armed conflict, i.e., that they have a sufficient nexus to an armed conflict. For example, there should be no doubt that the military confrontation in Afghanistan following the 11 September attacks was (and perhaps remains) an armed conflict. And a case can be made that the 11 September attacks are a part thereof. But it does not necessarily follow that the targeted killing of terrorist suspects by US authorities in Yemen a year after the 11 September attacks falls within that conflict and, therefore, is an event to which humanitarian law applies.

Identification of Beginning and End of Armed Conflict (Ratione Temporis)

According to the jurisprudence of the International Criminal Tribunals for the former Yugoslavia[30] and Rwanda,[31] as well as under the definitions of the newly established permanent International Criminal Court,[32] hostile acts must be 'protracted' in order for the situation to qualify as an 'armed conflict'. In fact, the Yugoslavia Tribunal has specifically stated that the reason for this requirement is to exclude the application of humanitarian law to acts of terrorism.[33] On the other hand, the Inter-American Commission on Human Rights says that intense violence of brief duration will suffice.[34] Likewise, it remains to be seen whether the mere gravity of damage resulting from the 11 September attacks will, in retrospect, become a 'decisive point of reference for the shift from the mechanisms of criminal justice to the instruments of the use of force'.[35] Whether or not the conflict needs be protracted, and whether or not intensity can take the place of duration, the beginning and end must be identifiable to know when humanitarian law is triggered, and when it ceases to apply.

Armed Conflict

The most important and most commonly forgotten element is that application of CA 3, like all other aspects of humanitarian law, depends on the existence of a particular quality of hostilities that amount to armed conflict. And yet, nowhere in the GCs or APs is the term 'armed conflict' defined. Where the question arises – 'Is there a state of international armed conflict (i.e., between or among states)?' – the analysis is relatively easy. The answer is 'yes' whenever there is 'any difference arising between two States and leading to the intervention of armed forces'.[36] The determination of non-international armed conflict, however, is more complex. One can start with the disqualifying criteria of AP II, Article 1.2 (internal disturbances and tensions such as riots, etc.),[37] but they are hardly precise. One can proceed to the inclusive criteria of the ICRC Commentary, reproduced earlier in this article, but there is no consensus on their legal authority. The ICRC Commentary also appears to presume that the non-state party to the conflict is acting within a determinate territory in revolt against, and attempting to displace, its own government. Must military means be used? Can the line between military and nonmilitary means be neatly drawn? This potential criterion is related to the question of intensity, which has been suggested as an alternative to the requirement that the conflict be 'protracted' (see above). Traditionally, acts of international terrorism were not viewed as crossing the threshold of intensity required to trigger application of the laws of armed conflict.[38] Some authority to the contrary is suggested by historical precedents involving the use of military force against extraterritorial non-state actors as indicative of 'war'. But these examples still fail to make the case that use of such force necessarily triggers the law of armed conflict.[39]

In Defense of Humanitarian Law

The Proper Limits of Humanitarian Law

The broadest, most significant criticism of humanitarian law seems to be that it should adopt provisions to cover so-called 'new forms of conflict'. Those who take this view are either wittingly or unwittingly calling for expansion of the concept of armed conflict, or the expansion of the scope of application of humanitarian law beyond armed conflict. The critics who claim that humanitarian law does not encompass the war on terror in the broad, rhetorical sense of that phrase are right. But inapplicability of humanitarian law to aspects of the war on terror that do not meet the criteria discussed previously should be viewed as a benefit rather than an obstacle or collision. Recall the compromise nature of humanitarian law: A license to kill enemy combatants, and to detain without charges or trials anyone who poses a security risk, is the price paid for rules designed to minimize human suffering. In peacetime, domestic and international criminal and human rights law prohibits and punishes homicide. Where the *lex specialis* of humanitarian law is active, however, those prohibitions are narrowed, and humanity is denied some very fundamental protections provided by other legal regimes.

This is not to imply that any state has explicitly suggested a need to move the boundaries between humanitarian law and other legal regimes. On the contrary, the position of most states leading up to the 'Informal High-Level Expert Meeting on the Reaffirmation and Development of International Humanitarian Law', sponsored by the Harvard University Program on Humanitarian Policy and Conflict Research early in 2003 was 'no development of humanitarian law'. However, we have also heard several disturbing, counterproductive and simply inaccurate assertions as to the content of humanitarian law, which if repeated often enough at influential levels, will become the functional equivalent of legal development.

Some Misguided Assertions Concerning Humanitarian Law

The War on Terror is an International Armed Conflict

US officials and other analysts have asserted that the global war on Terror is an international armed conflict[40] even when it is not a conflict between states, where the territorial boundaries of the conflict are undefined, where the beginnings are amorphous and the end undefinable and, most importantly, where the non-state parties are unspecified and unidentifiable entities that are not entitled to belligerent status. Since an international armed conflict under humanitarian law must be between two or more states, the better terminology for those aspects of the war on terror that do amount to armed conflict and that cross state boundaries, but that do not implicate two or more governments as parties to the conflict, would be 'transnational' or 'interstate'.[41] The error of the United States' choice of nomenclature is neither insignificant nor innocent. The US view, if accepted as a statement of law, would serve as a global waiver of domestic and international criminal and human rights laws that regulate, if not prohibit, killing. Turning the whole world into a rhetorical battlefield cannot legally justify, though it may in practice set the stage for, a claimed license to kill people or detain them without recourse to judicial review anytime, anywhere. This is a privilege that, in reality, exists under limited conditions and may only be exercised by lawful combatants and parties to armed conflict.

The targeted killing of suspected terrorists in Yemen in November 2002 by a CIA-launched, unmanned drone missile is a case in point. The killings are of dubious legality under humanitarian law for several reasons. First, unless the event is part of an armed conflict, humanitarian law does not apply, and its provisions recognizing a privilege to kill may not be invoked. The event must then be analyzed under other applicable legal regimes.[42] Second, even if humanitarian law applies, the legality of the attack is questionable because the targets were not directly participating in hostilities at the time they were killed,[43] and because the attackers' right to engage in combat is doubtful.[44]

No POWs in the War on Terror

On the other hand, in the recent war in Afghanistan – clearly an international armed conflict to which GC III Relative to the Treatment of Prisoners of War applies – the United States took the position that no detainees are entitled to prisoner of war (POW) status.[45] This is despite the plain language of GC III, Article 4.1, which states that POWs are members of the armed forces of a party to the conflict who have fallen into the power of the enemy. The United States has asserted that even the Taliban are not entitled to POW status since they failed to have a fixed, distinctive sign (uniforms) and did not conduct their operations in accordance with the laws and customs of war. These disqualifying factors are part of GC III, Article 4.2, which applies to militias and volunteer corps and not to regular members of the armed forces, who are covered by Article 4.1.

Even if these disqualifying criteria are relevant to regular members of armed forces, as some analysts suggest, their application is subject to two more provisions: GC III, Article 5, which calls for the convening of a 'competent tribunal' to determine POW status in case of doubt, and the even more specific language of US Army regulations calling for 'competent tribunal' determinations upon request of the detainee.[46] Both of these authorities can only be construed to require individualized determinations. Because the US administration has chosen not to make public any specific allegations, I do not pretend to know what it knows about the Taliban's alleged failure to conduct their operations in accordance with the laws and customs of war. It is obvious, however, that if the mere commission of war crimes by one or more members of armed forces can disqualify them all from entitlement to POW status, then there would never be a POW. Such an interpretation cannot stand, since it would defeat the very purposes for which the status of POW exists in humanitarian law.

While the weakness of the US interpretation is clear, the motives behind it are not. The most frequently stated suggestion is that since POWs are not obliged to provide information, granting that status would impede effective interrogation. This is misguided. POWs and non-POWs are equally subject to interrogation. It is also ominous because of the implicit, albeit false, suggestion that non-POWs may lawfully be subjected to interrogation techniques that may not be used against POWs.[47]

No Civilian Detainees in the War on Terror

Having denied its Guantanamo Bay detainees POW status under GC III, the United States also rejects application of GC IV for the protection of civilians, thus leaving them in a legal vacuum. This issue is clouded in emotional rhetoric that has far overshadowed the facts. The right of all persons to recognition before the law is a fundamental, non-derogable human right.[48] Consistent with that right, the ICRC Commentary takes the position that all armed conflict detainees are 'protected persons' either under GC III or GC, IV.[49] The idea of granting 'protected person' status to 'terrorists' is apparently unacceptable to the US administration. But first, not all detainees are terrorists. Those who are mere members of the enemy armed forces – the Taliban – are presumptively entitled to POW treatment 'until such time as their status has been determined by a competent tribunal'.[50] Second, others are civilians who may or may not have committed criminal (e.g., terrorist) acts. To recognize their entitlement to 'protected person' status under GC IV in no way prohibits their interrogation and detention for the duration of the conflict, so long as they remain a security risk.[51] Nor does it prohibit their prosecution and imprisonment beyond the temporal bounds of the conflict, if convicted of a crime.[52] They may even be subject to execution.[53]

The Principles of Distinction and Proportionality must Bend to the Realities of Modern Conflicts

The principle of distinction and the underlying principle of proportionality are the most fundamental principles of humanitarian law. The principle of distinction embodies the concept that the effects of war must be limited to combatants and military objectives as much as is feasible. Civilians and civilian objects should be spared and may not be targeted.[54] Combatants have a duty to take precautionary measures to implement the principle of distinction.[55]

The related principle of proportionality concedes, however, that it is not always feasible to limit damage to military objectives. Even if civilians are not the targets of attack, they may be affected. Otherwise legitimate military objectives are not rendered out-of-bounds simply because of a risk of 'collateral damage'. Thus, the principle of proportionality, like that of distinction, also requires that combatants take precautionary measures to minimize civilian harms and to refrain from attacks that are likely to result in incidental civilian damage or casualties that are excessive in relation to the concrete and direct military advantage anticipated.

Terrorism is, of course, a wholesale rejection of these principles.[56] Terrorists are not, however, the only ones to claim that the righteous and compelling nature of the cause for which they fight is relevant to the determination of what type of attacks are permissible. It has, for example, been argued that humanitarian intervention – a term unknown to humanitarian law – is a special case, allowing the 'humanitarian intervener' (but not the adversary) greater leeway in calculating proportionality than would be permitted in 'traditional' armed conflicts.[57] The argument has its attractions, but the principle is ultimately unworkable.

The view that humanitarian law should distinguish between the evil aggressor and the righteous warrior prosecuting the so-called 'just war' or acting in self-defense is untenable for two reasons. First, unless and until the Security Council declares it, or a criminal tribunal adjudicates criminal responsibility for it, there is no forum for distinguishing the aggressor from the aggressed. It is implausible that these determinations, which, in fact, might never be made, could occur in a manner that would permit their timely application to the field of battle. Secondly, recall that humanitarian law – the *jus in bello* – consists of two realms: one governing the conduct of hostilities, the other, the protection of persons in the power of the enemy (or persons not, or no longer, taking part in hostilities). As to the first realm, any humanitarian law that would simply prohibit the aggressor from engaging in hostilities would be a dead letter in practice – a rule of law that would simply undermine the integrity of law, since no aggressor is likely to obey a law prohibiting it from undertaking hostile acts. In addition, such a rule would impinge on the subject matter territory of the *jus ad bellum* – the legal regime that, quite apart from humanitarian law, determines when hostilities are, or are not, legal. As to the second realm, there can be no justification for a law that discriminates between members of the aggressor group, on one hand, and those of the victim group, on the other hand, be they civilians or combatants, if those persons are not, or are no longer, taking part in hostilities.

The absurdity of the proposition that the army, citizens and members of the aggressor group should rightfully be subject to cruelties that it may not impose upon its enemy or their citizens underscores why the *jus ad bellum* is distinct from, rather than consanguineous to, the *jus in bello*. The very essence of *jus ad bellum* is the distinction between just and unjust cause – between entitlement and prohibition to wage war. *Jus in bello*, on the other hand, rightfully recognizes no such distinction. While one party may be a sinner and the other a saint under *jus ad bellum*, the *jus in bello* must and does bind the aggressor and the aggressed equally.[58]

Another problem with these positions concerns the concept of collective guilt and punishment – a concept that is anathema not only to the principle of distinction upon which so much of humanitarian law rests, but to fundamental human rights and criminal justice values as well. The *modus operandi* of the terrorist is explicitly punitive in the collective extreme. On the other hand, the view from the 'humanitarian intervention' perspective that civilians may rightfully be subjected to greater burdens due to the nature of the conflict may be well intentioned. It has been suggested, for example, that an attack today that may be disproportionate in its own right due to the likelihood of excessive civilian consequences may become proportionate if reasonably calculated to prevent a greater civilian calamity tomorrow. But the principles of distinction and proportionality already incorporate a 'margin of appreciation'.[59] Attempts to dilute it create an unnecessary risk of appearing to endorse collective punishment, which can only fuel animosities and impede reconciliation.

A final criticism of the principle of distinction is that it puts lawful combatants at a disadvantage against unlawful ones, who remain civilians. This, however, ignores the fact that civilians forfeit their immunity from attack if and for such time as they take a direct part in hostilities.[60]

Customary Law will Fill in the Gaps

This somewhat technical claim is a dangerous one that could erroneously be used to apply humanitarian law where it does not belong. I have previously indicated that humanitarian law applies, as a general matter, when the Geneva Conventions and their Additional Protocols say it applies, namely, in the event of armed conflict. But these instruments are not the only sources of humanitarian law. There are, for example, other treaties both older and newer than the GCs and APs that establish additional prohibitions and requirements in armed conflict.[61] The very existence of these treaties, many of them in response to the post Cold War nature of armed conflict, belies the suggestion that humanitarian law is behind the times.

There is also an entire body of unwritten law–customary international humanitarian law – that supplements the rules of armed conflict found in treaties and in domestic law. In response to the assertion that the existing body of humanitarian law has a gap regarding the war on terror, some analysts suggest customary law as a gap-filler.[62] But it would be wrong to simply say that customary international humanitarian law can cover what the treaties do not. An important distinction must be drawn. Customary humanitarian law certainly does add to the content of treaty law, usually by providing a 'floor' or by filling gaps in protection for persons affected by armed conflict. There is no evidence, however, that it enlarges the scope of application of humanitarian law beyond armed conflict, as that term is understood in the GCs and APs. In other words, where the war on terror does not amount to armed conflict under the GCs and APs (and so, killings and detentions remain subject to the more restrictive legal regimes of international and domestic criminal and human rights law), customary humanitarian law adds nothing and should be seen to add nothing.

Conclusion

Humanitarian law is basically fine. Its boundaries are properly drawn in a respectful balance among interests of state security, individual security and civil liberties. It is effective when properly implemented. Its very vitality and relevance in the war on terror stems not from any claim that it is capable of encompassing all of the exigencies of terrorism and the efforts to combat it. The strength of humanitarian law lies, rather, in the fact that it is adequate to deal with such exigencies when they amount to armed conflict. There is little evidence that domestic and international laws and institutions of crime and punishment are not up to the task when terrorism and the war on terror do not rise to the level of armed conflict. But there are powerful reasons to conclude that the application of humanitarian law in those circumstances would do more harm than good.

Criticism of humanitarian law is also fine. Humanitarian law can be frustratingly vague, although sometimes for good reason.[63] It can appear to be internally contradictory and unduly burdensome. But some of the criticisms simply misread the law. These are relatively easy to address. Other criticisms correctly state the law and, in suggesting the need for change, misconstrue the law's purpose and function. Just as truth is the first casualty of war, logic is often a casualty in the effort to mold the laws of war, or at least their image, for parochial purposes.

The concept of war feeds the vision of an enemy that must be defeated, rather than a criminal problem to be solved. Viewing terrorism as crime, we might be permitted to consider its root causes. But to ask why they make war against us is to risk the appearance of sympathy. In the view of one commentator upon whose words I cannot improve, it is precisely by declaring war against them that we fall into their trap, following them in a scorched earth policy of burning bridges between civilizations and driving civilian populations with them over the precipice.[64]

The Geneva Conventions and their Additional Protocols did not anticipate 11 September or Al-Qaeda. And yet, the balance struck between humanitarian law and other legal regimes is probably more valid today than ever before. Civil rights, judicial guarantees, human rights and the rule of law are not impediments to human security. They are, in fact, the ultimate repositories of it. Humanitarian law, in particular, is a bulwark of human security in times of armed conflict, but only if invoked where it properly belongs and obeyed where properly invoked.

Notes

1. The terms 'international humanitarian law', 'humanitarian law', 'law of armed conflict', *'jus in bello'* and 'laws of war' are interchangeable. The term 'war' is somewhat archaic in international law, having been replaced by 'armed conflict.' The distinction reflects a change from past times, in which wars were declared, to the present, in which facts on the ground are rightfully given greater emphasis over the declarations of parties to conflict.

2. See, for example, Robert Kagan, 'Power and Weakness', *Policy Review* 113 (June/July 2002).

3. Humanitarian law is a *lex specialis* – a term used to indicate any specific branch of law that is triggered by special circumstances. *Lex specialis* prevails over conflicting *lex generalis*, or generally applicable law. Humanitarian law is a *lex specialis* applicable in times of

armed conflict. Some analysts assert that as a *lex specialis*, humanitarian law, when applicable, displaces legal regimes that apply in peacetime. This is clearly wrong as to international criminal law, a significant part of which is devoted to war crimes, covering a broader scope of prohibitions than humanitarian law. It is equally wrong with regard to domestic criminal law, which is also capable of covering war crimes and an even broader scope of other prohibitions than are covered by international criminal law. It is also wrong as to human rights law, as enunciated in the International Covenant on Civil and PoliticalRights (ICCPR), UN General Assembly Resolution 2200A16 Dec. 1966 or UN doc. A/6316 1967. The ICCPR recognizes that some rights may be subjectto derogation 'in time of public emergency which threatens the life of the nation', but identifies a 'hard core' group of rights from which there may be no derogation in any circumstances, including armed conflict. See ICCPR, Article 4.

4. The Geneva Convention of 22 Aug. 1864 for the Amelioration of the Condition of the Wounded in Armies in the Field, 18 Martens Nouveau Recueil (ser. 1) 607, 129 Consol. T. S. 361, entered into force on 22 June 1865.

5. Geneva Convention for the Amelioration of the Condition of the Wounded and Sick in the Armed Forces in the Field of 12 August 1949, 75 UNTS (1950) 31; Geneva Convention for the Amelioration of the Condition of the Wounded, Sick and Shipwrecked Members of Armed Forces at Sea of 12 August 1949, 75 UNTS (1950) 85; Geneva Convention Relative to the Treatment of Prisoners of War of 12 August 1949, 75 UNTS (1950) 135; Geneva Convention Relative to the Protection of Civilian Persons in Time of War of 12 August 1949, 75 UNTS (1950) 287. There are 190 states party to the Geneva Conventions.

6. Protocol Additional to the Geneva Conventions of 12 August 1949, and Relating to the Protection of Victims of International Armed Conflicts of 8 June 1977, 1125 UNTS (1978) 3; Protocol Additional to the Geneva Conventions of 12 August 1949, and Relating to the Protection of Victims of Non-International Armed Conflicts of 8 June 1977, 1125 UNTS (1978) 609.

7. David Rieff What Is Really at Stake in the US Campaign against Terrorism, http://www.crimesofwar.org/sept-mag/sept-home.html: 'The crisis of international humanitarian law was an accident waiting to happen. For when law and material reality no longer coincide, it is, of course, law that must give way'.

8. See Carsten Stahn, 'International Law at a Crossroads? The Impact of September 11', *Heidelberg Journal of International Law* 62 (2002) p. 195, citing W. J. Fenrick, 'Should the Laws of War Apply to Terrorists?', *American Society of International Law Proceedings* 79 (1985) p.112: 'There are times and places when it is appropriate to apply other regimes such as the criminal law of a State at peace... Premature application of the laws of war may result in a net increase in human suffering, because the laws of war permit violence prohibited by domestic criminal law'.

9. See note 3.

10. There are peacetime obligations under humanitarian law, but those are not relevant to the present discussion.

11. The reason there are two separate strands of humanitarian law is sovereignty. States are more willing to accept greater international controls on their international affairs than on their internal ones. Thus, Protocol I Additional to the Geneva Conventions Relating to the Protection of Victims of *International* Armed Conflicts runs to 102 articles, plus two annexes of 17 and 28 articles, respectively. There are 161 states party to AP I. (The United States is not a party to AP I, but considers much of its substance as 'either legally binding as customary international law or acceptable practice though not legally binding'. US Army, *Operational Law Handbook 2002* (Charlottesville, VA: 2001) p.5.) Protocol II Additional Relating to the Protection of Victims of *Non-International* Armed Conflict has 28 articles and no annexes. There are 156 states party to AP II.

12. AP I, Article 1.3 incorporates by reference GC Common Article 2 (CA 2) on scope of application. CA 2 provides:

In addition to the provisions which shall be implemented in peacetime, the present Convention shall apply to all cases of declared war or of any other armed conflict which may arise between two or more of the High Contracting Parties, even if the state of war is not recognized by one of them.

The Convention shall also apply to all cases of partial or total occupation of the territory of a High Contracting Party, even if the said occupation meets with no armed resistance.

Although one of the Powers in conflict may not be a party to the present Convention, the Powers who are parties thereto shall remain bound by it in their mutual relations. They shall furthermore be bound by the Convention in relation to the said Power, if the latter accepts and applies the provisions thereof.

13. The ICRC is acknowledged to be the guardian of international humanitarian law. It has published extensive commentaries to the Geneva Conventions and their Additional Protocols.

14. See J. S. Pictet, *Commentary of the First Geneva Convention for the Amelioration of the Condition of the Wounded and Sick in Armed Forces in the Field* (Geneva: International Committee of the Red Cross, 1952) p.32. The 'difference arising between two States' language suggests the requirement of a *causus belli*. This interpretation is not universally shared. See Jean-Francois Queguiner, 'The Contribution of the Jurisprudence of the International Criminal Tribunal for the Former Yugoslavia to International Humanitarian Law' (forthcoming).

15. 'In the case of armed conflict not of an international character occurring in the territory of one of the High Contracting Parties, each Party to the conflict shall be bound to apply, as a minimum, the following provisions...'

16. AP II: Part I. Scope of this Protocol
Art 1. Material field of application

1. This Protocol, which develops and supplements Article 3 common to the Geneva Conventions of 12 August 1949 without modifying its existing conditions or application, shall apply to all armed conflicts which are not covered by Article 1 of the Protocol Additional to the Geneva Conventions of 12 August 1949, and relating to the Protection of Victims of International Armed Conflicts (Protocol I) and which take place in the territory of a High Contracting Party between its armed forces and dissident armed forces or other organized armed groups which, under responsible command, exercise such control over a part of its territory as to enable them to carry out sustained and concerted military operations and to implement this Protocol.

2. This Protocol shall not apply to situations of internal disturbances and tensions, such as riots, isolated and sporadic acts of violence and other acts of a similar nature, as not being armed conflicts.

17. Pictet, (note 14) p.49. The International Criminal Tribunal for Rwanda also applied these criteria in the determination of armed conflict. See *The Prosecutor v. Jean Paul Akayesu*, 1998 ICTR-96-4-T para 619. The *Akayesu* court did not, however, see these criteria as minimum requirements for existence of non-international armed conflict. See also S. Boelaert-Suominen, 'Humanitarian Law Applicable to All Armed Conflicts,' *Journal of International Law* 13 (2000) p.619: 'In light of the ICTY jurisprudence since 1995, it can be safely concluded that the threshold suggested by the ICRC Commentary has failed to crystallise into customary law.'

18. Gerald I. A. D. Draper, 'The Geneva Conventions of 1949,' *Rec de Cours* 114 (1965) pp.65, 90.

19. I acknowledge, but exclude as unhelpful, the definition of terrorism found in the 1937 Convention for the Prevention and Punishment of Terrorism: 'criminal acts directed against a State or intended to create a State of terror in the minds of particular persons, or a group of persons or the general public.' A comprehensive list of treaties on terrorism can be found at http://untreaty.un.org/English/Terrorism.asp

20. UNGA Res. 51/210-17 Dec. 1996. See *Report of the Working Group, Measures to Eliminate International Terrorism*, A/C.6/56/L.9 (29 Oct. 2001).

21. Hans-Peter Gasser, 'Acts of Terror, "Terrorism" and International Humanitarian Law,' *International Review of the Red Cross* 84 (Sep. 2002) pp. 553–554: 'It is much more a combination of policy goals, propaganda and violent acts–an amalgam of measures to achieve an objective'.

22. Chibli Mallat, September 11 and the Middle East: Footnote or Watershed in World History? http://www.crimesofwar.org/sept-mag/sept-home.html: 'The problem is that terrorism as a concept remains so ill-defined that the idea of attacking it systematically transforms the use of violence–in international and domestic law the prerogative of States–into an open-ended project of endless war. And that, surely, is inconceivable, unless the American government now means to prosecute a series of wars to end all violence in the world'.

23. AP I, Article 1(4).

24. Stahn (note 8) pp.192–94.

25. Ibid., p.189. See also M. Cherif Bassiouni, 'Legal Control of International Terrorism: A Policy-Oriented Assessment,' *Harvard International Law Journal 43* (2002) pp.83, 99.

26. Jordan J. Paust, 'There Is No Need to Revise the Laws of War in Light of September 11', (2002), citing *Pan American Airways, Inc. v. Aetna Casualty & Surety Co.*, (2d Cir 1974) 505 F2d 989, 1013–1015 ('United States could not have been at war with the Popular Front for the Liberation of Palestine [PFLP], which had engaged in terrorist acts as a non-state, nonbelligerent, noninsurgent actor'). But see Yoram Dinstein, 'Humanitarian Law on the Conflict in Afghanistan', *American Society of International Law Proceedings 96* (2002) p.23: '. . . a terrorist attack from the outside constitutes an "armed attack" under Article 51 of the (UN) Charter'.)

27. Eyal Benvenisti, Terrorism and the Laws of War: September 11 and its Aftermath, http://crimesofwar.org/expert/attack-apv.html. See also *The Prosecutor v. Dusko Tadic, Decision on the Defence Motion for Interlocutory Appeal on Jurisdiction*, IT-94-1-AR72; See also Dinstein: 24, citing *Nicaragua v. United States*, (1986) ICJ 14, and the General Assembly's Consensus Definition of Aggression, General Assembly Resolution 3314 (1974).

28. Lindsay Moir, *The Law of Internal Armed Conflict* (Cambridge: Cambridge University Press, 2002) p.31.

29. For analysis of the legal consequences of the killings in Yemen, see Anthony Dworkin, The Yemen Strike: The War on Terrorism Goes Global, http://crimesofwar.org/onnews/news-yemen.html

30. *The Prosecutor v. (note 27) Dusko Tadic*, 1995 para. 70, p.37.

31. *The Prosecutor v. Jean Paul Akayesu*, (note 17) 1998 ICTR-96-4-T, para.619.

32. The Rome Statute of the International Criminal Court, UN doc. A/CONF. 183/9-17 July 1998, 37 ILM (1998) pp.999–1019, Article 8.2(f) contains this requirement, which may be seen as an expression of the drafter's belief that 'protracted' is a defining element of non-international armed conflict, or merely that ICC jurisdiction is triggered only in case a non-international armed conflict is protracted.

33. *The Prosecutor v. Zejnil Delalic (Celebici Camp Case), Judgment*, (1998) IT-96-21, para.184.

34. See *Abella Case*, Inter-American Commission on Human Rights, Report No. 55/97, Case No. 11.137, 18 Nov. 1997 paras.155–6.

35. Stahn, (note 8) p.188.

36. See note 14.

37. See note 16.

38. Stahn, (note 8) p.192, citing Elizabeth Chadwick, *Self-Determination, Terrorism and the International Humanitarian Law of Armed Conflict* (Boston: M. Nijhoff 1996), p.128, and noting the United Kingdom's denial of existence of armed conflict in Northern Ireland. In fact, the UK's ratification of AP I was accompanied by a statement that the term 'armed conflict' is distinguishable from the commission of ordinary crimes including acts of terrorism whether concerted or in isolation.

39. See Robert Goldman, Terrorism and the Laws of War: September 11 and Its Aftermath, http://crimesofwar.org/expert/attack-apv.html, noting the 1805 US military action in Tripoli against the Barbary Pirates and that of 1916 in Mexico against Pancho Villa and his band.

40. On the other hand, President Bush and others speaking on behalf of the US administration have clearly suggested that some aspects of the war on terror will not involve armed conflict, permitting us to conclude that in their view, those aspects, at least, will not be covered by humanitarian law. On 20 Sep. 2001, President Bush said in an address to a joint session of Congress and the American people, 'The war will be fought not just by soldiers, but by police and intelligence forces, as well as in financial institutions', http://www.whitehouse.gov/news/releases/2001/09/20010920–8.html. National security advisor Condoleezza Rice stated on *a Fox News* broadcast on 10 Nov. 2002: 'We're in a new kind of war, and we've made it very clear that this new kind of war be fought on different battlefields'. See http://www.foxnews.com/story/0,2933,69783,00.html

41. See Sec. II.B. 1. The exception to the 'between States' requirement for international armed conflict is armed conflicts 'in which peoples are fighting against colonial domination

and alien occupation and against racist regimes in the exercise of their right to self-determination ...' These are deemed international armed conflict by AP I, Article 1.4.

42. Sweden's Foreign Minister, Anna Lindh, used the term 'summary execution' and further stated: 'Even terrorists must be treated according to international law. Otherwise, any country can start executing those whom they consider terrorists'. Quoted in Walter Pincus, 'Missile Strike Carried Out With Yemeni Cooperation; Official Says Operation Authorized under Bush Finding', *Washington Times* 6 Nov. 2002.

43. See AP I, Article 51.3. The US position on this point is difficult to discern. The Yemen attack notwith standing, the U.S. State Department remains critical of Israeli targeted killings of Palestinian militants. Richard Boucher, Press Briefing, 5 Nov. 2002.

44. The criteria of GC III, Article 4, that the United States invokes to deny POW status to detainees it deems 'unlawful combatants' would also appear to apply to the CIA. The CIA is not part of the armed forces of the United States. Only members of the armed forces of a party to the conflict (other than medical personnel and chaplains) are combatants, entitled to participate directly in hostilities. AP I, Article 43.2.

45. This view is probably correct as to Al-Qaeda members detained in relation to the Afghan conflict. It is certainly correct as to others detained outside the context of armed conflict.

46. Section 1-6(b) Army Regulation 190-8, 'Enemy Prisoners of War, Retained Personnel, Civilian Internees and Other Detainees, Headquarters Departments of the Army, the Navy, the Air Force, and the Marine Corps' (Washington D.C.: 1 Oct. 1997).

47. See GC IV, Article 27, AP I, Article 75 and CA 3. See also 'Request by the Center for Constitutional Rights and the International Human Rights Law Group for Precautionary Measures under Article 25 of the Commission's Regulations on Behalf of Unnamed Persons Detained and Interrogated by the United States Government', filed with the Inter-American Commission on Human Rights, 13 Feb. 2003.

48. ICCPR, Arts. 16 and 4.2.

49. J. S. Pictet, *Commentary of the Fourth Geneva Convention* (Geneva: International Committee of the Red Cross 1952) 51: '[It is] a general principle which is embodied in all four Geneva Conventions of 1949 [that] every person in enemy hands must have some status under international law: he is either a prisoner of war and, as such, covered by the Third Convention, a civilian covered by the Fourth Convention, or again, a member of the medical personnel of the armed forces who is covered by the First Convention. *There is no* intermediate status; nobody in enemy hands can be outside the law'. Note, however, that nationals of the detaining authority and of neutral and co-belligerent states are not 'protected persons'. See GC IV, Article 4. Nevertheless, even they must have some legal status. See ICCPR, Arts. 16 and 4.2.

50. GC III, Article 5.

51. GC IV, Arts. 42, 78.

52. GC IV, Arts. 64–68.

53. GC IV, Article 68.

54. AP I, Arts. 48–49.

55. AP I, Arts. 57-58.

56. Thus, we should not be surprised by these comments attributed to Osama bin Laden, 'Letter to the American People', *The Observer* (24 Nov. 2002) http://www.observer.-www.observer.co.uk/international/story/0,6903,845724,00.html 'You may then dispute that all the above does not justify aggression against civilians, for crimes they did not commit and offenses in which they did not partake: ... the American people are the ones who choose their government by way of their own free will; ... (who) have the ability and choice to refuse the policies of their Government and even to change it if they want; ... who pay the taxes which fund the planes that bomb us in Afghanistan, the tanks that strike and destroy our homes in Palestine, the armies which occupy our lands in the Arabian Gulf, and the fleets which ensure the blockade of Iraq. These tax dollars are given to Israel for it to continue to attack us and penetrate our lands. So the American people are the ones who fund the attacks against us, and they are the ones who oversee the expenditure of these monies in the way they wish, through their elected candidates.'

57. See, e.g., Ruth Wedgwood, 'Propositions on the Law of War after the Kosovo Campaign: *Jus Ad Bellum* and the Personal Factor in History', *U.S. Naval War College International Law Series* 78 (2003) p.435. Asserting the 'consanguinity of *jus ad bellum* and *jus in bello*', professor Wedgwood states: 'whether one's framework is utilitarian or pure principle,

it is possible to admit that the merits of a war make a difference in our tolerance for methods of warfighting. This teleological view can be incorporated, albeit awkwardly, in the metric for "military advantage" in judging proportionality, for surely we do not value military objectives for their own sake'.

58. See Dino Kritsiosis, 'On the *Jus ad Bellum* and *Jus in Bello* of Operation Enduring Freedom', 96 *American Society of International Law Proceedings* 35 (2002), referring to the distinct spheres, histories, methodological traditions, stages of development and circumstances of application of these two legal regimes: 'As represented in the UN Charter, the laws of the *jus ad bellum* proceed from the general prohibition of the threat or use of force by member States of the United Nations 'in their international relations' (Article 2(4))', while the *jus in bello* of the (GCs and APs) applies *to* such use of force. Thus, the Preamble to AP I declares that 'the provisions of the Geneva Conventions and of this protocol must be fully applied in all circumstances to all persons who are protected by those instruments, without any adverse distinction based on the nature or origin of the armed conflict or on the causes espoused by or attributed to the Parties to the conflict.'

59. The Rome Statute of the International Criminal Court, Arts. 8.2(b)(i) and (ii) prohibit '*intentionally* directing attacks against the civilian population' and 'civilian objects', respectively; Art. 8.2(b)(iv) prohibits '*intentionally* launching an *attack* in the *knowledge* that such attack will cause incidental loss of life or injury to civilians or civilian objects … which would be *clearly* excessive in relation to the concrete and direct *overall* military advantage anticipated' (emphasis added).

60. AP I, Article 51.3.

61. 1899 Hague Declaration (IV, 2) Concerning Asphyxiating Gases and Hague Declaration (IV, 3) Concerning Expanding Bullets, *American Journal of International Law* 1 (1907) Supplement pp.155-9; 1907 Hague Convention IV Respecting the Laws and Customs of War on Land and its Annexed Regulations, Hague Convention V Respecting the Rights and Duties of Neutral Powers and Persons in Case of War on Land, Hague Convention VII Relating to the Conversion of Merchant Ships into Warships, Hague Convention VIII Relative to the Laying of Automatic Submarine Contact Mines, Hague Convention IX Concerning Bombardment by Naval Forces in Time of War, Hague Convention XI Relative to Certain Restrictions with Regard to the Exercise of the Right of Capture in Naval War, Hague Convention XIII Concerning the Rights and Duties of Neutral Powers in Naval War, *American Journal of International Law* 2 (1908) Supplement pp.90–127, pp.133–59, pp.167–74, pp.202–16; 1954 Hague Convention for the Protection of Cultural Property in the Event of Armed Conflict and its First Protocol, 249 UNTS pp.240–88, pp.358–64; 1999 Second Hague Protocol, 38 ILM (1999) pp.769–82; 1980 UN Convention on Prohibitions or Restrictions on the Use of Certain Conventional Weapons Which May be Deemed to be Excessively Injurious or to Have Indiscriminate Effects and Protocols and 21 Dec. 2001 amended version, 1980 Protocol I on Non-Detectable Fragments, 1980 Protocol II on Prohibitions or Restrictions on the Use of Mines, Booby-Traps and Other Devices, 1980 Protocol III on Prohibitions or Restrictions on the Use of Incendiary Weapons, 1342 UNTS (1983) pp.137–255, 1995 Protocol IV on Blinding Laser Weapons, 35 ILM (1996) p.1218, 1996 Amended Protocol II 35 ILM (1996) pp.1206–17; 1993 Statute of the International Criminal Tribunal for the Former Yugoslavia, UN doc. S/25704 of 3 May 1993, 32 ILM (1993) p.1192; 1994 Statute of the International Criminal Tribunal for Rwanda, UN doc. SC/5974 of 12 Jan. 1995, 33 ILM (1994) p.1598; 1997 Ottawa Convention on the Prohibition of the Use, Stockpiling, Production and Transfer of Anti-Personnel Mines and on their Destruction 36 ILM (1997) pp.1507–19; 1998 Statute of the International Criminal Court, UN doc. A/CONF.183/9-17 July 1998, 37 ILM (1998) pp.999–1019.

62. See Steven R. Ratner, Rethinking the Geneva Conventions, http://www.crimesofwar.org/expert/genevaConventions/gc-ratner.html

63. A case in point is the lack of any precise definition of 'armed conflict'. Every so often a call for precision arises, but ultimately gives way to an understanding that a certain degree of ambiguity is beneficial, so as to assure the laws' protections in close cases.

64. Frederic Megret, 'War'? Legal Semantics and the Move to Violence ', *European Journal of International Law* 132 (April 2002) pp.362–99.

11

Biological Attack, Terrorism and the Law

CLIVE WALKER

School of Law, University of Leeds, Leeds, United Kingdom

According to President George W. Bush, we are living amidst 'the first war of the twenty-first century'. How then should the United Kingdom react? It is suggested that at least two strands of legal policy and response should be considered. The first concerns the design of antiterrorism laws and policies. For the purposes of this paper, the remit will be confined to how antiterrorism laws have responded to the threat from biological attack. The second aspect concerns the laws and policies about terrorism risk management, part of the agenda of which takes us back to threats to health from biological attack.

Introduction

After the 11 September attacks, President George W. Bush avowed that we live amidst 'the first war of the twenty-first century'.[1] One can assume that the assertion is applicable to western states in general, including the United Kingdom, and not just to the United States, since the human casualties and financial damage of 11 September have been suffered in both jurisdictions. The number of British citizens killed in the World Trade Centre in September 2001 is reckoned to be sixty-seven.[2] In addition, the costs of the 11 September attacks will have an enormous impact on the London insurance and reinsurance markets, since many of the policies relating to buildings in New York are issued by companies based, or with a strong presence in, London.[3] How then should the United Kingdom react to the president's assertion? Should it be accepted at all? And if it is accepted that new forms of conflict have indeed emerged in the new millennium, including the use of weapons of mass destruction by non-state actors,[4] what are the laws and policies which will lead us to victory or at least allow us to live tolerable lives?

It is suggested in this paper that at least two strands of legal and policy response should be considered. The first concerns the design of antiterrorism laws and policies. For the purposes of this paper, the remit will be confined to the example of how the antiterrorism laws have responded to the threat from biological attack. The second aspect involves the laws and policies about terrorism risk management, part of the agenda of which takes us back to threats to health from biological, chemical and nuclear attack.

On the first aspect, the remit is set narrowly and is confined to the small picture (in terms of microbes and viruses) but some of the later agenda takes us towards the big picture (in terms of strategy and how a liberal democracy cohabits with endemic risk). In each case, this paper shall have regard to human rights implications, taking the European Convention on Human Rights as our guiding normative standard.[5] At the same time, it should be emphasised that there would be applied in a fuller survey a wider set of normative considerations which include not only a rights audit but also democratic accountability (explanations to Parliament and the public and clear v-alidation by Parliament and the public) and 'constitutionalism'[6] (this is a deliciously wide term which can simply mean 'be decent to your citizens' but might be concretized as requiring transparent laws and their lawful execution and judicial review of executive action).

To complete the contextualisation, these two aspects are but strands of legal and policy response, and other responses to terrorism are certainly advisable if not indispensable. Other strands include political engagement – the Good Friday Agreement of 1998[7] in Northern Ireland being a prime United Kingdom example of how to respond imaginatively and positively, albeit at some considerable risk of betrayal, to those groups demonized as terrorists for the long-term benefit of all.[8] The other vital strand is international cooperation, hopefully with respondent states comprising a wider coterie than simply the United States.

Biological Attack by Terrorists

The Threat

How should antiterrorism laws and policies be designed in a liberal democracy? A comprehensive answer is not being attempted here.[9] Instead, a snapshot will be given which is based on the apparently new terrorist threat of biological attack.[10] In reality, the phenomenon of biological terrorism is not new. For instance, towards the end of the nineteenth century anarchists were the imagined source of all ills, with accusations of them starting epidemics of cholera or yellow fever and of schemes 'to drop lice in the stalls from the galleries of theatres'.[11] Yet, biological attack has not previously figured in antiterrorism legislation, and so the phenomenon can, in that sense, be treated as a relatively new legal discourse.

Parts VI to IX of the Anti-terrorism, Crime and Security Act 2001[12] are lumped together for the purposes of this paper as they deal for the first time in terrorist-related legislation with the related issues of dangerous substances and acute vulnerabilities. Their genesis resides in the shock from the ferocious attacks of 11 September, attacks which sought mass destruction and deaths. The implication that the new breed of third millennium terrorism is unbounded in terms of its desire to inflict harm, as well as its flexible and transnational nature and organisation, seemed to be confirmed by the discovery of anthrax in letters to key political figures and to the media in the US, which resulted in eighteen persons being affected (eleven by inhalation, resulting in five deaths, and seven by cutaneous contact).[13] This dark episode brought to mind the only other notable use by terrorists of biological or chemical weapons, namely the sarin gas attacks by the Aum Shinrikyo sect in Japan on Matsumoto in 1994 (allegedly directed against judges deciding a land dispute affecting the sect: 307 persons were affected, including seven deaths) and the Tokyo underground in March 1995 (5,510 were affected, with eleven deaths).[14]

The reaction to this terror, reflected in the Anti-terrorism, Crime and Security Act 2001, was that it was necessary to tighten the laws relating to the possession and transfer of weapons of mass destruction (Part VI) and the security surrounding the possession and use of pathogens (something dangerous which grows on something else, in other words a virus, bacterium or fungus) and toxins (dangerous chemicals produced by living things such as snake serum) (Part VII). Hoaxes about such potential weapons were also of concern because of the restrictive wording of previous legislative sanctions. It was also necessary to improve the security of the nuclear industry (Part VIII) and the aviation industry (Part IX). The measures appearing under these headings were cobbled together in a very short space of time from various sources, including the work of the intergovernmental Australia group which had been undertaking work since 1985 to control the proliferation of chemical and biological materials which may be used in weapons.[15] The appearance of precipitate haste was, however, not entirely accurate since many clauses had already been resting on the legislative stocks or were at least in the legislative drawing room before 11 September. The Anti-terrorism, Crime and Security Act 2001 provided a suitable vessel in which all could be launched with a much shorter deadline than originally envisaged. Strategies alongside the legislative also included the provision of information about the nature of the threat and practical countermeasures. For example, counteraction (including against biological attack through the post) was posted at the government's website, UK Resilience.[16]

In all, these legislative changes are mostly worthwhile reforms, and there are reasons to be fearful of biological weapons such as anthrax. The materials can be readily obtained or produced – far more easily than, say, radiological or nuclear material. Infection can be achieved simply by aerosol spray or by person-to-person infection – there is no need for very sophisticated engineering and intricate machinery as required for a missile or nuclear weapon. The organisms can be made stable, more deadly and resistant to antidote. The modern urban environment, with high concentrations of high-mobility populations, facilities transmission and hinders treatment. Detection of the perpetrators is difficult when, unlike a bomb, the impact may not be noticed for some time. There is an enhanced element of panic or terror with chemical and biological weapons, so that the political impact may be much deeper than warranted by the actual casualties – the very core of what terrorism is all about. Finally, the threat is perceived to be clear and present. As is now notorious from the Hutton Inquiry into the death of the weapons expert David Kelly,[17] the government paper on Iraq's weapons of mass destruction in 2002 expressed the view that the production of chemical and biological weapons and the attempt to develop nuclear weapons were 'serious and current' on the part of a terrorist state and could be delivered within forty-five minutes.[18]

Analysts on both sides of the Atlantic have now come to question whether these threats were exaggerated, and the truth of the matter is the subject of intense political controversy. As for the anthrax attacks in the United States, the strain and properties of the weaponised anthrax found in the letters suggest strongly that it originated within the US bio-defence programme, where the necessary expertise and access are found. According to professor Barbara Rosenberg:[19]

> All letter samples contain the same strain of anthrax, corresponding to the AMES strain in the Northern Arizona University database (which has been used for identification). The AMES strain possessed by N. Arizona University is referred to herein as the 'reference strain.' That strain was obtained by [Louisiana State University] from Porton Down (UK) in 1997 (the sample was marked '10–32' meaning no. 10 of 32 samples sent); Porton had gotten it from Fort Detrick [the US Army Medical

Research Institute of Infectious Diseases, Fort Detrick, Maryland]. Fort Detrick got it from Texas A&M.

Thus, one wonders whether these threats of biological attack are sufficiently linked to terrorism or the responses to them sufficiently considered to have been included in the 2001 Act. In any event, the impact of the legislation is likely to be marginal, because administrative security in the United Kingdom is usually tight and effective, and because international cooperation is just as vital as national efforts but is far from universal, even amongst western states. Nevertheless, the details of the legislation will now be considered.

Offences of Possession, Transfer and Use (Part VI)
The Anti-terrorism, Crime and Security Act 2001 builds upon the controls already set out in the Biological Weapons Act 1974 and the Chemical Weapons Act 1996. This earlier legislation is based on international treaties, namely the Convention on the Prohibition of the Development, Production and Stockpiling of Bacteriological (Biological) and Toxin Weapons and on their Destruction, 1972 (the 'Biological and Toxin Weapons Convention')[20] and the Convention on the Prohibition of the Development, Production, Stockpiling and Use of Chemical Weapons and on their Destruction, 1993 (the 'Chemical Weapons Convention').[21]

The Biological Weapons Act 1974 implements in the United Kingdom the provisions of the Biological and Toxin Weapons Convention. The 1972 Convention supplements the Geneva Protocol of 1925 (Protocol for the Prohibition of the Use in War of Asphyxiating, Poisonous or other Gases, and of Bacteriological Methods of Warfare) which banned the use in war of chemical and biological weapons by banning in addition the development, production, stockpiling or acquisition of biological and toxin agents, as well as weapons or means of delivery designed to use such agents or toxins.

The continuing suspicion that Iraq had attempted to develop biological weapons created an impetus for negotiations on some form of effective verification regime from the mid-1990s onwards. However, in July 2001, the United States rejected the drafts of an Ad Hoc Group of States Parties which was established in 1996 to consider a verification protocol on grounds that the strategy would give false confidence and the procedures could compromise (US) biotechnology trade secrets and national security. This stance was broadly repeated in the Fifth Review Conference in November 2001. As a result, and in contrast to the Convention on the Prohibition of the Development, Production, Stockpiling and Use of Chemical Weapons and on their Destruction of 1993, there is no oversight body for biological weapons, though the World Health Organisation provides some assistance to states. At a national level, the Biological and Toxin Weapons Convention is monitored by the Department of Trade and Industry. The lack of international cooperation has been criticized by the Foreign and Commonwealth Office[22] and by the House of Commons Foreign Affairs Committee.[23] But the Foreign and Commonwealth Office is of the view that there is no international consensus[24] and that, while forty-eight countries favour an inspections regime, there would be no utility in adoption by western states alone (especially without the US).[25]

The Chemical Weapons Convention banned the development, production, stockpiling, transfer and use of chemical weapons and, as noted above, provided for a verification regime. Compliance is monitored by the Organisation for the Prohibition of

Chemical Weapons (OPCW),[26] which is based in The Hague and seeks to propose policies for the implementation of the Convention to the member states of the OPCW and to develop and deliver programmes with and for them. It is responsible for verifying destruction programmes, inspecting military facilities and civilian plants producing chemicals that could be used for weapons and carrying out monitoring and checks. The US government has again objected to parts of the inspection regime.

With this international superstructure in mind, the following offences were already in section 1 of the Biological Weapons Act 1974:

(1) No person shall develop, produce, stockpile, acquire or retain –
(a) any biological agent or toxin of a type and in a quantity that has no justification for prophylactic, protective or other peaceful purposes; or
(b) any weapon, equipment or means of delivery designed to use biological agents or toxins for hostile purposes or in armed conflict.
(2) In this section –
"biological agent" means any microbial or other biological agent; and
"toxin" means any toxin, whatever its origin or method of production.

Turning to the changes brought about by the Anti-terrorism, Crime and Security Act 2001, by section 43 the Biological Weapons Act 1974 is amended to make it an offence to transfer biological agents or toxins outside the United Kingdom or to assist another person to do so, provided the biological agent or toxin is likely to be kept or used (whether by the transferee or any other person) otherwise than for prophylactic, protective or other peaceful purposes and the person knows or has reason to believe that is the case. This offence is added as section 1(1A) and is clearly a reaction to the perceived foreign origins of the biological attack, which was vaguely thought to emanate from Afghanistan or Iraq. Incidentally, there is no corresponding alteration to the Chemical Weapons Act 1996 because that Act already makes it an offence to 'participate in the transfer of a chemical weapon' under section 2.

Next, section 44 extends United Kingdom jurisdiction over offences under section 1 of the Biological Weapons Act 1974 carried out overseas by a United Kingdom person. The corresponding measure in relation to chemical weapons already exists under section 3 of the 1996 Act. This extension is inserted as section 1 A in the 1974 Act. As a result, those British nationals who join terrorist training camps in Afghanistan, Somalia, Yemen or wherever can be prosecuted whenever they return home, no matter whom they intend to attack and in what location.

In addition, under section 50 it becomes an offence (with a sentence of up to life imprisonment) for a United Kingdom person outside the United Kingdom to assist a foreigner to do an act which would (for a United Kingdom person) be contrary to section 1 of the Biological Weapons Act or section 2 of the Chemical Weapons Act. These offences would not extend to either a United Kingdom–based foreign national, including a European Union citizen, who, while abroad, commits an act that, if committed by a British person, would be an offence or someone who, although not a British subject, has exceptional leave to remain in this country, and who commits such an act while on a foreign trip.[27] It is not clear why a more universal jurisdiction was not asserted.

Hoaxes (Part XIII)

By section 113(1), it becomes an offence for a person to use or threaten to use a noxious substance or thing to cause serious harm in a manner designed to influence the government or to intimidate the public. The serious harm is defined further by subsection (2) as that which (a) causes serious violence against a person anywhere in the world; (b) causes serious damage to real or personal property anywhere in the world; (c) endangers human life or creates a serious risk to the health or safety of the public or a section of the public; or (d) induces in members of the public the fear that the action is likely to endanger their lives or create a serious risk to their health or safety; but any effect on the person taking the action is to be disregarded. The latter caters for the situation where the attack has been disrupted before it has had chance to take effect, 'for example, where the police intercept a package of anthrax spores designed to kill the recipient before it reaches its target'.[28] The list overall is reflective of section 1(2) of the Terrorism Act, save that there is understandably no reference to electronic systems. By section 113(3), it is an offence to make a threat to carry out an action which constitutes an offence under subsection (1) with the intention to induce in a person anywhere in the world the fear that the threat is likely to be carried out. Offences under this clause carry a wide range of sentences – up to fourteen years and a fine on indictment and up to six months and a fine on summary process.

Section 114 deals with hoaxes with reference to 'a noxious substance or other noxious thing'. The law as it stood before the 2001 Act, in section 51 of the Criminal Law Act 1977 (as amended by the Criminal Justice Act 1991), made it an offence for someone to place or send any article intending to make another person believe that it is likely to explode or ignite and thereby cause personal injury or damage to property.[29] It was also an offence under section 51 for someone to communicate any information which he knows or believes to be false intending to make another person believe that a bomb is likely to explode or ignite. There were corresponding offences in Scotland (section 63) and in Northern Ireland (Criminal Law (Amendment) Northern Ireland) Order 1977.[30] A related offence deals with food contamination contrary to section 38 of the Public Order Act 1986.[31] It is an offence under subsection (1) to intend to cause alarm, injury or loss by contamination or interference with goods or by making it appear that goods have been contaminated or interfered with in a place where goods of that description are consumed, used, sold or otherwise supplied. It is also an offence to make threats or claims along these lines (section 38(2)) or to possess materials with a view to the commission of an offence (section 38(3)). Section 38 responded to a small number of well-publicised incidents of consumer terrorism, some of which involved animal liberationists.

It follows that there was a substantial range of offences in existence before 2001, but it was feared that there remained gaps. The offences in section 51 related only to hoax devices which are 'likely to explode or ignite'. The section 38 offences protected only the integrity of goods. Post–11 September 2001, the scare arose from the posting of anthrax powder in the US and the fear that groups like Al-Qaeda had possession of other biological or nuclear materials which could be extremely dangerous and harmful not just in the consumer chain but through any form of contact or distribution.

Accordingly, section 114(1) widens the offence by extending the *actus reus* to placing or sending 'any substance or article intending to make others believe that that it is likely to be or contain a noxious substance or thing which could endanger human life or health.' In the circumstances post–11 September, relevant actions might include 'scattering white powder in a public place or spraying concentrated water droplets around in an Underground Train'.[32] By subsection (2), it is an offence for a person to falsely communicate any information to another person anywhere in the world that a noxious substance or thing is or will be in a place and so likely to cause harm to endanger human life or health. The offence may be tried either way; the maximum penalty on indictment is imprisonment for up to seven years.

For the purposes of both sections 113 and 114, section 115 makes clear that 'substance' includes any biological agent and any other natural or artificial substance (whatever its form, origin or method of production). The word 'noxious' is not defined, but it is possible that the meaning will follow that given to the word in the context of an offence under section 23 of the Offences against the Person Act 1861 (to administer a noxious thing to endanger life). In that context, whether a substance is 'noxious' requires the jury to consider 'quality and quantity and to decide as a question of fact and degree in all the circumstances whether that thing was noxious'.[33] Section 115 also specifies that for a person to be guilty of an offence under section 113(3) or 114 it is not necessary for him to have any particular person in mind as the person in whom he intends to induce the belief in question. Thus, threats and hoaxes issued to the whole world, such as via the Internet, can be penalised.

The difficulties of detection remain formidable, so more effective counteractions against hoaxes has consisted of more sophisticated telephonic exchanges which allow quicker tracing of hoax calls, new packaging technology, stock records and consumer awareness.

Supplemental Matters

Further incidental matters are dealt with in sections 45 and 46, by which the customs and excise commissioners can enforce offences under the Biological Weapons Act 1974 and the Chemical Weapons Act 1996 (or under section 50 of the Anti-terrorism, Crime and Security Act 2001 relating to biological weapons) in cases involving the development or production outside the United Kingdom of relevant materials or the movement of a biological or chemical weapon across a border. Officers of the commissioners will be able to institute offences in England and Wales and Northern Ireland (provided the attorney general gives his consent under section 2 of the 1974 act and section 31 of the 1996 act). Sections 45 and 46 do not apply in Scotland.

Section 51 supplements the offences under sections 47 and 50 insofar as they relate to the acts of United Kingdom persons overseas. It is specified that the venue for trial may be anywhere in the United Kingdom. It is also possible to extend the coverage to bodies incorporated in the Channel Islands, the Isle of Man or any colony.

By section 52, there are granted powers of entry under a justice's or sheriff's warrant to officers of the secretary of state to search for evidence for the commission of an offence under sections 47 and 50. There is no provision for the police to obtain a warrant directly (presumably these are considered to be matters beyond their expertise), but they may be permitted to accompany authorised officers. It was promised in Parliament to preserve legal privilege under the order-making power in section 124[34] but no relevant order has yet appeared.

By section 53, the customs and excise commissioners can enforce offences under sections 47 and 50 in cases involving offences outside the United Kingdom or the movement of a nuclear weapon across a border. Officers of the commissioners will be able to institute offences in England and Wales and Northern Ireland (assuming the attorney general gives his consent under section 54). This section does not apply to the institution of proceedings in Scotland.

By section 55, the attorney general's consent is required for prosecutions under sections 47 and 50 in England and Wales and Northern Ireland.

By section 57, Her Majesty may by Order in Council direct that any of the provisions of Part VI shall extend to any of the Channel Islands, the Isle of Man or to any British overseas territory.

Comment on Offences

One is struck by the complexity and technicality of the changes. It cannot be said on the basis of the normative considerations that it was wrong to make these changes. The state has a duty to protect the right to life under Article 2 of the European Convention.[35] Furthermore, one cannot conceive that there is any human right to dabble with substances which are horrendously dangerous to fellow humans just as, outside the incredible American fixation with the right to bear arms as if part of a militia,[36] the United Kingdom Parliament's ban on handguns has been upheld as legitimate by the European Court of Human Rights.[37]

As for the utility of the legislation, police sources pointed especially to the difficulties caused by the gaps in the anti-hoax provisions. At the same time, there had been up to the end of 2001 no reported cases under those offences. Since then, and rather unexpectedly, it is the more exotic biological and chemical weapons offences which have been activated, though based on the pre-2001 catalogue. Thus, until 2001, the various offences could be viewed as mainly symbolic – a signal to the public and to the international community that the United Kingdom is tough on terrorism. But, consistent with symbolism, it followed that there had been no prosecutions of any terrorist-related defendants and even no prosecution of any kind under the 1972 or 1996 Acts. The picture began to change in November 2002 when three Algerians were arrested over a plot to make a chemical attack on the London underground. However, it was later reported that the actual charges were made under the less specific section 57 of the Terrorism Act (the possession of materials in preparation of terrorism).[38] But then there were further arrests in January 2003 after a raid in North London. The police allegedly found ricin and arrested seven Algerians,[39] four of whom were charged under the Chemical Weapons Act 1996. There then followed the stabbing to death of detective constable Stephen Oake in a raid in Manchester. Three persons were arrested;[40] one has been accused of murder and conspiracy to develop chemical weapons.

Administrative Controls (Part VII)

As well as the blunt instrument of the criminal law, the Anti-terrorism, Crime and Security Act 2001 also adopts a regulatory approach. This aspect must again be seen in context as not entirely new or unique. In particular, attention should be paid to the Export Control Act 2002, taking account of the recommendations of the Scott Inquiry[41] and the White Paper on *Strategic Export Controls*.[42] That Act includes powers to impose controls (by way of licensing) on exports of weapons, the transfer of technology and the provision of technical assistance overseas as well as controls on the acquisition, disposal or movement of goods or on activities which facilitate such acquisition, disposal or movement. Control orders may be imposed in order to prevent the carrying out of terrorism anywhere in the world (Schedule, paragraph

7E). However, one may wonder whether many biological scientists realize that they need a license to speak to other biological scientists at international conferences on pain of being labeled as terrorists.

Added to those controls on external traffic are new controls on internal movement. Part VII of the Anti-terrorism, Crime and Security Act 2001 is rather more self-contained than Part VI, for there is rather less in the way of international conventions or even domestic legislation in this field. However, as one would expect with deadly pathogens and toxins, there is some regulation, mainly through the office of the Advisory Committee on Dangerous Pathogens (ACDP). This non-statutory advisory body, based within the field of the Department of Health, has the task of advising the Health and Safety Commission, the Health and Safety Executive, Health and Agriculture ministers and their counterparts under devolution arrangements in Scotland, Wales and Northern Ireland on all aspects of hazards and risks to workers and others from exposure to pathogens.[43] The Public Health Laboratory Service (now part of the Health Protection Agency, as described later) issued a response to a deliberate release.[44] As already indicated, other aspects of contingency planning are dealt with by the Civil Contingencies Committee and Secretariat through the UK Resilience website.

The ACDP produces information on pathogens and has established a ranking system[45] which seeks to provide practical standards for the safe conduct of work with infectious biological agents in accordance with the Control of Substances Hazardous to Health Regulations 2002.[46] There is also guidance from the Health Services Advisory Committee (HSAC) on safe working in clinical laboratories,[47] while implementation of the advisory standards is done by the Health and Safety Executive (HSE). The supply of pathogens to laboratories requires those laboratories to have suitable facilities for the containment of those pathogens (Article 7 of the Control of Substances Hazardous to Health Regulations 1999), and such laboratories have to notify the HSE in order to be supplied with pathogens or to send them elsewhere (Schedule 3, paragraphs 12 and 13). The regulations (Schedule 3, paragraph 3(4)) define four levels of hazard from biological agents, and the ACDP defines four corresponding containment levels for laboratory work:

- Group 1: A biological agent unlikely to cause human disease.
- Group 2: A biological agent that can cause human disease and may be a hazard to employees; it is unlikely to spread to the community and there is usually effective prophylaxis or effective treatment available.
- Group 3: A biological agent that can cause severe human disease and presents a serious hazard to employees; it may present a risk of spreading to the community, but there is usually effective prophylaxis or treatment available.
- Group 4: A biological agent that causes severe human disease and is a serious hazard to employees; it is likely to spread to the community and there is usually no effective prophylaxis or treatment available.

Anthrax (*Bacillus anthracis*) is within Group 3, while smallpox (*Variola virus*) and Ebola viruses are Group 4. Most of the pathogens within Part VII of the Anti-terrorism, Crime and Security Act 2001 are within Groups 3 and 4.

Whilst extensive, these existing controls focus largely on health and safety, especially in relation to laboratory employees (of whom there are estimated to be around 230,000, mainly working with Group 2 pathogens) rather than security. Safe containment will have implications for defence from attack, and the notification process should prevent the supply of pathogens to unacceptable recipients. But there is little said about unauthorised access and entry or approval or imposition of security arrangements in the approximately fifty laboratories (most of which are in the National Health Service or university sectors).[48]

These security concerns are the focus of Part VII of the Anti-terrorism, Crime and Security Act 2001, and it proceeds not by licensing but by compulsory audit. It is necessary to define at the outset, in section 58, the dangerous pathogens and toxins which will be brought within the controls set out in Part VII. The relevant materials are described as 'dangerous substances', and they include anything which consists of, or includes, a substance for the time being mentioned in Schedule 5; or anything which is infected with or otherwise carries any such substance. The main threats are set out in Schedule 5, chosen by reference to their degree of hazard as well as their availability and usefulness to terrorists but above all simply borrowing from the established Australia list.[49] The secretary of state may, by order, modify the list provided the material is not simply dangerous but 'could be used in an act of terrorism to endanger life or cause serious harm to human health' (section 58(3)). An order has been made to allow some exceptions for pathogens and toxins under the Security of Pathogens and Toxins Regulations of 2002.[50]

Pathogens considered to pose the highest risk comprise: *Bacillus anthracis* (anthrax); *Clostridium botulinum* toxin (botulism); *Francisella tularensis* (tularemia); *Variola major* (smallpox); Viral haemorrhagic fever (viral and rickettsial diseases); and *Yersinia pestis* (plague). These are depicted as 'Category A Diseases/Agents', high-priority agents that include organisms that pose a risk to national security because they can be easily disseminated or transmitted from person to person; cause high mortality and have the potential for major public health impact; might cause public panic and social disruption; and require special action for public health preparedness. The government is not entirely satisfied with the Australia list and has circulated a wider 'Salisbury' list with which it has sought to encourage voluntary compliance [51] and which will eventually by order replace the Australia list.[52]

Building upon this framework, Part VII seeks to ensure that these substances are held in circumstances of high safety and security, out of harm's way as far as terrorism is concerned. Only in those prescribed conditions, likely to involve a small number of laboratories undertaking medical development and experimentation, may the substance be lawfully possessed. In this way, and in order to ensure that security regulations can be imposed, section 59 places a duty on the occupiers of premises to notify the secretary of state within one month before keeping or using any dangerous substance there. Further information can be demanded under sections 60 and 61. By section 60, the police can require occupiers to provide information about the presence and security of any dangerous substances kept or used on their premises. By section 61, the police can request information about persons who have access to dangerous substances or to the premises in which they are kept or used. It also places a duty on occupiers to ensure that other persons do not have access to the premises or substances. Where it is intended to give access to anyone else, notification must be given to the police, and access should be denied until thirty days following the notification unless otherwise agreed by the police. The police can also, under section 65, enter relevant premises following at least two days' notice, with any other persons, to assess security measures. In addition (for example, when there is urgency), under section 66 a justice of the peace or sheriff may issue a search warrant where the police believe that dangerous substances are kept or used on premises for which no notification has been given, or where it is believed that the occupier may not be complying with directions.

Having carried out their checks on the premises and relevant persons, the police can, under section 62, require the occupier of premises holding dangerous substances to make improvements to the security arrangements operating there. More drastic enforcement powers are given to the secretary of state who, under section 63, can require the disposal of any dangerous substances kept or used on premises where security arrangements are unsatisfactory, and, under section 64, can require that any specified person be denied access to dangerous substances or the premises in which they are held where this is necessary in the interest of national security or public safety. It is assumed that 'national security' can include 'international security'.[53]

By section 67, it is an offence for occupiers of premises to fail, without reasonable excuse, to comply with any duty or directions. A person guilty of an offence under this section is liable (a) on conviction on indictment, to imprisonment for a term not exceeding five years or a fine (or both); and (b) on summary conviction, to imprisonment for a term not exceeding six months or a fine not exceeding the statutory maximum (or both). Sections 68 and 69 deal with offences by bodies corporate, partnerships and unincorporated associations.

In view of the fact that personal employment, property and business rights might be severely constricted by these measures, a number of appeals mechanisms are set up. First, section 70 establishes the Pathogens Access Appeal Commission (PAAC) to receive appeals made by any person denied access on the direction of the secretary of state under section 64. By subsection (3), the commission must allow an appeal if it considers that the decision to give the directions was flawed when considered in the light of the principles applicable on an application for judicial review. A further appeal may be made with permission on a question of law under subsection (4) to the Court of Appeal or Court of Session.

Schedule 6 deals with the constitution and procedures of the PAAC. The commissioners are appointed by the lord chancellor and shall hold and vacate office in accordance with the terms of the appointment (paragraph 1); whether this is sufficient independence for European Convention purposes is very doubtful. The PAAC shall normally sit as a panel of three, including one person who holds or has held high judicial office (within the meaning of the Appellate Jurisdiction Act 1876 (paragraph 4)). By paragraph 5, in line with the precedent of the Proscribed Organisations Appeals Commission,[54] the rules of procedure may provide for full particulars of the reasons for denial of access to be withheld from the applicant and from any person representing him and enable the commission to exclude persons (including representatives) from all or part of the proceedings. These rules were set out by regulation in July 2002.[55] Where evidence is kept secret in this way, Schedule 6 follows the pattern established in the Special Immigration Appeals Commission Act 1997. A special advocate may be appointed under paragraph 6 by the relevant law officer. The use of a tribunal does of course allow for special rules of evidence and procedure and special privileges for sensitive sources. The model is the Special Immigration Appeals Tribunal. That is why the matter was not left to the ordinary courts. However, the issue could conceivably end up there through the operation of fair process requirements under the Human Rights Act.

Appeals aside from persons denied access (such as from occupiers of premises against directions relating to compliance with security directions, the disposal of dangerous substances or the provision of information about security arrangements) are provided for by section 71. The person may appeal within one month to a magistrates' court (with a further appeal to the Crown Court) against the requirement on the ground that, having regard to all the circumstances of the case, it is unreasonable to be required to perform that act. In Scotland, the route is the sheriff's court, to sheriff principal to Court of Session.

Initial surveys suggested that around half of the relevant laboratories (310 have been identified)[56] required some work.[57] From initial inquiries by the author within the university sector, it would appear that these measures have been taken on board alongside health and safety regulations. No prosecutions or closures have been reported under the 2001 Act, but health and safety legislation transgressions have occurred. For example,[58] convictions arose in 2001 concerning laboratory work which was undertaken at Imperial College, London, involving the propagation of high-hazard dangerous pathogens (related to HIV) at college premises in 1998 and 1999. Such laboratories are fumigated periodically as a routine precaution against infection. During a fumigation exercise in 1998 using formalin gas (formaldehyde vapour), gas escaped to floors above the laboratory, causing a maintenance worker to experience coughing and irritation to the eyes. In March 1999 an HSE specialist inspector discovered, while making a routine inspection visit, that the college had failed to ensure that the laboratory could be sealed so as to contain the fumigant (which is dangerous in itself if contacted in sufficient concentration) and the release of biological agents. Imperial College in London was convicted in Marylebone Magistrates Court in December 2000 and fined £20,000 at Blackfriars Crown Court on 2 March 2001 after pleading guilty to a charge brought by the Health and Safety Executive of failing to ensure that a laboratory was properly sealed. Universal Safety Consultants Ltd., the college's safety advisor, was also fined £20,000 for failing to ensure the health and safety of university employees. Imperial College was also prosecuted under the Control of Substances Hazardous to Health Regulations 1994 for a breach of Regulation 7(10) (safe working with biological agents). Universal Safety Consultants Ltd. was additionally prosecuted under section 3(1) of the Health and Safety at Work etc. Act 1974 (ensuring that its work does not affect the health and safety of others).

Despite the addition of a regulatory scheme to the threat of prosecution, doubts remain as to whether the scheme under Part VII is effective. The main concern lies in the quality of the training of staff and standard of equipment and security devices and less in the problem that the dangerous substances are readily available for appropriation by terrorists. The substances are generally held in minute quantities. Yet there are no security standards set in the 2001 Act, so the police (who have primarily carried out the inspections designated as Counter-Terrorist Security Advisers, despite their lack of expertise)[59] have had no waypoints for their inspections or, more precisely noth-ing more than provided already by the HSE – at least until a guid-ance document was issued in January 2004.[60] No individual has been barred from access.[61] In addition, it remains somewhat futile to impose increasingly strict physical protection in the United Kingdom if the measures are not replicated elsewhere. There remains a need for an international convention and, if it is not forthcoming, then one must think more in terms of protection from attack rather than prevention of attack.[62] A further potential gap is that the regulations do not apply to substances in transit where they are neither kept or used. While moves are afoot to ensure that diagnostic laboratories will be included within the Act,[63] it is not clear what detection and containment measures have been implemented within postal transit, despite the nature of the anthrax scare in the US.[64]

A report by the House of Commons Foreign Affairs Committee has preferred the idea of a central authority for the control of dangerous pathogens.[65] Its concern is not only ensuring that the Part VII scheme works effectively, but also that the human expertise on making biological and chemical weapons is not adequately controlled. There are at least two causes celebres which are often cited in this connection. First, Huda Salih Mahdi Ammash (designated as 'Mrs. Anthrax' in the popular press) earned a Ph.D. in microbiology from the University of Missouri in 1983, after earning a master's degree from Texas Woman's University in 1979. At some later point, she became the head of the Iraqi biological weapons programme. Second, Rihab Taba ('Dr. Germ') obtained a Ph.D. in plant toxins from the University of East Anglia in 1984. Dr. Taba's team grew 19,000 litres of botulinum toxin in Iraq.

Introduced in 1994, there is a voluntary vetting scheme of potential students in higher-education institutes within the United Kingdom. Those institutes are advised of concerns about proliferation and technology transfer whenever the student applicant comes from one of ten target countries and is interested in one of twenty-one disciplines.[66] But only 70 per cent of institutes take part (and not all departments within that cohort are aware of it), and it does not apply to the National Health Service or commercial laboratories where relevant work is more likely. Furthermore, applying these rules – devised with state weaponry and spying in mind rather than the more amorphous concept of terrorism – may be problematic as they may be as interested in micro-systems of delivery as in weapons of mass destruction.[67] The Foreign and Commonwealth Office (FCO) recognises a need to review the scheme,[68] but it rejects an overall central authority for the control of dangerous pathogens[69] even though regulatory powers are spread over at least three agencies–the Home Office,[70] the HSE[71] and the Department for Environment, Food and Rural Affairs.[72] However, the FCO is apparently pondering the worth of a scientific advisory panel to deal with restrictions on dual-use materials.[73]

Whatever their utility, the normative considerations mentioned at the outset do not prohibit state action in these respects. The laboratory owner's rights to property are more readily overridden than, for example, rights to liberty. Thus there was almost no mention in the debates on the 2001 Act of the intrusion into private property and the costs to businesses. The finding of public interest in much readier in property cases. Indeed, the very status of property rights in Protocol 1, Article 1 shows the doubts harboured in 1950 about the inclusion of private property possession as a 'right' which was not resolved until 1951, after doubts about the definition of 'property' and whether it can be counted as a civil right and not a social or economic attribute were overcome.[74] But even in the agreed text, under Article 1 of Protocol 1, the provisos are sweeping:

> Every natural or legal person is entitled to the peaceful enjoyment of his possessions. No one shall be deprived of his possessions except in the public interest and subject to the conditions provided for by law and by the general principles of international law.
>
> The preceding provisions shall not, however, in any way impair the right of a State to enforce such laws as it deems necessary to control the use of property in accordance with the general interest or to secure the payment of taxes or other contributions or penalties.

Risk Management and Terrorism

The second part of this paper will try to draw together some of the themes already discussed and take a broader view of the response to the risk of biological terrorism.

When we reflect upon issues like biological threat (as well as more traditional bomb threats and threats of assassination), we can perhaps discern a common theme, which is risk. In the case of terrorism, the objective of the terrorist is that the risk is meant to be perceived as pervasive. The destruction and injury are not to be taken too personally by the victims – the attack is symbolic, and the real impact is to be on the state. This observation about the nature of terrorist-related risk should lead to a state response which is equally mixed in its aspects, and often is mixed not only in terms of addressing liability and loss but also in terms of the reformulation of economic and political policies and policing and security policies which recognize the endemic nature of risk in our society. That if, for example, we create what appear to be sophisticated new benefits to society such as communications networks, genetically engineered crops, nuclear energy or the Channel tunnel, then we equally provide for new risks of injury, attack and failure. This shows the essentially organic nature of the processes of the 'risk society' – in the words of Ulrich Beck, 'an epoch in which the dark sides of progress increasingly come to dominate social debate'.[75] New risks result in novel understandings of risk and danger, for example, 'reflexive criminology' and 'actuarial justice'.[76] They also require new responses; as Beck states, 'risks presume industrial, that is, techno-economic decisions and considerations of utility'.[77]

The implication is that we must think less in terms of the eradication of risk, including even by the most draconian powers that we can conjure, and more in terms of risk management, both at the national and individual level. The future battle-grounds will not be just about repressive police powers but about insurance, private security and the preparedness to embrace risk by health and infrastructure agencies.[78]

In line with these observations, one can learn much about contemporary political economies as well as about the manifold nature of the threats to them, since terrorism can open up the social matrix surrounding the environment in which it occurs. Accordingly, the appropriate targets selected for this type of attack must be politically as well as economically important. In a globalised economy with meta-states such as the US, one can expect the targets to have global or meta significance. The same applies to those who perpetrate the terrorism – hence the earlier reference to 'third millennium' terrorism as practiced by a network like Al-Qaeda which does not define itself by modernist agendas such as nationalism or socioeconomic ideology. Meta-terrorism is unbounded by boundaries and may have designs against civilisations, orders or styles rather than sovereigns. Hence our current concern that, with those vast, inchoate targets in mind, terrorists will resort to weapons of mass destruction.

The management of terrorist risk remains primarily a matter for the security forces, and much of their effort is spent on preventive action designed to avert terrorism rather than to lead to prosecutions before public courts. It may be asked at the outset whether the risk management organisations are adequate.

Terrorism has long shaped policing organisations in the United Kingdom. Within the Metropolitan Police in London, the Special Branch was formed in 1883 to respond to an Irish bombing campaign at that time.[79] The Special Branch (SO12) remains the mainstay of police intelligence-gathering operations against political violence, and the London version has been replicated in other police forces throughout the country, most notably in Northern Ireland.[80] A separate Metropolitan Police squad with a more operational focus and responding to more defined threats and incidents emerged in 1970 in the shape of the Bomb Squad – renamed as the Anti-Terrorist Squad (SO13) in 1976, with national coverage.[81]

Further evidence of police attention to intelligence-gathering against terrorism was evidenced first through a reorganization of the policing of animal rights extremists by the setting up of a specialist unit in the National Crime Squad.[82] Another example is the establishment of the National Hi-Tech Crime Unit (NHTCU), launched within the National Criminal Intelligence Service (NCIS) in April 2001.[83] The NHTCU is tasked with the key role in the response to cybercrime, especially as practised by serious and organised crime. The NHTCU's ability to gather evidence has been reinforced by Part XI of the Anti-terrorism, Crime and Security Act 2001 which establishes that, under section 102, the secretary of state can issue a voluntary code of practice relating to the retention of 'communications data' by 'communications providers' which will give guidance to communications providers as to the basis for retaining, on national security and crime prevention grounds, communications data beyond the period that they require it for their own business purposes.[84] The enhanced perception of the vulnerabilities of networks to terrorist attack has also resulted in the appointment within the Cabinet Office of a Central Sponsor for Information Assurance and Resilience.[85]

In the background to the overt policing structures are the intelligence services – the Security Service (MI5) dealing with domestic threats and the Secret Intelligence Service (MI6) responding to international threats, as well as the surveillance agency, the Government Communications Headquarters (GCHQ), and Army Intelligence.[86] The central mechanisms for the coordination and resourcing of the intelligence agencies are based in the Cabinet Office. For GCHQ and the Secret Intelligence Service, the Joint Intelligence Committee (JIC), which includes the director general of the Security Service, approves the intelligence requirements and tasking, subject to ministerial approval. The Security Service's plans and priorities are reviewed annually by a separate Cabinet Office interdepartmental committee 'SO(SSPP)'.

The decisive step in explicitly allowing the secret agents into the world of policing was taken a decade ago when the increased threat from terrorism and organised crime prompted shifts in power. Consequently, the Security Service took over Special Branch's role as the lead terrorism intelligence-gathering agency in 1992. Next, the Security Service Act 1996 provided the Security Service with a greater profile in combating serious organised crime. Overall, the trend is away from local policing towards national agencies and, increasingly, away from policing to intelligence agencies. The trend has implications not only for the strategies being employed but also for issues such as democratic accountability.[87] The director general of the Security Service is now a public figure[88] and the service has even produced a glossy pamphlet about itself.[89] Yet, in the words of Tony Blair, 'a photo opportunity and brochure may be a historic moment by our standards of government secrecy, but giving us more facts about the security service is no substitute for being able to scrutinise it through genuine accountability'.[90] The Intelligence Services Act 1994, section 10, does set up a Parliamentary Intelligence and Security Committee, but its performance has been baleful. The other concern about this superstructure is its observance of individual rights. For example, will privacy be properly respected either during surveillance or in respect of the retention of records?[91] The tasking of externally oriented secret service agencies in ways which can involve activity within the United Kingdom (as under the Anti-terrorism, Crime and Security Act 2001, section 116) is further evidence of these worrying trends. Section 116(2) amends the Intelligence Services Act 1994 so as to ensure the full powers of the secret state (including the Government Communications HQ and the Secret Intelligence Service) can effectively be brought to bear against foreign terrorist threats by allowing both agencies to be authorised under section 7 to act in this country provided the intention is for those actions to have an effect only on an apparatus located outside the British Islands or on material originating from such an apparatus. Before this change, any authorised acts had to take place abroad. In addition, subsection (3) provides for the meaning of the prevention and detection of crime as set out in section 81(5) of the Regulation of Investigatory Powers Act 2000 to be applied to the Secret Intelligence Service. The same definition applies to the Security Service in the Security Service Act 1989. The effect is to clarify that the Secret Intelligence Service can act in support of evidence-gathering activities.

Focusing on the Security Service as the best-documented node in this intelligence web, under the Security Service Act 1989[92] the Security Service is allowed a wide mandate for its activities. It expressly includes by section 1(1) 'the protection of national security and in particular, its protection against threats from . . . terrorism . . . ' In practice, terrorism now forms the major part of its work during the past decade since the passing of the Cold War. This growing emphasis and expertise was given further impetus on 8 May 1992, when the secretary of state announced:[93]

> The Government have now decided that the lead responsibility for intelligence work against Irish republican terrorism in Great Britain should pass from the Metropolitan Police Special Branch to the Security Service.

The decision was prompted partly by concern about the failure to counter IRA activities in Britain, and it was also alleged that there was some pressure from the Security Service, searching for new work for agents at a loose end following the end of the Cold War. More rationally, the Security Service could argue that the police lacked the experience and skills necessary to penetrate the IRA, which was akin to counterespionage rather than anticrime techniques.[94]

Having made the switch in 1992, it is far from clear how successful the Security Service has been in its lead role, as many of its activities remain in the shadows and are also aimed principally at prevention and disruption rather than overt prosecution. However, there is evidence of impact at two levels. First, some cases have been reported in which it is clear that the secret services have taken the lead. For example, Fintan O'Farrell, Declan Rafferty and Michael McDonald were convicted in May 2002 of attempting to acquire weaponry for the Real IRA after being lured into a meeting in Slovakia with Security Service agents pretending to represent the Iraqi government.[95] Second, terrorism has become the prime focus for the Security Service. By 1993,[96] it accounted for 70 per cent of the workload of the Security Service, with 26 per cent expended on international terrorism and 44 per cent on Irish and other domestic groups; though this figure had fallen back to 53 per cent by 1999 because of the reduction in Irish terrorism (down to 30.5 per cent, compared to 22.5 per cent for international terrorism). But in 2002, the overall figure was rising again, with 28 per cent of resources devoted to Irish terrorism and 33 per cent to international terrorism.[97]

These structural developments, characterised by central control and an absence of close legislative or parliamentary scrutiny, have accelerated since 11 September 2001.[98] As part of an Action Plan on Terrorist Financing,[99] a Terrorist Finance Team has been established within the Economic Crime Unit at the National Criminal Intelligence Service.[100] There has also been established a National Counter-Terrorism Security Office (NaCTSO), a police unit working with the Association of Chief Police Officers, which provides a coordinating role for the police service in regard to counterterrorism and protective security and training. Next, the Police International Counter Terrorist Unit is a new partnership between the Security Service, the Police Special Branches and the Anti-terrorist Branch. The Joint Terrorism Analysis Centre (JTAC), formed in 2003, deals with threat intelligence assessment.[101] Finally, Sir David Omand became in 2002 the security and intelligence coordinator, and permanent secretary to the Cabinet Office.

There are almost endemic difficulties arising from institutional rivalry, leading to failure to cooperate in operations and the sharing of intelligence and uneven funding.[102] An attempt to reduce these problems, and also to give antiterrorism risk management a higher priority, is evidenced in the establishment post–11 September of the US Office of Homeland Security. The office has produced the US National Strategy for Homeland Security.[103] Many of the details of the national strategy are familiar, such as the emphasis on intelligence collection and analysis, border security, the targeting of finances, the protection of infrastructure and contingency planning and preparedness. However, significant differences from UK approaches may be noted in the following areas.

One difference is the extent to which a war model is pursued. The military are used against terrorism in Northern Ireland – there are still around 10,000 British troops in Northern Ireland. But they are not explicitly used in Britain. The constitutional settlement since the early part of the nineteenth century (long before the US Posse Comitatus Act)[104] is that policing should be undertaken by the police and not the military, even in cases of substantial disorder.

The next point, and building on the first, is that while both jurisdictions detain suspects primarily for information gathering, the rules and restrictions seem to be stricter here. There is no United Kingdom equivalent to Guantanamo Bay. Internment without trial under the Anti-terrorism, Crime and Security Act 2001, Part IV, is confined to the dozen foreign suspects who cannot be deported because of fear of torture and choose not to leave for distant shores (or rather, are too fearful of the consequences if they did).[105] The policy is deeply controversial. In its report of December 2003, the Privy Counsellor Review Committee viewed the system as objectionable in principle because of the lack of safeguards against injustice and also because it provides no protection against resident terrorists.[106] It argues for either a more aggressive criminal prosecution stance (perhaps aided by admissible electronic intercept evidence) or intrusive administrative restraints on movement and communications. In response, the Home Office Consultation Paper regards Part IV as essential and depicts the alternative strategies as unworkable.[107]

The third difference relates to the emphasis on foreign cooperation. This policy forms the very final part of the US strategic report and amounted to two-and-a-half pages. Of course, the world's most powerful country sometimes feels that it does not need help and that allies are either a luxury or a hindrance. The United Kingdom is by no means the weakest military power in the world, but the notion of cooperation is not simply a sign of weakness. It also represents sensible policy in global travel and finance networks. It was expressly indicated as part of policy by mention of the possible enactment of European Union measures under the Anti-terrorism Crime and Security Act 2001, section 111, even if its commitment proved ultimately pointless. Arguably more important is the Joint Contact Group formed with the US in April 2003.[108]

It remains doubtful whether the rather unwieldy Department of Homeland Security will provide effective coordination given its immense size and complexity. There is also the concern that security becomes the prime policy in all social life rather than an adjunct to other aims. The House of Commons Select Committee on Defence in its report, *Defence and Security within the United Kingdom*,[109] felt that a more modest body along the lines of a National Counter-Terrorism Service merited further attention. The House of Commons Select Committee on Science and Technology favoured an even more limited (but grander sounding), research-based Centre for Home Defence.[110] The only changes so far have been the appointment of a security and intelligence coordinator (David Ormand, ex-MI6) plus a new ministerial committee chaired by the home secretary.[111] But given the slow demise of the Home Office, as its functions seep away to bodies like the Department of Constitutional Affairs, one might posit that a Department of Homeland Security might offer a better description of its residual functions than the usual Ministry of Justice. In any event, it is hoped that Parliament seriously seizes the initiative in discussing these vital constitutional issues and does not again allow the prime minister's office to ignore it disdainfully, as happened with the abolition of the lord chancellor and his office.[112]

Aside from police-work aspects of terrorism, there is a wide array of scientific research, development and procurement as well as responses in the forms of contingencies planning, equipping and training, all with the aim of countering the threats from chemical, biological, radiological and nuclear (CBRN) weapons and materials. Here, at least, there is evidence of important recent progress in the United Kingdom.[113] Moving down from Ministerial Groups on Protective and Preventive Security and also Resilience, a CBRN Scientific Working Group was established in December 2001 and a Scientific Advisory Panel for Emergency Response, adding to the more operational work undertaken through the Defence Science and Technology Laboratory (DSTL) at Porton Down.[114]

Beyond the immediate confines of CBRN response, the Cabinet Office,[115] admittedly more concerned about the fuel price protests and localised flooding in the autumn and winter of 2000 than international terrorism, recognised in 2001 that the Civil Defence Act 1948 is no longer an adequate instrument and that new emergency planning legislation is needed. Local authorities are, however, to remain at the forefront of planning and leadership.[116] The House of Commons Defence Committee was critical of this undue emphasis, which it saw as ignoring the shortcomings of the Cabinet Office's Civil Contingencies Secretariat[117] which, in response to the scares post–11 September, fell casualty to red tape and 'departmentalism'.[118] It suggests a new and more prominent Emergency Planning Agency as part of any proposed legislation.[119] The Joint Committee on the Civil Contingencies Bill likewise suggested a Civil Contingencies Agency which would incorporate a dedicated inspectorate and act as a source of advice on a range of contingency planning issues and would report annually to Parliament through the home secretary.[120]

Yet the draft Civil Contingencies Bill 2002–03[121] and subsequent versions seek once again to put the entire emphasis for contingency planning on local authorities and services. Whilst it is a sound tactic to make use of local knowledge and to shorten lines of communication in an emergency, the idea that the planning phase can take place without tiers of responsibility being defined, without a central forum to deal with national infrastructure and resources (including the military), and without any form of central agency to provide advice, audit and accountability is fanciful in the extreme. The reasons for the reticence of central government to apply to itself the standards applied to others are not made explicit, but one might guess that the endemic British concern for official secrecy is at play. In other words, it is not the case that there are in fact no forums, contingency reserves of food and drugs, or plans – many have existed since at least 1945, but it is the general approach that they cannot be revealed to other branches of government, let alone the public or Parliament. Thus, the prime source of published guidance from the Cabinet Office, *Dealing with Disasters*,[122] never goes beyond a state of abstraction and falls far short of, say, US documentation on Emergency Support Functions numbers 1–12 under the Federal Response Plan.[123] How can we be sure that there are full and integrated plans and preparations if the frameworks are neither prescriptive nor comprehensive and there is no apparent central capacity for coordination?

The other key aspect of risk management where change has been occurring is in the area of health protection, which, of course, is especially relevant to biological attack. A variable state of preparedness was demonstrated by the National Audit Office, with readiness of biological or nuclear attack being lower than for mass attack or chemical attack.[124] A reform programme has emerged from the Department of Health in the light of flooding, the foot-and-mouth crisis and scares about anthrax attacks by terrorists.[125] Following a report by the chief medical officer, *Getting Ahead of the Curve*,[126] it proposed a Health Protection Agency which will provide information and training, surveillance and support services and will incorporate various public, national and localised health agencies. This idea received support from the Defence Select Committee and has been established as a special health authority on 1 April 2003 under the Regulatory Reform Act 2001.[127] This agency will helpfully unify the services of four distinct agencies: the Public Health Laboratory Board, the National Radiological Protection Board, the Centre for Applied Microbiology and Research, and the National Focus of Chemical Incidents. The chief medical officer's proposal for a new Inspectorate of Microbiology, which might affect the inspections in Part VII of the Anti-terrorism, Crime and Security Act 2001 has not been enacted, but surveillance is part of the function of the Health Protection Agency. More practical plans have also been put in place, including the development and distribution of protections suits and the stockpiling of vaccines, much of it overseen by the Medical Countermeasures Group set up in the Department of Health in 2001.[128] Another element is provided by the New Dimension Group programme for the fire service, which has produced seventy-seven incident response vehicles and 190 decontamination units.[129] With these reforms, the United Kingdom is making 'a concerted effort'[130] and in part mirroring good foreign practice, such as the unified Centers for Disease Control and Prevention in the US.[131]

Conclusions

The threat of the use of biological weapons by terrorists offers a paradigmatic insight into the endemic nature of risk in late modern society. The discourse starts with what we consider to be rare risks of diseases in nature such as smallpox or anthrax.

We feel relieved that we can contain some, such as smallpox, but realize that others, like anthrax and botulism, are at large in nature and so they cannot feasibly be eradicated. We then realize that it is not the diseases in nature that we should be frightened of so much as the people who might seek to abuse the harm they can cause. So, threatening people must be detained or put under surveillance, and technologies of surveillance can be developed to respond to that human risk.[132] But which people, and what about the risks either of not finding the right people or of the impact on everyone else in terms of inconvenience, cost and reminders of our insecurity?[133] As if those considerations were not troublesome enough, there comes the realization that it is not just people who cause threats but the very knowledge of how to threaten. So, we need to close of avenues of knowledge proliferation. But then, do we suppress the market in international students and forego opportunities to help developing countries (and also bankrupt several universities in the bargain)? And do we close down the confounded Internet which is of course the cause of all modern ills by allowing the free access to information about weaponry?

The conclusion to this situation must be to maintain a vibrant and inclusive democracy which can discern the difference between threat and potential violence and which can keep its nerve in the face of the heat and light of the terrorist spectacular and not lose sight of its own values such as rights. Liberal democracies cannot eradicate biological terrorism but can construct sufficient protections to make it unlikely to occur in a devastating form by the mobilization of both public and private resources which will reduce risk and reduce the losses from attack. The overt partnership of public and private is commonplace in policing circles[134] but is now set to make its mark in the antiterrorism field on a scale as never before. Beyond that predicted extension of law enforcement, it is proposed that we must seek to get on with our incredibly privileged western lives.

Notes

1. Duncan Campbell, 'Attack on America,' *The Guardian* 14 Sep. 2001, p.5.

2. Daniel McGregory, Tim Johnston, Philip Webster, and Richaard Beeston, 'Bush vows to fight terror on all fronts', *The Times* 15 Oct. 2002 p.1. Thirty-three were killed in the Bali bombing of 2002. See *Inquiry into Intelligence, Assessments and Advice Prior to the Terrorist Bombings on Bali 12 October 2002* (Cm. 5724, 2002) London: HMSO.

3. An estimate of costs is $40bn: James Moore, 'Insurance Firms Shun Terror Cover after September 11', *The Times*, 10 Sep. 2002. See further John. D. Wright, 'Insurance Coverage for War or Terrorism', *Construction Law* 12/10 (2001) p.27.

4. See further: Defence Committee, 'The Threat from Terrorism', HC 348-I (2001–02) para.79; Jessica Stern, *The Ultimate Terrorists* (Cambridge, MA: Harvard University Press 1999); John Alex Romano, 'Combating Terrorism and Weapons of Mass Destruction', *Georgetown Law Journal* 87 (1999) p.1023; Walter Laqueur, *The New Terrorism: Fanaticism and the Arms of Mass Destruction* (New York: Oxford University Press 1999); Nadine Gurr and Benjamin Cole, *The New Face of Terrorism: Threats from Weapons of Mass Destruction* (London: I. B. Tauris 2000); Ed Spiers, *Weapons of Mass Destruction: Prospects for Proliferation* (Basingstoke: "Macmillan Press 2000); Eric Herring (ed), *Preventing the Use of Weapons of Mass Destruction* (London: Frank Cass 2000); Walter Laqueur, *The New Terrorism* (London: Phoenix Press 2001).

5. These are, of course, now given domestic legal standing through the Human Rights Act 1998. Note also the Council of Europe, *Guidelines on Human Rights and the Fight against Terrorism* (Strasbourg: Council of Europe, 2002).

6. Clive Walker, 'Constitutional Governance and Special Powers against "Terrorism', *Columbia Journal of Transnational Law* 35(1997) p.1. For the latest official formulations of these criteria, see Privy Counsellor Review Committee, Anti-Terrorism, Crime, and Security

Act 2001 Review Report (2003-04 HC 100) Pt. C3; Home Office, Counter-terriorism Powers (cm.6147, 2004) Counter-Terrorism Powers (Cm. 6147, 2004) London: HMS. Pt. II para.1.

7. British-Irish Agreement Reached in the Multi-Party Negotiations (Cm. 3883, 1998) London: HMSO.

8. Rick Wilford (ed), *Aspects of the Belfast Agreement* (Oxford: OUP 2001).

9. But see Gerard Hogan and Clive Walker, *Political Violence and the Law in "Ireland* (Manchester: Manchester University Press 1989); Clive Walker, *The Prevention of Terrorism in British Law*, 2nd edn. (Manchester: Manchester "University Press 1992); Conor Gearty and John Kimbell, *Terrorism and the Rule of Law* (London: King's College London 1995); Laura Donoghue, *"Counter-Terrorism Law* (Dublin: Irish Academic Press 2001); Clive Walker, *Guide to the Anti-Terrorism Legislation* (Oxford: OUP 2002).

10. See further on biological weapons: Defence Select Committee, 'The Threat from Terrorism' (2001-2) HC 348-I (note 4) para.66; Ed Spiers, *Chemical and Biological Weapons* (Basingstoke: Macmillan 1994); Abraham Sofaer and George Wilson (eds), *The New Terror: Facing the Threat of Biological and Chemical Weapons* (Stanford: Hoover Institution Press 1999); Jonathan Tucker (ed), *Toxic Terror: Assessing the Terrorist Use of Chemical and Biological Weapons* (Cambridge, MA: MIT Press 2000); Barry Kellman, 'Biological "Terrorism', *Harvard Journal of Law & Public Policy 24(2001)* p.417; Parliamentary Office of Science and Technology, 2001 Report 166: Bioterrorism, http://www.parliament.uk/post/pn166.pdf; Tushar Ghosh, Mark Prelas, Dabir Viswanath and Sudarshan Loyalka (eds), *Science and Technology of Terrorism and Counterterrorism* (New York: Marcel Dekker Inc. 2002) chaps.4–10, 26.

11. John Quail, *The Slow Burning Fuse: The Long History of the British Anarchists* (London: Paladin 1978) pp.169–70. I am grateful to Professor Sir David "Williams, University of Cambridge, for this reference.

12. Clive Walker, *Guide to the Anti-Terrorism Legislation* (Oxford: OUP 2002).

13. Almost as shocking as the human casualties was the closure of congressional buildings during decontamination procedures. A short history is as follows (see further Philip. S. Brachman, 'The public health response to the anthrax epidemic', in Barry Levy and Victor Sidel (eds), *Terrorism and Public Health* (New York: OUP 2003) pp.105–9.

19 Sep. 2003: New York City – NBC received and opened letter containing anthrax.

4 Oct.: Boca Raton – First report of anthrax case (at media company, AMI).

5 Oct.: Boca Raton – Death of first anthrax victim (inhalation anthrax).

6–7 Oct.: Boca Raton – Spores found in second worker (mailroom worker) at AMI and on first victim's computer keyboard.

8 Oct.: Boca Raton – AMI mailroom worker becomes ill from what is later confirmed to have been inhalation anthrax.

10 Oct.: Boca Raton – Third AMI worker (also in mailroom) tests positive for anthrax.

12 Oct.: New York City – Cutaneous anthrax case reported at NBC offices (Tom Brokaw's assistant).

13 Oct.: Boca Raton – Six workers at AMI have tested positive for anthrax.

15 Oct.: Washington DC – Letter opened at senator Daschle's office is found to contain anthrax.

16 Oct.: New York City – Child visiting NBC office on 28 Sep. has cutaneous anthrax.

16 Oct.: Trenton, New Jersey – Two postal workers report what is diagnosed later as inhalation anthrax.

19 Oct.: New York City – Postal worker diagnosed with cutaneous anthrax.

21 Oct.: Washington DC – Several postal workers suspected of having inhalation anthrax. By 25 Oct., two were dead and two more ill, as well as a State Department mail handler.

31 Oct.: New York City – Hospital worker dies from inhalation anthrax.

16 Nov.: Washington DC – Letter containing anthrax to senator Leahy found unopened in bag of congressional mail held since Daschle letter received.

16 Nov.: Connecticut – Woman dies of inhalation anthrax; the source probably derives from some cross-contamination of mail.

14. Robert Lifton, *Destroying the World to Save It: Aum Shinrikyo, Apocalyptic Violence, and the New Global Terrorism* (New York: Henry Holt 1999); Ian Reader, *Religious Violence in Contemporary Japan: The Case of Aum Shinrikyo* (Honolulu: University of Hawaii Press 2000).

15. The Australia Group (http://www.australiagroup.net/intro.htm) is an informal arrangement which aims to allow exporting or trans-shipping countries to minimise the risk of assisting chemical and biological weapon proliferation. It consists of thirty-three states plus the European Commission and was founded in 1985.

16. http://www.ukresilience.info/home.htm

17. HC 247 (2003–04) http://www.the-hutton-inquiry.org.uk/

18. Cabinet Office, Iraq's Weapons of Mass Destruction – The Assessment of the British Government, http://www.pm.gov.uk/files/pdf/iraqdossier.pdf. Compare secretary of State Colin L. Powell, Remarks to the UN Security Council, New York, 5 Feb. 2003, http://www.state.gov/secretary/rm/2003/17300.htm. An inquiry is now being conducted by Lord Butler.

19. Barbara Hatch Rosenberg, Federation of American Scientists Working Group on Biological Weapons, http://www.fas.org/bwc/news/anthraxreport.htm

20. (Cmnd. 5053, 1972) London: HMSO.

21. (Cm.2331, 1993) London: HMSO, as discussed in Foreign Affairs Committee, Weapons of Mass Destruction (1999-00-HC 407) para.94 and *Government Reply* (Cm.4884, 2000). London: HMSO. See further on chemical weapons: Walter Krutzsch and Ralph Trapp, *A Commentary on the Chemical Weapons Convention* (Dordrecht: artinus Nijhoff 1994); Kevin J. Fitzgerald, 'The Chemical Weapons Convention', *Suffolk Transnational Law Review* 20 (1997) p.425; Michael Bothe, Natalino Ronzitti and Allan Rosas (eds), *The New Chemical Weapons Convention* (The Hague: Kluwer Law International 1998); C. Hunt, 'The Potential Contribution of the Chemical Weapons Convention', *Michigan Journal of International Law* 20 (1999) p.523; Walter Krutzsch and Ralph Trapp, *Verification Practice under the Chemical Weapons Convention* (The Hague: Kluwer Law International 1999); Parliamentary Office of Science and Technology, Report 167: Chemical Weapons, www.parliament.uk/post/pn167.pdf; M. Eshbaugh, 'The Chemical Weapons' Convention', *Arizona Journal of International and Comparative Law* 18 (2001) p.209; Tushar Ghosh, Mark Prelas, Dabir Viswanath and Sudarshan Loyalka (eds), *Science and Technology of Terrorism and Counterterrorism* (New York: Marcel Dekker Inc. 2002) chaps.17–25.

22. *Strengthening the Biological and Toxin Weapons Convention* (Cm.5484, 2002) London: HMSO.

23. *Biological Weapons Green Paper*, HC 671 (2002–03) paras.5, 6.

24. *Biological Weapons Green Paper* (Cm.5713, 2003) London: HMSO p.1.

25. *Biological Weapons Green Paper* (Cm.5857, 2003) London: HMSO paras.5, 6.

26. http://www.opcw.org

27. (2001-2) HC Deb. 375, col.719. 26 November 2001, Ben Bradshaw.

28. (2001-2) HL Deb. 629, col.1162. 10 December 2001, Lord Rooker.

29. Clive Walker, *The Prevention of Terrorism in British Law,* 2nd edn. ''(Manchester: Manchester University Press 1992) chap.12.

30. SI 1249. London: HMSO artiste 3.

31. S. Watson, 'Consumer Terrorism', *New Law Journal* 137 (1987) p.84; S. ''Watson, 'Product Contamination', *Law Society's Gazette* 84 (7 Jan. 1987) p.13.

32. Home Office Circular 7/2002, p.4.

33. Archbold, *Criminal Pleading Evidence and Practice,* 49th edn. (London: Sweet & Maxwell 2001) para.19–229.

34. (2001-2) HL Deb. 629, col.640. 3 December 2001, Baroness Symons.

35. *Osman v. United Kingdom*, (2001-2) App. no. 23452/94, Reports 1998-VIII.

36. US Constitution, Article II: 'A well regulated Militia being necessary to the security of a free State, the right of the people to keep and bear Arms shall not be infringed'.

37. Firearms (Amendment) Act 1997 and Firearms (Amendment) (No. 2) Act 1997. See the unsuccessful challenges to this legislation in *Andrews v. United Kingdom*, App. no.

37657/97, judgment 26 Sep. 2000; *London Armoury Limited and Others'v. United Kingdom*, App. nos. 37666/97; 37671/97, 37972/97, 37977/97, 37981/97, 38909/97, judgment 26 Sep. 2000; *C. E. M. Firearms Limited and Bradford Shooting Centre and 11 Others v. United Kingdom*, App.'nos.'37674/97, 37677/97, judgment 26 Sep. 2000; *Denimark Limited and 11 Others v. United Kingdom*, App. no. 37660/97, judgment 26 Sep. 2000; *Findlater v. United Kingdom*, App. no. 38881/97, judgment 26 Sep. 2000; *Slough & A. J. and W. King and 10 Others v. United Kingdom*, App. nos. 37679/97, 37682/97, judgment 26 Sep. 2000; *Ian Edgar (Liverpool) Ltd v. United Kingdom*, App. no. 37683/97,

   38. *R v. Rabah Kadre, Mouhoud Sihali and David Aissa Khalef, The Times* 18 Nov. 2002, 19 Nov. 2002 and 27 Feb. 2003.

   39. *R v. Mustapha Taleb, Mouloud Feddag, Sidali Feddag and Samir Feddag, The Times* 8 Jan. 2003, 13 Jan. 2003 and 14 Jan. 2003.

   40. *R v. Kamal Bourgass, The Times* 15 Jan. 2003, 18 Jan. 2003 and 1 Feb. 2003.

   41. HC 115 (1995–96).

   42. (Cm.3989, 1998) London: HMSO.

   43. http://www.doh.gov.uk/acdp/index.htm

   44. http://www.phls.co.uk/facts/deliberate_releases.htm, and see now http://www.hpa.org.uk/infections/topics_az/deliberate_release/menu.htm

   45. *Categorisation of Biological Agents According to Hazard and Categories of "Containment*, 4th edn. (Sudbury: HSE Books 1995).

   46. 2002 SI 2677. London: HMSO. Amended by 2003 SI 978. This implements various European Community Directives, including 90/679/EEC (on the protection of workers from risks related to biological agents at work) and 93/88/EEC (which contains a community classification of biological agents).

   47. *Health and Safety Executive, Safe Working and Prevention of Infection in Clinical Laboratories and Similar Facilities*, 2nd ed. (Sudbury: HSE Books 2003).

   48. Home Office, *Regulatory Impact Assessment: Security of Pathogens and Toxins* (London: Home Office 2001) para.2.

   49. *Counter-Terrorism Powers* (note 6) Pt. II para.67.

   50. Security of Pathogens and Toxins (Exceptions to Dangerous Substances) Regulations 2002 SI 1281. London: HMSO

   51. Privy Counsellor Review Committee (note 6) Pt. D para.294.

   52. *Counter-Terrorism Powers* (note 6) Pt. II para.68.

   53. *Secretary of State for the Home Department v. Rehman*, (2001) 3 WLR 877.

   54. Terrorism Act 2000 s.5, Sch.3. See Clive Walker, *Guide to the Anti-Terrorism Legislation* (Oxford: OUP 2002) chap.2.

   55. Court of Appeal (Appeals from Pathogens Access Appeal Commission) Rules 2002 SI 1844. See also Pathogens Access Appeal Commission (Procedure) Rules 2002 SI 1845. London: HMSO.

   56. Privy Counsellor Review Committee 2001, Beverly Hughes. HC 100 (note 6) Pt. D para.287.

   57. 2001-02 HC Deb. 375, col.723. 26 November 2001, Beverly Hughes.

   58. Health and Safety Executive Press Release E031:01–2 March 2001.

   59. See House of Commons Science and Technology Committee, The Scientific Response to Terrorism (2003-04 HC 415) para 191; Privy Counsellor Review Committee, Anti-Terrorism, Crime, and Security Act 2001 Report (2003-04 HC 100) Pt. D. para.288.

   60. Counter-Terrorism Powers (note 6) Pt. II para.70.

   61. Ibid., para.289.

   62. *Strengthening the Biological and Toxin Weapons Convention* (note 22) para.47.

   63. *Counter-Terrorism Powers* (note 6) Pt. II para.70.

   64. Foreign Affairs, Committee, Biological Weapons, Green Paper 100 (note 6) Pt. D para.296; Counter-Terrorism Powers (note 6) Pt. II para.75.

   65. Foreign Affairs, Committee, Biological Weapons, Green Paper 150 (2003–03).

   66. Foreign Affairs, Committee, Biological Weapons, Green Paper 415 (note 59) para.200.

   67. *Government Reply to the House of Commons Science and Technology Committee* (Cm.6108, 2004). London: HMSO para.141.

   68. *Biological Weapons Green Paper* (note 24) p.2.

69. Ibid.

70. Under the Anti-terrorism, Crime and Security Act 2001.

71. Biological Agents Directive 2000/54 and the Control of Substances Hazardous to Health Regulations 2002 (note 46).

72. Importation of Animal Pathogens Order 1980 SI 212. London: HMSO.; Specified Animal Pathogens Order 1998 SI 463. London: HMSO.; Plant Health (GB) Order 1993 SI 1320. London: HMSO.

73. The vetting scheme is also being looked at by HC 415 (note 59).

74. Gordon Weil, *The European Convention on Human Rights: Background, Development and Prospects* (Leyden: A. W. Sythoff 1963); P. van den Broek, 'Protection of Property Rights under the European Convention on Human Rights', *Legal Issues of European Integration* 13/1 (1986) p.52.

75. Ulrich Beck, *Ecological Enlightenment* (New Jersey: Humanities Press 1995) p.2.

76. D Nelken, 'Reflexive Criminology?', and M. Feeley and J. Simon, 'Actuarial Justice: The Emerging New Criminal Law', in David Nelken (ed), *The Futures of Criminology* (London: Sage 1994)

77. Ulrich Beck, *Risk Society* (London: Sage 1992) p.98.

78. Kenneth Abraham, *Distributing Risk* (New Haven: Yale University Press 1986); Tom Baker and Jonathan Simon (eds), *Embracing Risk* (Chicago: University of Chicago Press 2002); Barry Levy and Victor Sidel, *Terrorism and Public Health* (New York: OUP 2003).

79. Rupert Allason, *The Branch: A History of the Metropolitan Police Special Branch 1883–1983* (London: Secker &Warburg 1983).

80. http://www.met.police.uk/so/special_branch.htm. Home Affairs Committee, Special Branch HC 71 (1984–85); Home Office, *Guidelines on Special Branch Work in Great Britain* (London: HMSO 1994); Clive Walker, 'The Patten Report and Post-Sovereignty Policing in Northern Ireland', in Rick Wilford (ed), *Aspects of the Belfast Agreement* (Oxford: OUP 2001).

81. http://www.met.police.uk/terrorism/index.htm. National coverage was confirmed in 1990: (1990-91) HC Deb. 187, col.27 4 March 1991, Kenneth Baker.

82. Andrew Norfolk, 'New police squad for animal extremists', *The Times* 27 April 2001, p.2.

83. http://www.nhtcu.org/

84. Clive Walker and Yaman Akdeniz, 'Anti-Terrorism Laws and Data Retention: War Is Over?', *Northern Ireland Legal Quarterly* 54 (2003) p.159.

85. Defence Committee, Defence and Security in the United Kingdom HC 518 (2001–02) para.125

86. http://www.mi5.gov.uk/ http://www.cabinet-office.gov.uk/cabsec/1998/cim/cimrep3.htm; http://www.gchq.gov.uk/; http://www.army.mod.uk/intelligencecorps/. Pete Gill, *Policing Politics: Security Intelligence and the Liberal Democratic State* (London: Frank Cass 1994); Lawrence Lustgarten and Ian Leigh, *In From the Cold* (Oxford: OUP 1994); Nick Fielding and Mark "Hollingsworth, *Defending the Realm: Inside MI5 and the War on Terrorism* (London: Andre Deutch 2003).

87. Richard Norton-Taylor, *In Defence of the Realm?: The Case for Accountable Security Services* (London: Civil Liberties Trust 1990); G. Zellick, 'Spies, Subversives, Terrorists and the British Government: Free Speech and Other Casualties' *William and Mary Law Review* 31 (1990) p.773; Home Affairs Committee, Accountability of the Security Service, HC 265 (1992–93), reply at Cm.2197.

88. See especially Stella Rimmington, *BBC Dimbleby Lecture*, reported in Richard Newton-Taylor, 'Lights, Camera and Action Within the Law for MIS', *The Guardian* 13 June 1994, p.1.

89. *The Security Service* (London: HMSO 1993).

90. Richard Newton-Taylor, 'MIS Comes in from the Cold with Fact File', The Guardian 17 July 1993.

91. *Hilton v. UK*, App. no. 12015/86; *Hewitt and Harman v. UK,*. App. no. 12175/86; *Nimmo v. UK*, App. no. 12327/86; *R v. Secretary of State for the Home Department, ex p Ruddock*, (1987) 1 WLR 1482; *A. G. v Guardian Newspapers* (1987) 1 WLR 1248, (No.2) (1988) 2 WLR. 805, (1988) 3 WLR 776.

184   *C. Walker*

92. I. Leigh and L. Lustgarten, 'The Security Service Act 1989', *Modern Law Review* p.801; W. Finnie, 'The Smile on the Face of the Tiger', *Northern Ireland Legal Quarterly* 41 (1990) p. 64. The Secret Intelligence Service and GCHQ are governed by the Intelligence Services Act 1994. See J. Wadham, 'The Intelligence Services Act 1994', *Modern Law Review* 57 (1994) p.916.

93. (1992-93) HC Deb. 207, col. 297.

94. S. Farson, 'Security Intelligence v. Criminal Intelligence' (*Policing & Society* 2(1991-92) p.65.

95. Michael Evans, 'Restaurant Sting Traps Real IRA's Year-Runners', *The Times* 3 May 2002, p.3.

96. *The Security Service* (note 89). See also *Central Intelligence Machinery* 2nd ed. London: HMSO 1996).

97. http://www.mi5.gov.uk/threats.htm and http://www.mi5.gov.uk/major_areas_work/ major_areas_work.htm

98. Mario Matassa and Tim Newburn, 'Policing and Terrorism', in Tim Newburn (ed), *Handbook of Policing* (Willan: Cullompton 2003).

99. (2001-02)HC 372, col. 940. 15 oct. 2001, Gordon Brown.

100. http://www.ncis.co.uk/press/46_01.html; http://www.ncis.co.uk/ec.html.

101. Intelligence and Security Committee, *Annual Report 2002–03* (London Cabinet Office: 2003) para.62; *Government Reply to the House of Commons Science and Technology Committee* (note 67) para.15.

102. An earlier bout of rivalry prompted the appointment of Sir Maurice Oldfield as security coordinator in Northern Ireland in 1979: See Richard Deacon, *'C': A Biography of Sir Maurice Oldfield* (London: Macdonald 1985).

103. http://www.whitehouse.gov/homeland/book/.

104. US Code, s.1385. The Act was a reaction to the heavy-handedness of the federal army in southern states in the post-war reconstruction years. See: Furman, 'Restrictions Upon the Use of the Army Imposed by the Posse Comitatus Act' 7 *Military Law Review* , (1960) p.85; C. I. Meeks, 'Illegal Law Enforcement: Aiding Civil Authorities in Violation of the Posse Comitatus Act', "*Military Law Review*, 70 (1975) p.83; 'Note: The Posse Comitatus Act: Reconstruction Politics Reconsidered', *American Criminal Law Review* 13 (1976) p.703; C. A. Abel, 'Not Fit for Sea Duty: The Posse Comitatus Act, the United States Navy, and Federal Law Enforcement at Sea', *William & Mary Law Review* 31 (1990) p. 445.

105. The discriminatory nature of Part IV of the Anti-terrorism, Crime and Security Act 2001 convinced Mr. Justice Collins, in a Special Immigration Appeals Commission hearing, to declare the derogation to be in breach of Article 14 but the Court of Appeal reversed that judgment: *A v. Secretary of State for the Home Department*, (2002) EWCA Civ 1502. An appeal to the House of Lords is pending.

106. Thirty per cent of arrests under the Terrorism Act in 2003 affected British citizens: Privy Counsellor Review Committee (note 6) para.193.

107. Counter-Terrorism Powers (note 6) Pt. I paras.8, 34, Pt. II para.31.

108. HC 415 (note 59) para.184.

109. HC 518 (note 85) para.81.

110. *The Scientific Response to Terrorism* (note 59) para.48; Government Reply (note'67) para.4.

111. Home Office, *Counter-Terrorist Action since 2002* (London: Home Office 2002).

112. http://www.lcd.gov.uk/depfram.htm

113. *The Scientific Response to Terrorism* (note 59); Government Reply (note 67).

114. http://www.dstl.gov.uk/about_us/index.htm

115. Cabinet Office, *The Future of Emergency Planning in England and Wales* (London: Cabinet Office 2001).

116. Ibid., para.4.11.

117. Civil Contingencies Committee and Secretariat, http://www.ukresilience. info/role.htm. The Secretariat was established in 2001. It reports to the security and intelligence coordinator and through him to the Cabinet.

118. *Defence and Security in the United Kingdom* (note 88) para.158.

119. Ibid. para.181. Compare, in Canada, the Office of Critical Infrastructure Protection and Emergency Preparedness (http://www.ocipep.gc.ca/home/index_e.asp, the successor in 2001 to

Emergency Preparedness Canada and which has a duty to further these activities under the terms of the Emergency Preparedness Act 1988. In New Zealand, there is not only now the Civil Defence Emergency Management Act 2002 but an appointed director of Civil Defence Emergency Management (http://www.mcdem.govt.nz/memwebsite.nsf advising the Ministry of Civil Defence and Emergency Management and developing the National CDEM Plan, technical standards and guidelines. Note also in the US the Federal Emergency Management Agency (http://www.fema.gov, which is established under the Robert T. Stafford Disaster Relief and Emergency Assistance Act (42 USCode s.5121). See J. A. Bentz, 'The National Response Plan' and 'Government and Voluntary Agencies', in Tushar Ghosh, Mark Prelas, Dabir Viswanath and Sudarshan Loyalka (eds), *Science and Technology of Terrorism and Counterterrorism* (New York: Marcel Dekker Inc. 2002).

120. HL 184, HC 1074 (2002–03) chap.7.

121. *Draft Civil Contingencies Bill* (Cm.5843, 2003). London: HMSO. Also see the review ibid.

122. 3rd edn. (London: Cabinet Office) http://www.ukresilience.info/contingencies/dwd/

123. J. A. Bentz (note 119).

124. HC 36 (2002–03).

125. Department of Health, London, *Health Protection* (National Audit Office, Facing the Challenge: NHS Planning in England 2002).

126. Chief Medical Officer, Getting Ahead of the Curve, http://www.doh.gov.uk/mo/idstrategy/idstrategy2002.pdf

127. *Defence and Security in the United Kingdom* (note 85) para.256.

128. *The Scientific Response to Terrorism* (note 59) paras.55, 56, 150.

129. *Ibid*, para.108. The report criticizes the lack of equipment, by contrast, in'ambulances (para.153). The Home Office devised a decontamination programme in 2001 and has issued guidance (para.175).

130. *The Scientific Response to Terrorism* (note 59) para.245.

131. http://www.cdc.gov/

132. Richard Ericson and Kevin Haggerty, *Policing the Risk Society* (Oxford: "Clarendon Press 1997); Tom Baker and Jonathan Simon (eds), *Embracing Risk* (Chicago: University of Chicago Press 2002).

133. Adam Crawford (ed), *Crime, Insecurity, Safety and the New Governance* "(Cullompton: Willan Publishing, 2002).

134. Trevor Jones and Tim Newburn, *Private Security and Public Policing* (Oxford: Clarendon Press 1998).

12

Children, Terrorism and Counterterrorism: Lessons in Policy and Practise

ANDREW SILKE

School of Law, University of East London, London, United Kingdom

Children are all too often the victims of terrorist conflicts and, as the Beslan school siege tragically illustrated, this victimisation can be extreme, deliberate and intentional. While all victims of terrorism attract a special interest, child victims unquestionably attract the most. Following this, how terrorist groups and governments initiate and react to violence which kills and maims children can play a major role in how conflicts are perceived and in how campaigns unfold. A failure to appreciate the critical issues surrounding the victimisation of children risks undermining perceived legitimacy, eroding wider support and increasing the backing opponents enjoy. Drawing on a variety of case studies, this article provides a review of how the victimisation of children has impacted in recent terrorist conflicts. Implications for policy and practice are highlighted.

Vengeance for the blood of a small child
Satan has not yet created

Haim Nahman Bialik, Al ha-Shehitah (1903)

Introduction

Terrorism is often described as violence against the innocent, and no victims are more innocent than children. Sadly, children are all too frequently the victims of terrorist conflicts, both of long-running campaigns and also of more isolated major events. When Timothy McVeigh pulled up beside the Murrah building in Oklahoma City in 1995 he parked a truck bomb directly beneath the building's kindergarten. Nineteen babies and toddlers were killed in the resulting explosion. Long running conflicts take their toll too. Sixteen per cent of those killed as a result of The Troubles in Northern Ireland have been children (some six hundred children and teenagers killed).[1] Forty of these were babies or toddlers. Similarly, 16 per cent of all those killed by suicide bombers in Israel in the past three years have been children or teenagers.[2]

Sadly it is not just the terrorists who kill children. Government violence in response to terrorism frequently victimises children. In Northern Ireland, the British Army has killed more people aged seventeen or younger than any of the major loyalist paramilitary groups.[3] Of the paramilitary groups, only the Provisional IRA have killed more in this age category than the British Army. In Israel, government retaliatory assassinations against Palestinian militants have left a disturbingly high number of bystanders killed or injured. Currently, for every five militants killed in this way, at least one child is also killed in the attacks. Children are suffering especially badly in this latest conflict – Amnesty International reported in 2002 that after two years of violence at that stage, some 250 Palestinian children had been killed in the conflict, along with some seventy-two Israeli children.[4] The casualties continue to rise in these and other conflicts, and there are no signs that children are being any better shielded by the various protagonists.

High media coverage ensures we are all aware that terrorist attacks occur with disheartening regularity, and that the casualties to such attacks can be very high and very innocent. In an atmosphere where terrorism attracts great attention the statistic highlighted by Alex Schmid, that a person is more likely to be struck by lightning than to be killed in a terrorist attack, seems outlandish.[5] Media attention has negated such reassuring facts and fostered a widespread belief that terrorist attacks are both common and very dangerous. Worse, such biased media focus plays right into the hands of terrorists.

For the professional criminal, as with the terrorist, the victim is often incidental. But the needs for the two types of victimisation are quite different. The criminal's motivations are local and personal. In contrast, the terrorist seeks to send a wider message, and because of this his actions will have a relevance and impact on society in a way quite different to that of any other crime. Victims of terrorism are not simply victims of violent crime, and the threatening effects on society can not be expected to be on a par with those of crime.

Ultimately, the reason for the extra media attention is the similarity audiences feel they have with terrorist victims. Indeed, research has shown that it is factors relating to the victims – and not the terrorists – that determine the media attention given to terrorist incidents.[6] For example, the number of terrorists taking part in an attack does not affect the depth of media coverage, but the number of victims involved does. Not surprisingly, the more victims the greater attention. Following on from this, the seriousness of the victims' injuries increases coverage also, with the death of victims attracting a six-fold increase in media attention compared to if the victims are wounded but not killed. The nationality of the victims is important also, with domestic victims attracting over one hundred times more attention than foreign victims. While this research concluded that increased media attention did not lead to increased levels of terrorism, the effect on victims and on society was not considered. If the death of a compatriot attracts so much attention in the domestic media, it must inevitably increase awareness of terrorism and lead to heightened (and almost certainly unrealistic) expectations of the threat.

Justice and Just-Worlds

While all victims of terrorism attract a special interest, child victims unquestionably attract the most. Children are an especially clear lens through which to view the impact and dynamics of terrorism and counterterrorism. The principle reason for this is that in the muddied waters of culpability, responsibility and cycles of violence which invest terrorist conflicts, children stand aloof. They are not seen as initiators of violence or as provocateurs. Primarily, they are seen as the recipients of others' actions and intents, and in the case of terrorism these actions and intents can be appalling indeed.

Humans have many faults but as a species, psychologically speaking, we do have a keen awareness for justice. This is not justice in a strictly legal sense – cultures and societies vary dramatically in their legal codes and sanctions – but rather at an individual and small-group level. This is a trait humans share with other animals which live in close social groups. For such communities to work it is important that members fulfil roles and responsibilities, and that other members can detect shirkers and cheaters and react accordingly. Thus, at a psychological level, humans generally operate according to rules of fair play at least within their own immediate group.

An intricate element to this human sensitivity to justice is a capacity for sanction in the face of violation. Such sanctions may take the form of voiced displeasure, a lack of cooperation, a lack of support, isolating the offender, ostracising them and can also escalate to aggression and violence. A desire for vengeance and revenge is essentially a desire for punishment of a perceived wrong.

Cota-McKinley, Woody and Bell in psychological research defined vengeance as:

> the infliction of harm in return for perceived injury or insult or as simply getting back at another person…vengeance can have many irrational and destructive consequences for the person seeking vengeance as well as for the target. The person seeking vengeance will often compromise his or her own integrity, social standing, and personal safety for the sake of revenge.[7]

This observation is supported by a number of research studies. For example, in one Swiss study researchers gave students a cooperative task of the 'prisoner's dilemma' kind: All students in the study benefit provided each behaves honourably, but those who cheat will benefit more provided they are not caught. The students were rewarded with real money if they did well and fined if they did not. They were also able to punish fellow players by imposing fines but could only do this by forfeiting money themselves. This meant that those who punished others frequently would end up with considerably less than those who punished others only a little. Despite this, the research found that the participants tended to punish cheats severely, even though they lost out by doing so. People seem to hate cheats so much that they are prepared to incur significant losses themselves in order to inflict some punishment on the transgressors.[8]

Cota-McKinley, Woody and Bell highlighted that revenge can fulfil a range of goals, including righting perceived injustice, restoring the self-worth of the vengeful individual and deterring future injustice. Lying at the heart of the whole process are perceptions of personal harm, unfairness and injustice and the 'anger, indignation, and hatred' associated with the perceived injustice.[9]

Ultimately, the desire for revenge is tied both to the self-worth of the originally offended individual and also to a deterrent role against future unjust treatment. The vengeful individual 'sends the message that harmful acts will not go unanswered'.[10] Not only is the goal to stop this particular form of maltreatment in the future, it is to deter the transgressor from wanting to commit similar crimes; additionally, vengeance may stop other potential offenders from committing similar crimes or from even considering similar crimes.

In-group and out-group stereotyping, however, can leave opposing sides depressingly blind to such insight. As Cota-McKinley, Woody and Bell emphasised, revenge revolves around the idea of injustice and, more particularly, redressing injustice.

However, appreciating this reality sometimes involves accepting that your in-group has behaved in an unjust manner. In a conflict situation, however, stereotyping does not easily allow for accepting ignoble behaviour of the in-group. We are good, they are bad. God is on our side. Everything we do is justified, everything they do is provocative, inhumane and cruel. We are innocent, they are guilty. Or at least, we are more innocent than they are.

Children, however, bring an added dimension to this issue. Put simply, its not as easy to denigrate children as it is to denigrate adults, regardless of how repellent or hostile we may perceive the group they belong to. Humans invest very heavily in their offspring and in general we are very sensitive to the well-being of children, and sensitive too to their suffering.

Successful terrorist campaigns tend to have a number of characteristics but one of the most important concerns who is blamed for the violence. The attribution of blame is a critical factor. One might expect, for example, that victims of criminal violence would focus hostility and enmity arising from their experience solely against the perpetrators. But this is not the case. Research has shown that people tend to rate *the police* as more intimidating, oppressive and corrupt after they have been victimised by criminals. Such victims also tend to rate the police as being less efficient, sympathetic, pleasant, helpful and competent.[11]

Further, people not involved in the event can also be very prone to placing blame in unexpected places. Indeed, observers frequently blame the victims for their victimisation. This common reaction, sometimes referred to as victim derogation, first received significant attention in the context of rape victims. For example, one study on rape presented simulated newspaper accounts of a rape to 650 people. The situations included (1) stranger rape, (2) date rape and (3) rape after consensual sex. The participants were asked to judge the seriousness of the crime. Overall women judged rape to be more serious than men, however, the sentences suggested for the rapists were less severe when the rapist and victim knew each other.[12] Overall, research on rape victims has identified several factors which reduce the likelihood that a woman will be seen as having been raped by a date even though she rejects his sexual advances. Such factors include items such as having had an expensive date, having agreed to go to a man's apartment or having originally asked the man out. Within the context of a rape, such factors reduce the perceived illegality of the act and the perceived violation of the victim. Naturally, variables like these have no legal or moral relevance, but they do impact on how the event is perceived by wider audiences.[13]

This impact is a result of the just-world fallacy. This is a legacy of the human concentration on fair play. The just-world fallacy comes about because, cognitively, people perceive the world as a fair environment, and in a fair environment good things will happen to good people, bad things will happen to bad people. Unfortunately, the real world is not such a place, but is in general harsher and crueller. Yet, research in this area has shown that people find it very important to believe that they *do* actually live in a just world. The result, however, is that when they are confronted by a case of apparently flagrant injustice, people can distort matters so as to see the victim as deserving their fate. As already described, there is strong evidence that rape victims are often treated in this way.[14] It is likely that similar effects are seen in how the victims of violence resulting from terrorist conflicts – both those killed by the terrorists and by the state opposing them. Victim derogation is especially likely when the victims belong to the out-group. In contrast, victim exoneration is seen more for victims who belong to the in-group. *Our* people are generally innocent (and thus undeserving of their ill-fate), while *their* people must be guilty in some way (and thus deserving of their fate). The psychology of in-group/out-group competition all too easily allows such perceptions to become entrenched.

An example of such processes in action can arguably be seen even in efforts to provide an objective assessment of conflicts. Don Radlauer, for example, provided an assessment of casualties as a result of the latest phase of the Palestinian – Israeli conflict.[15] Radlauer argued that the casualties of this recent campaign of violence are often described in terms which are too simplistic and which paint a misleading and overly negative view of the Israeli role. Most reports of the Al-Aqsa conflict simply note that (at 27 July 2002) the violence had claimed 1,551 Palestinian lives compared to 578 Israelis. To the wider world the Palestinians were dying three times faster than the Israelis and this has generally been interpreted as the result of heavy-handed and unjust policies on the part of the Israelis.

Radlauer tried to counter such perceptions and pointed out, for example, that not all Palestinian fatalities were the result of Israeli actions. Many alleged collaborators had been killed by the Palestinians themselves, and there have also been sporadic clashes between rival Palestinian groups which have resulted in deaths. Further, there have been a number of 'own-goals' where Palestinians have died when weapons they were making or carrying exploded prematurely, not to mention the fact that suicide bombers are also included in the list of Palestinian fatalities. Thus, Radlauer argued, it was too simplistic to view the conflict as being quite as one-sided as the raw casualty totals seemed to portray.

This is certainly a valid point and it deserved to be made. Radlauer, though, undermined such legitimate observations when the study then engaged in some rather questionable sleights of hand to try and make the casualty statistics even less critical of Israel. Victim derogation research suggests that this can be achieved through attempting to portray the in-group as more innocent and undeserving of ill-fate and the out-group of being more guilty and hence deserving of unhappy endings.

Radlauer divided fatalities into two categories: combatants and noncombatants. This seems perfectly reasonable, but the fact that Radlauer's system allowed the inclusion of uniformed Israeli soldiers (who were carrying weapons) into the non-combatant category began to raise doubts about the overall picture being painted. Indeed, nearly 10 per cent of Israeli 'noncombatant' victims were armed and uniformed members of Israel's security forces. Most neutral observers, however, would have some serious (and warranted) difficulties about classing armed soldiers as non-combatants (especially given the wider context of an ongoing serious domestic conflict).

Yet if one belongs to or identifies with the group suffering casualties, there is a tendency to do just this. However, such an approach runs into particular difficulties in the case of children and this was something that was well illustrated in the Radlauer analysis. The report drew attention to the fact that a disproportionately high number of the Israeli victims have been female (177 compared to seventy Palestinian females). The report also suggested that Israelis have suffered more elderly victims compared to the Palestinians. While 172 Israeli 'noncombatants' killed were aged forty or over, there were seventy-four Palestinians in the same category. Such statistics certainly suggested that vulnerable sections of Israeli society were being disproportionately targeted. The report, however, then became reluctant to provide such blunt descriptions of especially young victims. In dealing with statistics on child fatalities the report started to talk in terms of proportions: the proportion of all Israeli victims which were children versus the proportion of all Palestinian victims which were children. This was the only way that Israeli casualties could be viewed as apparently equivalent. But why did Radlauer not focus attention on the actual figures (as opposed to proportions)? No reasons are given in the study. Amnesty International, however, reported that at roughly the time Radlauer published his report some 250 Palestinian children had at that stage been killed in the conflict, compared to just seventy-two Israeli children.[16] In other words, for every one Israeli child killed, 3.5 Palestinian children had also been killed. More recent figures by B'Tselem suggest this ratio has now climbed even higher and is more than four to one.[17] Radlauer was prepared to discuss such ratios with regard to female victims and victims over forty (where clearly more Israelis than Palestinians had died) but he did not follow the same pattern for children. Indeed, there is no discussion at all of the ratios or raw figures when it comes to child deaths. It is at least reasonable to suggest that this is because more straightforward reporting of child casualties did not support the general argument the research was intended to make.

Policy Lessons

Ultimately, a fundamental and simple truth is that it is extremely difficult for most people not to sympathise with child victims. The less connected people are with a conflict, the more uninhibited such sympathy will be. And sympathy with the victim contains within it condemnation of the perpetrator. If one identifies with the group the child belongs to, the emotions felt in response will be much stronger, but even if there is no prior affiliation, child victims will create identification. This issue becomes especially important for those conflicts where there is significant international awareness and interest in what is happening. International interest will focus on a narrower range of issues, and child victimisation is certainly a dramatically captivating and compelling issue. The result: Whoever hurts children takes great risks in terms of the perceived legitimacy of their cause, risks undermining their wider support and risks inflaming and augmenting the support their opponent enjoys in the conflict.

Political violence is messy and accidents happen. People are injured and killed who were not meant to be hurt and who were not intended to die. This applies to children too. Thus, both terrorists and governments kill and maim children – sometimes intentionally, more generally not. How they react to such events, however, can play a major role in how the conflict is perceived and in how campaigns unfold.

Terrorism related to Northern Ireland provides a good illustration of the significance of child victims. Over the course of the past thirty-five years, political violence related to that conflict has claimed nearly 4,000 lives and left some 50,000 people injured. In an average year prior to the 1994 cease-fires, some 900 terrorist attacks would take place, including shootings, bombings, mortar attacks, incendiary fire-bombings and so on. In the 1970s, the level of violence was even higher with some 4,000 attacks taking place each year. In the worst year, 1972, there were over 12,000 terrorist incidents.[18]

The wider impact of any given attack was generally low, but there are exceptions. A small number of incidents–a tiny proportion of the total–are universally recognised as having had a significant impact on the conflict. The conflict altered in its course after them. A significant characteristic of a surprising number of such watershed incidents are that their casualties included children. Among such events are Bloody Sunday in 1972 (thirteen Catholics killed, seven of whom were teenagers), the Shankill Road bombing in 1993 (nine Protestant civilians killed including two young girls) and the Omagh bombing in 1998 (twenty-nine dead including twelve children). These events altered the dynamics of the conflict, and always to the detriment of the group responsible for the deaths. After Bloody Sunday, IRA violence escalated alarmingly. In the three years before that day some 250 people had been killed in the conflict. In the twelve months which followed nearly 500 people died.[19] The Omagh bombing led to backlash against the perpetrators, the Real IRA. The organization's commander was locked out of his business premises in the Republic of Ireland, people openly protested outside his home and the group was forced to declare a surly cease-fire at a time when they had wanted to place increasing pressure on the peace process. As a movement, the organisation has never recovered. Though it restarted its campaign of violence in late 2000, support for the group has been paltry and the vast majority of its operations end in failure. Most new recruits are arrested and imprisoned without ever taking part in successful attacks, morale remains low, internal conflicts rife and there are no signs that the group can hope to change their fortunes.

The Provisional IRA's bomb attack in Warrington is another stark example of what happens when children are the victims of terrorism. On 20 March 1993, the IRA planted two bombs in litterbins in a crowded shopping area in Warrington. This attack was the latest in a series of litterbin bombings across the mainland UK. A few weeks previously a copycat litterbin attack in North London on a crowded high street had injured fifty-six people.

Two children, however, were killed in the Warrington attack. Jonathan Ball was only three years old and had been shopping for a Mother's Day present when the first bomb exploded. He died at the scene in the arms of a nurse. Timothy Parry was twelve years old and had been going to buy a pair of football shorts. He suffered horrific head injuries due to the second Semtex bomb as he was trying to run away from the scene of the first explosion. The second bomb utterly destroyed most of his face and it was three hours before he could be identified. He never regained consciousness and died six days later in hospital.

In a statement issued the day after the bombing, the Provisional IRA claimed that:

> Responsibility for the tragic and deeply regrettable death and injuries caused in Warrington yesterday lies squarely at the door of those in the British authorities who deliberately failed to act on precise and adequate warnings.

But the warnings had neither been precise or adequate. At 11:38 a.m. on the Saturday morning, the Samaritans in Liverpool had received a coded warning that a bomb had been left outside a Boots chemist's shop in the city.[20] A police radio alert was issued throughout the entire region, reaching as far as Warrington–a town which is twenty–five miles away (and as close to Manchester as it is to Liverpool). Thirty-four minutes after the warning the bombs detonated, killing the two boys and leaving fifty-one others injured.

Martin McGuinness, who at the time sat on the IRA's Army Council, later commented:

> I feel badly about the Warrington bomb, badly about those children and badly about the effect. I believe that the republican struggle was damaged as a result. I do not believe that the people involved in that intended for that to happen.[21]

Speaking later in 2001, he would add:

> The killing of Jonathan and Tim was wrong. It should not have happened and there is a responsibility on all of us to bring about a peace process.[22]

The republican struggle was certainly damaged as a result. The British government at the time of the bombing was already involved in secret negotiations with the IRA in the search for a cease-fire. The negotiations did not cease, though the tone changed after the bombing. In the public sphere, following the atrocity there was simply massive outrage both in England and in the Republic of Ireland. At a peace rally in Dublin, organised in response to the two deaths, people believed to be republican sympathisers were heckled and jeered:

> Well, it was called a peace rally, but it was obvious when we stepped into the street in Dublin that it was an anti-IRA rally; to me it was obvious ... the hatred coming from those people ... people came out totally against us ... They jeered and they shouted out and they spat on us and they tore up our posters.[23]

Riding a wave of revulsion, on 1 April 1993, the Irish government introduced new procedures which were designed to make extradition of IRA suspects to Britain easier. Meanwhile, throughout the Republic an increasing number of IRA weapons dumps were uncovered by security forces, as people with local knowledge refused to continue to turn a blind eye.

The manner in which the two boys had been killed had crossed a line. Former IRA member Eamon Collins said it best when he noted of IRA tactics that:

> The IRA – regardless of their public utterances dismissing the condemnations of their behaviour from church and community leaders – tried to act in a way that would avoid severe censure from within the nationalist community; they knew they were operating within a sophisticated set of informal restrictions on their behaviour, no less powerful for being largely unspoken.[24]

Warrington had broken these restrictions. As well as public apologies, the IRA changed tactics. The IRA's leadership recognised that Warrington damaged their cause and undermined their support. In response they changed tactics on the mainland UK to avoid similar harm. Bombings like Warrington were abandoned by the IRA teams operating in that theatre. Instead they solely focused on large-scale bombs aimed at economic targets (and for these great care was taken that plenty of 'appropriate warning' was provided to the authorities).

In the eyes of some, Warrington contributed significantly to the Provisional IRA's decision to call a cease-fire some seventeen months after the bombing. Very few claim that this cease-fire was the result of just one factor. Most accept that many forces combined to bring about that result. Yet, counterproductive and deeply unpopular attacks such as Warrington contributed. Monsignor Faul of Dungannon, a Catholic priest who played a significant role in the hunger strikes of the early 1980s and who has been an outspoken critic of both paramilitary and security force abuses in Northern Ireland, put it succinctly:

> [The IRA] had enough guns to carry on [but] they had no recruits. Derry was getting a lot of prosperity ... They were getting no recruits from Derry. They could keep it going in Belfast because in any big city you'll get an element that will fight ... The country people were getting fed up with it, too. And I say that because in the last two or three years the British Army and the police stopped a lot of the harassment on the roads, and the economic border disappeared. They did one disaster, Warrington; all these things made them dreadfully unpopular. So they were finished, anyway.[25]

One may speculate about the precise origins of the 1994 cease-fire, but there is certainly no denying that the Real IRA's 1998 cease-fire was entirely a reaction to the deathtoll of the botched bombing at Omagh. This atrocity was similar to Warrington in a number of respects. Both bombings were part of established campaigns using familiar tactics. In both cases, the disaster was caused by hopelessly inadequate warnings. The scale of destruction of Omagh was far greater, however – it remains the worst single atrocity of the entire Troubles. Twelve children died, and one of the women who was killed was heavily pregnant with twins.

The outrage, revulsion and condemnation expressed in the aftermath echoed Warrington forcefully. There were demonstrations and protests. Like the Provisionals, the Real IRA issued a statement the day after the bombing claiming that they had issued appropriate and adequate warnings adding 'We offer apologies to the civilians'. Again, the warning had been completely inadequate. The caller had said the bomb was parked outside the town's courthouse. The police quickly sealed off that area and shepherded people away. Unfortunately many people were guided towards the Dublin Road junction – a considerable and safe distance from the courthouse. But it was here that the car containing the 500 lb. bomb had been parked, and when it detonated it caused carnage.

The pressure brought to bear on the Real IRA was intense. The organisation's leader, Michael McKevitt, and his wife were openly named in the national press of both the UK and the Republic of Ireland. There were protests outside his home and his business was closed by the premise's landlords. Within three days the Real IRA had been forced to declare a sullen cease-fire – it was especially unwelcome as they had, after all, split from the Provisional IRA primarily because of that group's 1997 cease-fire. It would be nearly three years before the Real IRA felt bold enough to restart its campaign of violence (and then to only very limited effect). But the damage had been done. The bombing had leached support away from the group and it did not return. In the Republic of Ireland, the government introduced the most draconian counterterrorism legislation proposed by an Irish parliament in thirty years of conflict, and McKevitt would become the first person convicted and imprisoned under this legislation.

When one looks at the recent history of Northern Irish terrorism, one sees a conflict where the killing of children played a significant role, a role which was always to the detriment of the killers. In the aftermath of such incidents, the republican paramilitaries tried to lay blame elsewhere, offered apologies, changed tactics and even called cease-fires. Even then, the damage they suffered politically and socially was intense. The security forces, however, were often even more deficient in how they reacted to deaths. Bloody Sunday was dreadfully mishandled. The government certainly tried to lay blame elsewhere for the deaths but this was as inept and as biased as the IRA's efforts. Unlike the paramilitaries, no official apology for the deaths was forthcoming. The result was that Bloody Sunday remained a festering sore running through the conflict, a constant source of support and motivation for militant republicanism and an apparent sign of an oppressive and brutal government. Even today, six years after the signing of the Good Friday Agreement, Bloody Sunday remains the subject of official inquiries and public investigations. Had the incident received a more honest accounting in the immediate aftermath many things might have been different.

Conclusions

The lessons which can be drawn from incidents such as Warrington, Omagh and Bloody Sunday are not restricted solely to the folds of the British Islands. After all, there was an outpouring of reaction to these events across the world. This is to be expected. As outlined earlier, such reactions are the result of common characteristics of human psychology: how we react to acts of apparent injustice and how we perceive and respond to victims. Children occupy an especially important place because unlike many other groups, it is very difficult to denigrate children as victims. In some conflicts, particularly in the developing world, child soldiers are responsible for countless deaths and maimings.[26] Yet even then, they are regarded with more compassion and sympathy than any other group of killers.

Irish Republican terrorism has shown an awareness of these issues. The IRA – in its various incarnations – has reacted to these situations quickly. Clearly this is motivated out of the group's self-interest, but it would be wrong to say that genuine regret has not also been present for many. In comparison, governments are slower to react, slower to apologise and slower to change course. Why? Governments fear that such admissions may undermine the legitimacy of their cause and erode support. But this happens anyway. Being unwilling to compromise simply compounds the problem over the long term as the apparent injustice of the state is augmented. Bloody Sunday is a case in point. In the modern age, the most obvious example of similar practices probably concerns the Israeli response to Palestinian aggression. Palestinian suicide bombings and other terrorist attacks are highly destructive and there is a keenly felt desire to forcibly strike back in response. However, the manner in which the security forces currently act on this desire does further harm to Israel's cause.

Preemptive assassinations, for example, have become a cornerstone of Israeli counterterrorism policy. Indeed, the current Israeli campaign of 'targeted killing' has resulted in a disturbingly high number of innocent fatalities. Since the latest round of slayings began in November 2000 it is thought that over 126 Palestinian militants and activists have been deliberately assassinated by Israeli security services. However, this campaign of elimination has also resulted in the deaths of *at least* eighty-six innocent bystanders, including no fewer than twenty-four children.[27]

Yet advocates of these tactics are often blind to such collateral damage and its wider impact. The fact that the current campaign results in the death of nearly one bystander for every 'militant' is generally overlooked in assessments of the policy. Even the lessons of high-profile cases seem lost and quickly forgotten. In September 2000, the world was transfixed by television footage showing a Palestinian father and his twelve-year-old son cowering behind a water barrel in Netzarim. Israeli soldiers in a nearby outpost were shooting at the pair. The television footage showed the two were clearly unarmed and were simply desperate to get away. Bullets hit them both; the father was seriously injured while the son was killed and lay slumped in his father's lap. There was outrage in Palestinian areas, the Arab Middle East and the wider international community. In response, Israeli authorities prevaricated, attempted to lay the blame elsewhere, did not apologise and did not change tactics. In the three weeks after Netzarim, three more Palestinian twelve-year-old boys were shot dead by Israeli troops. The deaths helped fuel the descent into wider carnage.

For advocates of hard-line policies like targeted assassinations, the loss of assassinated members deals a steady stream of serious blows to the terrorist groups. The death of an experienced bomb-maker, for example, can disrupt planned attacks which must be postponed or abandoned until alternative sources of weaponry can be acquired. The reliability and quality of these alternative suppliers may be uncertain, resulting in less effective and more risky operations for the terrorists. The loss of senior leaders also necessitates internal reorganisation and again a period of adjustment for the group. Yet Israel's counterterrorism practices are currently taking a disturbingly high toll in bystanders and children. The Israeli-based human rights group, B'Tselem, maintains a database of casualties from the Al-Aqsa *intifadah*. It shows that as of 7 November 2003, Palestinian terrorist attacks had killed 104 Israeli children (aged seventeen or younger) since September 2000. This is a savage toll, but it is sobering to learn that B'Tselem reports that the Israeli security forces have killed 421 Palestinian children in the same period.[28] Such policies, on both sides, serve only to fuel the conflict and polarise positions. The discrepancy in the ratios, more than four Palestinian children killed for every one Israeli child, cannot help but place more opprobrium in the Israeli camp. Yaakov Peri, the former head of the Shin Bet, spoke out publicly against government policy in this regard in November 2003. In a scathing attack he said:

> We are heading downhill towards near-catastrophe. If nothing happens and we go on living by the sword, we will continue to wallow in the mud and destroy ourselves.[29]

In the end, what *are* good counterterrorism policies? One answer to this question – but not necessarily the one which always carries the most importance for policy-makers – is that they are processes which lead to a sustained reduction in the level of terrorist violence and ultimately to a *de facto* end to the terrorist campaign. Policy which can achieve such ends needs to be holistic in nature and it needs to consider carefully the question of what it is that will sustain a terrorist campaign. What do such campaigns of violence *need* to continue and to thrive? More than anything, terrorist campaigns need support if they are to endure. The more support they acquire the more resilient their efforts become, and the greater the threat they pose to the state opposing them. Losing sight of this key point – the hearts-and-minds question – is the first step in losing the initiative in the war against terrorism. Children are a lodestone for remembering this lesson. Ultimately, children are a nexus point in such struggles, and around them a great deal indeed can revolve.

> . . . we cannot take vengeance for the wrongs our people have suffered without lowering ourselves in the eyes of all whose abhorrence has been excited by the atrocities of our enemies . . . without whose favor and support our efforts must all prove in vain.

General Robert E. Lee (1807–1870)[30]

Notes

1. Marie-Therese Fay, Mike Morrissey and Marie Smyth, *Northern Ireland's Troubles: The Human Costs* (London: Pluto Press 1999).
2. This is based on a list of attacks maintained by the Israeli Ministry of Foreign Affairs. Analysis of this list indicates that 446 people have been killed in suicide bombings between 9 Sep. 2000 and 18 Nov. 2003 (this death toll excludes the bombers). Seventy-Three of these victims have been seventeen years old or younger. The list is available at http://www.mfa.gov.il/mfa/go.asp?MFAH0ia50
3. Fay, Morrissey and Smyth (note 1) pp.187–188.
4. See Amnesty International, Israel and the Occupied Territories and the Palestinian Authority Killing the Future: Children in the Line of Fire, http://web.amnesty.org/ai.nsf/Index/MDE151472002?OpenDocument & of=COUNTRIES/ISRAEL/OCCUPIED+TERRITORIES
5. Alex Schmid, 'Terrorism and the Media: Freedom of Information vs. Freedom from Intimidation', in L. Howard, (ed), *Terrorism: Roots, Impact, Responses* (London: Praeger 1992) p.101.
6. P. Nelson and J. Scott, 'Terrorism and the Media: An Empirical Analysis', *Defence Economics* 3/4 (1992) pp.329–339.
7. A. Cota-McKinley, W. Woody, and P. Bell, 'Vengeance: Effects of Gender, Age and Religious Background', *Aggressive Behavior* 27 (2001) pp.343–350. Quote taken from p.343.
8. C. Tudge, 'Natural Born Killers', *New Scientist* 174/2342 (2002) pp.36–39.
9. S. Kim and R. Smith, 'Revenge and Conflict Escalation', *Negotiation Journal* vol.9, No.1 (1993) pp.37–43.
10. Ibid., p.40.
11. J. Shapland, J. Willmore, and P. Duff, *Victims in the Criminal Justice System* (London: Gower 1985).
12. K. L'Armand and A. Pepitone, 'Judgments of Rape: A Study of Victim-Rapist Relationship and Victim Sexual History', *Personality and Social Psychology Bulletin* vol.8, No.2 (1982) pp.134–139.
13. R. Shotland and L. Goodstein, 'Sexual Precedence Reduces the Perceived Legitimacy of Sexual Refusal: An Examination of Attributions Concerning Date Rape and Consensual Sex', *Personality and Social Psychology Bulletin* 18/6 (1992) pp.756–764.
14. John Sabini, *Social Psychology*, 2nd edn, (London: Nortons & Company 1995).
15. Don Radlauer, An Engineered Tragedy: Statistical Analysis of Casualties in the Palestinian-Israeli Conflict September 2000 – June 2002, http://www.ict.org.il/articles/articledet.cfm?articleid=439
16. Amnesty International (note 4).
17. The Israeli Information Center for Human Rights in the Occupied Territories, Fatalities in the Al-Aqsa Intifada,: 29 Sept. 2000–7 November 2003, http://www.btselem.org/
18. Police Service of Northern Ireland, Security-Related Incidents 1969–2003, http://www.psni.police.uk

19. David McKittrick, Seamus Kelters, Brian Feeney and Chris Thornton, *Lost Lives* (London: Mainstream Publishing 1999) p.144.

20. Martin Dillon, *The Enemy Within* (London: Doubleday 1994) p.318.

21. Quoted in Kevin Toolis, *Rebel Hearts* (London: Picador 1995) p.325.

22. Quoted in Richard English, *Armed Struggle: A History of the IRA* (London: MacMillan 2003) p.378.

23. Quoted in Brendan O'Brien, *The Long War* (Dublin: O'Brien Press 1993) pp.62–63.

24. Eamon Collins (with M. McGovern), *Killing Rage* (London: Granta Books 1997) p.296.

25. Quoted in Jonathan Stevenson, '"We Wrecked the Place": Contemplating an End to the Northern Irish Troubles' (London: Free Press 1996) p.172.

26. Deborah Browne, 'Examining the Impact of Terrorism on Children', in Andrew Silke (ed), *Terrorists, Victims and Society* (London: Wiley 2003) pp.189–212.

27. The Israeli Information Center for Human Rights in the Occupied Territories (note 17).

28. Ibid.

29. BBC News Online, 'Ex-security Chiefs Chide Israel', http://news.bbc.co.uk/1/hi/world/middle_east/32704491.stm

30. Quoted in Peter Tsouras, *Warriors' Words* (London: Cassell 1992) p.70.

Human Rights Protection and Issues from Regional Perspectives

13

Protecting Human Rights in Times of Conflict: An Indian Perspective

SHRI P. R. CHARI

Institute of Peace and Conflict Studies, New Delhi, India

Human rights embody universal values that cannot be compromised but there are regional specificities and times of conflict when adherence to absolute values may not be possible. This is not to suggest that human rights in conflict zones can be trampled upon. What is argued here it that circumstances need being given due weight if an impartial view is to be adopted. This hypothesis is argued by reviewing the human rights situation in Kashmir, noticing the parties in contention, and the legal and judicial routes available for redress, before suggesting several remedies to improve the protection of human rights in this zone of conflict.

Genesis and Introduction

The terrorist attacks upon the United States on 11 September 2001 have profoundly heightened perceptions of this threat to national security in the international security system, which will in turn influence the discourse on human rights. State security has regained its ascendancy. It had come under review with growing internationalism, placing nationalism under pressure from a steadily globalising world. State actions against non-state actors in the war against terror are now past judgment, even if they are disproportionate to the actions being chastised. The *Economist* has noticed that 'governments everywhere have been restricting rights or enforcing existing laws more harshly, and thus reducing the freedoms that people used to enjoy'[1] before noting that 'they [governments] have reckoned, probably correctly, that the voters would be less forgiving of another terrorist attack made possible by excessive freedom than of the various new restrictions they have imposed. Security is uppermost in the minds of citizens these days, and the true price of an erosion of freedom becomes apparent only over time, which is to say the next election'.[2]

This enlarged authority of the state has serious implications for protecting human rights in zones of conflict and for citizens' protests to assert these rights against excesses committed by the state. The war against terror is far from over and Al-Qaeda remains largely intact, scattered over some fifty to sixty countries. Its capacity to undermine the maintenance of law and order was demonstrated in Afghanistan. Internal conflicts continue unabated in different parts of the world; indeed, the locus of global conflict has decisively shifted to the internal and domestic sphere,[3] which presages greater conflict within nations, more insurgent and terrorist challenges to state authority and further assaults upon human rights. It can be concluded that, with the expansion of conflict zones in developing and newly emerging countries, human rights will be in greater jeopardy in the future.

Amnesty International's latest annual report confirms these dire prognostications. It warns that the global war against terrorism has been taken advantage of by governments to limit civil liberties, and specifically notes, 'The war on terrorism, far from making the world a safer place, has made it more dangerous by curtailing human rights, undermining the rule of law and shielding governments from scrutiny'.[4] India has been indicted for 'misusing' new antiterrorist laws to 'target' political dissent in areas of 'armed conflict' – a fairly obvious reference to Kashmir.[5]

Human rights are generally discussed through a moral prism and in normative terms. Typically, concerned NGOs catalogue human rights abuses in relentless detail, condemn its perpetrators and appeal to the larger community within nations and the international system to provide redress. Ensuring greater transparency is an unarguable prerequisite to secure the mitigation of human rights abuses. The argument will be made in this paper that setting forth universal standards is unexceptionable, but a larger understanding must accrue of real-world situations in which human rights violations occur. In other words, the context in which these violations take place requires greater appreciation so that people can devise appropriate remedial measures. These general observations are of special relevance to South Asia.

The focus of this analysis has been narrowed down to Kashmir for several reasons.

- First, it has continued to remain a zone of conflict between India and Pakistan for almost six decades, and constitutes one of the oldest interstate disputes in the post–World War II era to defy any solution.
- Second, it has either been the major cause or the chief theatre of operations in the wars that were fought between India and Pakistan after they gained their independence in 1947. Indeed, the 1999 Kargil conflict occurred after their nuclear tests in May 1998 established them as nuclear powers, consolidating the global belief that Kashmir constitutes a 'nuclear flashpoint'.
- Third, the conflict in Kashmir possesses both an interstate and intrastate dimension, which adds to the complexities of finding a solution to this dispute.
- Fourthly, the loss of lives and property in Kashmir has been considerable. Official statistics say that 'terrorism in Jammu and Kashmir has taken a toll of more than 32,500, including over 11,000 civilians, since 1990. It has also caused enormous damage to the Kashmiri people and the economy of the State'.[6] The destruction of property has also been officially compiled to include 1,151 government buildings, 643 educational buildings, 10,729 private buildings and 337 bridges.[7]

Proceeding further, the genesis of the present violence in Kashmir, described as a 'proxy war' by India and 'freedom struggle' by Pakistan, can be traced back to the late 1980s. A combination of suppressive measures and misgovernance by the state government, growing unemployment among educated Kashmiri youth, unabashed rigging of elections to the state and central legislatures, and an insensitivity and high-handedness of the central government in dealing with these problems led to an explosion of discontent in the valley.[8] This view of the genesis of the Kashmir conflict contrasts sharply with the Indian government's version that lays the entire blame for this discontent on Pakistan, which had 'in 1989, undertaken to invest in instigating the local populace to engage in insurrection. The previous Afghan experience, which provided a ready-made trained manpower base and ready supply of arms from both western and Chinese sources, made it easier for Pakistan to sponsor militancy in J[ammu] & K[ashmir]'.[9] The violent protests that followed the resulting estrangement between Srinagar and New Delhi were indubitably taken advantage of by Pakistan to assiduously foment dissidence, militancy, violence and terrorism in Kashmir.[10] But it exaggerates to lay the reason for the 'insurrection' on Pakistani intransigence while ignoring local causes.

Indubitably, the influence of pan-Islamic forces is powerful in Pakistan, which has serious implications for the intensification of international terrorism that, in turn, affects global security. India would also be affected, and it needs underlining that the recent terrorism in Kashmir was characterised by the heightened role of foreign mercenaries, who mounted a number of suicide attacks, and cases of terrorists who sought refuge in religious places. The Ministry of Home Affairs has emphasized that some 60–70 per cent of the militants in Kashmir are from outside India, but are 'under the direct control of the Pak ISI (Inter-Services Intelligence)'. Local persons are 'playing the role of guides and porters'. An 'incremental use of suicide bombers' has also been highlighted, despite their numbers dropping from twenty-eight in 2001 to ten in 2002.[11] This issue of cross-border terrorism had embittered relations between India and Pakistan, and is a major issue in contention within their resumed bilateral dialogue.

The Parties in Disputation

Three parties are embroiled in the Kashmir conflict – India, Pakistan and the militant groups in Kashmir, which have both indigenous and cross-border origins and linkages. A 1999 Human Rights Watch report notes the presence of a fourth party:

> Since at least early 1995, Indian security forces have been making systematic use of state-sponsored counter military forces, frequently called 'renegades' by Kashmiris, composed of captured or surrendered former militants, in effect subcontracting some of their abusive tactics to groups with no official accountability. Many of these groups have been responsible for grave human rights abuses, including summary executions, 'disappearances', torture, and illegal detention. Although the Indian government denies any responsibility for the actions of these groups, they are organized and armed by the Indian army and other security forces and operate under their command and control. The government uses these groups principally to assassinate and intimidate members of militant organizations and political groups, especially the banned pro-Pakistan Jamaat-i-Islami.[12]

This policy of using surrendered militants in support of its insurgency and counter-terrorism operations was used by the government of India to deal with militancy in the Punjab region during the 1980s, which assisted in the eradication of the military from that state. It was extended to counterinsurgency operations in India's north-eastern states, with somewhat less success. In Kashmir the 'ikhwanis' (former militants) are greatly feared, and have been responsible for some of the worst human rights abuses that have only occasionally come to light.

In its 1999 report, Human Rights Watch evenhandedly noted that: 'Rising tensions in the region have made clear that both India and Pakistan have legitimate security concerns relating to Kashmir. But these concerns justify neither the abuses committed by Indian military and paramilitary forces nor Pakistan's support for fighters who have also committed serious human rights violations'.[13] None of the parties involved in the Kashmir conflict can be absolved, therefore, of human rights abuses. Thereafter, successive reports of Human Rights Watch have noted that, '[Human rights] abuses by all parties to the conflict were a critical factor behind the fighting in Kashmir'. Human Rights Watch noted 2002 in that 'the conflict in Kashmir remained a flashpoint for violence, as all parties failed to protect civilian non-combatants'. More distressingly, in 2003 'Attacks by militants continued to claim many civilian lives in the disputed region of Kashmir. The conflict in Kashmir persisted throughout 2002, as the safety of civilians and political leaders came under regular attack by militant groups. Hundreds were killed during, and in the weeks preceding, state assembly elections in September and October'.

The violence during these state elections held in September and October 2002 are significant because it reflected a concerted move by Pakistan-supported militants to thwart India's efforts to work with the democratic process in Kashmir. A sharp peak of terrorist attacks occurred during the preelection and polling periods, and 'as many as 261 civilians and 150 security personnel lost their lives up to the completion of elections. In addition, 48 political leaders/activists were killed in terrorist related incidents during this period'.[14] Though violent, these elections provided grounds for optimism that a resolution to the Kashmir crisis could be created, A 'healing touch' policy was initiated by the coalition government formed in Srinagar, which initiated a dialogue between New Delhi and political groups in Kashmir, including those representing separatist and pro-Pakistan elements. A 'hand of friendship' was also offered to Pakistan by the Indian prime minister in April 2003; this fructified into the resumption of bilateral dialogue between the two countries that has been carried forward into 2004.

Any compromise solution to the Kashmir issue, however, will necessarily have to be premised on New Delhi delegating greater administrative, legislative and financial powers to the state government, which is an issue that has long remained controversial. The legal quibble intruding here is that New Delhi favours a *larger devolution* of powers, while Srinagar demands *greater autonomy*. This controversy remains unresolved, casting some doubts on the viability of the entire peace process, but it is too early yet to reach any definite conclusions. At some time, moreover, the issue of past human rights abuses will have to be addressed within the Indian version of a 'truth and reconciliation' commission.

The Context for Human Rights Violations

The several contending parties involved in the Kashmir conflict have contributed to its complexities. Contrary to popular beliefs, and despite the creed of nonviolence preached by Mahatma Gandhi, South Asia is a very violent region. Incidents of violence, either casual or organized, regularly occur in some part of this area. Respect for human life and concern for human rights, regrettably, is not a live issue here. Witness, for instance, the efforts being made around the world to abolish the death penalty; this is not even within the public debate in India. There are other particularities illustrating the indifferent attitude towards human rights abuses. Communal riots occur regularly in India and take a sizeable toll of lives, but are soon internalised. A pernicious 'police culture' exists in the country, distinguished by high-handedness, lack of accountability and the routine use of third-degree methods to extort confessions. The police are feared but not respected; hence, public cooperation is generally unavailable to them, which greatly impedes the effectiveness of counter-insurgency and counterterrorist operations and results in an unending cycle of violence, retribution and human rights violations.

Internal security, however, is accorded high priority in India due to primordial fears that any loss of government control over the maintenance of law and order would encourage fissiparous tendencies and the unravelling of the state. This anxiety forms an indelible part of the South Asian historical experience and explains why national security is a holy cow; it is therefore considered antinational to criticise the security forces too strongly for human rights abuses, since they are believed to be keeping together the fragile structure of the country. These nuances are not understood by outsiders, but provide a prescient context for the human rights violations occurring in Kashmir. No excuse, obviously, can justify the violations of human rights occurring anywhere, including Kashmir. But the reason for these abuses being vociferously indicted by international NGOs, rather than locally, needs to be understood within the indigenous context: A proxy war is occurring in Kashmir which creates its own dynamics. As candidly admitted to human rights activists by a superintendent of police in the Doda district:

> . . . militants undertake a certain action and the security forces fight back. But contrary to the militants, we are accountable: We must answer to our superior officers . . . and we face inquiries, departmental and legal action. The population [in Doda district] is 48 percent Hindu and 52 percent Muslim. Any action has a reaction. Even Muslims are killed by the militants – 95 percent of the Muslims do not voluntarily support the militants . . . As for the actions by the security forces, mistakes do happen, but we repent, and it is not wilful. And even if it is not intentional, we have to answer to many forums. This is a proxy war. Collateral damage is much higher in this type of war. Things happen in the heat of the moment.[15]

What are the actions by the Indian security forces in Kashmir that precipitate human rights abuses? Their counterinsurgency operations are generally mounted in search of foreign militants, although local persons are responsible for a sizeable proportion (25–30 per cent) of incidents in Kashmir. The Indian government has dedicated specially trained infantry troops called Rashtriya [National] Rifles to conduct cordon-and-search and combing operations in Kashmir that often result in firefights between the militants and these troops. The human rights abuses that sometimes occur during these operations include the beating up of villagers suspected of harbouring militants, the torture of detainees, custodial deaths, the rape of women and destruction of property. Local citizens often get caught in the crossfire, and become part of what is euphemistically referred to as 'collateral damage'.

An especially poignant human rights problem in Kashmir is the issue of 'enforced or involuntary disappearances' (EIDs). It was officially admitted by the chief minister that this question was significant: 'Three thousand seven hundred and forty four are missing between 2000 and 2002, 1,533 persons got [*sic*] disappeared in 2000. 1,596 went missing in 2001 and 605 in 2002'.[16] The government argues that these disappearances were occasioned by young persons crossing over into Pakistan so they could be trained to become insurgents. But this explanation, though partially true, is facile, and several young persons – it is impossible to be certain about numbers – have quite probably been killed by the security forces and their bodies disposed off to avoid inquiry. This situation is particularly hard on their wives – 'half-widows', as they are referred to in Kashmir. Under the provisions of civil law they cannot claim a share in the 'disappeared' person's property unless it is proved that the person concerned is dead; moreover, these women cannot marry again under Muslim law for the same reason.

Legal and Judicial Processes

The legal processes enforced by the state to protect human rights can now be detailed. India has joined the Geneva Convention and the International Covenant on Civil and Political Rights, which prohibits derogation of the right to life, cruel, inhuman and degrading treatment, and bans torture. Considerable resentment was expressed, both inside and outside Parliament, before the draconian Prevention of Terrorism Act (POTA) was enacted in 2002. It was widely suspected of being intended to harass the opposition parties and the minorities. The National Human Rights Commission maintained that the 'existing laws are sufficient to deal with any eventuality, including terrorism, and there is no need for a draconian POTA'.[17] Its provisions define terrorism very broadly to include acts of violence carried out with 'intent to threaten the unity and integrity of India or to strike terror in any part of the people'. It makes not providing the authorities with 'information relating to any terrorist activity' a crime, permitting the police and security forces to exercise considerable discretion; and allows for preventive detention without charge for three months. Since POTA was first introduced, some efforts have been added to ensure due process, but these are deemed insufficient by its critics.

POTA continues to be attacked by media organizations, civil and human rights groups, academics, opposition parties and religious and secular institutions. Much depends on the efficacy of the judicial review procedures envisaged to protect persons detained under this special law from arbitrary or whimsical indictment. Ironically enough, the rigours of the POTA are likely to be less in Kashmir, as the coalition parties constituting the state government had opposed its enactment by the central government; it can be expected in consequence that the POTA will be used more judiciously and with greater circumspection in Kashmir. POTA has recently been abrogated, but cases launched under its provisions would continue unless they are withdrawn by the state.

Apart from POTA, the Jammu and Kashmir Disturbed Areas Act 1990 and the Armed Forces (Jammu and Kashmir) Special Powers Act 1990 are applicable in the state. In tandem, they permit the state or central government to declare Kashmir or parts thereof to be a 'disturbed area', whereby designated officers of the armed forces are empowered to '. . . fire upon or otherwise use force, even to the causing of death, against any person who is acting in contravention of any law or order for the time being in force in the disturbed area prohibiting the assembly of five or more persons or the carrying of weapons or of things capable of being used as weapons or of firearms, ammunition or explosive substances . . .' These laws empower the security forces to use lethal force in 'disturbed areas', and provide them immunity from any prosecution 'in respect of anything done or purporting to be done in exercise of the powers conferred' by these laws. The armed forces are further empowered 'to destroy any arms dump, prepared or fortified position or shelter from which armed attacks are made or are likely to be made or are attempted to be made, or any structure used as a training camp for armed volunteers or utilised as a hideout by armed gangs or absconders wanted for any offence'. The discretion available to the security forces is therefore very considerable, placing a large premium on their good faith.

At first sight these special laws may appear excessive. They are not, however, unconstitutional; otherwise public interest litigation would have ensured that they were struck down by the courts. Furthermore, these laws only amplify the legal provisions already existing in the Indian Penal Code and Criminal Procedure Code that were enacted in the latter half of the nineteenth century. It should also be appreciated that these special laws are required to deal with the insurgency and terrorism situation in Kashmir. What needs ensuring from the human rights perspective is that excesses are avoided, and that executive and judicial discretion is used in good faith, and not for biased or unjust ends.

What is a matter of concern, however, is the virtual breakdown of judicial processes in Kashmir and the inability of the state government to prosecute those indulging in militant activities (or abetting and collaborating with them) due to the impossibility of getting witnesses to testify against militants in criminal trials out of fear of reprisals. This leads to demands being made by the security forces for allowing detention without trial if adequate proof is available to prosecute the militants (subject to obtaining judicial satisfaction). There is already a predisposition in the security forces in times and areas of conflict, as copiously recorded by human rights NGOs, to indulge in extrajudicial procedures like sequential arrests of persons released by the courts and summary execution of captured militants (in false encounters or whilst 'escaping from custody') in pursuance of a 'no prisoners' policy. This does happen sometimes in Kashmir, which brings up the problem of ensuring the protection of human rights while also ensuring the normal functioning of the criminal justice system in zones of conflict. The need for some radical approach to holding judicial trials effectively and impartially in insurgency- and terrorism-affected areas requires much greater thought and consideration.

The 'common minimum programme' drawn up by the coalition government in Kashmir is of relevance here; its salubrious goals include,

> To heal the physical, psychological and emotional wounds inflicted by fourteen years of militancy, to restore the rule of law in Jammu and Kashmir state, to complete the revival of the political process which was begun by the recently concluded elections and to request the government of India to initiate and hold sincerely and seriously, wide ranging consultations and dialogue, without conditions, with the members of the legislature and other segments of public opinion in all three regions of the state to evolve a broad-based consensus on restoration of peace with honour in the state.[18]

Under this rubric, the 'healing touch' policy envisages discussions being held between the union government, the state government and the different representative groups in Kashmir,[19] the release of all political prisoners, investigations into cases of missing persons, an end to violence and a reining in the Special Operations Groups.[20] These sentiments cannot be dismissed as mere rhetoric or intended for public relations purposes; in fairness, the state and central governments have taken cautious steps to implement all these promises in the face of opposition from the hard-liners. A political dialogue has also been initiated between representatives of these hard-liners and the central government that would, hopefully, be invigorated after the impending general elections. The two governments need more time to flesh out this reconciliation process.

Finally, some reference must be made to the role of the Human Rights Commissions established by the state and central governments. The State Human Rights Commission (SHRC) is headed under statute by a retired judge of the Jammu and Kashmir High Court. It is officially claimed that all allegations of human rights violations are looked into and prompt action is taken against accused security forces personnel, which can involve suspension from service and arrest pending enquiry or court martial. Should the allegations be proved the punishments can include imprisonment, confinement, dismissal from service, compulsory retirement, reduction in rank or loss of seniority, apart from departmental penalties. Several officers and other ranks found guilty have been punished.[21]

The limitations of the state commission are also apparent: 'Its recommendations are not binding, and it does not take up cases pending before the High Court. Although it can undertake an investigation on its own, it cannot directly investigate abuses carried out by the army or other federal [central] forces. However, the commission can summon a representative from these agencies to report about the incident in question'.[22] A more critical appraisal of the SHRC denigrates it 'as a show-piece which was established to whitewash army and security personnel's excesses. The commission has no jurisdiction over the army and its recommendations are seldom taken seriously'.[23]

The National Human Rights Commission (NHRC) was established in India under the Protection of Human Rights Act 1993 with the 'goal of defending human dignity and thereby defending the human rights of the people of the country'.[24] A tradition has been established that the NHRC would be headed by the outgoing chief justice of the Supreme Court of India, which lends immense weight to its views and findings. The NHRC has taken a robust position about terrorism, and held that

> it aims at the destruction of civil society and the unravelling of the State; [hence] it is essential that it be firmly resisted by both. The Commission would therefore like to reiterate its conviction that the police and armed forces of the country, backed by all elements of civil society, have a duty to fight and triumph over terrorism. The Commission is additionally of the view, however, that this must be done in a manner that respects the constitution of the republic, the laws of the land and the treaty commitments into which the State has solemnly entered.[25]

The NHRC has specifically observed that the security forces 'when called upon to act in aid of civil power, must do so in close co-ordination with civil administration. This view is based on the experience of the Commission ... that violations of human rights are far less likely to occur when the role and the responsibilities of the civil authorities under the law are fully respected, not least in respect of cordon and search operations, arrest, interrogation and detention'.[26] These observations are of obvious relevance to Kashmir.

The NHRC's charter of duties also envisages its sensitising state governments to human rights issues. For instance, it issued directions to the chief ministers of all states, pointing out the law in regard to deaths attributed to the police or paramilitary forces under their control.[27] Such killings can only be justified under Indian law if they result from the exercise of the right of private defence under the Indian Penal Code, or section 46 of the Criminal Procedure Code which authorises the use of force, extending up to the causing of death, as may be necessary to arrest the person accused of an offence punishable with death or imprisonment for life. Information regarding such deaths must be inscribed in the police station registers and 'made over for investigation to some other independent investigation agency, such as the State CID'.[28]

It should be readily conceded that the establishment of the State and National Human Rights Commissions will not stop violations of human rights from occurring. Neither have they ceased. What they do provide is an institutional mechanism for establishing the checks and balances provided by a parliamentary democracy to protect the life and dignity of its citizens. They are of signal importance for this reason.

Remedies and Conclusions

The foregoing section clarifies that the rule of law is firmly established in India, which significantly reduces the scope for arbitrary conduct by the state and its security forces and entails a commitment to legal procedures being followed, even in times and zones of conflict. Mitigating the human rights abuses that do occur in Kashmir requires a political solution being found to the problem. Three parties are involved in the Kashmir conflict–India, Pakistan and the militants–and two sets of dialogue are needed to evolve a political *modus vivendi*. The first dialogue is required between India and Pakistan, which is currently in progress. It was being resisted by India since it required Pakistan to stop supporting cross-border terrorism, which it no longer denies. The second dialogue is required between New Delhi and Srinagar, but also with the various representative groups in Kashmir. These dialogues have only proceeded fitfully, punctuated by declarations of cease-fires and nominations of central government interlocutors to negotiate with them. Another such effort is in progress, as noted above, reinforced by the state's 'healing touch' policy. But it is still too early to opine on the fate of this initiative.

Whilst awaiting a political solution to emerge from these dual dialogue processes in play there are many steps that can be taken to remedy the human rights situation in Kashmir.

First, it is important to ensure the maximum transparency possible regarding security operations, subject to the imperative of not compromising security. It has been suggested that, wherever possible, a magistrate should accompany the security forces on cordon-and-search operations, which is a debateable proposition. Inviting external monitoring agencies to appraise India's human rights record in Kashmir would greatly assist in refurbishing the image of the security forces. A wholesome step in this direction of enlarging transparency is the Memorandum of Understanding (MOU) signed by the government of India with the International Committee of the Red Cross (ICRC) in June 1995, which permits its delegates access to detention centres for meeting arrested or detained persons in Kashmir. The ICRC has visited some fifty-three detention centres, and 7,777 detainees were registered as of October 2002.[29]

Second, the need to educate the public in human rights and humanitarian law is of the essence. This could be introduced in the curriculum of educational institutions in conflict zones like Kashmir, and a beginning could be made with state-funded schools and colleges. The state also needs to inculcate the practice of universal values like tolerance, secularism, respect for dissent and democratic practices in these institutions, and also invest in the education of its security forces to mitigate human rights abuses while appreciating their practical difficulties in functioning within conflict zones. The essential message needs constant reiterating that the security forces are dealing with their own citizens, not enemy aliens.

Third, NGOs working in the human rights field need to avoid the familiar malady of turf wars. They should monitor not only the human rights violations committed by the security forces and the militants, but also keep the NGO community under scrutiny to weed out organizations that serve partisan and nonsecular ends. Ensuring transparency in their functioning is important in South Asia, since the probity of NGOs, with honourable exceptions, is generally rated very low in the region. The possibility of human rights NGOs evolving a code of conduct for themselves is worth exploring, as is the feasibility of the NHRC and SHRC conducting training courses to instruct these NGOs in human rights legislation.

Fourth, the importance for evenhandedness to be observed (and also be seen to be observed) by NGOs and human rights organisations cannot be overstated. This is in the interests of their own credibility; hence, they need to balance their investigations/reports indicting the excesses of the security forces with publicising the excesses committed by the militants. Many of these NGOs are inclined to place the state perpetually in the dock but forgive the militants and terrorists their trespasses. The impression is therefore strong that the NGOs' natural inclination is to gloss over the misdeeds of militants but criticise the security forces.

Fifth, the continuance of the Armed Forces (Special Powers) Act, the Disturbed Areas Act and similar draconian legislation (including state laws like the Public Safety Act in Kashmir) should be periodically reviewed by Parliament and the state legislature to examine the necessity for their further continuance, and the government of the day should justify why the ordinary laws of the land are inadequate to deal with the situation. This review by the elected representatives of the people would also permit a debate to reevaluate the ability of these special laws to achieve their stated objectives.

Sixth, the relevance of the SHRC and NHRC would be enhanced by strengthening their investigating staff and equipping them with statutory powers to investigate complaints against the security forces. The state should be directed to act upon their findings with celerity to the satisfaction of the commissions; otherwise their views on the failure of the state to implement their recommendations should be placed before the state Legislative Assembly or the Houses of Parliament for their further consideration. Adding a statutory provision to this effect in the legislation governing the establishment of these commissions would greatly enhance their relevance.

Seventh, the policy of using surrendered or captured militants in counterinsurgency operations by the security forces requires urgent reconsideration due to the serious complaints that are regularly being received about their human rights violations and their extortion practices. Their role in counterinsurgency and counterterrorism operations should be restricted to providing information about their former associates and other material particulars. The rehabilitation of surrendered or captured militants in civilian avocations should be preferred to employing them in a counterinsurgent force. A proper programme for rehabilitating these former militants should be required.

Eighth, a conscious policy also needs to be devised to enable the return of internally displaced persons like the Kashmiri Pandits to their homes in the valley; 2 50,000–3 00,000 of them are living in pitiable conditions in refugee camps in Jammu and several other parts of India. An inventory of their abandoned property, lands and buildings should be drawn up and effective steps taken to keep them safe from encroachments. Naturally, these Pandits will be unwilling to return to their former homes unless suitable conditions are created for ensuring their safety and honour.

Human rights supporters are inclined to severely indict security forces. But they cannot ignore the murder of thousands of innocent civilians belonging to different communities in Kashmir – Hindus, Sikhs, Muslims and even nomadic graziers like Bakerwals and Gujjars – by the militants. They have indeed achieved a type of 'ethnic cleansing' by driving out Hindus from the Kashmir Valley; they have also targeted persons suspected of being informers; killed supporters of other militant groups; indulged in indiscriminate mining of areas; and engaged in bomb and grenade attacks to draw attention to their cause, especially before the visit of an important foreign dignitary.[30] Kidnapping for ransom is part of their repertoire, as also threatening journalists to ensure no criticism of their plainly criminal activities like smuggling. Such activities cannot be justified in any way as forming part of a 'freedom struggle'.

This recital is not intended to justify the human rights abuses committed by the state and its security forces in Kashmir. The essential point being made is that it would be unrealistic to judge human rights violations in times of conflict (and within conflict zones like Kashmir) on the same absolute scale as applicable in times of peace and normalcy. The provision of arms, training and political/ideological support to the militants in Kashmir has openly been continuing from across the border, and political organizations supporting them in Pakistan have yet to moderate these activities, despite some recent efforts being made by the state in Pakistan. Militant activities invite an inevitable reaction by India's security forces, leading to the Kashmiris suffering human rights abuses committed by all parties to the conflict. It remains doubtful how the killing of innocents, especially women and children, advances the cause which the militants and their handlers/supporters choose to espouse.

Notes

1. 'Civil liberties: for whom the liberty bell tolls', *The Economist* 364 (31 Aug. 2002) 8288 p.19.

2. Ibid, p.21.

3. The Stockholm International Peace Research Institute lists conflicts occurring globally, and has noted that 'in the 13-year post-cold war period 1990–2002, there were 58 different major armed conflicts in 46 different locations ... All but three of the major armed conflicts registered for 1990–2002 were internal'. Cf. *SIPRI Yearbook 2001: Armaments, Disarmament and International Security* (Oxford: Oxford University Press 2001) p.109. Further, 'In 2002 there were 21 major armed conflicts in 19 locations throughout the world ... The only interstate conflict that was active in 2002 occurred between India and Pakistan'. *SIPRI Yearbook 2003: Armaments, Disarmament and International Security* (Oxford: Oxford University Press 2003) p.109.

4. 'Amnesty International slams India', *The Hindu* 29 May 2003.

5. Ibid.

6. Government of India, *Ministry of Home Affairs, Annual Report 2002–2003* p.2.

7. Ibid. p.13.

8. A description of this deterioration in the Kashmir situation is available in P. R. Chari, Pervaiz Iqbal Cheema and Stephen Philip Cohen, *Perception, Politics and Security in South Asia: The Compound Crisis of 1990* (London and New York: RoutledgeCurzon 2003) pp. 34–64, cf. chapter on 'Kashmir: From Simla to Chaos'.

9. Government of India (note 6) pp.11–12.

10. The human rights issue in the Kashmir imbroglio is succinctly noted in Human Rights Watch's 1999 report *Behind the Kashmir Conflict: Abuses by Indian Security Forces and Militant Groups Continue* (New York: Human Rights Watch 1999) pp. 1–3.

11. Government of India (note 6) p.2.

12. Human Rights Watch (note 10) pp. 32–3.

13. *Ibid.* p.3.

14. Government of India (note 6) pp. 17–18.

15. Human Rights Watch (note 10) pp. 5–6.

16. This statement was made in the state Legislative Assembly on 25 Feb. 2003 as reported in Showkat A. Motta and Hilal Ahmad, 'Declare 'em Dead: Families of Disappeared Men Appeal [to] PM', *Srinagar Times* 18 April 2003.

17. http://hrw.org/un/chr59/counter-terrorism-bck4.htm

18. *Kashmir Times* (Jammu) Oct. 28 2002.

19. 'Mufti wants dialogue with all J & K groups', *The Hindu* 6 Nov. 2002.

20. Muzamil Jaleel, 'The Burden of Hope', *The Indian Express* 8 Nov. 2002; Editorial, 'Release them all', *Greater Kashmir* 12 Nov. 2002.

21. Government of India, Ministry of Home Affairs, Initiatives for Peace in the Valley: The Human Rights Scenario, http://mha.nic.in/pea.htm

22. Human Rights Watch (note 10) p.44.

23. http://www.Milligazette.com/Archives/01072002/0107200276.htm

24. Government of India (note 6) p.53.

25. Government of India, *National Human Rights Commission, Annual Report 1997–98* p.8.

26. Ibid, p.9.

27. National Human Rights Commission, *Important Instructions/Guidelines* (New Delhi: 2000) pp.33–35.

28. Ibid.

29. Government of India (note 6) pp.52–3.

30. For instance, on 20 March 2000, just before President Clinton's visit to India, thirty-six Sikh men were shot dead by militants in Chittisinghpura, Anantnag district. Extensive protests were made thereafter by the Sikh community demanding state protection, and by Muslim villagers who staged protests against the countermeasures taken by the Indian security forces. This course of events was perhaps anticipated by the militants, and designed to serve their political purpose of highlighting the Kashmir issue during the US president's visit to South Asia.

14

Human Rights Dilemmas in Using Informers to Combat Terrorism: The Israeli-Palestinian Case

HILLEL COHEN

Hebrew University of Jerusalem, Jerusalem, Israel

RON DUDAI

School of Oriental and Asian Studies, London, United Kingdom

Using informers is a basic tool in preventing terror attacks and the nature of current terror threats makes it even more crucial. This use, however, often leads to human rights violations, both of the informers and by them, and to many problematic ethical questions. Drawing on the Israeli–Palestinian example—where a main strategy of Israeli intelligence activity in the Palestinian areas has been an extensive use of informers—this article presents the main human rights dilemmas in the field, divided into three stages: recruitment, operation and post-operation obligations, and also points to the possible counter-productive consequences of such a use.

Introduction

Using informers is a basic tool in preventing terror attacks. The lack of HUMINT ('human intelligence') on terrorist groups such as Al-Qaeda is considered to be one of the main failures of American intelligence prior to 11 September, as a recent report by a US investigative committee shows.[1] Thus, since the announcement of the 'war on terror', increased efforts are being made to recruit informers in various organisations and communities. The use of informers, however, often leads to human rights violations of and by the informers. It also brings forth many problematic ethical questions, for which international law currently supplies only partial answers.

This article will focus on the Israeli-Palestinian case, where using informers has long been one of Israel's main strategies for intelligence activity in the Palestinian areas. After a short theoretical introduction and historical background on Israel's extensive use of Palestinian informers, we will present key human rights dilemmas related to using informers. We suggest an analysis according to three stages: recruitment, operation and post-operation obligations. Before concluding we will also briefly touch on the potential counterproductivity of using informers to combat terror.

It is worth emphasizing that, naturally, we do not question the general need – indeed, duty – of governments to protect civilians from terror attacks, nor do we generally question as such the tactical tool of using informers to these ends. We do, however, wish to highlight the dangers in operating unregulated systems of informers and to point out the ethical dilemmas and human rights problems that are involved in these systems.

Setting the Framework

Informers: Definitions and Features

Informers – individuals that do not belong to law enforcement agencies but supply them with information[2] – are considered a main tool in fighting crime and terrorism alike. As an American police manual states, 'From the dawn of our history, internal law and order has had to depend in greater or less measure on the informer'.[3] Being members of groups and communities which are under surveillance allows informers access to information not easily available by other means of intelligence gathering.

Greer suggested distinguishing types of informers according to their relationship with the activities and people about whom they inform: insiders and outsiders, single-event informers and multiple-event informers. This typology is complemented by a second distinction, between criminal and political informers, while the political sphere is divided into violent and nonviolent political movements.[4]

The objects of this study are the informers who work in the political arena in what we define as 'violence-related environments'. This definition aims to include political wings of violent groups, their welfare organisations (if they exist), their financial systems and their supporting communities, and is based on the lack of clear-cut dichotomy between violent and nonviolent organisations. They might be single-event or multiple-event informers, outsiders or insiders. Nevertheless, one should bear in mind that there is a spectrum between outsiders and insiders, and we would suggest the following subcategories, based on the actual work of counter-terror agencies:

- 'The archetypal insiders': people from within a political/terrorist group who were tempted or pressured to provide information about their colleagues.
- 'The archetypal outsiders': people who are merely casual observers and supply information voluntarily.
- 'Outsiders who turned into insiders': people with no connections to political/terrorist groups who are recruited by an intelligence agency and then sent to join such a group and provide information about it.
- 'Inside-outsiders': People who were recruited to be the 'eyes and ears' of the security services in their communities in general, and who are required to inform about anything which raises their suspicion as being connected to terrorist (or forbidden political) activity. These people are outsiders to the political group, but insiders in the community.

The Uniqueness of Counterterror Informers

The use of informers in current counterterror efforts differs from both anticriminal activity and interstate spying. Indeed, police intelligence units in the framework of their anticriminal activity have used all the above-mentioned types of informers. However, there are some differences which render the situation more complex and raise additional dilemmas. First, antiterror activity is most often carried out by secret service agencies, whose work is less transparent than that of police forces and is not usually fully legally regulated (or, in other cases, the regulations are internal and not open to public scrutiny)[5]. Second, in many cases these agencies operate under 'emergency law' regimes, which give less weight – or suspend – basic human rights.

Third, the fact that terrorist organisations pose a greater threat, or are at least perceived to do so, plays a major role in allowing the agencies charged with combating them greater freedom of action. Another factor that makes counterterror activity more complicated than counter-crime work is the fact that, in the case of the western 'war on terror', the target groups are usually of different ethnic or national origin.

Intelligence gathering in the framework of the 'war on terror' is also different from the type of espionage seen during the Cold War, or 'traditional' interstate espionage. The main difference is that 'traditional' espionage was generally limited to efforts to recruit informers among members of the diplomatic corps or the security services of rival countries. The elusiveness of the international terror networks, on the other hand, might cause intelligence services to apply surveillance methods, including operating informers on whole 'suspect communities', such as immigrant communities or religious groups.

The fact that these terror networks have no headquarters, bases or formal structures makes communications surveillance ('SIGINT') on them much more difficult. The nature of the target groups – small, closed, operating in remote areas and often fundamental – also makes infiltration by undercover agents very difficult: 'In the case of the Soviet Union, US spies shared some cultural and even physical characteristics, making it fairly easy to carry out operations on enemy turf. The typical American CIA agent, however, sticks out in places like the bazaars of Pakistan'.[6]

Hence the crucial role of inside informers. The persistent threat of mega-attacks by suicide bombers or by new methods not yet known makes taking preventive measures an urgent task.

Israeli Security Services and Palestinian Informers: Historical Background and Recent Developments

Fear of terror attacks has featured in the daily lives of Israelis since the mid-1960s, and more so since the occupation of the West Bank and Gaza in the war of 1967. Immediately after the war the Palestinian Fatah Movement (led by Yasir Arafat), as well as other Palestinian groups, tried to encourage popular resistance in the Occupied Territories in the form of guerrilla warfare and civil disobedience. Arafat and his aides infiltrated the territories and organised armed cells in various localities, and soon Israeli military and civilian targets came under attack.[7]

One of the main tools Israel used to combat these attacks was to establish a network of informers who would supply the Shabak, the Israeli General Security Service, with information about Palestinian underground cells and their activities. Based on former Jordanian secret agents and Palestinians who served Israeli intelligence prior to 1967, the foundations of the network were set up. Mass arrests of Palestinians, and strict Israeli military rule which employed the carrot-and-stick method, enabled Israeli intelligence officers to widen this network and to recruit activists from the rank-and-file of the resistance movement itself. Within a short period, an impressive intelligence network was created.[8]

Within the framework of Israel's security policy, which perceived the very emergence of Palestinian nationalism as a security threat, the role of informers (and collaborators in general)[9] was not limited to combating terrorism. In fact, Israel has used its informer network to prevent the Palestinian population in the Occupied

Territories from consolidating around the Palestine Liberation Organization (PLO, which was defined by Israel as a terror organisation until the Oslo Accords in 1993), to block the reemergence of the Palestinian national identity (which was suppressed during eighteen years of Jordanian rule from 1949 to 1967) and to thwart the process of nation-building promoted by the PLO. Thus, informers were not recruited from circles of the armed wings of the PLO only, but from all spheres of public life. Institutions of civil society such as universities, trade unions or local councils were all infiltrated by Israeli security services by way of their informers. And since institutional and political contacts with the PLO were regarded as a violation of the law, people involved in such contacts were put in risk of prosecution. In this way Israel tried to control the political and social lives of Palestinians in the occupied territories, and at the same time to prevent terror attacks on its citizens. In addition, in the late 1970s Israel established a political (though armed) organisation, known as the Village Leagues, to contest the pro-PLO leadership in the occupied territories.[10]

The Israeli system of control, which was based on informers, political collaborators and Palestinians who served in the military governance and the civil administration, collapsed during the first *intifada*, which erupted in December 1987. Hundreds of informers and members of the leagues were killed by Palestinian militants, and many others recanted and surrendered their weapons. Most Palestinian policemen, tax collectors and other civil servants resigned their posts, and during the second year of the *intifada* Israel became 'eyeless in Judea', to use the apt term of Salim Tamari.[11] This was a crucial problem for Israel, especially due to the fact that the eruption of the first *intifada* coincided with the emergence of Hamas, the Islamic resistance movement, which became a second strong movement in the territories.[12] At this point, Israeli security services began to reorganise their network of informers and increasingly used prisoners as a main source of manpower. Israeli intelligence officers approached two populations: political and military activists of all Palestinian factions, and criminals. The reward offered for collaboration was some measure of reduction in the term of imprisonment.

It is hard to ascertain how successful Israel's recruitment efforts were in that period, since the coming years brought upheaval on the Israeli-Palestinian scene. In September 1993, the PLO and Israel signed a mutual recognition agreement for the first time, in the framework of what is known as the Oslo Accords. As a result of these agreements, the Palestinian Authority (PA) was established in parts of the West Bank and Gaza, and Palestinian security services deployed in those areas. For the first time in the history of Palestine, internationally recognised, overt Palestinian armed forces took control of security matters in the country. Israel declared its prerequisite for the establishment of these forces in the agreements: The Palestinians had to cooperate with Israel in its combat against terror. Nevertheless, Israel continued its independent intelligence activities within the PA areas and inside the PA apparatus. The main change was institutional; since the PA was a foreign entity, an additional Israeli intelligence service started to operate Palestinian informers in the Palestinian territories alongside the Shabak, namely Unit 504 of the Israeli military intelligence. The activities of both agencies were directed towards terrorist groups and PA security agencies, yet people who did not belong to either of these circles were also recruited as informers. This is due to the Israeli method of 'recruit as much as you can'.

Indeed, the well-oiled machine of recruitment had to adjust itself only to minor changes. Contrary to widespread opinion, Israel has maintained its control over the

Palestinians in the territories after the establishment of the PA in many different ways. First, all access points to the PA from abroad are controlled by Israel. All entries and exits necessitate Israeli permission. Second, the PA consists of several enclaves inside Israeli-controlled areas and all movement between one area of the PA and another requires Israeli approval. In addition, Israel remains the sovereign power in more than half of the territories (areas 'C', in the Oslo terminology), with all the implications that has on the daily life of Palestinians. Another factor is that Israel has kept the right to detain residents of the territories, including those under PA control, for security reasons. All these means of control, and the fact that, up to the current *intifada*, tens of thousands of Palestinians made their living as commuting workers in Israel, helped sustain the pressure mechanisms which enabled recruitment of collaborators.

   The claim that this system of control and the expansion of the Jewish settlements in the territories were the main causes for the eruption of the second *intifada*, known as the Al-Aqsa *intifada*, in October 2000, is beyond the scope of this article.[13] However, the collapse of the Oslo peace process brought about an unprecedented wave of terror attacks, including dozens of suicide attacks in which hundreds of Israelis died. At the same time, the formal and semi-overt intelligence cooperation between the Palestinian intelligence apparatus and Israel ceased to exist. In the framework of its counterterror activity, which included targeted assassinations and reoccupying large parts of the PA, Israel intensified its intelligence gathering in Palestinian communities, using its network of informers extensively. The human rights dilemmas that characterized the use of informers during the years of direct Israeli occupation in the territories intensified as well.

Human Rights Dilemmas

There are numerous human rights dilemmas related to the use of informers. Here we will present the major ones as they relate to three stages: recruitment, operation and post-operation obligations.[14] There are additional issues that will not be covered here: the use of '*agent provocateur*', a method about whose use in the Palestinian territories we do not have sufficient data;[15] and the question of prosecutions based on informers' testimonies, which raises many questions regarding fair trials. The latter question was widely discussed in the literature about Northern Ireland,[16] but is not of much relevance in the Israeli-Palestinian instance, since in cases in which evidence is based mainly on informers, Israel tends to hold the suspects in administrative detention, i.e., without trial.

Recruitment

In his autobiography, summarizing some thirty years of service in Israel's security apparatus, the former head of the Shabak, Ya'akov Pery, states unequivocally: 'we have never recruited an informer by pressuring him'.[17] This is not true. More than anything, this statement illustrates the degree of denial of the ethical dilemmas involved in recruiting collaborators (in Israel/Palestine and elsewhere). As in other places, a small number of informers cooperate voluntarily, whether due to ideological reasons or other motivations; recruitment officers in the various intelligence services, however, pressure the vast majority of them into doing so. Indeed, the Shabak has attempted to pressure almost every Palestinian who comes into contact with the Israeli authorities for his daily affairs to collaborate. As Palestinians are dependant on Israeli permits for anything from traveling abroad or between the West Bank and Gaza Strip working in Israel, the Shabak has ample opportunity to recruit collaborators in this manner. This practice has been used since the beginning of the occupation of the territories in 1967 until the present.

The testimony given by H., a resident of the town of Dura in the West Bank, to B'Tselem, The Israeli Centre for Human Rights in the Occupied Territories, illustrates this practice. H. was planning to study in a university in Egypt. In order to do so, he first had to travel to Jordan through the Allenby Bridge.

> On May 15, 1992, I was at the Bridge, with an exit permit for studies in Egypt, but it was returned to me with no explanation. The next day I went to the Civil Administration at Dura, where the officer Fuad Halhal told me that everything was in order and that I could leave. Two days later, I was at the bridge again and was sent back without being told why. The officer at the bridge said it depended on the computer and that I should check with the Civil Administration, the *Shabak* or a lawyer. The next day I went to Attorney Muhammad Khalil, in Hebron, who submitted a request to the Civil Administration in Beit-El. On July 22 I received a letter stating that there was no obstacle to my going.[18]

H. tried once again to leave for Jordan. It was already August 26. He was sent back again. He went to the military governor of Hebron to inquire why he had not been let through. The governor called a Shabak agent who took H. to an interrogation room. Another agent that sat there said: 'No one can approve your departure except me. Your entire future is in my hands. You want my help now, and in return I want your help'.[19]

In this case H. declined the offer and decided not to turn into an informer. In many other cases people do accept the offers made to them by the Shabak.

Another example is the case of N. from a village in the southern West Bank. In 2002, N.'s son and daughter required medical treatment. His daughter, thirteen years old, had a large mole on her face, which made her feel unattractive and made her parents worry about her chances of getting married. The son, ten years old, suffers from a disability. In the summer of 2002, after a long wait, a charity in Jordan told N. that it would fund medical treatment for both children. N. was to accompany them to Jordan. When he went to obtain a permit to go to Jordan, he was directed to an intelligence officer, who told him unequivocally that if he wanted the permit he would have to collaborate with him.[20]

Another severe form of pressure is imprisonment. Some have argued that one goal of the mass arrests of Palestinians in the current *intifada* is to recruit informers.[21] Such claims are not new, but it is still difficult to determine their reliability. In one case, at least, a prisoner applied to a military tribunal through the Israeli human rights organisation, HaMoked: Center for the Defense of the Individual asking to be released. He argued that he was arrested because he refused to become a collaborator. The judge, a colonel in the Israeli Defense Forces (IDF), decreed that despite the proved attempts to recruit him, his arrest was unrelated to these efforts. The judge did state, however, that it would be illegitimate to arrest a person only in order to force him to collaborate.[22] Nevertheless, there are some indications that this practice is used by the Shabak.[23]

In terms of international law, the fourth Geneva Convention[24] forbids an occupying power from such actions against protected persons. Article 31 states that 'no physical or moral coercion shall be exercised against protected persons, in particular to obtain information from them or from third parties', and the official commentary of the International Committee of the Red Cross (ICRC) elaborates that 'the prohibition . . . is general in character and applies to both physical and moral forms of coercion . . . whether the pressure is direct or indirect, obvious or hidden'.[25] Furthermore, article 51 states that 'the Occupying Power may not compel protected persons to serve in its armed or auxiliary forces. No pressure or propaganda which aims at securing voluntary enlistment is permitted', and the official commentary adds that 'the prohibition is absolute and no derogation from it is permitted'. The statute of the International Criminal Court (ICC) defines as a war crime the act of 'compelling the nationals of the hostile party to take part in the operations of war directed against their own country'.[26]

Notwithstanding this clear prohibition in international law, its applicability might be limited. Israel has not ratified the ICC statute, and its position regarding the Geneva Conventions is ambiguous, rejecting its applicability to the West Bank and Gaza (as these are not 'occupied') but promising to abide by the 'humanitarian clauses'.[27] In other contexts, the prohibition – at least to some extent – would be limited to international armed conflict (in the case of the ICC), and to occupation status (in the case of the fourth Geneva Convention). In any case, security services would probably argue that they couldn't base their counterterror intelligence operations on ideological volunteers and demand that the law make allowances for some degree of pressure to be applied when attempting to recruit informers.

If these demands were accepted, the question that remains is to what extent it is legitimate to use this power: Is there a difference between proactive and reactive measures? Should some forms of pressure (e.g., preventing medical care) be banned while others (e.g., preventingstudies or travel for holiday) be permitted?[28]

One should be cautious in sanctioning any form of pressure. It is clear that a sweeping policy of putting pressure on almost any Palestinian, whatever their background, is illegitimate.

In a more subtle analysis, one can argue that two parameters are relevant when determining what means of pressure are legitimate. The first one should be the degree of involvement of the would-be informer in terrorist activity. When there is reliable information that an individual belongs to a terrorist group, intelligence services should have more freedom in their efforts to recruit him: e.g., while it might be illegitimate to prevent a neighbour or a family member of a terrorist from studying abroad in order to recruit him, it might be legitimate to do it to a member of a terrorist cell. Using the subcategories of insiders-outsiders mentioned above, it might be legitimate to pressure an archetypal insider, but not another member of the community (inside-outsiders or archetypal outsiders).

The second parameter is proportionality: A clear imminent risk to human lives should be treated differently from an attempt to circumvent political activities (whether and how security services can be trusted with identifying clear and imminent danger is a separate issue).

A second dilemma regarding recruitment is the legitimacy of using minors. Cases where persons under eighteen, in some cases as young as thirteen, were operated by Israel were reported by Arab sources.[29] These reports were based on testimonies collaborators gave to Palestinian security services during interrogations. As in other cases of confession under pressure, one should be cautious about these accounts' accuracy; nevertheless, the former head of Shabak has admitted that the organisation uses minors to gather information.[30]

The use of children in hostilities has been an issue of concern in international law in the last decade. It is important to note that definitions of 'child soldiers' make it clear that these do not have to be gun-carrying combatants, but can also be those who participate in activities such as spying.[31] The ICC statute defines 'conscripting or enlisting children under the age of fifteen years into the national armed forces' as a war crime.[32] This wording shows that 'conscripting or enlisting' means that consent or volunteering is irrelevant; it is also sufficient that the accused was 'wilfully blind to the fact that the child was under fifteen years of age in order to establish criminal liability'.[33]

In some cases recruitment of children under fifteen was indirect, i.e., the security service recruited an adult, who in turn used a child, usually his son or another minor relative. If the operator 'should have known' that this would be the result he might be liable under the 'superior responsibility' principle (see next section below).

With regards to children between the ages of fifteen and eighteen, matters are more complicated. There is a trend toward prohibition of their participation in conflicts. Currently, an optional protocol to the Convention of the Rights of the Child prohibits all participation of persons under eighteen in the armed forces apart from voluntary noncombat roles.[34] Israel signed this instrument but has not ratified it, and as it has not yet reached customary law status it is not binding.

However, even if this practice may be legal, it still raises ethical questions. It creates a psychological burden for the child and exposes him to physical danger. A child would be much more vulnerable to the types of pressures presented above. In cases where the informer is given power that has the potential to result in his committing human rights violations (see next section below), children are less likely to understand the limits of their power. Given that, any use of children should be limited as much as possible.[35]

The categorisation of insiders-outsiders might be useful in the case of minors as well. To be more specific, recruitment of a high school student who is involved in violent political activity seems to be more justifiable than recruiting a nonactive student who happens to be in the same school with political activists. The parameter of proportionality should be applied here as well. There is a difference between recruiting minors who have access to information about nonviolent (though defined as subversive) activity and attempting to prevent suicide attacks. It should be noted when discussing this point that both informers' lives would be put at risk.

A third sensitive question arises from the profiles of the potential recruited persons. In 1995, after a series of scandals, the then head of the CIA, John Duetch, issued rules that required field officers to get headquarters' approval before recruiting anyone with a criminal or human rights – abuse record. Some argued that these rules hampered the CIA's efforts to infiltrate terrorist organizations and should, at least partially, be blamed for the intelligence failure on 11 September.[36] A US Congress investigation committee called for the reversal of the rule. The Israelis, on the other hand, recruited criminals quite frequently to serve as collaborators both inside and outside prisons.[37] When can it be justified to sacrifice the rights of the potential victims of the 'informer as criminal' in order to secure information from the 'informer as spy'?

Whereas the first two dilemmas have to do with the human rights *of* informers, the last one concerns violations carried out *by* them. The next section, which analyses the actual operation stage, will also deal with these two types of questions.

Operation

A serious problem arises when informers are used to commit human rights violations that their operating agencies are themselves forbidden from committing. An important issue is the use of Palestinian informers to torture individuals suspected of terrorist activity.[38] A common practice in Israeli police, military and Shabak interrogation facilities is using informers, known as 'birds'. These informers introduce themselves to new detainees as activists and force them to prove that they are not collaborators by telling who they are, what they did and who were the people that sent them on their missions. Many young activists fall into this trap and give full details of their activities. Their confessions are recorded, or written, by the informers, and then brought as evidence during their trials. While this can be a legitimate means of deception, 'birds' also torture the detainees that refuse to disclose information.

The prohibition on torture is one of a few absolute prohibitions in international law, from which no derogation is allowed under any circumstances.[39] Use of torture by informers, whether ordered, solicited or merely tacitly approved, should clearly be banned.

In addition to the moral and public problems in using someone else to do the 'dirty work' while maintaining the state's clean image, it should be noted that state officials who are in charge of informers that apply torture could face legal challenges themselves. They could be liable under the 'superior responsibility' doctrine, a principle that puts liability on commanders, even if they did not order the crime – in some circumstances, even if they were not aware of it – if they failed to prevent it.[40] There are three requirements for this concept to be used: a superior/subordinate dinate relationship; the superior 'knew or should have known' about the crime; the superior failed to take reasonable measures to prevent or punish the violations. It seems that all of these conditions are met in cases of torture by informers, and thus criminal responsibility may rest with their operators, even if they were not directly involved in the torture and even if they did not order it. The same principle may be applied to indirect recruitment of children (see above).

A second recurrent issue is the intrusion of privacy exercised by the informers, which in many cases is inherent in their work. Unlike the right to be free from torture, the right to privacy is not an absolute right; it is well established that in conflict with national security, for example, governments can derogate from this right and impose measures that will intrude on people's privacy. Such measures were common after 11 September, and some were approved by judicial bodies.[41]

However, while violating privacy may be tolerated in principle, there might be a need to define more accurate limitations on the actions of informers. State agents operate within legal guidelines. Phone tapping and secret surveillance inside Israel require the approval of a judge on a case-by-case basis. The potential of informers to violate privacy is almost unlimited, and stricter definitions are needed. Should the same legal limitations that are imposed on state agents be imposed on the informers themselves? Should the sanctioned violation of privacy be in proportion to the perceived threat? Who will determine the boundaries of this proportionality? As the actions of informers and the orders they get are secret, these questions often go unanswered. While the lines may be difficult to draw, there should at least be legal supervision and regulation of this aspect of informers' work.

Two other ethical issues arise from the specific nature of the relationship between informers, their society and their operators. The first relates to family relationships. Is it legitimate to demand an informer to report on his family members' whereabouts and activities, knowing that this kind of activity affects family ties and loyalties, or should they be 'exempt' from spying against their own families? Such exemptions are often granted to regular police officers or judges, who are disqualified from dealing with cases that involve their relatives. In the case of inside informers, this principal would be difficult to apply, as access and intimacy are often the very reasons for their recruitment.

Another question is illustrated by the case of 'Alan Bani Odeh of the town of Tammun in the northern West Bank. Bani Odeh was a Hamas member who was recruited as an informer by the Shabak in February 2000. According to his testimony, the Shabak had revealed he was having an intimate relationship with a woman from his town and threatened to expose it. In November of that year, while in a meeting with his handler, Shabak explosives experts booby-trapped his car. Bani Odeh was then told to lend it to his cousin, who was active in the armed wing of Hamas. The following day, while his cousin, Ibrahim, was driving the car in Nablus, it exploded and Ibrahim was killed. A few days later, Bani Odeh turned himself in to the Palestinian police. He was brought to the State Security Court, and after a short trial was sentenced to death. He was executed in January 2001.[42]

Putting aside the debate over the legitimacy of targeted assassinations, an ethical question rises from this case: the legitimacy of using unwitting collaborators. Alan Bani Odeh had no intention to kill his cousin and was involved in this operation without his knowledge. He was used not as a human being but as a tool of the security services. Moreover, such deceit can put the informer's life in danger, as was proved in the case of Bani Odeh. Though the informer may theoretically not be legally liable (as he was unaware of the plot), he would be exposed to revenge by his society. Such risks are the subject of the next section, which deals with the obligations of the state to the collaborators once they have completed their missions or been exposed.

Post-Operation Obligations

When caught by their 'own side', informers are faced with harsh punishment. Treatment of those considered 'traitors' would almost always be severe; many countries that have abolished the death penalty in general retain a special clause allowing its use for the offence of 'treason'. In war – or warlike – situations the chances of receiving a fair trial in these circumstances are usually very low.

Palestinian informers who are caught are exposed to extremely harsh treatment. Since the outbreak of the current wave of conflict, dozens of informers have been killed in acts of 'street justice'. Others have been prosecuted in the Palestinian Authority State Security courts, which often violate basic fair trial standards.[43]

While a government would do everything in its power to rescue its own agents in such circumstances, it seems not to be the case with regards to informers. For example, one can assume that if the Palestinian Authority announced that it was going to execute a Jewish-Israeli soldier, Israel would have used all means available to prevent this. Yet, Israel took no action in the weeks between the sentencing of Bani Odeh to death and his actual execution, or after the verdicts of other collaborators had been announced. The question is whether they should get the same treatment as state agents and soldiers: What are the government's legal and moral obligations to them?

This question relates in general to all informers who complete their operations. Even if they are not caught, quite frequently one hears them claim that Israel has abandoned them, especially when they are deemed less 'valuable' by the security services. In fact, since the Oslo Accords in 1993 hundreds of collaborators were relocated from PA-controlled areas into the state of Israel and given financial aid for resettlement. Nevertheless, many of them argue that they do not receive enough support to enable them to live in dignity. In addition, many others argue that they have not received Israeli citizenship despite the fact that they assisted the Israeli security agencies.[44]

With regards to compensation, an official in the Israeli Ministry of Justice told the Israeli newspaper *Ha'aretz* that the Israeli authorities distinguish between 'spies' i.e., Israeli Jews, and Palestinian collaborators. Although sent on similar missions, 'spies' are entitled to a variety of rewards, while 'collaborators' are not.[45] Moreover, an Israeli court decided that relatives of collaborators are not entitled to compensation when their family members are murdered, since the law of remuneration to victims of terrorism refers only to Israeli citizens, and, in the territories, only to Jews.[46]

Treating informers differently from a country's own agents, i.e., as meriting lesser obligations, is tantamount to viewing them as lesser people or mere tools, and will inevitably result in violating their human rights. Legal contractual obligations might be hard to ascertain in these circumstances, though regulating the relationship between informers and their operators along the guidelines of an employer/employee relationship may not be implausible. But even without it, there is a strong moral case against leaving these people to their fate.

Abandoning informers may also be counterproductive, from the intelligence services' point of view, as it adversely affects the efforts to recruit new ones. The next section will briefly touch on larger counterproductive implications of the policy of using informers in general.

Counter-Productivity? The Long-Term Consequences

Whereas the previous analysis presented dilemmas based on the assumption that using informers is an efficient tool to combat terror attacks (and thus the dilemmas concern the need to balance the security 'gain' with the human rights 'loss'), here we briefly want to note that in the long run, and especially during a peace process, the efficiency as such might also be dubious.[47]

The Israeli policy of recruiting and using informers, carried out in large numbers and over a long period of time, created a culture of suspicion, which is a well-known phenomenon in societies which are under political surveillance. In addition, it affected the building of a civil society.[48] This culture of suspicion also hampered the emergence of groups and individuals who genuinely pursued moderate agendas, as they were immediately branded as 'collaborators'.

The possibility of Israeli-Palestinian security cooperation (which was a central component of the Oslo Accords) was also adversely affected by the decades of operating Palestinian informers by Israeli intelligence officers. Not only did some Israeli officials treat Palestinian officers as no more than informers (as a previous head of Shabak has admitted),[49] but also Palestinian opposition groups constantly identified Palestinian security forces as traitors. This identification was widely accepted in Palestinian political discourse, and has caused many members of the Palestinian security forces to want to 'clear their names'. When the Al-Aqsa *intifada* broke out in October 2000, they took the opportunity to halt security cooperation with Israel against Hamas, and join Hamas in its fight against Israel.[50]

This can be the counterproductive result of creating a culture of suspicion. In general, it was this culture of suspicion that stood in the way of creating accountable and independent Palestinian institutions – the very institutions that could have helped stop the terror. This consequence could be attributed to Israel's blindness to the long-term effects of its policy, or to the fact that these were indeed the 'hidden' goals of this policy – not only to combat terror but also to create a system of social control.

While the various dilemmas presented above could be evaluated vis-a-vis the immediate results of intelligence received through informers, these long-term effects should also be taken into account.

Conclusions

As with many other counterterror measures, such as detention without trial, the use of informers poses grave challenges to governments who must take into account the need to protect civilians from terrorist attacks on the one hand and the obligation to protect human rights on the other. The global 'war on terror' has resulted in an erosion of human rights standards on local and international levels[51] and the justified need to protect lives has too often been used to violate the human rights of individuals and communities. While most other measures come under some public scrutiny and judicial examination, this aspect of intelligence work is usually conducted far from the public eye. Some of the activities presented above, like torture by proxy, should be banned outright. Others present ethical dilemmas that stem from the need to balance individual rights and public security. Thus, it is imperative to develop a regulating framework that would provide the appropriate ethical and legal guidelines in this field. Such a framework should be created by means of an informed and open debate. It should be as transparent as possible, and should aim at retaining accountability even in this clandestine aspect of law enforcement. When the potential for abuse is left unattended it will almost always be fulfilled, and the possibility of having counterproductive results should also not be ignored. When American and British security services are seemingly about to embark on an effort to create such informer networks, whether in Muslim countries or in their own Muslim communities, the lessons from the Israeli-Palestinian experience must be acknowledged.

Notes

1. See House Permanent Select Committee on Intelligence and the Senate Select Committee on Intelligence, *Report of the Joint Inquiry into the Terrorist Attacks of September 11, 2001* (2003). The report stated that: 'Prior to September 11, 2001, the Intelligence Community did not effectively develop and use human sources to penetrate the Al-Qaeda inner circle. This lack of reliable and knowledgeable human sources significantly limited the Community's ability to acquire intelligence that could be acted upon before the September 11 attacks' (p.93).

2. As such, they are distinguished from 'undercover' law enforcement agents.

3. Quoted in Gary T. Marx, 'Thoughts on a Neglected Category of Social Movement Participants: The Agent Provocateur and the Informant', *American Journal of Sociology* 80/2 (September, 1974) p.402.

4. Steven Greer, *Supergrasses: A Study in Anti-Terrorist Law Enforcement in Northern Ireland* (Oxford: Clarendon Press 1995) pp.1–26. For other theoretical definitions see Justice, Madeleine Colvin, *Under Surveillance: Covert Policing and Human Rights Standards* (London:

1998) p.41; and Daniel Nsereko, 'Police Informers and Agents Provocateurs: Accomplices or Handmaidens of the Law?', *Criminal Law Forum* 9 (1999) p.151.

5. For example, the new Israeli General Security Service (Shabak) Act 2002 does not refer to informers and the legal questions related to their recruitment and handling at all. The internal regulations are classified.

6. Abraham McLaughlin, 'A Matter of Ethics for the Cloak and Dagger Set', *Christian Science Monitor* 5 Oct. 2001.

7. Shlomo Gazit, *The Stick and the Carrot: The Israeli Administration in Judea and Samaria* (Tel Aviv: Zonora-Bitan, 1985) pp.282–84.

8. David Ronen, *The Year of the Shabak: Deployment in Judea and Samaria – The First Year* (Tel Aviv: Ministry of Defense Press, 1989); Yaakov Pery, *Strike First* (Tel Aviv: 1999).

9. The informers were the cornerstones of the Israeli control system in the territories, but there were other types of collaboration, such as land selling, which enabled Jewish settlement (and spatial control); political collaboration whose goal was to weaken the mainstream national movement; and distributing pro-Israeli propaganda; for the origins of these categories in the 1917–48 period see Hillel Cohen, *An Army of Shadows: Palestinian Collaborators in the Service of Zionism* (Jerusalem: Ivrit, 2004) [in Hebrew].

10. Salim Tamari, 'In League with Zion: Israel's Search for a Native Pillar', in N. Aruri (ed), *Occupation: Israel over Palestine* (London: Zed Books, 1984) pp.377–90.

11. Salim Tamari, 'Eyeless in Judea: Israel's Strategy of Collaborators and Forgeries', *Middle East Report* 164/165 (May-August 1990) pp.39–45.

12. For a detailed analysis of the emergence of Hamas see Ali Jirbawi, *The Intifada and Political Leaderships in the West Bank and Gaza Strip* (Beirut: al-Tali'ah 1989) pp.102–30.

13. See, for example, Edward Said, ' The End of Oslo', *The Nation* 30 Oct. 2000.

14. For ethical questions in using informers in a counter-crime context, see Paul Cooper and Jon Murphy, 'Ethical Approaches for Police Officers When Working with Informants in the Development of Criminal Intelligence in the United Kingdom', *Journal of Social Policy* 26/1 (January 1997) pp.1–20; Colin Dunnighan and Clive Norris, 'The Detective, the Snout, and the Audit Commission: The Real Costs in Using Informants', *The Howard Journal* 38/1 (February 1999) pp.67–86.

15. As is well known, the Israeli Shabak used such an agent in the radical right wing in Israel (named Avishay Raviv) who was later prosecuted for not informing the Shabak of the plans to assassinate Israeli premier Yitzhak Rabin. On the question in other contexts see Greer (note 4) and Nsereko (note 4).

16. See Greer (note 4); P. Taylor, *Provos: The IRA and Sinn Fein* (London: Bloomsbury 1998) pp.254–65.

17. Pery (note 8) p.259.

18. Yizhar Be'er and Saleh Abdel-Jawad, *Collaborators in the Occupied Territories: Human Rights Abuses and Violations* (B'Tselem, The Israeli Information Center for Human Rights in the Occupied Territories, Jerusalem, 1994) pp.35–6.

19. Ibid., and see there for other examples of recruitment using this practice. See also Gershom Gorenberg, 'The Collaborator', *New York Times* 18 Aug. 2002; and Yehezkel Lein, *Forbidden Roads: The Discriminatory West Bank Road Regime* (Jerusalem: B'Tselem, The Israeli Information Center for Human Rights in the Occupied Territories, 2004) p.33.

20. This information comes from firsthand knowledge. A family member of N.'s asked Hillel Cohen to help N., and was subsequently put in touch with a human rights organisation that successfully handled the issue. Another case of making medical treatment conditional on collaboration is mentioned in Be'er and Abdel Jawad (note 18).

21. For example, see the claims by Saleh Abdul Jawad, a prominent Palestinian scholar on informers; see Catherine Taylor, 'How Israel Builds Its Fifth Column', *Christian Science Monitor* 22 May 2002.

22. Megido Military Court, Files AMM 793/98 and 392/98, *Ahed Abu Sbeih v. The IDF Commander in the West Bank*.

23. A number of released detainees told one of the authors that they were not interrogated during their detention but were made the offer to become collaborators.

24. Geneva Convention Relative to the Protection of Civilian Persons in Time of War, 1949.

25. http://www.icrc.org

26. Rome Statute of the International Criminal Court, Article 8 (2)(b)(xv), 1998. For commentary see Auto Triffterer, *Commentary on the Rome Statute of the International Criminal Court: Observers Notes, Article by Article* (Baden Baden: Nomos Verlges 1999) pp.235–7.

27. Israel's position has been widely contested by other governments and experts. See, generally, B'Tselem, *Israeli Settlement in the Occupied Territories as a Violation of Human Rights: Legal and Conceptual Aspects* (Jerusalem: Yuval Ginbar, 1997) pp.4–9.

28. It should be noted that offering rewards–or bribes–in exchange for information (such as the price on the heads of Udai and Qussai Hussein that apparently led to information about their whereabouts) could be a legitimate exercise.

29. *Al-Quds* 18 July 1995; based on an article published earlier that month in *Al-Sharq al-Awsat*.

30. In his memoirs, Pery, the former head of the Shabak, recounts the case of a high school student he recruited who was later murdered by Palestinians, see Pery (note 8) p.52. It is worth noting that many high school students are active in violent political activity, hence the desire of the Shabak to recruit informers in schools.

31. Triffterer (note 26) p.261.

32. Rome Statute of the International Criminal Court, Article 8 (2)(b)(xxvi), 1998. A similar prohibition appears in The First Optional Protocol to the Geneva Conventions, (1977) Article 77. While Israel has not ratified the ICC statute nor the protocol, this prohibition has reached the status of international customary law, and is therefore binding on all states.

33. Triffterer (note 26) p.262.

34. Optional Protocol to the Convention on the Rights of the Child on the Involvement of Children in Armed Conflict, 2000.

35. For the use of minors in counter-crime activities, see Justice (note 4) pp.42–3.

36. See the July 2002 report of the House Permanent Select Committee on Intelligence (HPSCI), Subcommittee on Terrorism and Homeland Security 'Counterterrorism Intelligence Capabilities and Performance Prior to 9–11' (Washington, DC 2002) p.99.

37. B'Tselem, (note 17) p.37–9.

38. See information by B'Tselem, at http://www.btselem.org/english/Collaboration_ Suspects/index.asp

39. Convention against Torture and other Cruel, Inhuman or Degrading Treatment or Punishment, 1984. See also Steven Ratner and Jason Abrams, *Accountability for Human Rights Atrocities in International Law: Beyond the Nuremberg Legacy* (Oxford: OUP 2001) pp.117–9.

40. Ilias Bantekas, 'The Contemporary Law of Superior Responsibility', *American Journal of International Law* 93/3 (July 1999) pp.573–95.

41. Electronic Privacy Information Center (EPIC), Privacy and Human Rights Survey Report, http://www.privacyinternational.org/survey/phr2002

42. *Haaretz* 8 Dec. 2000; *Al-Ayam* 14 Jan. 2001.

43. 'Alan Bani Odeh was among the first sentenced to death and executed, see the Palestinian daily *Al-Ayam* 14 Jan. 2001. Dozens of suspected collaborators were killed by militants with no judicial process during the *intifada*. See Associated Press (AP) report, 'Suspected collaborator executed in public square', http://www.smh.com.au/articles/2003/05/19/ 1053196527247.html. The same article reports on an execution that took place in a public square in Nablus and on the responses of the members of the public. On treatment of collaborators by the Palestinian Authority before the Al-Aqsa *intifada* see The Palestinian Human Rights Monitoring Group, *Human Rights and Legal Position of Palestinian 'Collaborators'* (Jerusalem:2001), http://www.phrmg.org/monitor2001/jul2001.htm. Regarding their treatment during the *intifada* see Human Rights Watch, *Justice Undermined: Balancing Security and Human Rights in the Palestinian Justice System* (Washington DC: 2001) pp.22–5, 37.

44. Dozens of collaborators applied to the Israeli Supreme Court of Justice asking to receive compensation for their services, mainly Israeli identity cards. See, for example, the petition of *Unnamed and Others v. The Prime Minister and Others*, 1972/97; *Abraghit v. The Government of Israel* 9007/96.

45. Baruch Kara, 'Jailed for Seven Years in an Enemy Country; The State: They Are Only Collaborators, *Ha'aretz* 27 Dec. 2001.

46. Moshe Reinfeld, 'The Court: No Compensation for Collaborators whose Family Member was Murdered as Suspected Collaborator', *Ha'aretz* 9 June 1998.

47. This still relates only to the tactical sphere, without touching on the more strategic solution, political settlement, as the best way to reduce terror.

48. For studies on the influence of life under surveillance on the citizens of the USSR see Merle Feinsod, 'Controls and Tensions in the Soviet Union', *The American Political Science Review* 44/2 (June 1950) pp.266–82; Paul Hollander, 'Research on Marxist Societies: The Relationship between Theory and Practice', *Annual Review of Sociology* 8 (1982) pp.319–51; Donna Bahry and Brian Silver, 'Intimidation and the Symbolic Uses of Terror in the USSR', *The American Political Science Review* 81/4 (December 1987) pp. 1065–98; Louise Shelley, *Policing Soviet Society: The Evolution of State Control* (London: Routledge, 1996).

49. Pery (note 8) p.254.

50. See Hillel Cohen, 'The Palestinian "Treason Discourse" during the Oslo Period (1993–2000) and the Failure of the Palestinian-Israeli Security Coordination', (forthcoming).

51. For example, see Human Rights Watch, In the Name of Counter-Terrorism: Human Rights Abuses Worldwide, http://www.hrw.org/un/chr59/counter-terrorism-bck.htm; Liberty, *Anti-Terrorism Legislation in the United Kingdom* (London: 2002).

15

The Security Imperative in Counterterror Operations: The Israeli Fight Against Suicidal Terror

SERGIO CATIGNANI

Department of War Studies, King's College London,
London, United Kingdom

Israel has had a long tradition of fighting international and Palestinian terror. This article looks at how Israel counterterrorism strategy and tactics have developed since the establishment of the State in 1948. By initially providing a working definition of terrorism, the article then goes to show how Israel has sought to defend itself from different Palestinian terror tactics. This article shows how Israeli security forces have struggled safeguarding, and sometimes disregarded Palestinian human rights. This article concludes by arguing that given the responsibility of democratic governments of defending their citizens from imminent terror attacks, such governments often find themselves paradoxically violating human rights. Despite attempts to reduce such human rights abuses, governments will never do so at the expense of their own security.

Introduction

Israel has had a long tradition of fighting international and Palestinian terror. Thus, the following paper will look at how Israel counterterror strategy and tactics have developed since the establishment of the state in 1948. At the same time, this paper will show how Palestinian terror in particular has strategically changed over the last two decades from being used as a negotiation and political tool to being exploited mostly as an instrument of terror with genocidal intent.

The following paper concurrently will show how the Israeli security services have augmented the number of ways and the level of force used whilst trying to fight suicidal terrorism, occasionally at the expense of safeguarding human rights, because of the security imperative. By providing the *extreme* case of Israel, the paper will show that, despite a state's good intentions, human rights issues tend to gradually lose their importance as the severity of suicidal terrorism and the desperation to eradicate it increase.

The paper will finally conclude by suggesting that as the suicide terror campaign increases against not only Israel, but other western democratic societies most involved in the fight against terror – that is the US, Australia and the UK – the problem and necessity of safeguarding human rights will not only increase, but so will human rights violations as governments become more desperate to provide security for terror-stricken citizens. However, before dealing with such issues, it is important that a working definition of terrorism is provided and that the issue of whether or not terrorism itself is a valid, morally justifiable, instrument of political violence is examined.

Defining Terrorism

Terrorism is such a broad term that one can argue it has lost any significant meaning within international relations. In fact, 'the definitional problem has grown so great that Christopher Hitchens called terrorism "a cliche in search of a meaning"'.[1] Moreover, though scholars do not agree on the definitions of either political violence or terrorism 'without some solution to the definitional problem, without isolating terrorism from other forms of political violence, there can be no uniform data collection and no responsible theory building on terrorism'.[2]

Another problem that has arisen when scholars or statesmen have tried to define terrorism has been the use of the cliche that 'one man's terrorist is another man's freedom fighter'. However, it would be too simplistic to judge the world of terrorism by proposing such a cliche as a justification of terrorism as just another type of political violence. When it comes to terrorism there should be no room for moral relativism. Consequently, if the term 'terrorist' is used with the care and consistency urged in this paper then 'one man's terrorist is simply another man's terrorist'.[3]

Hence, this paper will try to propose a definition of terrorism that will help the reader understand its immoral and inhuman nature. Such a definition is the one put forward by the US State Department, which defines terrorism as '... premeditated, politically motivated violence perpetrated against non-combatant targets by sub-national groups or clandestine state agents, usually intended to influence an audience'.[4]

The most notable aspect of terrorism is that the immediate price in property or human life is only incidental, to the terrorist's primary objective: the impact on the target government and its citizens. Such an impact can take on the guise of 'political extortion through specific demands, media exposure, drawing public attention to the terrorists' cause and agenda, the propagation of a general climate of fear, the embarrassment to governments of appearing impotent and at times the dividend of baiting governments into overreacting and becoming (or appearing) oppressive'.[5]

Furthermore, most terrorism is either politically or religiously motivated, and while the putative cause may be just (e.g., the liberation or autonomy of an oppressed group), the means used are usually inconsistent with any just vision or humane agenda. Hence, terrorists' actions are frequently counterproductive to their cause. In fact, it is ironic that terrorism almost always obtains its short-term tactical goals – violence, destruction, media coverage, public reaction and political crises. However, terrorism almost never obtains its ultimate strategic aim, which in the Palestinian terror groups' case is, *at least*, the full withdrawal of Israel from the territories occupied after the 1967 Six-Day War. Lawrence Freedman *et al.* reinforce this position by stating that 'overall, the record of terrorism in the past two centuries is not one to inspire confidence in it as a method. It has often failed to achieve anything like the intended results'.[6]

Nevertheless, just because terrorism never really achieves the goals it strives for does not answer the question of whether it is morally justifiable in certain contexts. It is, nonetheless, difficult to state whether terrorism is morally justifiable in certain contexts within international relations because of the pejorative connotation given to the term *terrorism* itself by certain groups.

In fact, a large part of the international community has consistently dismissed terrorism in all of its forms. In May 1986, for example, the heads of state at the G7 summit in Tokyo declared that 'terrorism has no justification. It is such a morally contemptible means of struggle that it is absolutely wrong in all circumstances'.[7] Again, the United Nations Security Council adopted on 20 January 2003 Resolution 1456, which reaffirmed that:

> Terrorism in all its forms and manifestations constitutes one of the most serious threats to peace and security [and that] any acts of terrorism are criminal and unjustifiable, *regardless of their motivation*, whenever and by whomsoever committed and are to be unequivocally condemned, especially when they indiscriminately target and/or injure civilians.[8] [author's emphasis]

Thus, many states have even written off the fundamental notion that terrorism is the resort to premeditated violence by marginal groups unable or unwilling to advance their cause by nonviolent democratic means. That is, terrorism is used as a weapon of last resort and as an act of political desperation. Consequently, many states since 11 September have 'adopted a policy of controlling terrorism by downplaying its political character and emphasising its criminality'.[9]

Such a position is understandable, because it can be argued that terrorism is actually not a 'natural, if unfortunate, result of the fervour and even the panic of people engaged in a desperate struggle. In fact, terrorism is usually very calculated and is a weapon that is deliberately chosen for deliberate purposes'.[10] Furthermore, there are other forms of protest available to oppressed groups which are more effective than terrorism. Civil disobedience and violent demonstrations, particularly those aimed at Israeli security forces, are just two examples of alternative tactics that Palestinians used during the first *intifada* and which were 'a more worrisome and persistent challenge than the paramilitary one'.[11]

Consequently, the 'means-to-an-end' justification that most terrorists uphold when asking the question of whether it is acceptable to use evil to obtain good (i.e., the consequentialist method) is actually fallacious. This fallaciousness can be explained by the fact that this form of justification always provides answers that 'depend on the ideological position of the people asking the question and the value they place on the resulting good' and not on the moral significance of the act *per se*.[12] Furthermore, while intellectually appealing, consequentialism has never succeeded in quantifying and weighing moral values and outcomes. Today this method has largely been discredited because the '"felicific calculus" that [consequentialism] requires eludes real calculation and, even if calculable, would be a dubious moral yardstick'.[13]

Is Terrorism Morally Justifiable?

We are, thus, still left with the question of whether terrorism is morally justifiable in certain instances. If, finally, we distinguish terrorism from other forms of political violence we can actually decide whether it is morally justifiable. In order to distinguish terrorism from other forms of political violence we have to analyse in depth its core characteristic, because 'while all terrorism is political violence, not all political violence (even on a small scale) can be considered terrorism in the strict pejorative sense'.[14] Thus, what distinguishes terrorism from other forms of political violence is the choice of target, which is a moral consideration in itself. More generally, Schmid and Jongman state, 'one reason why terrorist violence is different from other political violence is that it is widely perceived as more inhuman. The victims' guilt or innocence is immaterial to the pure terrorist'.[15] Moreover, not only are such acts inhuman, but according to UN General Assembly Resolution 49/60, also 'aim at the destruction of human rights, fundamental freedoms and the democratic bases of society'.[16] As Yonah Alexander aptly puts it:

> Since terrorism represents the use of indiscriminate and unrestrained psychological extra-legal force typically directed against innocent victims, it is in complete disregard of fundamental human rights, contrary to international law, and flouts the letter and spirit of the UN Charter and other relevant multilateral treaties.[17]

Hence, a valid, if general, moral benchmark exists: The self-evident censurable aspect of most of the violence that constitutes the central or conventional meaning of *terrorism* is the targeting of innocent persons. But who can be classified as an innocent victim? Is it just noncombatants? And on what criteria can an individual distinguish a combatant from a noncombatant? Such questions are of a more political rather than moral nature and are constantly asked when analysing terrorism. Nevertheless, the distinction given above provides the only clear delimitation for a 'morally forceful, but politically neutral, definition of the term'.[18] No definition will naturally satisfy everyone and vast grey areas remain and must be tolerated because moral judgement itself cannot always be unequivocal.

Unfortunately, terrorists come to believe that no one is innocent in their struggle against the *status quo*. For example, terrorist George Habash once said that 'in today's world there are no innocent victims'.[19] However, it is quite clear that noncombatant immunity is a core principle of the laws of warfare. Hence, 'as a minimum standard, what is impermissible in war – specifically and especially the intentional targeting of civilians – should be impermissible outside of the war zone'.[20] Under this 'laws-of-war approach', terrorism would comprise all acts that deliberately target civilians.

Palestinian Terrorism and Israeli Counterterrorism

Since its creation, the state of Israel has had to deal with waves of terrorist activity at its borders, in the territories[21] and inside Israel itself. Palestinian and other Arab *fedayeen* elements were intent on carrying out small-scale cross-border terror raids into Israel. Such attacks were initially targeted against property; subsequently, however, they quickly escalated into the murder of civilians who were situated in the pioneering *kibbutz* outposts along the 1949 Armistice borders. Indeed, 'in 1950 there were 50 civilian casualties, 97 the following year, and 182 in 1952'.[22] Such cross-border terror operations were carried out in order to cajole the Israel Defense Forces (IDF) into retaliating. Such retaliation would hopefully, in turn, escalate tensions between Israel and its Arab terrorist-hosting neighbours to the point of bringing about a full-scale war, which would with any luck redress the Arab nations' and Palestinian people's defeat of 1948.

Israel initially attempted to impede such terror raids through diplomatic channels, using force solely to fend off attacks within its own territory. Yet, when such actions proved unfruitful, the Ben-Gurion government authorised in 1953 reprisal raids, which according to Michael Walzer, are 'appropriate to periods of insurgency, border strife, cease-fire, and armistice'.[23] Such reprisal raids were often carried out into neighbouring states. Their main rationale was that of deterring Arab governments from aiding and hosting any terrorist groups bent on attacking Israeli civilians and civilian installations. However, in 1955 it was clear to then chief of staff, general Moshe Dayan, that:

> We [i.e., Israel] cannot guard every water pipeline from explosion and every tree from uprooting. We cannot prevent the murder of a worker in an orchard or a family in their beds. But it is in our power to set a high price on our blood, a price too high for the Arab community, the Arab army or the Arab government to think worth paying.[24]

Thus, from its inception, Israeli counterterror policy was well aware that terrorism could not be fully eradicated. Counterterrorism could only lower the effects of terror to a tolerable level whereby Israeli civil society could function normally, despite the grave risks it faced and still faces today. Such a limited counterterror goal was due to the fact that Arab terror has predominantly been viewed by Israeli politicians and security officials as a tactical rather than strategic threat. For example, when addressing the Knesset on 21 October 1985, the late defence minister Yitzhak Rabin stated that terrorism 'hurts, it is annoying and disruptive, but it does not constitute a threat to the country's very existence'.[25] Thus, deterrence by punishment was the Israeli counterterrorist method adopted during the early years of its fight against terror.

Nonetheless, despite the inability of terrorism to threaten the existence of Israel, the security establishment did not refrain from addressing the threat head-on. Thus, in 1953 a former intelligence officer, major Ariel Sharon, was chosen to form a special raiding unit, called Unit 101, which soon gained a reputation for daring and hard-hitting operations. However, the lack of discipline within this IDF unit led to a reprisal raid, which was carried out in the village of Kibya in October 1953. The raid resulted in the deaths of over sixty Arab civilians. This led to the unit's disbanding, only to be reformed shortly after into a much more disciplined and professional fighting company called Unit 202, which was led again by Ariel Sharon.

Units 101 and 202 set the standards of subsequent Israeli counterterror policy, both in terms of relying operationally on the rapid and silent covert approach and in terms of relying mostly on special forces units. Indeed, since the formation of Units 101 and 202, in the IDF counterterrorism operations have been fulfilled by several elite units able to conduct both conventional and special operations.

Over the years, in fact, the principal duty in the IDF for counterterrorism has been shared by five elite units: Sayeret Matkal, the General Staff Reconnaissance Unit, Sayeret Tzanchanim, the reconnaissance company of the 35th Paratroop Brigade, Sayeret Golani, the reconnaissance company of the 1st Golani Infantry Brigade, Sayeret Giv'ati, the reconnaissance company of the Giv'ati Infantry Brigade, and Kommando Yami, the IDF's naval special warfare unit.[26] The IDF has generally formed, on a mission-specific basis, task forces consisting of *ad hoc* mission groups drawn from some or all of these units, occasionally supported by other units such as the Engineering Corps.

During the 1950s and 1960s, Israeli counterterror operations were motivated by three factors. First, they were principally counter-force assaults on terrorist forces, centres and installations. Second, they normally caused collateral damage given that terrorist bases were commonly situated in civilian areas. Indeed, Israel has always tried to reduce any collateral damage, but has argued that people living close to terrorist infra-structures and who back or tolerate terrorist operations must anticipate Israeli counter-terror attacks. According to Israeli policy-makers, the risk of collateral damage would possibly weaken the civilian population's desire to shelter or collaborate with terrorists, or even tolerate the presence of terrorist organisations within their communities.

Finally, Israeli counterterror attacks were normally carried out in the sovereign territory of a neighbouring Arab state and were planned to pressure the target state into withdrawing support for terror groups stationed within their territory. Opera-tions deep into enemy territory were, moreover, preferred as they had a greater possi-bility of attaining strategic surprise and inflicting a superior psychological effect on the terrorists. Former chief paratroop and infantry officer Emmanuel Shaked, who played a crucial part in the establishment of Israel's specific approach to special operations, stated that 'I always believed . . . that an operation 200 km from the bor-der is less dangerous than an operation near the border, since surprise is assured'.[27]

Perimeter Defence

Furthermore, defensive measures were also undertaken at quite an early stage of Israel's fight against terror and guerrilla infiltrations. Israel built up fortified out-posts along its borders, created minefields all along easily accessible crossing routes and supported these outposts and minefields with lightly armoured patrols all in order to stop Arab terrorist access into Israel. In any case, over the years the IDF's 'perimeter defence system has continually expanded to incorporate such assets as ultra-sophisticated electronic equipment, maritime and airborne reconnaissance, border fences and patrol roads'.[28] This integrated perimeter defence system, has not been able to stem all cross-border terror attacks over the years, but nonetheless proves essential in lowering the number of overall successful terror attempts. More-over, as shall be seen below, this system has been even less successful in offsetting terror attacks within Israel that originate from the territories.

Intelligence

Key to any counterterror operation has always been the gathering, analysis and use of intelligence. The three branches of Israeli intelligence gained major responsibilities in fighting terror, particularly after the occupation of the territories in 1967.[29] The General Security Services (GSS) in particular set up a major HUMINT (human intelligence) network of Palestinian collaborators, which enabled the IDF and other security services to keep the territories under tight supervision and to eliminate any terrorists that were in the process of carrying out imminent terror operations. Fur-thermore, the extensive use of the 1945 British Defence (Emergency) Regulations enabled the Israeli security services to carry out extensive interrogations of security detainees, but often at the expense of their human rights. According to such regula-tions, individuals could be detained without charge or trial for a period of six months; furthermore, such detentions could be renewed every six months for an indefinite amount of time. Hence, Israeli security officials were able to detain indefi-nitely any suspect without any legal representation, or judicial hearing for that matter. Quite often such detainees were subjected to interrogations involving torture and humiliating living conditions.

Thus, Israeli counterterror policy by 1967 had been firmly established. It was generally defined as a strategy of retaliation and prevention based on deterrence. Counterterror operations were generally reactive and between 1968 and 1969 were primarily focused on the Palestine Liberation Organisation (PLO) bases that formed in areas bordering the Israeli-Jordanian cease-fire lines; subsequently, their emphasis shifted to South Lebanon, where the main PLO operatives had been exiled to by Jordan after the 1970 'Black September' open Palestinian insurrection fiasco against the Hashemite Kingdom. By then Israel was not only carrying out special task force reprisal raids, but also targeting PLO bases through small-scale aerial and artillery bombardments.

International Terror: Hostage-Taking and Airline Hijacking

As the PLO and other Palestinian terror organisations were being systematically targeted by the IDF, the Palestinian terror organisations' traditional cross-border terror campaign began to falter. This was also due to the fact that the defeated Arab states were less interested at the time in supporting PLO raids and more intent on licking their wounds (and pride) after the humiliating Six-Day War defeat. With no real presence in the territories, no substantial diplomatic backing and the fear of the Palestinian national liberation cause being forgotten, the Palestinian terror organisations decided to internationalise their cause by targeting Israeli assets and citizens abroad.

Thus, during the 1970s, the PLO carried out spectacular aeroplane hijackings (e.g., the July 1968 El Al and the May 1972 Sabena Airlines hijackings) and hostage-taking operations (e.g., the 1972 Munich Olympics massacre).[30] Such terrorist operations were not only intended to bring international attention to the Palestinian national cause, but were also used as negotiation opportunities. The Palestinian terror organisations would, in fact, often use a hostage crisis as a way of exchanging imprisoned terrorists for their hostages. At the same time various terrorist-guerrilla groups, primarily operating out of Lebanon, carried out audacious missions into Israel. For example, in April 1974 three terrorists killed sixteen civilians in Kiryat Shimona; the following month other terrorists took schoolchildren hostage in Ma'alot, resulting in twenty-four pupils killed and sixty-two wounded during the rescue operation.

However, the Israelis as a matter of policy never carried out negotiations with terrorist groups during hostage crisis situations unless they were deliberately used as a decoy for an antiterror salvage operation. This is due to the fact that they have always believed that such negotiations rarely achieve success, because 'the danger to the hostages and the counter-terrorist forces grows greater the longer the siege continues, with the gunmen becoming more alert and trigger-happy as their deadline approaches'.[31] On the whole and with the exception of the 1972 Munich Olympics massacre – Israeli special forces were not allowed to intervene in this case – Israeli counterterrorist operations dealing with hostage-taking and aeroplane hijacking situations were successful.

'Conventional' Terror

Following the 1975–76 Lebanese Civil War, the PLO managed to fill a power vacuum in South Lebanon given that the Syrian-Israeli 'Red Line' agreement brokered by the US barred any Syrian presence in southern Lebanon. This led to a significant conventional military buildup by the PLO and the beginning of an ongoing artillery and missile campaign – as well as traditional cross-border terrorist infiltrations – specifically targeted against the civilian population of northern Israel. Israeli reactions continued to be retaliatory and punitive in nature so as to deter further attacks, which in any case continued.

However, with the advent in 1977 of the first right-wing government in Israel's history, Israel shifted its counterterror strategy from tit-for-tat retaliation to sustained counterterror operations. Thus, preventive as well as preemptive operations began to be carried out by not only special forces units, but also increasing numbers of regular infantry, armour and artillery units. To be sure, such a change led to sporadic large-scale raids by air, sea and land against the growing PLO terrorist and guerrilla infrastructure in South Lebanon, which culminated in the two-month-long 'Litani Operation' in 1978 and ultimately escalated in 1982 into a major three-year war and the subsequent fifteen-year occupation of South Lebanon.

The Lebanon invasion was driven by the fact that prime minister Menachem Begin, defence minister Ariel Sharon and the Likud party in general envisaged a new perception of the Israeli-Palestinian conflict. Rather than viewing the conflict as a national and interstate one, they now perceived the conflict as an intercommunal and internecine war. Indeed, from the War of Independence until the elections of 1977, Israeli governments had always accentuated the regional, interstate nature of the conflict, simultaneously looking to diminish its national and internecine component. This made it possible to distinguish between current and existential security. Thus, until then, terrorist groups were normally punished with limited force in the form of special forces reprisals.

However, Israeli security policy saw the PLO 'for the first time as a strategic danger and not only as a nuisance terror'.[32] The cost of PLO terror to Israel, especially in the civilian sphere, was becoming unbearable. Indeed, the PLO as a whole seldom carried out counter-force attacks against Israeli military units and installations. 'Of 353 terrorist attacks in Israel that caused casualties between June 1967 and October 1985, 25 involved IDF or security forces personnel and none were aimed at military installations'.[33]

Accordingly, transferring emphasis from the interstate to the intercommunal levels of the conflict mainly influenced two spheres: (1) in the operative-military sphere it lowered the threshold at which Israel would go to war, thus increasing the chances of war breaking out over intercommunal conflict, such as in response to terrorist activity; (2) in the political-strategic sphere it emphasised the political, intercommunal aspect of the conflict, thus reducing the chance for an interstate territorial compromise in the West Bank and Gaza.[34]

The Intifada

With the PLO in complete disarray and its exile in Tunis – and eventually in the Arabian Gulf – the Palestinians no longer had any local or international champion that could carry on the struggle for national liberation. Economic deprivation, twenty years of 'benign' Israeli occupation and the absence of any military or political-diplomatic solution led to the spontaneous and popular uprising known as the *intifada*, which for the most part was fought through mass demonstrations involving women and children, the establishment of self-helping and self-governing committees of solidarity that tried to establish *de facto* self-rule (and thus sever any relations with the Israeli military government in the territories), the throwing of projectiles such as rocks and occasionally Molotov cocktails and sporadic terror attacks. Suffice to say that with the explosion of the *intifada* in December 1987, Israel would confront one of the greatest threats to its existence since its establishment in May 1948.

The source of such a threat was not to be found in the power of missiles, tanks and airplanes, but in the power of a civilian rebellion, which would eventually drag all of Israel – its leadership, its armed forces and its citizens – into a diplomatic and domestic (but most of all, moral) quagmire because of the numerous human rights violations that occurred whilst the IDF, the police and the intelligence agencies tried to put a lid on the seething cauldron of Palestinian self-determination. Arbitrary arrests, the targeted assassination of many demonstrators, Rabin's infamous policy of 'force, might and beatings' and the use of military forces in carrying out policing duties demoralised the IDF, Israeli society and led to the eventual recognition on the part of the Rabin government that the Palestinian people, the territories and their need for self-determination had to be addressed before radical Islamic terror groups, such as Hamas and the Palestinian Islamic Jihad (PIJ), could gain even more influence within the territories and beyond.

The Oslo Peace Process

Thus, the Oslo process, which began in September 1993 and abruptly ended with the beginning of the Al-Aqsa *intifada* in September 2000, tried to establish peace, based on UN Security Council Resolutions 242 and 338, between Israel and the Palestinians.[35] The Oslo process, however, was predicated on the formula of peace-for-security. That is, the process would continue as long as the Palestinian Authority would crack down on terrorism and other political violence directed at Israel and Israelis residing in the territories.

Still, during the Oslo process Palestinian terrorism not only carried on, but actually augmented because of the lax efforts of the PLO-dominated PA in trying to crack down on Hamas and the PIJ. Yasser Arafat, in fact, was – and still is – allegedly not interested in peace with the state of Israel, but has been trying to implement over the last twenty years the 'Doctrine of Stages', which was adopted at the twelfth meeting of the Palestinian National Council (PNC) in 1974. Such a doctrine articulated a major alteration in the strategy of the PLO, shifting from an inflexible doctrine of unbending armed struggle for the liberation of the whole land of Palestine (including pre-1967 Israel), to the acceptance of a gradualist liberation process, as permitted by the prevailing diplomatic and security conditions, but without yielding the principles of armed struggle and without compromising one inch of the whole of Palestine. Obviously, the reader could assume that such a doctrine was the mere product of revolutionary rhetoric, especially given the fact that Yasser Arafat, the PLO and ultimately the PA actually took part in the peace process.

Nonetheless, the Al-Aqsa *intifada*, which contrary to popular belief was planned months before Ariel Sharon's visit to the Temple Mount Mosque on 28 September 2000,[36] demonstrated that ultimately Arafat's rhetoric has proved to be fundamental policy shared by many members of not only the PLO, but of all other organisations that have been fighting Israel either by means of terrorism or guerrilla warfare over the last four years. The reader must understand that the political solution is merely a tactical ploy in order to one day reach the Palestinians' much-desired 'historic solution,' which in the eloquent words of Sakher Habash, a member of the central committee of Fatah and its recognised chief of ideology, is based on the assumption that:

> ... without establishing a Palestinian state on the *entire land*, peace cannot be achieved ... The Jews must get rid of the Zionism that rules them ... They must become citizens of the state of the future, the democratic Palestinian state.[37] [author's emphasis]

This is not to say that during the peace process the Rabin, Peres, Netanyahu, and Barak governments ever provoked the Palestinians with a deliberate increase in settlements so as to change 'facts on the ground' or by continuing counterterror operations that often breached not only the Oslo I & II Accords, the Hebron Protocol and the Wye Plantation Agreement, but also domestic and international human rights law. However, it is hard to fathom any moral equivalence between building more Israeli settlements (on land the status of which was to be determined, in any case, by the final agreement of the Oslo process) and Palestinian suicide terror attacks, which grew bloodier as the peace process carried on.

Yasser Arafat's lack of cooperation in fighting terror during the Oslo era was somewhat encouraged by the fact that both the Rabin and Peres governments of 1992–96 disassociated the peace process from reactions to terrorist attacks against Israel. That is, the peace process continued, despite Israeli threats of stopping it altogether, even after mass-murder attacks in Israel. Moreover, counterterrorist-operations carried on notwithstanding the formal or informal limitations required by the peace process.

During the hawkish Netanyahu government (1996–99), which demanded linkage between the continuation of the peace process and military calm, 'only three terror attacks occurred compared to the 21 suicide bombings under the previous government. The number of shooting incidents, hand grenades and bombs dropped from around 1,000 during the Rabin and Peres' governments to 250 under Netanyahu; the number of Israelis who were killed in terrorist attacks fell from 245 to 70'.[38] This, though, did not come at the price of respecting Palestinian human rights, as the Netanyahu government made ample use of various punitive and collective measures such as closures, deportations, administrative arrests and the destruction or sealing of homes associated with terrorists.

The Al-Aqsa Intifada

On the other hand, the Barak government, which came close to an historic final status agreement with the PA at Camp David and Taba, lost all credibility in the eyes of the Israelis due to the fact that it failed to retaliate against the architects of Palestinian terror and guerrilla violence during the Al-Aqsa *intifada*. Though it continued to negotiate under fire as had the Rabin and Peres governments previously, this time the level of violence was much greater (and more perplexing, given the extent of the peace concessions Barak was, nevertheless, willing to offer). Consequently, at the February 2001 elections Barak lost to Ariel Sharon by a margin of 63 per cent to 37 per cent, the widest in Israeli history.

The majority of the Israeli population was, in fact, tired of making concessions to the PA whilst at the same time absorbing growing terrorist attacks from not only

Hamas and PIJ, but also from a growing number of members of the Palestinian Security Service (PSS)-affiliated militias (i.e., Tanzim, Force 17), the PLO-affiliated Al-Aqsa Martyrs Brigade and eventually the PSS itself, which was paradoxically set up by the Oslo process in order to combat Palestinian terror. Indeed, Shin Bet statistics show that, during the first two years of the Al-Aqsa *intifada*, out of the 145 suicide bombers '52 were Hamas men and 35 belonged to Islamic Jihad, whilst 40 belonged to Fatah'.[39]

Consequently, despite being called the Al-Aqsa *intifada*, the second *intifada* was not, apart from the first five weeks – that is, until November 2001–a popular uprising. Indeed, in this current conflict, the term '*intifada*' is a misnomer, because the violence used by Palestinians has been of a different nature: the 'activists of the Al-Aqsa uprising have employed starkly different tactics and weaponry, transforming a civil uprising into an urban guerrilla war' and terror campaign.[40]

The terror campaign intensified into 'Lebanese-style roadside bombs, mortar attacks and large-scale ambushes and shooting incidents,' which gradually began to be carried out by all of the Palestinian militias and terror groups.[41] This led Sharon to state in a televised address to his nation that:

> A war has been forced upon us. A war of terror. A war that claims innocent victims every day. A war of terror being conducted systematically, in an organised fashion and with methodical direction.[42]

Sharon's Response

Thus, with the ushering of Ariel Sharon into power the Israeli response to escalating Palestinian violence became fierce. This was possible due to the fact that the majority of the Israeli population hardened their resolve in wanting to combat Palestinian aggression. In fact, whereas in the first *intifada* an increasing segment of the Israeli population had begun to favour a political solution over a military one, the second *intifada*, mainly due to the Palestinians' disproportionate use of terrorist and guerrilla tactics, had shifted Israeli public opinion to the right: For example, '53 percent of the sample in 1997 fully supported trading land for peace .... In the 2002 survey that percentage dropped to 37 percent.' Moreover, favouring the military option, in 2002 '75 percent believed that [the *intifada*] could be controlled by military activity'.[43]

Such a shift in public opinion enabled Sharon to employ extensive coercive measures against the Palestinian population, including wide-ranging curfews, closures, house demolitions, the burgeoning of IDF checkpoints on many main Palestinian roadways in the territories and the withholding of Palestinian tax revenue from the PA.

Furthermore, the military response has been even greater than in previous Israeli-Palestinian flare-ups. In fact, the IDF has introduced more of its major weapons platforms into the conflict together with the implementation of expanded counterterrorism measures against the Palestinians in the territories. Artillery barrages, naval bombardments, and 'surgical' air strikes by F-15I and F-16 aircraft as well as AH-64A Apache and AH-1 Cobra attack helicopters have been particularly commonplace during the current *intifada*.[44]

The use of the major weapons systems has, thus, brought about cases of excessive use of force and has consequently led to the occasional acknowledgement of such disproportionate force on the part of IDF military commanders. For example, in early October 2002, following an attack by Palestinian gunmen on IDF troops attempting to build a wall blocking Palestinian smuggling from Rafah into Egypt, an IDF tank responded with four shells, killing six Palestinians, which included women and children. This incident led the commander of the army in Gaza, brigadier-general Yisrael Ziv, to concede that 'the army used an exaggerated amount of force. The tank fired four shells when one was enough'.[45]

Nonetheless, the use of greater firepower and aggressive retaliation have been the result of the Sharon government's policy of making sure that the PA understands that 'the days are over when we [i.e., Israelis] were willing to negotiate in the morning and go to the funerals of terror victims in the afternoon' and that the Israeli government considers the PA to be fully responsible for the escalation of violence and terror during the current conflict.[46]

Operation 'Defensive Shield'

Moreover, since the Seder Night Massacre on 27 March 2002, the Israeli government initiated a second stage to the conflict. Until then, in fact, the IDF had retaliated to terror and guerrilla attacks by carrying out short reprisal raids, but as of April 2002 the IDF has adopted a more proactive stance. The Seder Night Massacre, in fact, represented a 'major psychological watershed ... and prompted Sharon to declare that Israel was in a "state of war" ', which entailed a substantial increase in the size and depth of the IDF's military operations, 'including the mobilisation of 20,000 reservists'.[47] It has adopted a more aggressive stance by trying to actively neutralise the terrorist infrastructure and by entering former PA-controlled 'A' areas and conducting massive preventive and preemptive operations that, as current US President George W. Bush pointed out after 11 September, will hopefully take 'the battle to the enemy, disrupt his plans, and confront the worst threats before they emerge'.[48]

Indeed, according to current chief of staff Moshe Yaalon, Operation 'Defensive Shield was the turning point of the IDF's transition to initiative Israeli action rather than reaction'.[49] The three-week operation's goal was to attack the infrastructure of Palestinian terrorism. The IDF hoped to catch as many terrorists as possible, to discover and destroy arms caches and bomb-making laboratories, and to gather the intelligence necessary to thwart future attacks. In order to carry out such an operation, the IDF reoccupied Ramallah, Nablus, Tulkarem, Bethlehem, Jenin and other cities in the West Bank. 'Operationally, this translated into the encirclement of a city and the slow cautious entry of infantry forces [normally a brigade, sometimes two of them, with support forces], supported by tanks ... and by attack helicopters'.[50] The encirclement of the areas targeted before the entry of troops actually augmented the chances of hunting down terrorists and guerrillas who had nowhere to run to.

Thus, the operation generated significant arrests of terrorist and guerrilla suspects, the partial destruction of the terrorist and guerrilla infrastructure within the areas targeted and ultimately yielded groundbreaking evidence of the level of the PA's connection to terrorist activity. For example, correspondence between the PA and terrorist groups, procurement requests for ammunition and bombs by terrorist groups, numerous rocket-propelled grenade launchers, short-range Kassam rockets and suicide-bomber belts, amongst other things, were found in Arafat's Mukata compound in Ramallah alone.

Despite the relative success in arresting or killing many terror suspects whilst carrying out operations during 'Defensive Shield', its follow-up Operation 'Determined Path' (and other subsequent ones) used a highly controversial method for apprehending terror or guerrilla suspects – 'neighbour practice'. The 'neighbour practice' has, in reality, repeatedly been used to get wanted men out of houses within highly populated Palestinian areas, and despite assurances of the IDF to the Israeli High Court of Justice (IHCJ) that such a counterterror method would be eradicated. Basically, the 'neighbour practice' involves the use of the wanted man's neighbour as a 'living shield' for IDF troops, whereby he is sent to call on the suspect to come out. In spite of this fact, one officer argued that the "neighbour practice is a military method, an efficient and effective method" ... Former justice Minister Yossi Beilin called the practice "immoral and un-Jewish" and warned that [the Sharon government] "is teaching the army the worst practices, and *is turning the concept of purity of arms into slander*",[51] [author's emphasis].

Indeed, despite the fact that such massive incursions have enabled the IDF and the GSS to find plenty of evidence of PA complicity with (and activity in) terror attacks, to obtain valuable intelligence, to arrest and occasionally assassinate numerous incumbent terrorist martyrs and to gradually reoccupy the former autonomous 'A' areas for the sake of security, many, such as the former head of the Israel Security Agency Ami Ayalon (1996–2000), have come to question Sharon's counterterrorism strategy by arguing that:

> War against terrorism is part of a vicious cycle. The fight itself creates ... even more frustration and despair, more terrorism and increased violence ... [And that] it is not a fleeting battle that ends in either victory or defeat.[52]

Counterterrorism's Relative Success

Notwithstanding remarks such as the one stated above, there have been signs that the IDF's continuous sorties, reprisals and incursions into the Palestinian terrorist- and guerrilla-infested cities and refugee camps have had some positive results. The number of terror attacks against Israeli civilians has actually diminished. The frequency of suicide attacks has, in fact, dropped considerably since the deterrent effects of the IDF's reoccupation of Palestinian-controlled West Bank 'A' areas have finally come to fruition. To be sure, during the months of November 2002 and January 2003 there was *just* one suicide attack, whereas December 2002 reported none. 'During the same three-month period, the IDF reports that 36 [suicide] missions were thwarted ... [And] in the first two months of 2003, 123 various terror attacks were averted'.[53]

'There were no attacks in February; three in March; and only two' in April. This was due to the fact that the Israeli security forces have been able to arrest '150 would-be suicide bombers since the start of the *intifada*, [that] 'Israel's prisons are housing about 5,000 Palestinians suspected of involvement in acts of terror or membership in terror organisations and that the security forces operations have led to a shortage of military-grade explosives'.[54] Such 'success' has, however, not come at a low cost, because it has involved growing numbers of IDF incursions in to areas, such as Gaza, whose Palestinian population was relatively less active in carrying out terror or guerrilla attacks against Israeli civilians or troops until recently.

Moreover, whilst incursions into Gaza were initially one- or two-day tactical raids carried out on a sporadic basis, they have lately become longer in duration, more frequent and have involved greater amounts of IDF personnel and materiel.

Indeed, such an escalation and penetration of IDF operations into areas initially left out of the conflict have been the result of a deep-seated belief that, as stated by chief of staff Yaalon in *Yediot Ahronot* in August 2002, 'the only solution is to achieve an unequivocal victory over the Palestinians' and that such a victory would not come at a low price or immediately.[55] 'Counter-terrorism, however, is a form of conflict management, not conflict resolution'.[56] Thus, it is hard to see how the IDF alone will be able to impose an 'unequivocal victory' or political solution.

To be sure, Sharon has stated that 'it [i.e., terrorism] is not something that we can fight and destroy quickly. It takes time. It demands commitment and hard work ...' At the same time, knowing how deleterious an effect the protracted conflict can have on the IDF operational capabilities and combat motivation, Sharon has been quite clear that he does not want the IDF bogged down forever in the territories: 'I don't want to sit in Nablus forever. I do not want to have our country mobilised forever to sit in Nablus'.[57] Hence, prime minister Sharon's recent unilateral disengagement plan from Gaza has begun to gain significant momentum despite opposition from the IDF general staff and the Israeli Right.

The Human Rights and Security Dilemma

And yet, Israel has relentlessly pursued terrorists and fought major conventional wars in order to defend itself and maintain its existence. Thus, the defence of state of Israel and its wider interests has been carried out in spite of the ethical and legal dilemmas and international censure it has faced over the years. Indeed, as a western democratic state, Israel has had to fight a form of warfare which has on occasion brought the worst out of it and which has required it to act against the democratic and moral foundation upon which it stands. This has particularly been the case during the last twenty years of the Israeli-Palestinian conflict, which has been radicalised by the mushrooming of suicide terrorism and callous terrorist organisations that have deliberately used civilian areas as their base of operations.

Hence, every security operation that has been carried out by the IDF has had the potential of causing gross human rights violations. This has been particularly the case when the IDF has subjected the Palestinian populations to extensive bouts of curfews, checkpoints, border closures and the destruction of property such as orchards, homes and other buildings in the name of security.[58] Nonetheless, in Israel's desperation to stop buses from blowing up in Tel Aviv, Haifa and Jerusalem; suicide bombers detonating themselves in crowded theatres, nightclubs and bars all over the country; sniper, mortar and missile attacks being carried out against both settlements in the territories and border towns in the Israeli heartland; Israel has had to intermittently violate Palestinian human rights in order to carry out vital counter-terror missions.

Then again, the number of such violations pales if compared to the number of violations Palestinian terrorist groups have deliberately carried out against Israeli civilians. Moreover, if one takes into consideration the number of counterterror and counterinsurgency operations the IDF has participated successfully in without blatantly abusing human rights, then the number of such violations are overall relatively small.

Moreover, the necessity and obligation of a state to defend its own citizens is of primary importance, particularly when confronting an unremitting terror campaign, and is clearly enshrined in the principle of self-defence, which is explicitly acknowledged in Article 51 of the UN Charter and by customary international law. Both actually permit every state to respond with force to an armed attack, granted such force is necessary and proportionate.

However, the UN Security Council in several cases (most involving Israel) has seemed to judge proportionality by measuring the response on a quantitative basis to the single attack that preceded it. Nonetheless and contrary to its track record, the Security Council should consider Israeli retaliatory responses in relation to a continuing pattern of attacks rather than the last one. 'Tit-for-tat' does not mean disregarding an accretion of violent incidents in judging the appropriate response. Moreover, the concept of proportionality would have to take into account how much force would have to be wielded in order to cause the terrorist to change his expectation about the costs and benefits of his terror strategy. In the case of suicide terrorists, imprisonment or death have been the only two viable options.

Furthermore, whereas the principle of self-defence can be applicable to retaliatory operations – given the fact that self-defence can only be called upon after an armed attack has occurred – the principle of necessity allows for preventive and pre-emptive counterterror operations if the use of force is imminent. Israel has consistently justified its counterterror operations in the international arena by using the principle of necessity, particularly with the growth over the last twenty years of suicide terrorism, which has given rise to the phenomenon of 'ticking bombs'.

Such 'ticking bombs' are known terrorists that have undergone all the martyrdom rituals and suicide training and are ready to strike at Israeli civilian targets in Israel and within the territories. Thus, 'pursuing terrorist leaders therefore has a dual function: prevention of future terror and punishment of those responsible for the attacks. Major-General Amnon Shahak, then head of intelligence, explained the justification of striking at terrorist leaders in April 1988: "In my opinion, terrorist leaders are a proper target for elimination. Anyone who conducts terror against us ought to be a target"'.[59]

As a result, Israel has conducted a campaign of 'targeted killings' in order to pre-empt any egregious and deadly terror attacks, despite the fact that the summary execution of an individual is considered a human rights violation. Moreover, many international critics have argued that killing potential terrorists and their political leaders and carrying out large-scale counterterror operations such as Operation 'Defensive Shield' causes greater numbers of revenge attacks by the targeted terrorist organisations. Although that might be true in the short-term, in the long-term the consistent targeting of terrorist organisations' personnel and materiel will decrease such attacks, 'because the number of suicide attacks depends upon more factors than simply the number of willing martyrs'.[60] Successful suicide bombings depend on highly specialized capabilities, particularly in terms of making the explosives and the detonation of complex mechanisms, and most of those capabilities have been reduced 'by arresting or killing terrorist leaders, seizing bomb-making equipment and sealing off [Israel's] borders'.[61]

Notwithstanding the fact that UN Secretary General Kofi Annan has declared that 'terrorist acts are grave violations of human rights', he also reiterated that 'to pursue security at the expense of human rights is short-sighted, self-contradictory, and, in the long run self-defeating'.[62] Israel, for all its blunders and violations, has tried to fight terror on a similar understanding. To be sure, given the extensive internal debate, critical domestic media coverage, Knesset and Israeli High Court of Justice supervision and Israeli, Palestinian and international human rights organisations' whistle-blowing regarding the Israeli security services' human rights track record, not many other countries could do such an effective job in fighting terrorism as Israel has done.

Indeed, despite vitriolic international criticism, Israel has cracked down on individuals and military units that have violated Palestinian human rights. For example, over the last two years the IDF judge advocate general has investigated over 1,200 complaints of human rights violations and other criminal activities. '360 investigations have been conducted regarding the conduct of soldiers during fighting with terrorists. These included 134 alleged property violations, 153 allegations of violence, and 55 allegations of inappropriate shooting. The investigations [so far] have yielded 44 indictments'.[63] A border police company suspected of systematic abuse and harassment of Palestinians in Hebron was disbanded recently.

Furthermore, calls by the attorney general Elyiakim Rubinstein and by many Knesset members for the current Sharon government to end targeted killings have increased, but have fallen so far on deaf ears.[64] The Knesset Law Committee has begun a monitoring programme of IDF roadblocks in order to prevent any human rights abuses on the Palestinian population,[65] and the IHCJ has consistently heard, and sometimes ruled in favour of, Palestinian petitions against IDF human rights abuses (e.g., in September 1999, the ICHJ banned the use of 'moderate physical pressure' on security prisoners; however, since then, abuses have still occurred).

Attempts at reducing the likelihood of casualties is the reason why Operation 'Defensive Shield' in Jenin was carried out solely by infantry and engineering units without any armour, artillery or air force cover. Yet, due to an ingenious Palestinian disinformation campaign, the world believed that 5,000 Palestinians were massacred (eventually the accusation dropped down to 'only' 500) and that extensive damage to civilian houses was carried out by the IDF. This obviously was far from the case as subsequent UN and IDF reports showed. Moreover, according to international law, civilian buildings that function as military outposts become legitimate military targets. Due to the fact that the houses in Jenin were infested with snipers and booby traps, one cannot consider the destruction of such makeshift refugee homes a human rights violation, as many in the international community declared after the military operation.

In any case, the Israeli Ministry of Defence is even trying to obviate the difficulty of killing terrorist snipers without causing collateral damage by developing an automatic antisniper gun, called 'Believer', which in effect could locate precisely the source of enemy fire in less than one-third of a second and return fire with the help of highly sophisticated infrared thermal technology. Not only is this system being developed to reduce collateral damage, but also to deter the sniper as 'the shooter knows that as soon as he's fired off the first shot, he's dead'.[66] The 'Corner Shot' non-line-of-sight weapon system has also been developed. It allows the soldier to engage a target from behind a corner because of its swing-hinge front section, which includes a high-resolution camera and an independent firing system, thus helping the soldier avoid exposure to hostile fire when in close-quarters combat.[67]

Moreover, the necessity of reducing cases of misbehaviour carried out by Israeli soldiers during combat and routine security duties, especially at checkpoints, has led to the establishment of a legal and moral code of conduct. Such a code, which is based on eleven key rules of conduct, has been taught over the last year-and-a-half to both regular and reservist ground force units. It provides extensive role-playing drills on the dilemmas of how to treat civilians and civilian property and, more importantly, on the dilemmas of what rules of engagement are acceptable in densely populated urban theatres of operations.[68]

Conclusion

Despite such Israeli attempts at reducing the likelihood of human rights violations, the elimination of all of them would be impossible given the gargantuan task of fighting suicide terrorism. Terrorist organisations, in any case, are fully conscious of the human rights dilemmas associated with any counterterrorist measures and will try cunningly to exploit such dilemmas in order to undermine the legitimacy of the government against which they are fighting. In addition, the sympathy garnered with an occupied people will always prevail no matter how heinous the strategy to gain national independence adopted by such a people is. Indeed, 'victim status is becoming a prized commodity in international politics, because it is a means by which a group with no capacity of its own can acquire powerful external allies'.[69] This trend can be seen in the current Anglo-American occupation of Afghanistan and Iraq.

Thus, in a strategy that not only targets the opponent's civilian population, but also holds to ransom its own, the probabilities of human rights abuses when fighting terrorism are never-ending, no matter how much effort is made to avoid such abuses. Nonetheless, as long as western democratic states continue to alter their policies and practices to accommodate human rights guidelines and laws, their moral fight will ultimately succeed. Such accommodation, conversely, can never occur at the expense of their own security, especially in the nasty and brutish world of international relations in general and counterterror war in particular, even more so when various Islamic or Middle Eastern terror groups and states are intent on developing terrorist weapons of mass destruction and on deliberately striking their enemies' civilian centres.

Notes

1. R. Kennedy, 'Is One Person's Terrorist Another's Freedom Fighter? Western and Islamic Approaches to 'Just War' Compared', *Terrorism and Political Violence* 11/1 (1999) p.4.

2. A. P. Schmid and A. J. Jongman, *Political Terrorism: A New Guide to Concepts, Theories, Data Bases and Literature* (New Brunswick: Transaction Books 1988) p.3.

3. A. R. Norton, 'Drawing the Line on Opprobrious Violence', *Ethics & International Affairs* 4 (1990) p.124.

4. US Department of State, Office of the Ambassador-at-Large for Counterterrorism, *Patterns of Global Terrorism: 1985* (Washington DC: Government Printing Office 1986), inside cover.

5. J. Scheuer, 'Moral Dimensions of Terrorism', *Fletcher Forum of World Affairs* 14/1 (1990) p.146.

6. L. Freedman *et al.*, *Terrorism and International Order* (London: Routledge & Kegan Paul 1986) p.18.

7. Ibid., p.8.

8. S/RES/1456-20 Jan. 2003.

9. M. Hofnung, 'States of Emergency and Ethnic Conflict in Liberal Democracies: Great Britain and Israel', *Terrorism and Political Violence* 6/3 (1994) p.345.

10. C. C. Harmon, 'Terrorism: A Matter for Moral Judgement', *Terrorism and Political Violence* 4/1 (1992) p.3.

11. R. M. Beitler, 'The Intifada: Palestinian Adaptation to Israeli Counterinsurgency Tactics', *Terrorism and Political Violence* 7/2 (1995) p.65.

12. J. R. White, *Terrorism: An Introduction* (Pacific Grove, CA: Brooks/Cole Publishing Company 1991) p.116.

13. Scheur (note 5) p.151.

14. Ibid., p.148.

15. Schmid and Jongman (note 2) p.17.

16. United Nations General Assembly Resolution 49/60, Measures to Eliminate International Terrorism, 17 Feb. 1995.

17. Y. Alexander, 'Democracy and Terrorism: Threats and Responses', in Y. Dinstein (ed), *Israel Yearbook on Human Rights*, No. 26 (The Hague: Martinus Nijhoff Publishers 1997) p.257.

18. Scheuer (note 5) p.148.

19. B. T. Wilkins, *Terrorism and Collective Responsibility* (London: Routledge 1992) p.9.

20. Norton (note 3) p.124.

21. That is, the West Bank and Gaza.

22. G. E. Rothenberg, 'Israeli Defence Forces and Low-Intensity Operations', in D. A. Charters and M. Tugwell (eds), *Armies in Low-Intensity Conflict: A Comparative Analysis* (London: Brassey's Defence Publishers 1989) p.56.

23. M. Walzer, *Just and Unjust Wars* (New York: Basic Books 1977) p.216.

24. Rothenberg (note 22) Israeli Defence p.56.

25. Foreign Broadcast Information Service, 'Rabin Addresses Knesset on Terrorism', *Tel Aviv IDF Radio*, 1404 GMT, 21 Oct. 1985 p.16.

26. M. Eisenstadt, 'Special Operations against Terrorism: The Israeli Approach', in Barry Rubin (ed), *Terrorism and Politics* (London: MacMillan 1991) pp.23–39.

27. Ibid., p.36.

28. D. Rodman, 'Combined Arms Warfare in the Israel Defence Forces: An Historical Overview', *Defence Studies* 2/1 (Spring 2002) p.123.

29. These branches are: 1) the General Security Service (GSS – Shabak in Hebrew), 2) the IDF Intelligence Branch (A'man in Hebrew) and 3) the MOSSAD, the Israeli intelligence agency.

30. S. Reeve, *One Day in September: The Story of the 1972 Munich Olympics Massacre* (London: Faber 2000).

31. C. Dobson and R. Payne, *Terror! The West Fights Back* (London: MacMillan 1982) p.100.

32. Y. Peri, 'Coexistence or Hegemony? Shifts in the Israeli Security Concept', in D. Caspi, A. Diskin, and E. Gutmann (eds), *The Roots of Begin's Success: The 1981 Israeli Elections* (London: Croom, Helm, 1984) p.206.

33. W. V. O'Brien, *Law and Morality in Israel's War with the PLO* (London: Routledge 1991) p.16.

34. D. Horowitz, 'The Israeli Concept of National Security', in A. Yaniv (ed), *National Security and Democracy in Israel* (Boulder, CO: Lynne Rienner Publishers 1993).

35. I. Rabinovich, *Waging Peace: Israel and the Arabs at the End of the Century* (New York: Farrar, Straus & Giroux 1999); U. Savir, *The Process: 1,100 Days That Changed the Middle East* (New York: Vintage Books 1999); and W. B. Quandt, *Peace Process: American Diplomacy and the Arab-Israeli Conflict Since 1967* (Berkeley: University of California Press 2001).

36. On 2 March 2001, Pakistani an Authority communications minister Imad Falouji declared that the Al-Aqsa *intifada* 'had been planned since Chairman Arafat's return from Camp David' (i.e., July 2000, two months prior to Sharon's visit). Quoted from 'Intelligence Briefs: Israel/Palestinians', *Middle East Intelligence Bulletin* 3/3 (March 2001) http://www.meib.org/articles/0103 ipb.htm

37. Lt.-Col J. D. H. (Anonymous), 'Why Peace Failed: An Intelligence Assessment of Palestinian Motives', *The Review* 28/1 (Jan. 2003) p.12.

38. B. Ganor, 'Israel's Counter-Terrorism Policy: 1983–1999, Efficacy versus Liberal Democratic Values', 15 Sep. The International Policy Institute for Counter-Terrorism, http://www.ict.org.il/articles/articledet.cfm?articlesid=447

39. A. Harel, '*Shin Bet*: 145 Suicide Bombers Since the Start of the *Intifada*', *Ha'aretz* 1 Oct. 2002.

40. J. Sinai, '*Intifada* Drives Both Sides to Radical Arms', *Jane's Intelligence Review* 13/5 (May 2001) p.33.

41. D. Eshel, 'The *Al-Aqsa Intifada*: Tactics and Strategies', *Jane's Intelligence Review* 13/5 (May 2001) p.37.

42. 'Sharon Equates *Intifada* and Terror', *The Middle East Reporter* 101/1171 (15 Dec. 2001) p.10.

43. A. Arian, *Israeli National Public Opinion on National Security 2002*, Memorandum No. 61 (Tel Aviv: Jaffee Centre for Strategic Studies 2002) pp.13, 35.

44. S. Rodan, 'Interview: Maj. Gen. Dan Halutz, Commander-In-Chief of the Israel Air Force', *Jane's Defence Weekly* 37/3 (16 Jan. 2002) p.32.

45. A. Harel, 'Top IDF Officer Admits "Exaggerated" Force in Rafah Shelling Incident', *Ha'aretz* 30 Oct. 2002.

46. B. Ben-Eliezer, 'Israeli Defence Policy: Responding to Challenges Near and Far', *Peacewatch* 364 (12 Feb. 2002) http://www.washingtoninstitute.org/watch/Peacewatch/peacewatch2002/364.htm

47. M. A. Heller, 'Operation "Defensive Wall": A Change in Israeli Strategy?', *Tel Aviv Notes* 34 (4 April 2002) p.1.

48. S. Mofaz, 'The Israeli-Palestinian Conflict: What Next?', (13 Sep. 2002), *The Washington Institute for Near East Policy*, http://www.washingtoninstitute.org/pubs/speakers/mofaz.htm

49. M. Yaalon, 'Press Release of the Third Herzliya Conference on the Balance of Israel's National Security', *Herzliya*, 3 December 2002.

50. Shlomo Brom, 'Operation "Defensive Shield": An Interim Assessment', *Tel Aviv Notes* 35 (11 April 2002) p.1.

51. J. Lis and B. Kra, 'Officers Defend "Human Shield" Practice', *Ha'aretz* 16 Aug. 2002.

52. A. Ayalon, in R. B. Satloff (ed), 'Fighting Terrorism—Lessons from, the Front Lines', *War on Terror: The Middle East Dimension* (Washington DC.: The Washington Institute for Near East Policy 2002) p.4.

53. Z. Schiff, 'Thwarting Suicide Missions Is Not Enough', *Ha'aretz* 6 March 2003.

54. G. Alon, '150 Would-Be Bombers Nabbed During *Intifada*', *Ha'aretz* 30 April 2003.

55. R. Hazut, 'The Palestinians Are an Existential Threat: Iraq Is Not', *Yedioth Ahronoth* 23 Aug. 2002: *Israel Resource Review*, http://israelvisit.co.il/cgi-bin/friendly.pl?url=Aug—23—02!IDF

56. M. Levitt and S. Wikas, 'Defensive Shield Counter-Terrorism Accomplishments', *Peacewatch* 377 (17 April 2002) http://www.washingtoninstitute.org/watch/Peacewatch/peacewatch2002/377.htm

57. C. B. Glick, 'Sharon: No Military Solution to the War With the Palestinians', *Jerusalem Post* 26 Sept. 2002.

58. For extensive reports on Israeli (and Palestinian) human rights violations see http://www.btselem.org/ and http://web.amnesty.org/library/eng-isr/index

59. B. Ganor, 'Israeli Counterterrorist Activity', *The International Policy Institute for Counterterrorism* 5 July 2003. http://www.ict.org.il/counter_ter/Is_ct.htm. See also G. Luft, 'The Logic of Israel's Targeted Killing', *Middle East Forum* 18 Feb. 2004, http://www.meforum.org/pf.php?id=515

60. J. Chait, 'Exploding Myths', *The Review* 27/6 (June 2002) p.12.

61. Ibid.

62. UN security council press release SC/7523 (4 Oct. 2002) http://www.un.org/News/Press/docs/2002/sgsm8417.doc.htm

63. D. Izenberg, 'IDF Tell Knesset Committee It Probes Human Rights Allegations', *Jerusalem Post* 22 June 2003.

64. A. Benn, 'A-G Urges Sharon to Only Use Targeted Killings as Last Resort', *Ha'aretz* 30 Dec. 2002.

65. D. Izenberg, 'Knesset Committee to Monitor Soldiers' Behaviour at Roadblocks', *Jerusalem Post* 7 July 2003.

66. B. Opall-Rome, 'Israel Tests Anti-Sniper System in Combat', *Defence News* 15/21 (July 2002) p.34.

67. Army Technology, http://www.army-technology.com/contractors/machine_guns/corner_shot

68. For a detailed account of the IDF Code of Conduct see Amos Guiora, 'Balancing IDF Checkpoints and International Law: Teaching the IDF Code of Conduct', *Jerusalem Issue Brief* 3/8 (19 Nov. 2003) http://www.jcpa.org/brief/brief3-8.htm

69. L. Freedman, 'The Coming War on Terrorism', in L. Freedman (ed), *Superterrorism: Policy Responses* (Oxford: Blackwell Publishing 2002) p.48.

16

Terrorism, Human Rights and Law Enforcement in Spain

ROGELIO ALONSO AND FERNANDO REINARES

Unit for Documentation and Analysis on Terrorism,
Universidad Rey Juan Carlos,
Madrid, Spain

Terrorism systematically violates human rights and disrupts basic political processes common to liberal democracies. Combating terrorism is thus necessary in order to protect these fundamental rights and maintain the well functioning of tolerant polities. However, state initiatives put in place to cope with terrorism may also damage human rights, even when these measures are formulated by elected accountable authorities and implemented in the context of open societies. Spain has precisely been among those European countries most affected by the wave of terrorism initiated more than three decades ago across western industrial societies, and thus where violations of fundamental rights as well as obstacles to the exercise of civil liberties as a consequence of such violence became particularly severe. Also, a case where effective rule of law was temporarily damaged in the fight against the ethno-nationalist terrorism perpetrated by ETA (an acronym for Euskadi ta Askatasuna, meaning Basque Homeland and Freedom) but successfully restored by efforts from both state institutions, as a result of an effective division of power, and civil society. It is therefore an experience providing substantive knowledge and valuable insights on how to counter terrorism in accordance with the principles and procedures of democracy. Accordingly, this paper aims at a better understanding on the interrelated issues of terrorism, human rights and law enforcement in a context of political change.

Terrorism, Public Opinion and Victimisation

Spaniards have consistently perceived terrorism as one of their main public concerns since the late 1970s, as their polity was undergoing a process of democratization following nearly four decades of dictatorship, until the present day. Nowadays it is no longer considered a major threat to democratic stability, as was the case some twenty years ago, but a protracted violent phenomenon that systematically violates fundamental rights and impairs the free exercise of civil and political liberties. Until the massacre perpetrated in Madrid by radical Islamists on 11 March 2004, the real problem has been that of ETA, a terrorist organization formed during the 1960s, amidst the crisis of Francoism (1939–75) as a radicalized expression of Basque ethnic nationalism. ETA has claimed responsibility for well over 80 per cent of the more than 1,000 people killed in the country as a result of terrorist actions between 1968 and 2001.[1] This terrorist organisation has remained a major source of concern for the citizens of Spain as a whole, and for the residents of the Basque Country in particular, in spite of its violence having progressively declined in frequency throughout the 1980s and more so during the 1990s and the first years of the new century. Current and recent levels of violence are clearly a long way from the dramatic escalation which took place precisely during the period when the country underwent a process of regime change.

The average yearly number of fatalities occasioned by ETA was eighty-one between 1978 and 1980, thirty-four between 1981 and 1990, and sixteen between 1991 and 2000. ETA's murderous campaign has progressively declined since then. In 2001 the group killed thirteen people. The following year ETA caused five fatalities followed by three killings in 2003. It should be noted that this terrorist organisation perpetrated an average of seven assassinations per year between 1968 and 1977, which was under the dictatorship and before the first free elections were held in Spain. Paradoxically, though, this operational decline, caused by changing political conditions and governmental responses has modified both internal structures and victimisation patterns of the terrorist organization. For instance, the range of targets has been successively expanded, from mainly military and police personnel at the beginning to civilians (often highly indiscriminately killed outside the Basque Country) and, finally, Basque-elected politicians from the local to the national levels of government, university lecturers, journalists, businessmen and judges, among other categories of people explicitly known for not endorsing nationalist propositions. In addition, the terrorist organization established new expressions of daily violence (practiced by a number of supporters in their late teens and early twenties) intended to harass and prosecute non-nationalist sectors of Basque society, which account for half the population in the autonomous community.[2] This tactic was designed as a complement, on a more routine basis, to the periodic attacks perpetrated by fully engaged militants. As a result of this intense phenomenon, Basques themselves agree with the rest of Spanish citizens in considering terrorism their main issue of public concern. In this sense, particularly relevant are social surveys periodically conducted by the University of the Basque Country which show that a significant percentage of Basque citizens are afraid of participating in politics, expressing also an extremely worrying lack of freedom to voice their views in public because of fear. Interestingly enough, almost half of Basque society admits to this fear and lack of freedom, feelings that are more common among non-nationalist citizens than their nationalist counterparts.[3]

It came as no surprise when, at the beginning of February 2001, the Council of Europe Commissioner for Human Rights visited the Basque Country. According to the report he submitted one month later to the Committee of Ministers and the Parliamentary Assembly of the same international organisation, the visit was prompted by the continuing violations of human rights in that autonomous community as a result of terrorist activities. However, the report identified as major causes of the human rights violations suffered by ample segments of Basque society not only the assassinations, kidnappings, threats and extortion activities perpetrated by members of ETA, but also the more diffused urban or street violence, locally known as *kale borroka*, carried out on a daily basis (although especially during weekends) by trained gangs of youngsters who openly support the terrorist organization.[4] This violence included attacks on shops, the burning of buses, acts of street vandalism, personal attacks against elected municipal councilors, regional parliamentarians, schoolteachers, journalists, university faculty, students and even relatives of such individuals. ETA's terrorism as well as the violence perpetrated by the group's juvenile sympathisers has resulted in the systematic violation of fundamental human rights. This combination of tactics has created a climate of fear among a wide section of the population since many individuals, on the left and right of the ideological spectrum, have felt severely restricted in the exercise of their civil and political rights as citizens of a democracy, with the only reason being that they have chosen to defend the constitutional order and to articulate non-nationalist ideas and openly criticize terrorism.

Regime Change, Justice and Terrorism

Francoism confronted insurgent terrorism through indiscriminate repression and the use of militarized institutions. Official violence was, under these circumstances and particularly when deployed against ETA, conducive to the loss of state legitimacy in the Basque Country and to an increasing sympathy of public opinion towards the terrorist organization. During the democratic transition and the years of democratic consolidation, the emerging political elites had to remove those practices and reform those agencies, introducing new ones in accordance with the rule of law and the principles of an open society. But due to the intrinsic characteristics of the political change experienced, many of these reforms took place rather slowly, to the extent that indiscriminate repression by police forces when presumably performing operations against terrorism happened while the existing legal framework was being replaced. All this resulted in the counterproductive application of some legislative and coercive measures against terrorism which, during some critical years, contributed to sustain a significant amount of lasting popular support for the terrorists. It is estimated that nearly half of the Basque adults perceived ETA members as either patriots or idealists in 1978, whereas only 7 per cent of those interviewed in public opinion surveys would call them plain criminals. In 1989, less than one-quarter of the same citizens refer to the terrorists as patriots or idealists, and those who portray them simply as criminals more than doubled from the previous decade.[5] A more recent survey conducted in 2004 shows that never before, since the end of Franco's dictatorship, has Basque society rejected ETA's activists so strongly. Nowadays the majority of Basque citizens regard ETA's activists as 'terrorists' (69 per cent), 'criminals or murderers' (17 per cent) and 'fanatics' (13 per cent).[6]

In January 1977, the National Court was created in Madrid to deal with serious organised crime and terrorist offences. This implied a fundamental jurisdictional change, since terrorist crimes would be dealt with, from that moment on, by ordinary judges instead of military courts as was previously the case. Likewise, following the broad Pactos de la Moncloa (Moncloa Agreements) which were signed in October 1977 by most of the parliamentary parties in order to secure the democratization process despite a severe economic crisis, the fragmented and confusing legislation on terrorism inherited from the dictatorship became progressively replaced by new provisions adapted to both the international environment and the emerging political context. But it would not be until December 1978, when terrorist activity had already started its dramatic escalation, that the first constitutional law to combat terrorism was proclaimed, including special provisions on increasing condemnatory sentences, extending otherwise normal detention periods and establishing limitations to the judicial control over searches of domiciles and the interception of private communications. As it will be argued, some of these provisions were intended to facilitate police investigation. But enforced by state security agencies that were still unreformed and largely devoid of a professional culture adapted to the emerging democratic regime, far from effective for these purposes, such legislation resulted instead in a worrying number of proven cases when detainees were subject to mistreatment and even torture.[7]

Interestingly enough, a significant change in the ideological orientation of the governing party, from the liberal conservative position of the Union de Centro Democratico (UCD) to the moderate leftist orientation of the Partido Socialista Obrero Espanol (PSOE) following the 1982 general elections, did not initially result in a different legal approach to terrorism. On the contrary, the Socialist Party, thanks to its absolute majority in both houses of the Spanish Parliament as a result of the general elections held in October 1982, promoted a new law in December 1984 along the same lines of existing laws. Such legislation, probably the most important of its kind (as well as controversial), was applied during 1985 and 1986. However, the Constitutional Court overturned some of these new provisions at the end of 1987, among them the extension of the detention period to ten days. This especial antiterrorist legislation was finally derogated in May 1988, not only because of the unconstitutional provisions already mentioned but also because of the political consensus on antiterrorist measures reached early that year, when the Ajuria Enea Agreement (Pacto de Ajuria Enea) was signed by the main Spanish political parties, including all the formations represented in the Basque Parliament with the exception of ETA's political wing, Herri Batasuna (HB). Some of the unquestioned provisions contained in the derogated especial legislation were subsequently incorporated into the ordinary legislation. For instance, Articles 571 to 580 within Chapter V of the new penal code approved in November 1995, when the PSOE was still in control of the central government, are devoted to terrorist crimes.

Early in 2001, the penal code was modified so as to include new provisions adapted to changes observed in terrorist practices since the middle of the 1990s, as mentioned earlier. Reacting to widespread popular mobilizations against ETA inside the Basque Country, leaders of this underground organisation designed a plan to complement terrorist actions such as car bombs or assassinations perpetrated by formal militants with other kinds of violent activities, typically committed during the weekends by fanatical teenagers. The terrorist group intended through these means to strengthen the systematic harassment and intimidation of Basque citizens who declared themselves not to be nationalists. Therefore, and in response to this new strategy instigated by ETA, terrorist offences also include criminal actions intended to intimidate part of a given population as well as entire social or political collectivities, and violent activities aimed at subverting the constitutional order and at seriously altering public peace.

Moreover, terrorist actions perpetrated by individuals aged between eighteen and twenty-one who otherwise will face special juvenile courts, as well as the praise or justification of terrorism; and the humiliation of victims and their relatives are also regarded as terrorist offenses in these new legal provisions adopted. Likewise, those condemned for terrorist offences will no longer be eligible for public office during a period of at least twenty years, and terrorist actions against elected representatives in local institutions have become equated with those suffered by members of other state bodies. Coinciding with the incorporation of these new offences, judges belonging to the National Court, chiefly among them magistrate Baltasar Garzon, initiated legal action on the financing of terrorism and on entities providing support to terrorist organisations, simply by applying the penal code. As a result, some youth gangs, groups seeking to maintain control over ETA members in prison and even a newspaper sympathetic to the ethno-nationalist gunmen (all of them belonging to the complex network created over the years by leaders of the terrorist organisation) were finally declared illegal.

Batasuna Outlawed to Protect Democracy

One of the most controversial measures implemented by the Spanish authorities as a response to ETA has been the banning of the terrorist organisation's political wing, formerly known as Herri Batasuna. The basis for the banning of Batasuna rests in the belief, supported by an overwhelming amount of evidence, that the party constitutes a part within the network of organisations ultimately led by ETA which complement terrorist actions, being all of them a movement that shares objectives as well as overlapping membership.[8] Legislation introduced in June 2002 resulted in the banning of the party that has traditionally represented ETA's interests. This law was strongly criticised by the totality of nationalist parties in the Basque Country, including more moderate formations such as the Partido Nacionalista Vasco (PNV), which has held power in the region since the inception of autonomy in the early 1980s. Irrespective of their party allegiance, nationalist representatives agreed on defining the banning of Batasuna as a serious violation of political rights and liberties. Subsequently, nationalist parties joined forces in the Basque Parliament and voted against the banning of Batasuna.

Sympathisers of ETA saw nationalist disagreement with the legislation put forward by the Spanish government as evidence of the lack of freedom and democracy suffered by Basque citizens. This was a view that many nationalists from the main party in the region, the PNV, also endorsed as illustrated by the Basque government's decision, announced in September 2003, to formally accuse the Spanish state of violating Articles 6, 7 and 11 of the European Covenant of Human Rights. However, on February 2004 the European Court of Human Rights unanimously agreed to reject the Basque government's claim in relation to the banning of ETA's political wing. The European body concluded that an autonomous government within the state was unable to sue its own state. This rejection of the Basque government's claim had been endorsed by previous pronouncements by the highest judicial bodies in Spain: the Constitutional Court and the Supreme Court. The latter had declared in March 2003 that the benefit derived from the banning of ETA's political wing was the protection of democracy and the safeguarding of citizens' rights in the Basque Country. This view was contrary to the Basque government's demand before the European Court of Human Rights arguing that fundamental rights and liberties had been suspended as a result of the banning of a political party.

At the core of these opposing arguments lays a very important debate about human rights and terrorism. In a clear attempt to distort the real nature and intention of the banning of Batasuna this measure has been deliberately presented by the majority of nationalist politicians as a denial of the civil rights of a section of Basque society. The term 'apartheid' has been widely used by ETA's sympathisers to describe the situation provoked by the banning of the party that has traditionally supported the terrorist organisation. Moreover, the representatives of the main nationalist parties in the region have lent some credibility to the alleged discriminatory and repressive intentions of the Spanish state, as illustrated by the demonstration held in Bilbao in June 2002 that was backed by all nationalist formations under the following slogan: 'For all the projects, for all the ideas, for all the people. Not to the banning'. However, and as Katherine A. Sawyer has concluded, 'political parties are obliged to operate within the bounds of the Constitution and of established notions of democracy. If a given party, in aligning itself with a terrorist organization, chooses not to do so, it may not, then, invoke those same constitutional principles as shield nor seek legal refuge in the very provisions that it has chosen to violate'.[9]

When discussing human rights in the context of intrastate violent conflicts it is not uncommon to assume that violations of rights and liberties originate mainly from the state. It is often ignored that terrorist organisations and their supporters do violate human rights and that liberal states must deploy measures that guarantee that such a serious infringement does not occur. Democracies are vulnerable and they should have mechanisms to prevent even the electoral expression of groups who advocate violent, racist, genocidal or discriminatory ideas. It is with this intention that the Spanish Parliament opted for the banning of a political party, a measure that had been previously implemented by several European states and which is contemplated by the legislation of others. Therefore, and contrary to what the main Basque nationalist parties have argued, such a controversial initiative has to be seen as a protection of rights that were being abused rather than as an unjust and illegal restriction of those rights. In fact, and contrary to what nationalist politicians had foreseen, the illegalization of the party has not resulted in an increase of violence but has contributed to the gradual weakening of ETA, as illustrated by the constant arrests and the decrease in the group's terrorist activities, including the actions of urban terrorism locally known as *kale borroka* that have practically disappeared.

As we have already emphasised, ETA has pursued a systematic campaign of violence and intimidation against Basque citizens who do not share a nationalist ideology. The extent of these threats and abuses of human rights led the Spanish judge Baltasar Garzon to accuse ETA and Batasuna of pursuing a campaign of 'ethnic cleansing'.[10] Garzon's report argued that both organisations had promoted the 'depuration of the census' in the Basque Country through the elimination of those citizens who would prevent a nationalist hegemony. These allegations have to be seen in the context of the strategy advocated by ETA since the 1990s which resulted in the massive targeting of civilians and politicians as a deliberate attempt to spread fear and terror beyond the traditional targets of the violence perpetrated by the terrorist organisation. This strategy coincides with ETA's concerns, as expressed in an internal document dated July 1999, on the need to establish a 'national census' as well as the 'definition of who is a citizen of Euskal Herria' and who is entitled to vote.[11] The ideological hunt that has derived from such a rationale has resulted in the premeditated harassment and intimidation of more than 42,000 people, as estimated by the Basque non-gubernamental organisation Gesto por la Paz (Gesture for Peace).[12] Journalists have also been among the targets, forcing the International Press Institute to strongly criticise ETA's attacks on the freedom of expression.[13] The European Parliament has explicitly and repeatedly condemned ETA's human rights violations.[14] In the same line prominent intellectuals from across the globe denounced in 2003 the terrible conditions under which local elections took place in the Basque Country due to the terrorist threat. Bernard-Henri Levy, Gunter Grass, Gianni Vattimo, Jorge Edwards, Michael Burleigh, Nadine Gordimer, Paolo

Flores d'Arcais, Paul Preston, Mario Vargas Llosa and Susan Sontag, among others, criticised the undemocratic conditions in which non-nationalist citizens in the region had to vote as well as their lack of freedom to exercise such a fundamental right.[15]

Under these circumstances it is not difficult to understand that Juan Jose Ibarretxe, the head of the Basque government, also known as the Lehendakari, recognised in January 2003 that in the Basque Country 'human rights are violated in a terrible and barbaric way'. In his opinion, 'ETA continues killing and violating the most fundamental right, the principle without which there is no other right, the human life'.[16] Such a critical acknowledgment by the main authority in the region demonstrates the seriousness of the situation and the extent to which fundamental rights are not guaranteed by the very government Ibarretxe represents. It has to be stressed that the Basque autonomous government has full control over the Ertzaintza, a fully autonomous police force consisting of over 7,000 members that has engaged in counterterrorism as of 1986. Therefore of particular concern ought to be the distortion by the main Basque nationalist parties, as summarised above, of the rationale behind the banning of Batasuna and the effects of this important antiterrorist measure. The banning of Batasuna has been instrumentalised to reinforce a nationalist discourse aimed at delegitimising Spanish democracy, as illustrated by a PNV document published in April 2003 which called for the restoration of democracy since it alleged that the Basque people are 'ruled against their will' by an 'external majority' represented by the non-nationalist parties.[17] Not only does this attitude represent an attempt to constrain the multiplicity of Basque identities that characterises this society into opposing and exclusively nationalist allegiances, but it also fulfills ETA's wishes of polarisation. This is further emphasised by the disparagement that nationalist representatives have directed towards pacifist groups from civil society that have supported the banning of Batasuna, mainly Basta Ya! (That's Enough!), an organization which was unanimously awarded by the European Parliament in 2000 the prestigious Sajarov Prize for its defence of human rights and liberties in the Basque Country. As a way of example, an article published in *Deia*, the PNV's newspaper, described ¡Basta Ya! as 'the main obstacle to understanding' between the Basque people since, according to the author, both ETA and the pacifist organization look for 'the extermination of those who think differently'.[18] Xabier Arzalluz, former president of the PNV, accused ¡Basta Ya! of creating the context for a 'dirty war',[19] associating the civic group with the Grupos Antiterroristas de Liberacion (GAL or Antiterrorist Liberation Groups), a vigilante terrorist organization linked to some state authorities and members of the security agencies that was responsible for the death of twenty-seven people between 1983 and 1987.

A comparison with the Northern Ireland conflict helps to highlight the unfairness of these claims by a party that supported the appointment of Jose Antonio Urrutikoetxea Bengoetxea, also known as Josu Ternera, as member of the Human Rights Commission of the Basque Parliament since 1999. Ternera, a leading member of ETA during the 1980s and allegedly responsible for the murder of eleven people – five of them children – in a terrorist attack perpetrated in 1987, is currently on the run after being summoned by a Spanish judge investigating this atrocity. Those who are and who have been the targets of ETA's terrorism have not responded with violence but with peaceful and massive demonstrations. Had they followed the example of terrorist organisations in Northern Ireland that have wrongly justified their violence as an alleged defence of their community, the situation in the Basque

Country would have worsened considerably. Basque society has prevented its 'Ulsterisation' thanks to the peaceful resistance of those who have been the victims of ETA's terrorism and who have welcomed the actions taken by the Spanish state against Batasuna as a means of defence which is entirely respectful of the law. This attitude seems absolutely coherent with the belief expressed by Joseba Egibar, a leading politician from the PNV who, nonetheless, has denounced the Spanish government for the banning of Batasuna. In July 1997, Egibar stressed that Batasuna 'is an organization led by ETA'. In his view, ETA holds the political and military direction of the radical movement to which Batasuna belongs. Therefore, Egibar added, Batasuna's actions were of complete submission to ETA.[20] It is precisely because of this narrow relationship that the action taken by the state against Batasuna has proved to be an extremely effective antiterrorist initiative, as the significant decrease in terrorism shows.[21]

Politics, Internal Security and Terrorism

Concerning the police response to terrorism, it is important to remember once again that, during the immediate post-Francoist, democratic transition period, security agencies and agents were those of the previous authoritarian regime. Surely affected by conditions of uncertainty, the two existing and still militarised security agencies, namely the Policia Nacional (National Police) and the Guardia Civil (Civil Guard) were then unreceptive and even opposed to the conflict regulation initiatives adopted by the government to deal with terrorism in general and the threat posed by ETA in particular. Information services within these security agencies were in precarious positions and lacked any coordination. Security agents, trained and indoctrinated under the previous authoritarian regime, were prone to disloyalty and their officials were often involved with both domestic and foreign right-wing extremists. Certainly, police branches associated with the surveillance and persecution of political dissent during the dictatorship were dismantled at the end of 1976. However, some of the state functionaries who belonged to these units later became assigned to new antiterrorist operation branches starting in 1977, when the incidence of terrorism was relatively low and violent actions perpetrated by left-and right-wing terrorists appeared even more worrying than similar incidents attributed to ETA. Nevertheless, terrorism was not a priority in the governmental agenda and police responses adopted in this period denote a rather low profile if compared with those common during the first half of the 1970s, when Spain was still under the dictatorship. The fact that the new authorities shared certain distrust toward the existing security forces also explains this kind of response.[22] Political elites were still thinking that the demise of terrorist organisations would be a likely outcome of democratization. This belief lasted until the middle of 1978, when terrorist violence initiated a dramatic escalation which lasted nearly two years. That is, precisely the critical years when the Constitution was drafted and promulgated, and when the Basque statute of autonomy was negotiated and approved.

As terrorism perpetrated by ETA escalated at the end of the 1970s, the government of Spain finally decided to establish special police units in the Basque Country in a rather unsuccessful attempt to coordinate resources between agencies. The National Police was the agency preferred by the UCD politicians who were responsible for internal security issues in those days. At the same time, the then minister of interior went abroad looking for advice on how to properly counter terrorism. In

July and November of 1978, for instance, he traveled to the Federal Republic of Germany and the United Kingdom, respectively, to find out about specialised antiterrorist units and appropriate information-gathering systems. The executive wanted to increase the number of agents, articulate adequate intelligence services and modernize technical resources within the police in order to improve the efficiency in the fight against terrorism, a threat that by then was undoubtedly perceived as a major danger. However, as terrorism continued to escalate, the then civilian minister of interior was replaced in April 1979 by an army general. This could be seen as an anomaly in the context of functioning democracies which can only be understood by taking into consideration the menace of a military uprising as a result of deliberate terrorist provocation, and the fact that such an appointment actually lasted less than one year. During this period, a delegation of the central government for security matters was opened in the Basque autonomous community and also in the autonomous community of Navarre, headed by another general linked to the National Police. In February 1980, special operations groups and antiterrorist units from both the National Police (the Grupos Especiales de Operaciones) and the Guardia Civil (the Unidades Antiterroristas Rurales) were deployed in the Basque Country.

It was not until the middle of 1980 that a new minister of interior, again a civilian, decided for the first time to create a unified command that would be in charge of the fight against terrorism and that would be headed by a police commissioner. The same minister successfully ordered the suppression of violent extremist right-wing bands that were still committing acts of terrorism against left-wing parties and their sympathisers. Following the unsuccessful *coup d'etat* in February 1981, four army companies were assigned to antiterrorist operations in the Basque Country, though these were strictly limited to frontier surveillance that lasted only until the end of the summer, when these army companies were replaced by units belonging to the Guardia Civil. Again in 1982, military personnel were assigned to the protection of public buildings and installations. Beyond surveillance and protection in these years, the democratic government of Spain was always cautious enough not to involve the armed forces in internal security issues, contrary to the experience of Northern Ireland. Besides, surveillance operations by army companies turned out to be inefficient for the containment of terrorism. When the Socialist Party came to power as a result of the October 1982 general elections, the new governing politicians opted initially for continuity in issues concerning the police response to terrorism. Soon, however, the new minister of interior decided to favour the Guardia Civil as the preferred agency in the fight against terrorist organisations. This prominency became particularly notorious by the end of the 1980s, and has persisted until the present day throughout the time in which Partido Popular (PP) was the party in government between 1996 and 2004. It was on March 2004 that the Socialist Party won the general election, enabling its candidate Jose Luis Rodriguez Zapatero to form a new government.

Counterterrorism, Police and Legitimacy

What about police efficacy and efficiency in the fight against terrorism as these parameters evolved in the transition from authoritarian rule to a consolidated new democracy? It is estimated that only one-third of the nearly 5,700 people arrested between 1977 and 1987 by the state security agencies for alleged terrorist offences in relation to ETA were finally prosecuted by judges.[23] Clearly, between the late 1970s and the best part of the 1980s, the main purpose of detentions seemed to be that of obtaining information on the terrorist organisation and its collaborators with the intention of subsequently using this information in specific police operations. Lack of information useful in operations to counter terrorism prompted a large number of detentions by the police for the simple and primary purpose of collecting information on the terrorists and those who were offering them direct support. All this no doubt facilitated further police responses and therefore had effects on the terrorist organisation itself, contributing to a decrease in its violent activities.

Nonetheless, it seems also true that such behaviour produced widespread anger and resentment among large affected sectors of the Basque population because of police abuses and not uncommon cases of torture, thus facilitating the reproduction of effective adhesion and even a significant amount of popular support for ETA. Unfortunately, this facilitated its persistence over time as a protracted terrorist organisation. Accusations of torture allegedly committed by state agents on detainees held on suspicion of terrorist offences have continued over the years. Most of these accusations have proved to be unfounded, originating in ETA's own instructions to their activists to systematically claim torture when arrested, as was revealed in an internal document of the terrorist group. The United Nations Special Rapporteur concluded in 2004 that torture or maltreatment of prisoners in Spain is not a systematic practice. He also observed that the system made torture possible, particularly in *incommunicado* detention, and recommended the recording of the interrogation of detaines to prevent any infringement of their rights.[24] However, police trade unions have frequently rejected such a practice, as the disclosure of their identities would seriously endanger their work, and also put their lives at risk.[25]

The Special Rapporteur also briefly referred to the dispersal of ETA prisoners in prisons around Spain. This measure was introduced in 1989 as an attempt to reinforce the policy of social reinsertion based on individual pardons, from which 250 militants and collaborators had benefited by 1990. ETA perceived that reinsertion measures negatively affected the maintenance of the organisation and tried to dissuade activists from taking that path by murdering in September 1986 a female member of the terrorist directorate who had decided in 1985 to accept the social reinsertion offered by the state. Dolores Gonzalez Catarain, known as Yoyes, was gunned down while she was walking with her four-year-old son through the main square of a small village in Guipuzcoa where she had been born. As the effectiveness of social reinsertion measures declined, the authorities introduced in May 1989 penitentiary provisions aimed at dispersing across the country imprisoned members of terrorist organisations in general and the then nearly 500 members or collaborators of ETA. The aim was to make it more difficult for the terrorist leaders to exert strict control over the inmates and their relatives. This inititative, which aimed at undermining the internal cohesion of jailed militants and of the terrorist organisation at large, has been criticised by nationalist politicians and church leaders in recent years. To some extent the progressive and deep weakening of ETA has made the dispersal of ETA prisoners redundant. Nonetheless, the concentration of prisoners in a few prisons closer to their homes faces important technical and logistical difficulties, a situation which does not only affect individuals sentenced because of offences related to ETA.

If the mistreatment of suspects in the past benefited the terrorist organisation, similar consequences in terms of popular discontent and lasting sympathy towards

ETA can be attributed to the terrorist violence practiced by right-wing extremists during the transition from authoritarian rule. These included individuals of Basque origin and a number of Italian neofascists associated with reactionary members of the state security agencies who killed ten people in France and twenty-three others inside Spain between 1975 and 1981, victims presumably chosen because of their direct or indirect relationship with ETA. The terrorist campaign perpetrated by the already mentioned GAL between 1983 and 1987 had the same effect.[26] This terrorist organisation was secretly augmented by police officials who recruited mercenary assassins among the organised criminals of Marseille and Lisbon, some of them already implicated in previous terrorist activities against ETA and its supporters. GAL benefited from the passivity and allegiance of some prominent politicians. They targeted members and sympathisers of ETA who were living across the border in southwestern France, though surprisingly around half of the twenty-eight people killed had no links whatsoever with the ethno-nationalist terrorist organisation. Spain, fortunately, proved to be a functioning democratic regime and the rule of law was finally applied to these policemen, gangsters and some politicians belonging to the Socialist Party who were involved with the GAL. They received severe court sentences for their illegal activities. The families of their victims have received monetary compensation through funds extracted from the state budget, the same procedure as in the case of relatives whose beloved ones were killed by other terrorist organisations, including ETA.

Police counterterrorist operations became much more discriminate and selective after 1988. No single episode of illegal violence in the state response to ETA has been reported since that time. For instance, the number of people suspected of crimes associated with this terrorist organisation who were detained by security agencies between that year and the end of 1997 amounts to nearly 970, which is about one-fifth of all those arrested during the previous decade. More importantly, well over 60 per cent of all those arrested were formally prosecuted by the judiciary. Interestingly enough, despite the decreasing number of suspects arrested and the selective character of police detentions since the end of the 1980s the terrorist activity of ETA continued to decline. This factor itself led to an increasingly selective policing of terrorism, in addition to reforms within the state security agencies and, of course, political decisions adopted with that purpose as part of the already mentioned Ajuria Enea Agreement.[27] Moreover, the Basque autonomous police, fully and exclusively dependent on the Basque autonomous government and established as a result of the statute of autonomy approved by a large majority of the Basque population in the referendum held in 1979, engaged in counterterrorism starting in 1986, though it would not be until the end of 1989 that the Ertzaintza, as this law enforcement agency is also known, proactively acted against the gunmen of ETA. As expected, the terrorist organisation then reacted, killing four autonomous police officials during the 1990s.

Politics in a Terrorised Society

All these changes observed in the police response to terrorism have been crucial in emotionally dissociating important segments of the Basque population from ETA and have contributed to the progressive reduction of support for the terrorist organisation. Basque public opinion throughout the 1980s increasingly exhibited very strong negative attitudes towards the militants of ETA. Since the late 1980s, and throughout the 1990s, citizen mobilisations against violence became generalized and articulated in a number of associations, such as the Gesto por la Paz, which became a prominent social feature in villages and cities across the Basque Country.[28] Since the mid-1990s, ETA and their followers have reacted to this social trend by physically and aggressively confronting demonstrations against terrorism and, as earlier indicated, by targeting in particular Basque citizens who are not nationalists, often elected political representatives at various levels of government who belong to either the Basque section of the PP or that of the PSOE. Between 1996 and 2000, as a matter of fact, almost 5,000 episodes of street harrassment and intimidatory actions against these people and their families (a variety of more limited terrorism practiced by gangs of youngsters outside formal membership in ETA but in open support of the terrorist organisation) have been reported in the Basque autonomous community and Navarre. This form of violence has to be seen as an addition to the more common terrorist attacks perpetrated by ETA gunmen, which during that same period (the second half of the 1990s), caused forty-seven fatalities.

Although new legal measures, increasing police efficiency and growing international cooperation continue to debilitate ETA and its supporting network, around 42,000 Basque citizens live under daily threat from the terrorists and its supporting gangs. At the same time all the popularly elected politicians who are non-nationalists, from the local to the regional or autonomous level of government, have to go around with bodyguards in order to protect them from attacks by radical ethnonationalists. Possibly this is the only case in Europe where a situation exists where the non-nationalist opposition parties and elected representatives, though backed by half of the Basque electorate, have to develop their political activities under intimidation and terrorism coming from an ethno-nationalist totalitarian movement–a movement often tolerated by moderate nationalists who since 1980 control the Basque autonomous government. It should be noted that the main nationalist party in the region, the PNV, reached a pact in 1998 with the terrorist organisation by which they agreed to 'abandon all the agreements with the forces whose objective is the destruction of Euskal Herria and the building of Spain [PP and PSOE]'.[29] This alliance between a democratic party and those responsible for the physical extinction of their political adversaries has shed many doubts over the PNV's commitment in the fight against terrorism. Although mainstream Basque nationalists unequivocally condemn ETA's violence, their actions often ignore the consequences that terrorism has on a terrorised society.

This flawed analysis was very evident in the contents of the political initiative put forward by the Lehendakari Ibarretxe in 2002. The nationalist leader has made great efforts to ensure the success of a proposal that demands a new status between the Spanish state and the Basque Country based on the 'free association' of the Basque people to Spain after they have so decided in referendum. It is extremely revealing that Ibarretxe presented his proposal as a peace plan ignoring that ETA, and not the Spanish state, is the main obstacle for the achievement of that elusive peace. In spite of the painful evidence of thousands of Basques who suffer ETA's terrorism and who are unable to freely decide their future, the prominent nationalist politician announced his plan establishing dangerous equivalence between ETA's violence and a Spanish state that was accused of being authoritarian and responsible for restricting basic human rights and liberties.[30] Given ETA's long campaign of terror in the region, great concerns have arisen regarding certain sections of Ibarretxe's proposal which deal with a hypothetical referendum in the Basque Country. Certainly, tens of thousands of those persons threatened end up leaving their own country and settling in other regions within Spain. All this indicates that the Basque Country most probably remains the only area in the European Union where systematic violations of human rights still occur. It is also significant that victims are mainly, and almost exclusively, non-nationalist Basque citizens. The fact that those who systematically violate human rights are radical ethno-nationalists relying on terrorist violence places an important degree of responsibility on mainstream nationalist parties. And at the end of the day the most important nationalist party is the PNV, which has always held power in the region since the inception of autonomy in the early 1980s. Therefore, there is no other way for democratic institutions and collective actors than acting, in accordance with the rule of law, to guarantee fundamental rights and civil liberties for all Basque citizens.

Notes

1. The web page of the Ministry of Interior provides very useful information and statistics on the terrorist attacks perpetrated in Spain by different organisations for the last thirty years. See for example http://www.mir.es/policia/linea/ter prin.htm, http://www.guardiacivil. org/terrorismo/index.jsp and http://www.mir.es/oris/infoeta/index.htm

2. On this issue see for example Francisco Llera, 'La Red Terrorista: Subcultura de la Violencia y Nacionalismo en Euskadi', in Antonio Robles Egea (ed), *La Sangre de las Naciones. Identidades Nacionales y Violencia Politica* (Granada: Universidad de Granada 2003) pp. 265–96. Percentages of the evolution of the vote in the Basque Country showing how the electorate is evenly divided between nationalists and non-nationalists can be found in Jose Luis Barberia and Patxo Unzueta, *Como Hemos Llegado a Esto. La Crisis Vasca* (Madrid: Taurus 2003) pp.306–315.

3. The *Euskobarometro*, as these surveys conducted by a team from the Politics Department at the University of the Basque Country are known, are periodically updated and can be consulted at http://www.ehu.es/cpvweb/pags_directas/euskobarometroFR.html

4. Office of the Commissioner for Human Rights, *Report by Mr. Alvaro Gil Robles, Commissioner for Human Rights, On His Visit to Spain and the Basque Country* (Strasbourg: Council of Europe 2001) p.2.

5. Francisco J. Llera, *Los Vascos y la Politica. El Proceso Politico Vasco: Elecciones, Partidos, Opinion publica y Legitimacion en el Pais Vasco, 1977–1992* (Bilbao: Universidad del Pais Vasco 1994) pp.97–119; Juan J. Linz, *Conflicto en Euskadi* (Madrid: Espasa Calpe 1986) pp.617–65.

6. University of the Basque Country, *Euskobarometro* (May 2004) http://www.ehu.es/cpvweb/pags_directas/euskobarometroFR.html

7. Oscar Jaime, *Policia, Terrorismo y Cambio Politico en Espana 1976–1996* (Valencia: Tirant lo Blanch 2002) pp.219–62.

8. This thesis was formulated by judge Baltasar Garzon as far back as 1997 in his 'Con Esperanza en el Futuro ... ', in Sagrario Moran (ed), *ETA entre Espana y Francia* (Madrid: Editorial Complutense 1997) pp.XV–LIV. For a thorough analysis of the complex system of organisations linked to ETA, their actions and the nature of their relationships see Jose Manuel Mata, *El Nacionalismo Vasco Radical. Discurso, Organizaciones y Expresiones* (Bilbao: Universidad del Pais Vasco 1993).

9. Katherine A. Sawyer, 'Rejection of Weimarian Politics or Betrayal of Democracy?: Spain's Proscription of Batasuna under the European Convention on Human Rights', *American University Law Review*, 52 (2003) pp.1531–81.

10. The judicial report containing these allegations was fully reproduced in the main Basque newspaper, *El Correo*, in Oct. 2002: http://servicios.elcorreodigital.com/vizcaya/pg021018/actualidad/politica/200210/17/RC_auto_garzon.html

11. Florencio Dominguez, *Las Raices del Miedo. Euskadi, una Sociedad Atemorizada* (Madrid: El Pais Aguilar 2003) pp.260–61. Euskal Herria, the ethno-linguistic unit claimed by Basque separatists as their homeland, is made up of the three Spanish provinces that

contain the Basque Country (Guipuzcoa, Alava and Vizcaya), as well as another Spanish province outside the Basque Autonomous Community, Navarre, and the French Departments of Labourd, Soul and the Lower Navarre portions of Pyrenees.

12. 'Gesto por la Paz Estima que 42,000 Personas Sufren la Amenaza Directa de los Etarras', *El Pais* 9 Nov. 2002.

13. 'El Instituto Internacional de Prensa Denuncia los Ataques de ETA Contra la Libertad de Expresion', *El Correo* 19 March 2003.

14. Committee on Citizen's Freedoms and Rights, Justice and Home Affairs, *Report on the situation as regards fundamental rights in the European Union* (2003/2006) (INI), Alima Boumediene-Thiery (European Parliament 2003); and Committee on Citizen's Freedoms and Rights, Justice and Home Affairs, *Report on the situation as regards fundamental rights in the European Union* (2002/2013) (INI), Fodé Sylla (European Parliament 2002).

15. Basta Ya! Iniciativa Ciudadana, *Euskadi, del Sueno a la Verguenza* (Barcelona: Ediciones B 2004) pp.363–64.

16. Quoted in *El Correo*, 9 Jan. 2003.

17. 'De la Ofensiva Electoral a la Guerra Politico Judicial', eaj-pnv.com April 2003. There are plenty of examples of speeches and articles by nationalist politicians comparing Spanish democracy with Franco's dictatorship as a means of attacking the legitimacy of the Statute of Autonomy. Euzkadi Buru Batzarra, 10 April 2003, http://www.eaj-nv.com/documentos/documentos/Ilegalizacion%20Batasuna030410.doc

18. Koldo San Sebastian, 'Yo Estoy de Acuerdo con Manolo Huertas', *Deia* 19 Feb. 2003.

19. Quoted in *Deia*, 24 Feb. 2003.

20. Quoted in Patxo Unzueta, 'No Permitiremos que nos Llamen Ambiguos', *El Pais* 20 March 2003.

21. The annual assessments compiled by the Spanish Ministry of Interior provide ample evidence of this success in countering ETA's terrorism. See for example http://www.mir.es/oris

22. Oscar Jaime (note 7) pp.167–217.

23. Florencio Dominguez Iribarren, *De la negociacion a la Tregua: ¿el Final de ETA?* (Madrid: Taurus 1998) pp.201–21.

24. *Civil and Political Rights, Including the Question of Torture and Detention. Report of the Special Rapporteur on the Question of Torture, Theo van Boven.* United Nations Economic and Social Council, Commission on Human Rights, (2004) E/CN.4/2004/56/Add.2

25. It should be mention that ETA has often used television footage to identify their targets. Recently police discovered TV footage of a raid in Cahors (France) in which three ETA members were arrested with 500 kilos of explosives. The policemen who were coming in and out of the house raided had been identified as targets by another group of terrorists.

26. On the GAL, see Paddy Woodworth, *Clean Hands, Dirty War* (Cork: University Press 2001).

27. Fernando Reinares and Oscar Jaime, 'Countering Terrorism in a New Democracy: The Case of Spain', in Fernando Reinares (ed), *European Democracies Against Terrorism. Governmental Policies and Intergovernmental Cooperation* (Aldershot, Hampshire: Ashgate 2000) pp.119–45.

28. Maria J. Funes, 'Social Responses to Political Violence in the Basque Country: Peace Movements and Their Audience', *Journal of Conflict Resolution* 42 (1998) pp.493–510.

29. *Gara*, 30 April 2000.

30. Juan Jose Ibarretxe formalised his proposal in the Basque Parliament in 2002 and 2003. The parliamentary speeches on this initiative can be read in full in *El Correo*, 28 Sep. 2002, 26 Sep. 2003 and 26 Oct. 2003. At the time of writing Ibarretxe was still pressing for the implementation of his proposal in spite of having been rejected by parties such as the PSOE and PP.

17

Russia and the United States After 9/11

CAROLINE KENNEDY-PIPE

Department of Politics, University of Sheffield,
Sheffield, United Kingdom

STEPHEN WELCH

School of Government and International Affairs,
University of Durham, Durham, United Kingdom

We begin by briefly surveying and discussing approaches to the study of Russian foreign policy after the Cold War. These largely descriptive approaches fail to provide much purchase on the new circumstances obtaining after 9/11. Instead we consider the 'war on terror' from a broadly constructivist perspective as a new international paradigm. We describe its main features, and then consider its implications for Russian-American relations in three policy areas: Chechnya, neighbouring states, and internal security. We find in these areas both opportunities and dilemmas for Russian foreign policy.

In this article, we explore the implications for Russian foreign policy of the terrorist attacks of 11 September 2001 and the ensuing 'war on terror' promoted and prosecuted mainly by the United States. In adopting this focus, we make an immediate commitment to the view that 9/11 matters: that the terrorist attacks constitute a disjuncture in international relations and represent the starting point of a new period. However, we adopt this view in a manner consistent with a broadly 'constructivist' view of international relations,[1] utilizing the interpretive device of an 'international paradigm' of the war on terror. The implication is that 9/11 is important in large part because states (powerful states in particular) have chosen to make it so.

With such a view, we do not need, or wish, to assert that absolutely everything about foreign policy changed on 9/11. There is, for example, legitimate scope for examining Russian foreign strategies in terms of the traditional options and outlooks that have arisen from its geopolitical situation and political history. We explore some of these continuities in the first section, along with interpretations that emphasize the decisive role of the current Russian leader, Vladimir Putin.

The bulk of our argument is, however, premised on the view that a 'war on terror' paradigm exists and provides both opportunities and difficulties for Russian foreign policy. In the second section some key aspects of the war on terror paradigm are outlined. In subsequent sections we discuss the implications of the paradigm for Russia, its foreign policy and its relations with the United States. We first examine the case of Chechnya, which appears to offer a 'fit' between existing Russian policy and the paradigm's claim that the new security challenge to powerful states is that of groups of terrorists operating across borders and inspired by radical Islam. We then discuss more complex cases, in which tensions arise between the adoption of the war on terror paradigm and Russia's interests in influencing, if not controlling, key former Soviet republics. We also point to what seems to us to be the crucial paradox of the Russian adoption of the war on terror paradigm, in connection with Russia's own possession and possibly weak supervision of substantial terrorist resources, human and material. Although 9/11 seemed to offer Russian foreign policy-makers a coherent framework through which to operate, it actually poses significant problems for Russia, its internal sovereignty and its relations with the United States.

Russian Foreign Policy After the Cold War

The post-Cold War world presented particular challenges for world leaders, certainly for Russian leaders but for others too. If Russia, like Britain after World War II, had 'lost an empire but had yet to find a role', the United States, correspondingly, had lost an *enemy* and had yet to find a new one. The decade of the 1990s may come to be seen as an 'interregnum' in which the overall shape of international relations was uncertain. Analysts, of course, sought to give it shape. The 'end of history' and the 'clash of civilizations' were early contenders, each however quite abstract and distant from direct policy implications.[2] Another theme arising during the 1990s was that of 'humanitarian intervention'. Some commentators promoted,[3] and some claimed to observe,[4] the development of a new international norm whereby sovereignty (increasingly seen as a kind of fetish)[5] could be violated on humanitarian grounds in cases of large-scale suffering such as genocide–though with some implicit provisos as to when this would be feasible and politic and when not.[6] Indeed, this descriptive and normative analytical discourse can be located within a broader one that turned attention away from states and their 'billiard ball' interactions in the realm of military security towards a set of interactions at the economic, social and administrative levels that ultimately promised to replace 'government' with 'governance'.[7]

For Russia, the implications were complex. In the first phase of the interregnum, hopes for a new-model Marshall Plan, providing large-scale transitional assistance to Russia from the West, were high. It failed to materialize. Instead, the West seemed to be encroaching on Russia in the conventional old way–territorially–and even its economic aid, such as it was, came with a high degree of 'good governance' conditionality that could also seem threatening. Moreover, a heightened international concern with human rights was potentially uncomfortable for a regime struggling with various secessionist and insurrectionary movements, most notably but not only in Chechnya.

In this context, Russian foreign policy seemed to lack coherence. In discussing Russia's response to the rapidly changing international environment, analysts have categorized the outlooks competing for predominance in Russian foreign policy-making into two strands.[8] In so doing they have in essence refurbished the traditional division in world outlooks, familiar from nineteenth-century radical thought in Russia, of 'Westernizers' and 'Slavophiles'.[9] In the refurbished version, 'Westernizers' or 'Atlanticists' are seen to have been predominant in the late Soviet period, finding expression in Gorbachev's 'new thinking'.[10] But as the Soviet Empire collapsed and the CIS failed to take on any real coherence, more conservative and nationalistic voices began to emerge. These conservatives/nationalists argued for a reassertion of Great Russian policies.[11]

This posture could not, however, seriously impede American and West European dominance in Europe and elsewhere. Specifically, Moscow, whatever the rhetoric of the Yeltsin years, could do little to halt the formation of an American-led coalition in the first Gulf War and had few cards to play to prohibit the expansion of the NATO alliance even into central and eastern Europe. It could more plausibly seek the preservation of a Russian sphere of influence in some, but by no means all, of the former Soviet space. This 'Eurasianist' policy outlook is indeed a throwback to the past trajectory of Russian continental expansion, and can include virulent nationalist and Great Russian chauvinist ideas such as those of Vladimir Zhirinovsky. However, it need not (and quite often does not) take this radical form, nor need it be seen as mere policy recidivism. To the south and east lie important resources and strategic sites, and as western Europe is no longer the unique pole of world progress that it was in the nineteenth century a turning away from it is not necessarily a turn backward.[12]

Analysts have formalized this policy outlook as the 'Monroeski Doctrine'. The term suggests similarities with the nineteenth-century American Monroe Doctrine which had been designed to protect US interests in its own hemisphere.[13] The doctrine was a bid to place emphasis on the 'near abroad' and the protection of both Russian strategic interests and ethnic Russians in newly sovereign post-Soviet states. Even this formulation, presented as it is in terms of regional predominance arising out of familiar kinds of self-interest, has led some commentators to argue that Russia was on a quest to reanimate its Soviet Empire.[14]

There is some risk involved in the formulation of descriptive categories such as 'Westernizers' and 'Eurasianists'. It needs to be remembered that they are descriptive categories, not exhaustive and mutually exclusive logical alternatives. At best they are 'ideal types', if indeed they are not radical oversimplifications. There is a risk of assuming an unbroken continuity of Russia's traditional options, thus overdetermining policy outcomes. Looking closely at such typologies, as Adomeit has argues, can suggest their decomposition into ever more finely differentiated subgroups.[15] A contrasting mode of analysis responds to this possible oversimplification by stressing the preferences of the key policy-makers–a strategy that on the face of it promises some advantage in the case of relatively constitutionally unconstrained leaders like Yeltsin and Putin, and emphasizes, in contrast to the policy traditions approach, the possibility of a dynamic response to a changing environment.

Yeltsin's foreign policy was characterized by a lack of coherence and by frequent policy turns, which indicated that the emphasis on the near abroad was not the only or dominant strand of thinking.[16] During the Yeltsin years, there was a record of cooperation (albeit a patchy one) with the West and especially the United States. Better relations with France and Germany too seemed to offer avenues for the advancement of Russia's economic and political ambitions.[17]

The election of Vladimir Putin as president was taken as a sign by some analysts that there would be a more consistent approach to the making of Russian external policy. Initially it seemed that Putin, with his KGB background and his stated enthusiasm for a renewal of the war in the Chechen Republic, would emphasize a Eurasianist policy rather than a pro-Western one.[18] Putin has in fact proved to be a pragmatist.[19] He has sought to construct a strong and unified Russia within a coherent CIS. He has also, though, sought a sustained engagement with many of the leading western nations and most particularly with the United States. Putin has made it clear that Russia needs a far greater integration with the leading capitalist nations and presidential ambitions have of late centred around incorporation into the G8 and the WTO. A recent token of this is Putin's signal that he may be about to restructure the state gas monopoly Gazprom, proposing to lift the ban on foreign ownership of domestically traded shares.[20] Analysts have pointed to the relative strength of Putin's position after his success in the 2004 elections. His approval ratings are high and are based not just on a rapidly improving economy but are bolstered, some argue, by the comparison with the erratic character of Boris Yeltsin.

Some, though not all, of the developments incipient in the late 1990s, whatever their implications for Russia, were thrown into serious doubt (or even reversed in practice) by 9/11. The terrorist attacks, and the US response to them, changed the foreign policy environment for Russia, as for other states. In the Russian case, both new opportunities and new threats were created by the ensuing 'war on terror' prosecuted by the United States. Many states have encountered dilemmas resulting from this new environment. Russia's dilemmas, we will argue, are among the most severe.

The War on Terror Paradigm

The proclamation of a 'war on terror' by President Bush in the aftermath of 9/11 was greeted, especially outside the United States, with a degree of scepticism that even now has not completely abated. There was an immediate assumption that it was a piece of rhetoric on the analogy of the 'war on poverty' of the 1960s or the 'war on drugs' of the 1990s:[21] significant rhetoric, to be sure, that expressed the determination of the government to take the enemy seriously, but all the same hyperbolic. Visitors from Europe to the United States, however, have been surprised to note how readily and unself-consciously the terminology has been adopted as a description of US policy. This surprise, and the scepticism it reflects, may be a function of the far greater exposure of European populations and political leaders to domestic terrorism, and a degree of inurement to it as a 'fact of life' (an 'acceptable level of violence' in the infamous phrase pertaining to British military control of Northern Ireland).[22] Europeans had grown accustomed to the use of undramatic methods such as surveillance, infiltration and informing in the control of terrorism, and may even have tended towards the conclusion, which the German example and somewhat later the Northern Irish one would suggest, that terrorism might ultimately be worn down by these methods rather than by outright confrontation. It is possible, indeed, that the 'postmodern' European state, as characterized by Robert Cooper,[23] accepted terrorism at a certain level as part of its international openness and its coming to terms with reduced global and military power in the postwar period.

A European–American divide in the response to 9/11, opening up more deeply by the time of the invasion of Iraq, has been readily apparent,[24] though of course the generalization immediately needs to be qualified in the light of equally obvious divisions within Europe. However, more is at stake than American 'can-do' mentality (or naivety) and European realism (or ennui). The war on terror has had enormous importance in reorienting policy beyond the United States both because of the large military preponderance that the US can bring to bear in prosecuting its war, and also because there is at least some plausibility in the idea that terrorism itself has risen to a new level of threat. The war on terror has become a powerful discourse both because of the material power (cultural power flows to some extent in its wake) of its leading sponsor, but also because it evokes, and purports to respond to, a threat that can at least be made to seem both plausible and unprecedented. The war on terror is thus not only a discourse, still less a mere piece of rhetoric, but rather an *international paradigm.*

The term 'paradigm', following Kuhn,[25] has usually been applied to the analytical or theoretical frameworks employed by scholars or scientists. But the 'action-guiding' feature of a paradigm, whereby it channels not only perception but also responses and routines (this is indeed Kuhn's main emphasis), allows the concept to be fruitfully employed in the analysis of policy frameworks and shifts too.[26] By an 'international paradigm' we mean a way of intellectually grasping the leading contours of the world order that prioritizes some issues at the expense of others, that recasts some issues within its framework and that has implications for the corresponding ranking of policy options. No international paradigm, by definition, provides a comprehensive account of international reality. The Cold War, to take a prominent earlier example, neglected (indeed suppressed) issues such as development, and reconstituted some emergent events, such as the Cuban revolution, in its terms. This lack of complete fit between paradigm and reality is one source of policy dilemmas for states.

The contents of this paradigm merit extended discussion; more than we can provide here. We are at present interested in explaining the implications of the paradigm for Russian foreign policy–and in particular the complexities and dilemmas that arise out of its adoption and application. Two features of the paradigm need to be emphasized. It asserts that terrorism has reached a new level of threat due (among other things such as an alleged change in the ethical threshold formerly maintained by terrorists) to its 'transnational' organization in international networks, of which the exemplar is Al-Qaeda. But the paradigm also asserts that international terrorism flourishes where states either are supportive or only weakly oppose it. Terrorism is thus seen both as an insidious existential threat to states (and the ways of life they shelter) and also an occasion for violating sovereignty in the service of its eradication. As a result, the war on terror tends to reorder the world of states along a single dimension of more or less adequate opponents of terrorism–with the United States in the role of chief adjudicator.

Separatism and Terrorism in Chechnya

The idea of a new division in international politics, determined by opposition to 'international terrorism', immediately provided Russia with scope for aligning itself with the United States, and thus simultaneously reversing its post-Cold War marginality in world affairs and legitimating some of the activities that had exacerbated that marginalization–in particular its hard-line policies in Chechnya. In 'territorializing' terrorism by focusing on terrorist bases and supportive states, the war on terror has licensed military efforts, up to and including invasion, as a means of eradicating the threat. By virtue of its analysis of, and actions in, Chechnya, Russia could claim to be in the vanguard of this effort.

The Chechen crisis and terrorism in the republic predated 9/11 by a number of years. The roots of the modern struggle may be dated to the summer of 1991 when general Dzhokav Dudayev declared Chechen independence. Over the next few years the Yeltsin regime was too weak to force the issue of sovereignty and the republic remained in a state of *de facto* independence. The Russian Federal Security Service attempted a coup in 1994, following a spate of bus hijackings,[27] and the failure of this was rapidly followed by an air and ground invasion. This too failed, the Russian military proving incapable of waging effective counterinsurgency operations and suffering from low morale and poor preparation. A subsequent withdrawal and treaty of 1997 left basic constitutional issues unresolved, which meant the continued presence of security risks. After Chechen raids into the neighbouring territory of Dagestan and a series of bombings in Moscow, Putin in 1999 sent troops back into Chechnya. This time, with almost double the number of troops (some 100,000), reflecting a stronger political commitment, Russian forces were successful, capturing Grozny and other major cities and forcing the separatists into mountain areas.

In 1999, on the occasion of the second Russian intervention, Putin argued that the war in Chechnya was not a civil war but a war declared by Russia against international terrorism. He insisted that the Chechen insurgency formed part of the general international terrorist threat to the stability of established and democratic governments. He also stressed the novelty of the threat by linking it to globalisation and international criminality, asserting: 'Terrorism and drugs are absolutely kindred phenomena. They have common roots and similar destructive power'.[28] He stated that the Chechen terrorists were financed from abroad and emphasized the role of the Wahhabis from Saudi Arabia in attacks. In effect, Putin anticipated the war on terror paradigm by linking territorial conflict to a 'transnationalized' threat of terrorism.[29] An essentially territorial (in this case secessionist) conflict was thus reconfigured as a distinct and novel threat, licensing vigorous counter-measures.

Russian policy and actions in Chechnya had met a somewhat fluctuating though on the whole tolerant response from the Clinton administration.[30] In the context of the developing humanitarianism of the interregnum, Russian tactics could certainly be questioned. The Clinton administration, however, was not blind to the more general threat that might be posed by Chechen terrorism (indeed it was arguably more alert to this and similar threats than the Bush administration prior to 9/11). Before 9/11, when, it has been argued, the Bush administration paid insufficient attention to terrorist threats,[31] Russian action in Chechnya raised some concern among American policy-makers. Condoleezza Rice, for example, expressed a view with potentially conflictual implications for the US–Russian relationship in suggesting that the Russian war in Chechnya was a reminder of the 'vulnerability of the small new states around Russia and the interest of America in their independence'.[32] After 9/11, however, a favourable response from the Bush administration could be expected. For example, in June 2002, Colin Powell stated rather more supportively: 'Russia is fighting terrorists in Chechnya, we understand that'.[33] The occurrence of suicide bombings in Russia–in July 2003 at a rock festival held at the Tushino airfield near Moscow and again in Moscow in December 2003 when a female suicide bomber staged an attack only metres from the Russian Parliament underlined the nature of the threat to Russia. The hostage crisis of October 2003, in which Chechen separatists imprisoned a Moscow theatre audience, also helped reinforce the connections between separatist insurrection and international terrorism. When Putin decided to end the theatre crisis by authorising the use of gas to kill the terrorists (and as a by-product 118 hostages) President Bush defended Putin by invoking the fight against terrorism. He argued that 'these people were killers just like the killers that came to America'.[34]

Thus the war on terror retrospectively legitimated Russian actions in Chechnya by virtue of the linkages Putin had *already* been asserting between separatist insurrection and international terrorism. It allowed Putin to position Russia as a partner with the United States both in the experience of terrorism and in the struggle against it.[35] This example clearly illustrates the opportunities and advantages created for Russia by the diagnosis and treatment promoted by the war on terror paradigm.

Instability and Control in Neighbouring States

The picture is more complicated in the case of Russia's relationship with neighbouring states in the context of the war on terror. The balance of advantage and disadvantage to Russia from the wider prosecution of the war on terror is less clear, as it has involved a considerable expansion and enhancement of American influence in and control over the region neighbouring Russia to the south.

The American-led invasion of Afghanistan was the first major expression of the war on terror proper. It proved controversial for the Russian leadership, unavoidably evoking echoes of the Soviet invasion, with which the rapid success of the American demolition of the Taliban regime was a stark and unflattering contrast. Putin argued that the Soviet frame of reference (in particular its conception of spheres of influence) was irrelevant and that Russia should not be afraid of its neighbours within the CIS developing relationships with other states.[36] Accordingly, Russia did not oppose the establishment of American bases in Tajikistan from which coalition forces could attack the Taliban from the north. It also provided vital intelligence on conditions in Afghanistan, the Taliban and terrorist networks.[37]

The assumption of the war on terror paradigm is that the eradication of terrorist bases is most effectively achieved by military intervention. The validity of this assumption is not completely clear at the time of writing, as Osama bin Laden remains at large and substantial surviving organizational capability is suggested by alleged Al-Qaeda involvement in the Madrid train bombings. Somewhat problematic for Russia is the additional implication that it can at best be only a somewhat infirm junior partner in this military enterprise. Putin may be justified in arguing that Soviet history provides no basis for Russian opposition to the substantial enhancement of American influence, including the establishment of bases, in the region. However, in this broader case, in contrast with that of Chechnya, Russia may have cause to question the sufficiency of the war on terror paradigm as justification of current trends.

The case of Georgia illustrates the complexities. Russia's relations with this former Soviet republic had grown increasingly strained during the 1990s. Russia had supported autonomist and indeed separatist demands from Ajaria, Abkhazia and South Ossetia in Georgia, partly because of the presence of large numbers of ethnic Russians in these areas. However, by offering support to the majority Muslim populations there, Russia also hoped to offset some of the damage done to Moscow's legitimacy in the eyes of Russia's own substantial Muslim minority by the Chechen campaigns. Moreover, Russia increasingly suggested that Georgia harboured Chechen terrorists. This view was endorsed by the United State as part of its attempt to justify intervention in Iraq when in his 5 February 2003 address to the UN Security Council, Colin Powell linked Islamic militants arrested in France with terrorist activities in Georgia and Chech-nya (a connection about which other countries expressed doubt).[38]

But while the war on terror entailed some convergence of concerns about Georgia between the US and Russia, the outcome that has occurred with American support–the consolidation of the authority of the Georgian state under its new leader Mikhail Saakashvili–runs counter to previous Russian support for autonomy and separation in Georgia's regions. Russian self-interest here threatens to undercut the programme of the war on terror of reinforcing territorial sovereignty in regions inhabited by terrorists.

Moreover, the presence of 'mixed motives' on the American side would also be hard to deny. Georgia is to become a major supplier of oil from the Caspian Sea and a crucial link between Europe and Asia. The oil pipeline currently being built is eventually expected to deliver some 1 m barrels of crude oil per day to western markets. This will help the United States to diversify its oil supplies. The US currently spends $1 bn on foreign aid to Georgia. Saakashvili–American-educated, with an American wife and quite clearly pro-American in his public utterances–may readily be identified by Russia as an American client. The change of regime in Tbilisi has certainly not eased tensions with Moscow. In the spring of 2004 Georgian forces attempted to enter Ajaria but were turned back at the border by Russian forces emerging from their Georgian bases – a territorial presence which Russia does not seem ready to abdicate.

Thus, in offering both public support and tactical assistance to the territorial manifestation of the war on terror in Afghanistan (not, however, in Iraq–an overextension of the war on terror paradigm in the eyes of Russia and other states broadly sympathetic to its general aims), Russia has been obliged to cede much of its influence over its unruly southern neighbours to the United States. In Uzbekistan, for example, a spate of terrorist attacks in the spring of 2004 seriously undermined confidence that the Karimov government could contain the threat posed by Islamist insurgents. At least forty-two people were killed in less than a week. General Colin Powell argued that the US would provide assistance as the Uzbek regime appeared to be under attack by groups linked to Al-Qaeda. The United States has thousands of troops based in the south of the country and assistance is likely to be in the form of counterinsurgency training for Uzbek security forces.[39] The war on terror as manifested in the former Soviet republics both licenses intrusion into the region while also implying Russia's relative incapacity to undertake it. Even so, Russia retains its bases in Georgia and continues to use them to support autonomist and separatist regions – even as the American-backed Georgian leader seeks to consolidate sovereignty in these very areas. Here Russia and the United States clearly differ over the implications and application of the war on terror paradigm.

Security and Terrorist Resources in Russia

Although the war on terror has been noteworthy for its territorialization of the struggle against terrorist networks, its domestic security agenda is equally important. This second aspect may prove to be an even sharper double-edged sword for Russia. For the idea that terrorism is now international, involving transnational networks and interfacing with globalization counter-products such as arms and drug trafficking, can be seen as promoting a new kind of 'good governance' agenda. By means of this agenda, emerging in 1989 World Bank Report on Sub-Saharan Africa, both international organizations and other states have pressed for changes in the target states' internal political and legal systems and policies as precautions of aid.[40] By analogy, we can speak of the war on terror as promoting an agenda of 'good security governance'. The threat posed by terrorism, construed in the war on terror paradigm as large, growing and existentially fundamental (a threat, as Communism was held to be during the Cold War, to a 'way of life'), necessitates drastic modification in internal, domestic security arrangements.

Enhanced border and transportation security, risk profiling, investigatory drag-nets and innovative incarceration regimes (as at Camp X-ray and Camp Delta) have all been part of this response in the United States. Such measures have of course been controversial, though in a somewhat muted way, with questions raised not only about their political acceptability and constitutionality,[41] but also their efficacy. However, the thesis of the transnationality of terrorism entails that such responses be promoted elsewhere in the world too. One small token is the threat to fingerprint visitors to the US and to exclude airlines which do not conform to developing American aircraft security procedures.

What this amounts to is a programme of good security governance which, given the global reach of terror, in principle needs to be promoted globally. Of course, like the territorial dimension of the war on terror, there are practical limits to this impo-sition. Just as North Korea, for example, is not a feasible target for military inter-vention given its possession of nuclear weapons and its extreme isolation nor, is it vulnerable to pressure through aid conditionality or institutional interconnections via NGOs or at a sub-diplomatic level.

But the good security governance agenda may pose significant problems for Russia. It is a large potential source of ingredients for, as well as expertise in, the manu-facture of weapons of mass destruction such as 'dirty bombs'. Its economic and admin-istrative resources are thinly spread, and the rule of law is not uniformly or securely established. Drastic changes since the end of the Cold War in the rewards and status available to technicians, scientists and military personnel involved in weapons research, production and storage have increased incentives for wrongdoing.[42] The closed cities that housed Soviet nuclear production facilities–built in isolated areas with little obvious alternative employment–were particularly affected, with implications for approximately 756,000 scientists and technicians.[43] It has been argued that Taliban envoys attempted to recruit at least one former Soviet nuclear expert in 2000.[44] In short, 'international terrorism' and its networks need not necessarily be confined to Russia's periphery. In Jessica Stern's words, 'The most significant threats to US national security now arise not from Russia's military might but from its weakness'.[45]

Before 9/11, the United States had responded to this potential danger in two ways. The more benign of these, from the Russian point of view, was exemplified by the Nuclear Cities Initiative launched by the US Department of Energy in 1998.[46] However, officials in the Bush administration before 9/11 had expressed the somewhat more hostile view that Russia was an 'active proliferator' and was 'willing to sell anything to anyone for money'. There was some suggestion also of reducing funding for nuclear decommissioning.[47]

The dilemma for Russia, then, is that in endorsing and in some respects promot-ing the war on terror, as well as compromising its control of its own vicinity and in principle (and already to a large extent in practice) ceding this to the United States, Russia may be validating its own problematic exposure to a developing good security governance agenda. Russia has seen in the war on terror an opportunity for partner-ship with the US, though (like others) it has also had to recognize its junior status in this partnership. American unilateralism has probably passed its zenith with the invasion of Iraq, whose messy aftermath has reminded US policy-makers of the significant limits faced even by a military 'hyper-power' (limits not so much on regime demolition as on regime reconstruction).[48] Even so, the war on terror remains a reality, its substance largely dictated by American existential anxieties, American strategies and American criteria of security. Russia has the dilemmatic position of a forceful opponent of international terror, but also the weak possessor of some of terrorism's most dangerous potential resources.

Conclusions

We began by reviewing some conventional approaches to the analysis of Russian foreign policy, influenced both by long-standing historiographical themes (comparing western and Asiatic orientations in Russian foreign-policy outlooks) and by interpretive methods that focus on personal policy-making styles. These have some utility in sorting out the array of claims and actions that initially confront's the student of foreign policy. However, as largely descriptive approaches with little causal weight they take analysis only so far. Our main concern has been to explore the implications for Russia of the American-led war on terror, which we have characterized as an 'international paradigm' that seeks to impose a practical and political world order by first establishing an intellectual one. No paradigm, by definition, is exhaustive–and to the resulting tensions between it and events and processes in the world should be added in this case internal tensions too. The war on terror paradigm tends to homogenize and hypostatize terrorism as an interconnected and existential threat to states (both claims possibly exaggerations) necessitating the reinforcement and in extreme cases the replacement of governments. It both reaffirms, and licenses the violation of, sovereignty. It has a military–territorial aspect as well as a novel stress on what we have termed 'good security governance'.

We have explored the implications of these features of the war on terror for Russian foreign policy. These are simplest and least problematic in the case of Russian handling of the ten-year-old Chechen insurgency, allowing Russia to position itself as partner and indeed pioneer in the struggle with 'international terrorism'. More problematic are the implications for Russian relations with its immediate neighbourhood, where American doubts about Russia's capacity to impose the requisite order, alongside other imperatives of the war on terror, have led to a rapid escalation and potentially permanent establishment of an American military presence. In Georgia, we suggested, the complexities of minority ethnic politics and economic interest make uncritical endorsement by Russia of America's conception of security requirements unlikely.

The same may be true of the implications of the good security governance agenda for Russia itself. Aid for Russia's efforts to dismantle its substantial military-industrial (and particularly nuclear) legacy from the Cold War is one thing (even here one could expect some sensitivity regarding the extent and timing of the dismantling and the nature of direct American participation in it). Quite another is to be targeted for criticism as a reservoir of inadequately secured potential terrorist resources, human and material. Heightened American attention to this problem is an inevitable concomitant of the war on terror. Foreign policy analysts will need to pay increasing attention to this kind of 'sovereignty–security' dilemma so long as the war on terror remains dominant in international affairs.

Notes

1. Nicholas Onuf, *World of Our Making: Rules and Rule in Social Theory and International Relations* (Columbia, SC: University of South Carolina Press, 1989); Martha Finnemore, *National Interests in International Society* (Ithaca, NY and London: Cornell University Press, 1996); Alexander Wendt, *Social Theory of International Politics* (Cambridge: Cambridge University Press, 1999).

2. Francis Fukuyama, *The End of History and the Last Man* (London: Penguin 1992); Samuel P. Huntington, *The Clash of Civilizations and the Remaking of World Order* (New York: Simon and Schuster 1997).

3. Nicholas J. Wheeler, *Saving Strangers: Humanitarian Intervention in International Society* (Oxford and New York: Oxford University Press 2000).

4. Martha Finnemore, 'Constructing Norms of Humanitarian Intervention', in Peter Katzenstein (ed.), *The Culture of National Security: Norms and Identity in World Politics* (New York: Columbia University Press 1996).

5. Gwyn Prins, *The Heart of War: On Power, Conflict and Obligation in the Twenty-first Century* (London and New York: Routledge 2002).

6. Prime Minister Tony Blair's account of these provisos is in his speech 'Doctrine of the International Community', Economic Club, Chicago, 24 April 1999, available at www.number10.gov.uk. For a discussion of Blair's 'just war theory' see Caroline Kennedy-Pipe and Rhiannon Vickers, 'Britain in the International Arena', in Richard Heffernan *et al.* (eds), *Developments in British Politics 7* (Basingstoke: Palgrave, 2003). For a critique of such provisos, see Noam Chomsky, *The New Military Humanism: Lessons form Kosovo* (London: Pluto Press 1999).

7. Barry Buzan, Ole Wæver and Jaap de Wilde, *Security: A New Framework for Analysis* (Boulder, CO and London: Lynne Rienner 1998), and see the discussion in Stephen Welch and Caroline Kennedy-Pipe, 'Multi-level Governance and International Relations', in Ian Bache and Matthew Flinders (eds), *Multi-level Governance* (Oxford: Oxford University Press 2004).

8. See the discussion in John O'Laughlin, Gearóid Ó Tuathail and Vladimir Kolossov, 'A "Risky Westward Turn"? Putin's 9-11 Script and Ordinary Russians', *Europe-Asia Studies*, vol. 56, no. 1 (January 2004), 3–34, at pp. 14–15.

9. See for instance Tibor Szamuely, *The Russian Tradition* (London: Secker and Warburg 1974).

10. Archie Brown, *The Gorbachev Factor* (Oxford: Oxford University Press 1996).

11. See Iver B. Neumann, *Russia and the Idea of Europe: A Study in Identity and International Relations* (London: Routledge 1996), pp. 190–3.

12. David Kerr, 'The New Eurasianism: The Rise of Geopolitics in Russia's Foreign Policy', *Europe-Asia Studies*, vol. 47, no. 6. (Sept. 1995), 977–88, at pp. 983–5.

13. Andranik Migranian, 'Podlinnye i mnimye orientry vo vneshnei politike', *Rossiiskaia Gazeta*, 4 August 1992, p. 7.

14. Zbigniew Brzezinski, 'The Premature Partnership', *Foreign Affairs*, vol. 73, no. 2 (March-April 1994), 67–82.

15. Hannes Adomeit, 'Russia as a "Great Power" in World Affairs: Images and Reality', *International Affairs*, vol. 71, no. 1 (January 1995), 35–68, at pp. 50–2.

16. Leon Aron, *Boris Yeltsin: A Revolutionary Life* (London: Harper Collins 2000).

17. See Mark Webber, 'Introduction: Russia and Europe – Conflict or Cooperation?', in Mark Webber (ed.), *Russia and Europe: Conflict or Cooperation?* (Basingstoke: Macmillan 2000).

18. See Paul Kubicek, 'The Evolution of Eurasianism and the Monroeski Doctrine under Vladimir Putin'. Paper prepared for the International Studies Association 45th Annual Convention, Montreal (March 2004). For a view of Putin as committed to a pro-Western line, see Thomas M. Nichols, 'Russia's Turn West: Sea Change or Opportunism?', *World Policy Journal*, vol. 19, no. 4 (Winter 2002–03), 13–22, at p. 22, available at www.worldpolicy.org.

19. Archie Brown, 'Russia as a "Normal" Object of Study in International Politics', in Bengt Sundelius (ed.), *The Consequences of September 11: A Symposium on the Implications for the Study of International Relations*, Swedish Institute of International Affairs, *Conference Papers* 30 (2002), p. 165.

20. *The Economist*, 20 March 2004, p. 34.

21. For the use of the rhetoric of war in US politics, see Michael S. Sherry, *In the Shadow of War: The United States since the 1930s* (New Haven, CT and London: Yale University Press 1995).

22. Michael Dewar, *The British Army in Northern Ireland* (London: Arms and Armour Press 1985). See Paul Wilkinson, *Terrorism and the Liberal States* (London: Macmillan 1986).

23. Robert Cooper, 'The Post-Modern State and the World Order', *Demos Paper* 19 (1996).

24. Robert Kagan, *Paradise and Power: America and Europe in the New World Order* (London: Atlantic Books, 2003).

25. Thomas S. Kuhn, *The Structure of Scientific Revolutions* (2nd edn, Chicago: University of Chicago Press, 1970).

26. See for example Peter A. Hall, 'Policy Paradigms, Social Learning, and the State: The Case of Economic Policymaking in Britain', *Comparative Politics*, vol. 25, no. 3 (1993), 275–96 and Adomeit (note 14).

27. A. Politovskaya, *A Dirty War: A Russian Reporter in Chechnya* (London: Harvill 2001); Dmitri Trenin, Aleksei Malashenko and Anatol Lieven, *Russia's Restless Frontier: The Chechnya Factor in Post-Soviet Russia* (Washington, DC: Carnegie Endowment for International Peace 2004).

28. 'Speech by President Vladimir Putin at a Meeting of the Security Council of the Russian Federation', Moscow (28 September 2001), available at the Russian Ministry of Foreign Affairs website, www.ln.mid.ru. See also Vladimir Putin, 'State of the Nation Address to the Russian Parliament', BBC Monitoring Former Soviet Union (26 May 2004, 10.21 am).

29. Another prefiguration of the war on terror paradigm is the fact that Russia had been a near victim of the only known incident of radiological terror against civilians when in November 1995 Chechen militants placed high-isotope caesium in a Moscow park. See Ian Bremmer, 'The Russian Roller Coaster' in *World Policy Journal*, vol. 20, no. 4 (Winter 2003–04), 22–9, available at www.worldpolicy.org. See also Gail Lapidus, 'Putin's War on Terrorism', *Post-Soviet Affairs*, vol. 18, no. 1 (January–March 2002), 41–9; Mark A. Smith, 'Russian Perspectives on Terrorism', Conflict Studies Research Centre Paper C110 (January 2004), available at www.da.mod.uk/CSRC; Ralph Davis and Robert Bruce Ware, 'Was Aslan Maskhadov Involved in the Moscow Hostage Crisis?', *Journal of Slavic Military Studies*, vol. 16, no. 3 (September 2003), 66–71.

30. Michael McFaul, 'US Policy and Chechnya: A Joint Project on Domestic Politics and America's Russia Policy', Euro-Atlantic Initiatives Policy Paper, The Century Foundation and The Stanley Foundation (March 2003), available at www.stanleyfoundation.org.

31. Richard Clarke, *Against All Enemies: Inside America's War on Terror* (New York: Free Press 2004).

32. Condoleezza Rice, 'Exercising Power without Arrogance', *Chicago Tribune*, 31 December 2002.

33. 'Bush Defends Putin in Handling of Siege', *Washington Post*, 19 November 2002, p. A16

34. Ibid.

35. *Economist* (note 19), p. 34.

36. O'Loughlin *et al.* (note 8), p. 14.

37. Dmitri Trenin, 'Russian–American Relations, Two Years after 9/11', Carnegie Moscow Center Briefing Papers, vol. 5, no. 9 (August 2003), available at www.carnegie.ru; see also Aleksandr Iurin, 'Russia and U.S.: Partners, No Matter What', *International Affairs: A Russian Journal*, no. 2 (2003), available at www.ciaonet.org (subscription required). *Economist* (note 19), p. 34.

38. Colin L. Powell, Remarks to the UN Security Council, 5 February 2003, available at www.un.int/usa/. See also Jean-Christophe Peuch, 'Russia: Moscow Levels Fresh Terrorism-Related Charges against Georgia', 11 February 2003, available at www.rferl.org/features/Default.aspx.

39. 'Tashkent Militants Take Hostages in Clash', *The Times*, 1 April 2004, p. 37.

40. As we have argued elsewhere, the promotion of 'good governance' by organizations and donor states should really be understood in terms of *government*: it is 'largely a specification, arguably a quite narrow one, of good government, or indeed of the scope of government (limited) and its economic policy (neoliberal).' Welch and Kennedy-Pipe (note 7), pp. 128–30. But we will nevertheless conform to established usage by using the term 'governance' in the present context.

41. We should however note the history of deference of the US courts to government arguments invoking 'national security'. See Thomas M. Frank, *Political Questions/Judicial Answers: Does the Rule of Law Apply to Foreign Affairs?* (Princeton, NJ: Princeton University Press, 1992).

42. Jessica Stern, *The Ultimate Terrorists* (Cambridge, MA and London: Harvard University Press, 1999), pp. 89–106.

43. Matthew Bunn, Oleg Bukharin, Jill Cetina, Kenneth Luongo and Frank von Hippel, 'Retooling Russia's Nuclear Cities', *Bulletin of the Atomic Scientists*, vol. 54, no. 5 (September–October 1998), available at www.bullatomsci.org. See also Jon B. Wolfsthal, 'Surveying the Nuclear Cities', *Bulletin of the Atomic Scientists*, vol. 57, no. 4 (July–August 2001), 15–17.

44. Matthew Bunn, Anthony Wier and John P. Holdren, *Controlling Nuclear Warheads and Materials: A Report Card and Action Plan*, Nuclear Threat Initiative (March 2003), p. 18, available at www.nti.org.

45. Stern (note 41), p. 88.

46. 'Agreement between the Government of the United States of America and the Government of the Russian Federation on the Nuclear Cities Initiative' (1998), full text available at www.nti.org. Article 3 specifies for example co-operation in the selection of projects for diversification and the development of entrepreneurial skills among displaced nuclear employees.

47. McFaul (note 28), quoting respectively Donald Rumsfeld and Paul Wolfowitz.

48. The term 'hyper-power' (*hyperpuissance*) was coined by Hubert Vedrine, French Foreign Minister 1997–2002. For a discussion of the difficulties of state-building see Michael Ignatieff, *Empire Lite: Nation-Building in Bosnia, Kosovo and Afghanistan* (London: Vintage 2003).

Index